Praise for *Wonderfully Wordless*

"Martin's book captures the rich diversity and international flavor of sequential art in all its forms. It is the definitive guide to the wordless novel."—**Stefan Berg, graphic novelist and author of *Let That Bad Air Out***

"Wordless books are wonderful in that they encourage creativity, imagination, and visual understanding. All of these are indispensable for human development but have been neglected in our society. This book will make it easier to find these beneficial books and reap their benefits. It is the fruit of patient research. But if you read the list of categories, which feels like a poem, you will find that there is a lot of heart in this book, too. For me this is important."—**Giora Carmi, art therapist and author of *The Basis of Psychotherapy through Art***

"*Wonderfully Wordless* is truly wonderful—this comprehensive survey documents the variety and nuance of visual language employed by artists across decades and around the globe."—**Mary DePalma, author of *Bow, Wow Wiggle-Waggle*, a Bank Street College of Education Best Book**

"Comprehensive, concise, and engaging, a great handbook for anyone interested in the art of telling stories with pictures. It is the only book of its kind and long overdue!"—**Rebecca Dudley, author of *Hank Has a Dream***

"William Martin has done an astounding job in gathering wordless book titles that he has meticulously classified into themes that would make any teacher or parent—or avid reader for that matter—find something that would be of interest to them at specific points in their lives: be it for babies, tweens, adolescents, or adults. This is a definitive resource of wordless graphic novels and picture books painstakingly organized into themes such as 'acts of kindness,' 'creative journeys,' 'fabulous friendships,' 'weird encounters,' 'edifying exploits,' and 'marvelous mysteries,' just to name a few. This is a labor of love, indeed, and as an avid bibliophile fascinated with visual literacy and the many wonders that wordless books have to offer, I would make it one of my life's mission as a reader to find the book titles that he has included here."—**Bacsal Rhoda Myra Garces, assistant professor and coordinator of high-ability studies and gifted education at the National Institute of Education, Singapore**

"*Wonderfully Wordless* is a comprehensive and timely resource for educators and speech language pathologists who are working with children and adolescents. It will definitely be listed as a resource on my syllabi addressing intervention for children with language delays and disorders."—**Sandra Gillam, professor in the Department of Communicative Disorders and Deaf Education at Utah State University**

"What began on cave walls nearly 50,000 years ago continues today on pages and screens—visual storytellers leading our eye from panel to panel and page to page, driven by that ever-burning question of a good story: 'And then what happened?' How wonderful to have as knowledgeable and insightful a guide as Bill Martin leading us into these modern caves to point out many a hidden room and vast stores of forgotten treasure."—**Jamichael Henterly, teacher of illustration and drawing at Western Washington University**

"Dr. Martin's *Wonderfully Wordless* does an amazing job of organizing and distilling a wide variety of wordless graphic novels and picture books into useful categories to help us find those that are most worthy of reading. Overall, it's a great list of recommended titles and includes many remarkable wordless book creators from Lynd Ward and Tana Hoban to Shaun Tan."—**Lita Judge, author of *Good Morning to Me!***

"All the words you'll ever need to find that perfectly wordless read."—**Stephen Michael King, award-winning author of *Bella's Bad Hair Day***

"This is an invaluable guide to the entire range of picture stories for all ages. If you're a fan of wordless books or if you are just discovering this vital art form, William Martin's *Wonderfully Wordless* is an essential roadmap to this silent universe."—**Peter Kuper, illustrator of *Mad* magazine's *Spy vs. Spy* comic strip and lecturer at Harvard University**

"*Wonderfully Wordless* is an awe-inspiring sourcebook! By gathering 500 of the greatest achievements in this fascinating art form, William Martin places nearly a century of ideas and information within your grasp. If you love picture books, you should own and read this book."—**Jeff Mack, illustrator of *Hurry! Hurry!*, a *School Library Journal* Best Book**

"It is with huge enthusiasm that I welcome William Patrick Martin's compendium, *Wonderfully Wordless: The 500 Most Recommended Graphic Novels and Picture Books*. At last an authoritative list, gathered from all over the world, appealing to all ages and all tastes, a formal and useful recognition that these kinds of books deserve a category of their own. I am particularly charmed by the titles of the categories Martin uses, thirty-two in all: 'Acts of Kindness,' 'Lost and Found,' 'Dreamy Departures,' and 'Concepts Galore' are a few that appeal particularly to me. . . . This is a perceptive list full of unusual and wonderful books, and I for one will be clearing my bookshelves to make space for some exciting new titles I had not known about before."—**Domenica More-Gordon, author of *Archie* and *Archie's Vacation***

"*Wonderfully Wordless* is a fantastic book. I had no idea there were so many wordless picture books out there, let alone great ones. Martin has provided a valuable resource to readers everywhere."—**Josh Simmons, author of the graphic novels *The Furry Trap* and *Black River***

"More than a mere list, this informative, well-organized compilation of illustration-only titles provides a curiosity igniting spark that will no doubt lead to multiple excursions to my local library and bookstore!"—**Brad Sneed, author of *Picture a Letter***

"William Martin should not only be excused for using an abundance of words in *Wonderfully Wordless*, he should be applauded. His expansive, insightful, and ambitious survey of the 500 most recommended wordless graphic novels and picture books is an indispensable resource for librarians, educators, and parents who value exposing children to an endlessly ethereal world of rich stories dependent not on objective text but on evocative imagery. Bravo."—**Bob Staake, author of *Bluebird***

"The aptly named *Wonderfully Wordless*, with its concise descriptions and thoughtful selections, will be an indispensable resource to all collectors and scholars who appreciate visual storytelling and want to dig a little deeper into this graphic tradition. The accessible nature of the visual narrative has an innate appeal for many different types of students. This book provides an excellent resource encompassing everything from essential xylographic novels to board books."—**George A. Walker, graphic novelist and professor at the Ontario College of Art and Design**

Wonderfully Wordless

The 500 Most Recommended Graphic Novels and Picture Books

WILLIAM PATRICK MARTIN

ROWMAN & LITTLEFIELD
Lanham • Boulder • New York • London

Published by Rowman & Littlefield
A wholly owned subsidiary of The Rowman & Littlefield Publishing Group, Inc.
4501 Forbes Boulevard, Suite 200, Lanham, Maryland 20706
www.rowman.com

Unit A, Whitacre Mews, 26-34 Stannary Street, London SE11 4AB

British Library Cataloguing in Publication Information Available

Library of Congress Cataloging-in-Publication Data

Martin, William P. (William Patrick)
  Wonderfully wordless : the 500 most recommended graphic novels and picture books / William Patrick Martin.
      pages cm
  Includes bibliographical references.
  ISBN 978-1-4422-5477-0 (hardcover : alk. paper) — ISBN 978-1-4422-5478-7 (ebook)
  1. Picture books for children—Bibliography. 2. Picture books—Bibliography.
3. Graphic novels—Bibliography. 4. Best books. I. Title.
  Z1033.P52M36 2015
  011.62—dc23   2015019482

Printed in the United States of America

For Mar, who finds value in everything.

Contents

Acknowledgments

If a single picture is worth a thousand words, then multiple picture-only titles are surely worth a book. But my book is not the first to survey this text-free world. One other title deserves special recognition. I am indebted to Virginia H. Richey and Katharyn E. Puckett, who in 1992 published the groundbreaking *Wordless / Almost Wordless Picture Books: A Guide*.

I am grateful to my editors Charles Harmon and Robert Hayunga for their guidance and confidence in my work.

Thank you, Casey, for first opening my eyes to the wonder of wordless picture books. After *Flotsam*, I never looked at children's picture books the same way. Many thanks to Matt, Katie, and Rob for your encouragement.

There are no words to express how thankful I am to Marianne, who has been thoughtfully and lovingly proofreading my work for a very long time.

Introduction

Books without words—it almost sounds like a paradox. But there is no contradiction in the minds of those who have experienced the wonder of stories that spring from a sequence of images rather than a sequence of words. Their only question is, Where can I find more of these rare and compelling books?

Wonderfully Wordless: The 500 Most Recommended Graphic Novels and Picture Books is the only comprehensive guide to illustration-only books on the contemporary scene. Distilling the opinions of a diverse group of educators, journalists, critics, and librarians from around the world,[1] it identifies the best wordless graphic novels and picture books in a way that is more complete and authoritative than the judgment of any single person or organization. The book artists included in this international collection include representatives from Argentina, Australia, Belgium, Brazil, Canada, Chile, France, Germany, Great Britain, Holland, Hungary, Indonesia, Italy, Japan, Netherlands, Norway, Poland, Russia, South Korea, Spain, Sweden, and Switzerland.

This reference will be valuable to school, public, and academic libraries, providing needed help to children, teenagers, and adults looking for the wordless and almost wordless books that are most worth reading. With concise descriptions and suggested age ranges, it will be an indispensible resource to all parents and teachers who appreciate visual storytelling and to those who recognize the unique value these books have with different types of students, including preschool, limited-English-proficiency, gifted and talented, creative, and special-needs children. Even adults who are not yet readers can benefit from this guide, gaining immediate access to books that can be shared with others and help on the path to literacy. This compendium will interest a wide audience, but it will have special value to the community of comic artists and children's book illustrators, providing the first complete overview of the essential titles in the wordless genre, encompassing everything from board books to woodcut novels.

Wonderfully Wordless is a composite of book entries gathered from 135 expert sources and over seventy-two hundred listings, entered into a database with the capacity to sort and rank the most recommended titles. The five hundred books that emerged from this review—in essence a tabulation of votes—are the titles upon which most authorities agree. The blue-chip sources used to create *Wonderfully Wordless* are recommendations from reference books, award lists, book reviews, professional journals, and literary blogs, as well as the best-book lists and collections of many of the most prominent libraries in the United States and other English-speaking countries. Departing from the customary best-book guide model, this uniquely authoritative guide asks, Why settle for the opinion of a single expert, when you can leverage the opinion of a multitude of experts?

The US libraries include the Boston Public Library, Carnegie Library of Pittsburgh, Denver Library, Louisville Free Public Library, New York Public Library, and Seattle Public Library, as well as the academic libraries at Bank Street College, Bloomsburg University, Miami University, Michigan State University, Penn State University, Stanford University, Temple University, and University of Chicago. The international libraries include the British Council Library India, British Library, Hong Kong Public Libraries, National Library of Australia, National Library of New Zealand, National Library of the Philippines, Toronto Public Library, Trinity College Library (Dublin), University of British Columbia, University of Oxford, and Vancouver Public Library.

The first wordless picture book for children was Ruth Carroll's *What Whiskers Did* (1932), published in the same period as several remarkable wordless woodcut novels, most notably Lynd Ward's *Gods' Man* (1929). After many years of dormancy, the wordless picture book genre took off in the 1960s, with multiple titles being created by masters such as Mitsumasa Anno, John S. Goodall, Fernando Krahn, Mercer Mayer, and Tana Hoban, followed by a second wave of award-winning artists such as Peter Spier, Alexandra Day, David Wiesner, and Barbara Lehman. By the 1990s, wordless graphic novels were also attracting significant attention, with works such as Eric Drooker's *Flood! A Novel in Pictures* (1992) and Peter Kuper's *Speechless* (2001) leading the way. Today, some of the most exciting and critically acclaimed titles are wordless—for example, Shaun Tan's *The Arrival* (2007), Jerry Pinkney's *The Lion & the Mouse* (2009), Aaron Becker's *Journey* (2013), and Marla Frazee's *The Farmer and the Clown* (2014).

Wordless graphic novels and picture books come in many varieties. They tell stories, create enigmas, launch adventures, teach basic concepts, mask hidden images, make people laugh, explore complex relationships, dazzle with different visual perspectives, devise imaginative journeys, educate about culture and history, invent strange new worlds, rail against social and economic injustice, celebrate traditional values, unleash streams of consciousness, thrill with mystery and suspense, and more. In short, wordless graphic novels and picture books are a lot like mainstream literature, except that the absence of language creates more opportunities for divergent interpretations. Relying only on images, wordless books require readers to actively translate and creatively explain what is happening on the page, with each viewer reading the sequence of images in his or her own way. In the world of wordless books, readers are the storytellers.

Not everyone appreciates the value of sequential art books. Although the tide has turned, some teachers still treat graphic novels as unproductive distractions from time-tested content. A few educational traditionalists even equate wordless picture books with the decline of literate culture, while others, accustomed to scripted teaching, see wordless books as problematic because there is no script. Meanwhile, some achievement-driven parents try to bypass picture books altogether, pushing their preschoolers to spend all their time on books with text, thinking this will give them a leg up on the academic competition that lies ahead.

Yet a growing body of research and classroom experience shows the crucial role that wordless picture books can play in promoting discussion, inspiring creativity, and boosting language development. Research at the University of Waterloo and Utah State University[2] has shown that parents actually use more sophisticated language when sharing wordless stories than when they simply read to young children. Savvy parents and teachers dealing with this preschool- and primary school–age population recognize that literacy is about not just decoding words but also interpreting images and using one's imagination. Thus, picture literacy is not a threat or a competitor but a partner and gateway to print literacy. For children who are not yet readers, wordless books teach them that reading follows a left-to-right pattern and that stories have a structure from which they can make inferences, generate predictions, and see causal relationships. With text-based books, parents and teachers read to children, but with wordless picture books, they are more likely to read with them. Image-only titles invite children to invent a narrative in a way that conventional books, for all their obvious merits, do not. Likewise, graphic novels do a tremendous job of motivating and engaging students, making subject matter much more accessible, especially to reluctant students. No longer considered an underground format, graphic novels are being successfully integrated into many parts of the school curriculum.

Wonderfully Wordless begins with a chapter that highlights several classic books, followed by chapters that group books by theme or format. Chapters for the youngest readers, titled, for instance, "For and about Babies" and "Concepts Galore," come first, with the more advanced-content chapters, such as "Graphic Novels for Teens" and "Woodcut Novels," appearing toward the end. Each chapter lists its books by popularity, beginning with the most recommended books.

Readers should have no problem zeroing in on their favorite topics. There are thirty-one chapters organized by topics such as Christmas cheer, character values, comedy capers, pet mischief, creative journeys, and marvelous mysteries. What's more, *Wonderfully Wordless* also sorts the collection into over thirty additional categories, including Caldecott Awards and Honors, circus and clowns, cultural diversity, extraterrestrial beings, fables and fairy tales, good deeds, history, magic, seek and find, and time travel. These additional classifications make up chapter 32, "Special Interests."

Chapter 33, "24 Wordless Book Artists You Should Know," sheds light on the book collection by providing basic information about some of the extraordinary author-illustrators who created the books. This fascinating group includes established contemporaries as well as great pioneers. The chapter includes Mitsumasa Anno, who was drafted into the Japanese army and taught mathematics before becoming an artist; Arthur Geisert, who currently resides in an Iowa farm town and lives in a building that was once a bank; Tana Hoban, who didn't publish her first children's book until she was fifty-three years old but went on to create scores of photography books for young children; Bill Thomson, a professor of illustration who did some of his best work while working as a high school track coach; Fernando Krahn, who was a political caricaturist forced to flee his home in Chile to avoid persecution; Peter Kuper, who lectures at Harvard University and draws *Mad* magazine's *Spy vs. Spy* comic; Barbara Lehman, who worked at many odd jobs, including movie theater ticket seller, ice-cream server, lifeguard, and house painter before becoming an award-winning artist; Frans Masereel, who is considered the most influential woodcut artist of the twentieth century and whose work was burned by the Nazis when they took power; Peter Spier, who spent time in a Nazi concentration camp; and Lynd Ward, whose legendary woodcut novels were among the original graphic novels.

Some wordless and nearly wordless books are incredibly popular, seeming to appear on everyone's booklist. The ten most recommended reads are

1. *Flotsam.* By David Wiesner. (Clarion Books, 2006.)
2. *The Snowman.* By Raymond Briggs. (Random House, 1978.)
3. *The Red Book.* By Barbara Lehman. (Houghton Mifflin, 2004.)
4. *The Lion & the Mouse.* By Jerry Pinkney. (Little, Brown, 2009.)
5. *Zoom.* By Istvan Banyai. (Viking, 1995.)
6. *Tuesday.* By David Wiesner. (Clarion Books, 1997.)
7. *A Ball for Daisy.* By Chris Raschka. (Schwartz & Wade Books, 2011.)
8. *Wave.* By Suzy Lee. (Chronicle Books, 2008.)
9. *Time Flies.* By Eric Rohmann. (Crown, 1994.)
10. *The Arrival.* By Shaun Tan. (Arthur A. Levine Books, 2007.)

Appendix 1 continues this list, showing the rank order of all five hundred books, while Appendix 2 sorts all the titles by chapter.

Pulitzer Prize–winning cartoonist Art Spiegelman once observed, "Wordless novels are filled with language, it just resides in the reader's head rather than on the page." So, in a sense, this guidebook is about giving my language a change of residence. I've moved thousands of words from head to page, making sure that everything is clearly boxed and organized, hoping nothing important has been left behind, but always mindful that the packages belong to me. Readers, and the parents and teachers who assist them, will make up their own minds about these wonderfully wordless books. They will make their own interpretations, unpack their own storehouses of language, and translate these visual treasures into their own stories, none of which will be exactly alike.

Notes

1. Leveraging the power of collective wisdom has a strong pedigree. Aristotle is widely credited with the realization that, under the right circumstances, the judgment of the group is often superior to that of the individual. English polymath Sir Francis reached a similar conclusion when he visited a county fair and observed a contest involving guessing the weight of a butchered ox. Hundreds of villagers, including livestock experts, participated in the exercise, but not one person got the weight exactly right. Afterward, when the eminent statistician averaged the guesses, he discovered something quite remarkable. The group average was closer to the ox's actual weight than the vast majority of the individual estimates. Social science research has borne out this insight about communal judgment, which James Surowiecki articulates well in his *The Wisdom of Crowds: Why the Many Are Smarter Than the Few and How Collective Wisdom Shapes Business, Economies, Societies, and Nations* (New York: Doubleday, 2005). Two of my books, *A Lifetime of Fiction: The 500 Most Recommended Reads for Ages 2 to 102* (Lanham, MD: Rowman & Littlefield, 2014) and *The Mother of All Booklists: The 500 Most Recommended Nonfiction Reads for Ages 3 to 103* (Lanham, MD: Rowman & Littlefield, 2014), use a similar aggregating methodology to identify other canonical reading lists.

2. University of Waterloo, "Reading Wordless Storybooks to Toddlers May Expose Them to Richer Language," *ScienceDaily*, last modified April 29, 2013. http://www.sciencedaily.com/releases/2013/04/130429164821.htm. The research, conducted by Daniella O'Neill of the Department of Psychology at Waterloo and graduate student Angela Nyhout, was reported in the April 2013 issue of *First Language*; Utah State University, "Maternal Input during Book Sharing: Wordless vs. Printed Books," *Utah State Today–University News*, last modified June 9, 2012. http://www.usu.edu/ust/index.cfm?article=49877. The research, led by professors Sandra Gillam and Lisa Boyce, was presented at the Annual Convention of the American Speech Language and Hearing Association in Philadelphia.

CHAPTER 1

Classic Titles

Whereof one cannot speak, thereof one must be silent.

—Ludwig Wittgenstein

1. *Flotsam.* By David Wiesner. (Clarion Books, 2006.) David Wiesner won his third Caldecott Medal for *Flotsam,* a story about a curious boy who finds an old-fashioned camera washed up on the shore of a beach. He develops its film, finding an array of fantastical underwater photographs, including an octopus in an armchair, miniature aliens, windup fish, and tiny people living on the shells of sea turtles. The boy also discovers a succession of photos of children from different times and places whose images were captured by the magical camera. After adding a selfie to this collection, the boy tosses the camera back into the surf, where it makes its way to its next lucky recipient. *Flotsam* is a wordless picture book of the first rank, created by an artist and storyteller almost without peer in his ability to conjure up imaginary new worlds. (Ages 4–8.)

2. *The Snowman.* By Raymond Briggs. (Random House, 1978.) This Boston Globe–Horn Book Award winner is a softly hued visual adventure about a boy who builds a snowman who comes to life. The boy and his frosty friend explore the young lad's home, play together, go on a magical flight, and return home—where the snowman melts away.

Intended as story about mortality, *The Snowman* became a Christmas favorite and a heartwarming tribute to the wonder and innocence of childhood. Its dreamy wintertime imagery has made the book a perennial favorite among children and adults. The book has been adapted for the stage and was made into a wordless animated film, earning an Academy Award nomination. (Ages 3–8.)

3. *The Lion & the Mouse.* By Jerry Pinkney. (Little, Brown, 2009.) In Jerry Pinkney's interpretation of this beloved fable, a mouse is captured and his life unexpectedly spared by a fierce and regal lion, who is later rewarded for his good deed when the diminutive rodent returns the favor by freeing the beast from a hunter's trap. This wonderfully wordless Caldecott Medal story, done in pencil and watercolor with many dramatic close-up illustrations of its protagonists, is set in the African Serengeti. This story of surprising kindness and unlikely friendship is further amplified in back endpapers, where the mouse and lion appear with their families, with the mouse and her children hitching a ride on the lion's back. Children will be drawn into the story by the characters' varied facial expressions and will be touched by the message that no act of kindness is ever wasted. (Ages 3–5.)

4. *Truck.* By Donald Crews. (Tupelo Books, 1997.) Making effective use of arresting geometrical shapes, Donald Crews follows the progress of a big red truck as it goes across the country on a lively journey. Loaded with boxes of tricycles, the tractor-trailer makes its way from New York City to San Francisco to make its delivery. Along the way, the truck encounters traffic jams, tunnels, bridges, foggy weather, road signs, and enough material to serve as an excellent introduction to highway travel and the trucking industry. This American Library Association Notable Book for Children was also named a Caldecott Honor book. For kids obsessed with trucks, and they are many, there is no better book. (Ages 4–8.)

5. *The Arrival.* By Shaun Tan. (Arthur A. Levine Books, 2007.) Shaun Tan captures the universal immigrant experience of isolation, confusion, and wonder in his tale of a middle-aged man who journeys to a bizarre and awe-inspiring new country hoping to build a future for himself and his family. In a stunningly imaginative series of small square panels done in sepia, the man encounters alien creatures, surreal cityscapes, and incomprehensible text as he struggles to adapt himself to the strange environment and make friends. Replete with compassion and hope and fittingly resembling a worn family album, *The Arrival* concludes with pictures of the man's family finally joining him in their new homeland. This critically acclaimed graphic novel is frequently used in high school and university courses and has been adapted for the stage and orchestra. (Ages 12+.)

6. *Anno's Journey.* By Mitsumasa Anno. (Puffin Books, 1997.) This ambitious picture book will be a blessing for children and adults who like to linger and look closely at illustrations to savor all that is going on. This detail-rich art sequence follows Mitsumasa Anno as he rides on horseback on winding paths through northern European hamlets ripe with activity and culture. Seeing the unfolding panorama from a bird's-eye perspective, readers will find famous characters from literature and fairy tales, subtle jokes, and even a hint of time travel, juxtaposing things old and new. *Anno's Journey* is an engrossing, multilayered education in architecture, landmarks, and landscape, sure to prompt return visits to the book, each inspection revealing more hidden treasures. (Ages 5–9.)

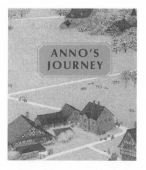

7. *Deep in the Forest.* By Brinton Turkle. (Puffin Books, 1992.) A bear cub leaves his mother to explore a cabin deep in the forest. In this clever retelling of the famous Goldilocks story, the curious little creature wreaks havoc in the frontier dwelling while its human inhabitants are out for a walk. The baby bear samples the family's three bowls of porridge, tries

their chairs on for size, breaking the smallest rocker, and jumps on their beds, falling asleep in the child-size one. The twist is made complete when the family returns. A chubby Goldilocks shrieks at the cub's mischief, making him run back to his own family. Children who are familiar with the original tale will especially love the book. (Ages 3–7.)

8. *Noah's Ark.* By Peter Spier. (Doubleday, 1977.) This interpretation of a seventeenth-century poem retells the biblical story of how pairs of every type of creature climbed aboard the enormous vessel and survived the flood. Noah is seen constructing his ark and rounding up his menagerie, leaving the corrupt, war-torn world behind. He is pictured on the ship caring for his animals, and when the water recedes, the survivors arrive in a promising new world. With detailed and breathtakingly beautiful illustrations, Peter Spier demonstrates that he is a master of his craft. *Noah's Ark* received numerous honors and awards, including the Caldecott Medal and the American Book Award, and was designated as a best book by the American Library Association and the *New York Times.* This excellent book will appeal to secular and sectarian audiences. (Ages 3–8.)

9. *Gods' Man.* By Lynd Ward. (Dover Publications, 2004.) *Gods' Man* was the first American wordless novel and a key influence in the development of graphic novels. Comprising 139 intricate black-and-white wood engravings, this classic is an allegory of the Faustian bargain that a poor artist makes with life. Lynd Ward's autobiographical work, first published in 1929, shows the artist signing a contract with a dark stranger who gives him a magic brush. With it, he experiences material success but is deeply disillusioned by greed and corruption. After much tumult and turmoil in the city, including being chased by a mob, he escapes to the woods and lives a happy family life until the stranger, a harbinger of death, returns. Ward was a social activist and inspiration to many writers and artists. (Ages 14+.)

10. *The Adventures of Paddy Pork.* By John S. Goodall. (Harcourt, Brace & World, 1968.) While on a shopping trip with his pig mother, Paddy Pork catches a glimpse of a circus wagon passing through town. He gets the idea to join the traveling show and sneaks away while his mother is busy. Along the way the protagonist gets lost in the forest and finds himself alone. He meets a wolf and goes with him to his house, barely escaping being eaten by the treacherous animal. When he catches up with the circus performers, his clumsiness makes him ill-suited to becoming one of them. Thanks to a sympathetic bunny, the upset piglet finds his way home. John S. Goodall, a beloved British illustrator, launched a successful series of small-format Paddy Pork books based on the popularity of this breakout porcine character. (Ages 5–8.)

11. *Little Red Riding Hood.* By John S. Goodall. (Margaret K. McElderry, 1988.) Casting a mouse in the role of the red-hooded heroine, this retelling of the famous fairy tale classic does not sugarcoat the climactic ferocity and drama of the original Brothers Grimm story. In this rendering, Little Red Riding Hood strolls through the woods, encountering many friendly animals along the way, including a helpful squirrel, a courteous frog, and an appealing family of ducks, before being greeted by the hungry wolf, who has been following her. The wolf, dressed in an ascot and top hat, then scurries ahead to devour grandma and wait for little Red to arrive with her basket of goodies. True to the original tale, a woodcutter saves the day, but not without spilling the predator's blood. (Ages 5–8.)

12. *Flood! A Novel in Pictures.* By Eric Drooker. (Four Walls Eight Windows, 1992.) This melancholy masterpiece, set in New York City, shows the final days of the twentieth century before the apocalypse. In the first part of the novel, an artist takes the subway from his home to his job, learning that the factory has been shut down. After an evening with a young woman, he returns to his apartment and finds that he is being evicted. The final section shows an isolated and

powerless protagonist roaming a dark and rain-saturated cityscape. Eric Drooker, who does cover art for the *New Yorker*, employs a black-and-white, scratchboard style reminiscent of woodcut novels. *Flood!* is an intellectual and artistic tour de force. It was a winner of the American Book Award, a New York Times Notable Book of the Year, and a *Los Angeles Times* fiction prize finalist. (Ages 14+.)

13. *The Tortoise & the Hare*. By Jerry Pinkney. (Little, Brown, 2013.) Following up on the success of the Caldecott Medal–winning *The Lion & the Mouse* (2009), Jerry Pinkney created another amazing retelling of an Aesop's fable in this spare-text picture book. Set in the desert landscape of the American Southwest, this familiar tale pits the plodding but diligent tortoise against the brash and foolhardy hare, who famously naps and loses the race. Gorgeously illustrated, the book shows the lively animal spectators dressed in human garb, wearing hats and bandanas, with the tortoise wearing an engineer's hat and the hare sporting a checkered vest. Pinkney cleverly delivers the moral of the story—slow and steady wins the race—by cumulatively adding just one word at a time to mark each stage of the race. (Ages 3–8.)

14. *What Whiskers Did*. By Ruth Carroll. (Scholastic Books, 1965.) First published in 1932, *What Whiskers Did* is considered the first wordless picture book for children. It is the story of a Scottish terrier who breaks away from his girl owner in the woods and is chased by a vicious fox until he takes refuge in a rabbit hole. With the bushy-tailed predator blocking his exit, Whiskers wanders into the warren, where he finds an affectionate and welcoming family of rabbits. They invite him to join them in a meal of carrots, and then the fluffy dog frolics with the young bunnies. After the family verifies that the coast is clear, Whiskers bids farewell to his new friends and reunites with the girl, who gives him a hug. (Ages 3–7.)

15. *Harry Potter and the Sorcerer's Stone: A Deluxe Pop-Up Book.* By J. K. Rowling and Jill Daniels. (Scholastic, 2001.) This visual retelling of the first novel in the phenomenally successful Harry Potter series is ideal for younger children and prereaders who want to understand why their older siblings are so bewitched by the bespectacled wizard and the Hogwarts School of Witchcraft and Wizardry. Full of inventive pull-tabs, pop-ups, and three-dimensional imagery, the book depicts six pivotal scenes from the original book that launched J. K. Rowling into publishing history. The cartoon artwork, similar to illustrator Mary GrandPre's well-known American edition book covers, will reassure novices that they are entering the authentic magical world celebrated in books, movies, and all manner of paraphernalia. (Ages 4–10.)

16. *Puss in Boots.* By John S. Goodall. (Margaret K. McElderry Books, 1990.) Half pages alternate with those of regular size in John S. Goodall's signature format to retell one of Charles Perrault's classic stories, first written by the Frenchman at the end of the seventeenth century. Goodall's interpretation is true to the original story in his depiction of the adventures of a cat who uses his intelligence and guile to advance the interests of his master. Wearing red boots and a large feathered hat, the flamboyant feline travels with his penniless master to win the hand of a princess, defeat a hideous ogre, and gain ownership of the monster's castle and wealth. Goodall's watercolors capture the major events of the story, but someone who has read Perrault's book may be needed to help fill in the gaps. (Ages 4–8.)

17. *Harold and the Purple Crayon.* By Crockett Johnson. (HarperCollins, 2005.) First published in 1955, this spare-text classic is about an imaginative four-year-old boy who one night goes on an adventure walk with his purple crayon. With his crayon he magically draws a moon to light his way, a path for walking, an oceangoing boat, and finally his own

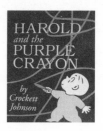

home and a bed for sleeping. The *School Library Journal* has listed *Harold and the Purple Crayon* among its top one hundred picture books of all time. The original creative premise behind the book, that children can create a world by simply drawing it, is one of the most borrowed in children's literature. (Ages 2–6.)

18. *How Anansi Obtained the Sky God's Stories.* By Janice Skivington. (Children's Press, 1991.) All the characters featured in this classic West African story—the sky god, snake, hornet, leopard, and Anansi the spider—appear on the book's attractive cover. The only missing piece is the storyteller, a woman holding a story bag, who is shown at the start and finish of the book telling her tale to appreciative children gathered around her in an African village. The kernel of the story is that Anansi, a legendary trickster, wants the stories of the world contained in the sky god's bag. To receive his reward, the black spider must first trick and capture the snake, hornet, and leopard, but there are unexpected results. Janice Skivington provides a written account of the story at the end of the book, filling in some gaps in the visual narrative. (Ages 5–9.)

19. *Where's Waldo? The Wonder Book.* By Martin Handford. (Candlewick Press, 1997.) *Where's Waldo?* is the first title in the famous wordless picture book series, setting the standard for books that hide images in densely illustrated spreads. Elaborately detailed and teeming with tiny figures and visual gags, *Where's Waldo?* helped make the bespectacled wanderer dressed in a bobble hat and red-and-white striped sweater widely recognizable. This enduring classic will provide hours of challenging fun searching for the intrepid protagonist, as well as many other objects listed at the end of the book. Book publishers routinely claim that their titles are for all ages; in the case of *Where's Waldo?*, this assertion is almost certainly true. (Ages 5+.)

CHAPTER 2

For and about Babies

Children (even from their infancy almost) are delighted with pictures, and willingly please their eyes with these lights.

—John Amos Comenius

1. *New Baby.* By Emily Arnold McCully. (Harper & Row, 1988.) The youngest mouse wakes to find elation in his large family when his mother has a new baby. Feeling resentful about losing his central role as the baby of the family, he seeks attention through immature antics such as sucking from the infant's bottle and climbing into its carriage. All ends well for this multigenerational family when the little mouse realizes that there is enough love to go around. Parents familiar with sibling rivalry will recognize that some children never quite recover from this emotional shock. Still, they will appreciate the value of Emily Arnold McCully's book as a necessary palliative and opportunity for conversation with the children in their life. (Ages 3–6.)

2. *Of Colors and Things.* By Tana Hoban. (Greenwillow Books, 1989.) A simple concept book consisting of bright glossy photos of familiar objects such as toys and food, *Of Colors and Things* is the perfect choice for babies and toddlers. Each page is separated into four boxes, three of which have subjects of the same color. This child-friendly offering is an

excellent tool for teaching the major hues, and the crisp, textured photos will command the attention of most preschoolers. From pinwheels to jellybeans, the images are sure to stimulate verbalization. Tana Hoban makes ample use of the colors red, yellow, green, orange, blue, brown, gray, and black, but for some reason she omits the colors pink and purple. (Ages 1–4.)

3. *Frere Jacques.* By Jonas Sickler. (Workman Publishing, 2011.) *Frere Jacques,* based on the classic French rhyme, is part of Workman Publishing's Indestructibles series, known for being impervious to baby chews, pulls, rips, bends, drools, and sucks. Its nontoxic material can be repeatedly washed and seems able to withstand virtually any assault a baby or toddler can muster. The sleeping main character, a pastry chef, dreams of goodies flying over the streets of Paris with buildings made of confections. The pictures are bright and include Notre Dame Cathedral and the Eiffel Tower. Jonas Sickler's other books for babies in this ruggedly rhyming series are *Mary Had a Little Lamb* (2010), *Humpty Dumpty* (2010), and *Hey, Diddle Diddle* (2010). (Ages 1–3.)

4. *Who Are They?* By Tana Hoban. (Greenwillow Books, 1994.) Parents introducing infants to their first book would be wise to begin with this one. With solid black silhouettes of ducks, pigs, dogs, cats, and sheep on white backgrounds, the images are precisely the kind of sharp-contrast figure-ground visuals that capture the attention of the youngest minds. Starting with one lamb and working up to five ducklings, each double-page spread has an adult animal with incrementally more babies. The animal images are realistic, not cartoonish, and are posed in a pleasing variety of ways. Parents will be able to use *Who Are They?* to teach animal and baby animal names and to introduce counting from one to five. (Ages 1–3.)

5. *Wiggle! March!* By Kaaren Pixton. (Workman Publishing, 2009.) For toddlers and younger children who literally sink their teeth into books, Kaaren Pixton, mother of triplets, created books that won't end up as soggy bits and pieces in the mouths of babes. *Wiggle! March!*, part of a series of nontoxic, baby-proof books, shows eleven farm animals, one to a page. With colorful images set against textured backgrounds, it is a perfect first book for babies and excellent for discussing how various animals navigate by crawling, wiggling, or by using paws, hooves, or webbed feet. Three other excellent Pixton books in the Indestructibles series are *Creep! Crawl!* (2009) and *Plip-Plop Pond* (2010). (Ages 1–3.)

6. *Flutter! Fly!* By Kaaren Pixton. (Workman Publishing, 2009.) Marketed chiefly for its safety and durability, *Flutter! Fly!* is part of a popular series of brightly illustrated books intended for the youngest children. This title shows how various animals use their wings to fly through nature. Lighter and more rugged than a board book, it is published on paper-like material that poses little risk for choking or toxicity when placed in the mouth. The eye-popping images of flying animals will keep the attention of babies as much as any book can. On the assumption that it is never too early to introduce babies to books, *Flutter! Fly!* would be the ideal gift for expectant parents. (Ages 1–3.)

7. *What Is That?* By Tana Hoban. (Greenwillow Books, 1994.) Tana Hoban's *Who Are They* (1994) features black silhouettes of animals displayed against a white background; in *What Is That?* she reverses the figure and ground to wonderful effect with a variety of solid white silhouettes on glossy black pages. This high-contrast, baby-friendly board book shows familiar objects, such as a balloon, pacifier, stuffed animal, and baby carriage. Hoban is such a prolific creator of preschool books that parents might begin to confuse them. Her similarly titled *What Is It?*

(1985) also features common objects that children will immediately recognize, but the book is a collection of color photographs. (Ages 1–3.)

8. *Kite in the Park.* By Lucy Cousins. (Candlewick, 1992.) What do you say about a nontoxic and washable cloth book known chiefly for how safe it will be for a baby to suck on? The taste and texture of the book are not that different from those of any other sturdy fabric, but its eight soft pages will be a vivid sight for wandering young eyes. The illustrations are bright and colorful, one image to a page, populated with objects that babies may already love, such as dogs and trees, or may soon learn to love, such as kites in the sky. In addition to many board books, Lucy Cousins has also produced the cloth books *Flower in the Garden* (1992), *Teddy in the House* (1992), and *Hen on the Farm* (1992), as well as a more recent series of cuddly fabric books featuring Maisy the Mouse. (Ages 1–3.)

9. *Find the Duck.* By Stephen Cartwright. (Usborne, 2000.) Young readers who are not yet ready for finding Waldo on a densely illustrated page will get an excellent chance to become familiar with the hidden-picture genre with *Find the Duck.* Toddlers will be eager to locate the yellow duck toy in scenes of a child's bath time. Motivated youngsters will not have too much trouble spotting the duck nestled near clothing, a sink, a potty, and a bathtub before they are whisked off to bed. This board book has gone through some changes in later editions to include simple rhyming text and a puppet. Stephen Cartwright has created several hidden-animal books that challenge children to find a duck, puppy, teddy, kitten, or piglet lodged in familiar settings. (Ages 1–3.)

10. *Waiting for Baby.* By Annie Kubler. (Child's Play International, 2000.) *Waiting for Baby* is designed to get young children ready for the birth of a new brother or sister. The board book does a great job of covering trips to the doctor's office, buying new toys, decorating the playroom, receiving visits from grandparents, and going to the hospital for the delivery. Annie Kubler also has an excellent follow-up board book, *My New Baby* (2000), showing a young boy getting used to his new sibling. The publisher has another version of *Waiting for Baby* (2009) with pictures and text, illustrated by Rachel Fuller and featuring a multiracial mother and child on the book's cover. (Ages 2–5.)

11. *My New Baby.* By Annie Kubler. (Child's Play International, 2000.) Followers of Annie Kubler's progressive family books will not be disappointed with *My New Baby.* With Kubler's usual expressive illustrations, toddlers and preschoolers will have an easy time understanding what will happen with the arrival of a new sibling. The board book shows mom nursing and dad changing diapers, doing some cooking, and carrying the baby, while both parents make sure the older boy has things to do and does not feel left out. Grandma and grandpa are also on the scene, helping to make the new addition to the family a joyful event. The colorful illustrations of toys and other familiar objects will also keep young children interested. (Ages 2–4.)

12. *Baby! Baby!* By Vicky Ceelen. (Random House, 2008.) More than anything else, babies and toddlers love pictures of animals and of babies and toddlers. It must be in our DNA. By this measure, Vicky Ceelen's board book is a standout success because her endearing photographs capture the remarkable similarities between human babies and animals. Each spread features the juxtaposition of two photographs, one of an animal and one of a similarly posed human baby. The babies and their animal counterparts, including frogs, lions, kittens, turtles, and ducklings, are just as cuddly and adorable as one would expect for tender psyches. Parents will also be charmed by this collection of look-alikes, which is a blessing because their children will be endlessly fascinated, wanting to examine the book again and again. (Ages 1–4.)

13. *Mrs. Mustard's Baby Faces.* By Jane Wattenberg. (Chronicle Books, 2007.) Reissued in a larger format than its original 1990 publication, this accordion-style board book features twelve sets of color photos of a multiethnic caste of babies making expressive faces. Each child is shown twice, first cheerful and smiling and then cranky and crying. This book will garner the rapt attention of infants and toddlers and has the added value of being easily stood up near the child for additional entertainment. If there were such a thing as a canon of essential books for babies, it would include *Mrs. Mustard's Baby Faces.* Parents should also consider getting *Mrs. Mustard's Beastly Babies* (1990), an accordion foldout book that pairs human and animal faces. (Ages 1–3.)

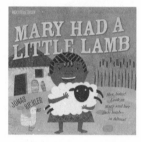

14. *Mary Had a Little Lamb.* By Jonas Sickler. (Workman Publishing, 2010.) The cover of *Mary Had a Little Lamb* shows a sweet little girl clutching a puffed up lamb, with a thatched-roof hut in the background and a curious duck standing beside her. This refreshing multicultural spin on the classic childhood rhyme sets the story in an African village, bringing new interest to the traditional rhyme printed on the back cover. Jonas Sickler's illustrations are pleasing and informative, but the experience would have been more meaningful to young readers and parents if he had integrated the text with the pictures in the conventional way. Presumably, the point is to illuminate the rhyme, not make up a new story. Still, *Mary Had a Little Lamb* is a fine addition to the Indestructibles series, known for its baby-proof materials. (Ages 1–3.)

CHAPTER 3

Concepts Galore

I found I could say things with color and shapes that I couldn't say any other way—things I had no words for.

—Georgia O'Keeffe

1. *Shapes, Shapes, Shapes.* By Tana Hoban. (Greenwillow Books, 1986.) Tana Hoban, the queen of preschool concept books, has photographed everyday objects to make young children more aware of the shapes that permeate their world. Her excellent color photos—a full gamut of circles, squares, stars, triangles, hearts, rectangles, hexagons, parallelograms, and more—are amazing in their clarity and elemental appeal. This book features eleven shapes that young readers are asked to find in twenty-seven photographs. Children will come away with a greater awareness of geometric forms and will certainly pay closer attention to their surroundings by finding shapes everywhere. Hoban's work has been exhibited at New York's Museum of Modern Art and in galleries throughout the world. (Ages 4–8.)

2. *Look! Look! Look!* By Tana Hoban. (Greenwillow Books, 1988.) By viewing photographs first through small die-cut holes and then in full, young readers learn the basics of prediction and recognize that things can be perceived in different ways. This book is a wonderful way to get children to look

15

for details and make educated guesses. *Look! Look! Look!* is fun but has a limited life span. The element of surprise and interest disappear as the images become known and commonplace. Kids who enjoyed *Look! Look! Look!* will also like Tana Hoban's *Look Again!* (1971), *Take Another Look* (1981), and *Look Book* (1997), each employing the die-cut format. (Ages 4–8.)

3. *Is It Larger? Is It Smaller?* By Tana Hoban. (Greenwillow Books, 1985.) Tana Hoban's *Is It Larger? Is It Smaller?* would be a helpful but not essential addition to a preschool or family library. Her close-up color photographs demonstrate the difference between large and small using easy-to-recognize items such as toys, pigs, fish, bowls, boats, balls, dolls, snowmen, cars, and shoes. As always, Hoban's photography is first rate and a pleasure to observe. This size-relativity concept book would be a nice companion to Hoban's other books for young readers, but when it comes to showing such basic differences, parents and teachers might be better off using actual objects in the child's environment to make the point. (Ages 2–5.)

4. *The Colors.* By Monique Felix. (Creative Editions, 2013.) Swiss artist Monique Felix's story of a curious mouse would be an excellent choice for parents who are teaching their children colors. The book shows the primary colors and how they can combine to produce secondary hues. First published in 1991, *The Colors* proceeds from the same premise as her other mouse books that work so well with toddlers, in which an inquiring rodent eats its way into a book, senses the possibility for adventure, and transforms the blank sheets of paper into something more. Fans of *The Colors* may also enjoy *Mouse Paint* (1995) by Ellen Stoll Walsh and Felix's other concept books, such as *The Wind* (2012) and *The Alphabet* (2012). (Ages 1–3.)

5. *Shadows and Reflections.* By Tana Hoban. (Green-willow Books, 1990.) Hoban scores another impressive win with her photography concept book on the ubiquity of shadows and reflections. In fourteen pairs of color photographs, she finds loveliness in the commonplace with her shots of a street sweeper, a bouquet of flowers, an iron chair, a bicycle, sailboats, planks on a fence, and reflections of people in glass, metal, and other surfaces. There is even a self-portrait of the photographer taking her own picture reflected in a mirror. In its investigation of different colors, textures, and concepts, *Shadows and Reflections* will be a visual delight for all ages and serve as an important learning tool for the youngest readers. (Ages 3–7.)

6. *Circles, Triangles, and Squares.* By Tana Hoban. (Macmillan, 1974.) You can judge Tana Hoban's book by its black-and-white photographic cover showing circles, triangles, and squares being drawn in chalk on a sidewalk by two girls. The kids on the cover are assembling the geometric shapes in human form. Inside the book the shapes are shown in a variety of photos of everyday scenes and objects, such as windows, bubbles, and tires. This first lesson in geometry will be a hit with children eager to acquire the basic vocabulary and concepts essential to describing the contents of their world. Kids will feel encouraged to see photographically as they identify the circles, triangles, and squares in their immediate environment. (Ages 3–6.)

7. *Is It Red? Is It Yellow? Is It Blue? An Adventure in Color.* By Tana Hoban. (Mulberry Books, 1987.) This well-designed concept book is ideal for introducing colors to toddlers and preschoolers. Children will enjoy matching photographic details with the colored circles at the bottom of each page. The color photos are of city scenes, populated by cars, fire hydrants, trash bags, construction sites, a box of fruit, a child in a puddle, and a youngster with a giant lollipop of

many colors. The mix of high-quality pictures can also be used to discuss the concepts of shape and size and to notice the sometimes unappreciated beauty of an urban environment. *Is It Red? Is It Yellow? Is It Blue?* was originally published in 1978. (Ages 2–5.)

8. *Freight Train.* By Donald Crews. (Greenwillow Books, 1978.) A colorful freight train hurtles through tunnels, over trestles, past cities, and through the countryside, always picking up speed. Illustrated using strong graphic design, this Caldecott Honor book creates the excitement of movement as the colorful cars blur together. This minimal-text book provides the names of colors and the words for different train cars. Train lovers, young and old, will be impressed with the detail and realism of the pictures. *Freight Train* will enable youngsters to learn the parts of a train and can be used to start a general discussion about transportation. The 1996 edition was published as a board book. (Ages 2–6.)

9. *Dylan's Day Out.* By Peter Catalanotto. (Orchard Books, 1989.) In this celebration of all things black and white, Dylan, a Dalmatian dog, dreams about egrets, zebras, and pandas, before fleeing his home to explore the area and romp in the countryside, as canines are inclined to do. Dylan's day is a kind of primer on black-and-white objects, animals, and people, including soccer balls, dominoes, crossword puzzles, and nuns. He becomes the goalie in a soccer game between skunks and penguins, leading the penguins to victory. Not everything in this energetic book is monochromatic, as some of the objects and landscape come in an attractive variety of hues. This sparsely worded book will challenge children to make their own list of black-and-white items in their environment. (Ages 3–6.)

10. *Is It Rough? Is It Smooth? Is It Shiny?* By Tana Hoban. (Greenwillow Books, 1984.) This simple concept book introduces the concept of touch through color photographs of many everyday objects with different textures and surfaces. Tana Hoban includes quite a range of items, from gleaming coins, to sticky taffy apples, to the rough and wrinkled skin of an elephant. The book can also be used to discuss other fundamental attributes such as size, shape, number, and color, all of which come into play in labeling and classifying objects. *Is It Rough? Is It Smooth? Is It Shiny?* is a great first science book and a useful addition to the large Hoban library of photo books that teach the most basic vocabulary and concepts. (Ages 3–7.)

11. *Snail, Where Are You?* By Tomi Ungerer. (Blue Apple Books, 2005.) Originally published in 1962, Tomi Ungerer's playful concept book shows that the spiral shape of a snail's shell can be discovered hidden in many guises, such as in the curl of a wave, the hat of a jester, the curly tail of a pig, a ringlet of hair, an elephant's curled trunk, and even the letter *S* in the book's title. This 2005 edition still has old-fashioned pictures, but they are reimagined with text, die-cuts, and lift-the-flap features. The question "Snail, where are you?" is repeatedly asked and answered, as young children are able to put their fingers in holes in each painting and lift the flap to see what is revealed. This edition stretches the meaning of "almost wordless" to the point where some readers may prefer the book's 1962 version. (Ages 4–7.)

12. *Exactly the Opposite.* By Tana Hoban. (Greenwillow Books, 1990.) This concept book, one of Tana Hoban's best, uses a variety of animals, people, and everyday objects in pairs to illuminate the multifaceted idea of opposites. The pleasantly colored photographs are challenging and open-ended, as more than one type of opposite can be introduced for most pictures. For example, the pair of turquoise sneakers (and socks) on the cover can be construed as antonyms for shoes that are tied versus untied, clean versus dirty, and other contrary notions. Hoban is simply the master of preschool photo concept books, and *Exactly the Opposite* is exactly what we have come to expect from an artist at the peak of her powers. (Ages 3–8.)

13. *Color Zoo.* By Lois Ehlert. (HarperFestival, 1997.) This work of bold graphic design combines simple geometric shapes and vivid color saturation to make a variety of animal faces. The minimal-text board book comprises a series of cutouts that, with every turn of the page, reveal a succession of familiar animals, such as a lion, tiger, mouse, goat, and fox, that will enable children to identify the creatures and configurations. Kids will be captivated by the shapes and fascinated by how the animals transform as you move through the book. *Color Zoo* won Caldecott Honors and was picked by the American Library Association as a best book of the year. (Ages 3–7.)

14. *Beach Ball.* By Peter Sis. (Greenwillow Books, 1990.) At the beach, Mary's ball blows away, forcing her to chase it across the sandy landscape. The pursuit becomes a game rich in concepts and fun. The little girl's search is the pretext for counting from one to ten, introducing the letters of the alphabet, discovering shapes and colors, learning opposites, and finding quirky images in minutely drawn chaotic scenes reminiscent of the Where's Waldo? series. The book also has sight gags that will appeal to different age groups, such as a depiction of the Beach Boys rock group and a little elf sitting under a mushroom umbrella. *Beach Ball*'s double-page spreads are so visually stimulating that children will beg their parents to visit the beach. (Ages 3–8.)

15. *Spirals, Curves, Fanshapes & Lines.* By Tana Hoban. (Greenwillow Books, 1992.) Tana Hoban scores another success in delivering a book of attractive color photographs of various child-friendly objects—birthday cakes, musical instruments, zoo animals, vegetables, fossils, shells, and loaves of bread—but the book has slightly less value as a concept book than some of the gifted photographer's other titles, several of which already deal with shapes. Still, Hoban's photos are stimulating, and her book will encourage children to pay closer attention to forms and patterns that are often overlooked. *Spirals, Curves, Fanshapes & Lines* will encourage children to see photographically, sharpen their perceptions, and enlarge their vocabulary for describing everyday objects. (Ages 4–8.)

16. *So Many Circles, So Many Squares.* By Tana Hoban. (Greenwillow Books, 1998.) The book cover nicely summarizes what is inside, in its attractive depiction of round brown cookies on a checkered blue-and-white plate resting on red table with a glass of milk (seen as a circle viewed from above). Tana Hoban supplies twenty-nine colorful photos, including shots of wheels, signs, pots, onions, grapes, bicycles, dishwashers, and teapots. Some teachers and parents will rightly fault the book for being less than precise in a few of its examples. The grapes and onions are not exactly circles, while some of the squares are actually rectangles and parallelograms. If the whole point of the book is to teach basic concepts, the pictures should get them right. (Ages 3–7.)

17. *I Read Symbols.* By Tana Hoban. (Greenwilllow Books, 1983.) Symbols so permeate our public spaces that they constitute a universal language. In keeping with her mission to create practical concept books, the award-winning photographer here assembles these everyday signs so ordinary that they can easily be overlooked in the education of youngsters. *I Read Symbols* collects twenty-seven wordless signs in full color, one image to a page, including railroad crossings, detours, deer crossings, restrooms, first aid, school zones, do not walk, and no smoking. The value of these close-up photographs is that they give preschoolers time to absorb them, as many are only glimpsed while riding in the backseat of a car. All the signs and their meanings are listed at the back of the book. (Ages 3–8.)

18. *Blue Sea.* By Robert Kalan and Donald Crews. (Greenwillow Books, 1992.) This concept book introduces size differences and special relationships by showing fish chasing one another in the sea and swimming through different-size openings, with one of them getting stuck in a coral reef. Simple text

married to bright and colorful graphics will help pre-schoolers understand basic ideas, but the book will probably not keep their attention for long, except to have them worry about big fish swallowing little ones. Large text and uncluttered deep-blue backgrounds will help young children understand the difference between small, smaller, and smallest and big, bigger, and biggest. Robert Kalan and Donald Crews have also teamed up to produce *Rain* (1991), another minimal-text picture book. (Ages 3–5.)

19. *My Very First Book of Shapes.* By Eric Carle. (Philomel, 2005.) Legendary picture book artist Eric Carle's simple introduction to shapes asks young children to match common objects, such as dome-shaped ladybugs and diamond-formed kites, with their corresponding silhouetted shapes. This split-page board book improves upon the original 1974 publication by using top and bottom pages that are separately moveable. Toddlers will enjoy seeing simple shapes in collage illustrations used to create bugs, trains, and watermelon slices. The shapes are labeled and the pages can be flipped to make the appropriate matches, making it more of a game than a reading exercise. The board book is also available as a bilingual edition titled *My Very First Book of Shapes = Mi primer libro de figuras* (2013). (Ages 1–3.)

20. *Bow-Wow Orders Lunch.* By Mark Newgarden and Megan Montague Cash. (Red Wagon Books, 2007.) Bow-Wow is back with a concept book sure to make him a toddler's best friend. In this simple minimalist cartoon, the little orange terrier is shown making a multilayered sandwich, alternating between slices of bread and cheese, that finally becomes a very tall feast. With each page adding another ingredient, including meat, the six-word book teaches the concept of patterns. Fun, informative, and brief, *Bow-Wow Orders Lunch* is a Children's Book of the Month Club selection. Other books in the popular series are *Bow-Wow Naps by Number* (2007), *Bow-Wow Hears Things* (2008), and *Bow-Wow's Colorful Life* (2009). (Ages 2–4.)

CHAPTER 4

Numbers and Letters

Art, as I see it, is any human activity which doesn't grow out of either of our species' two basic instincts: survival and reproduction.

—Scott McCloud

1. *Anno's Counting Book.* By Mitsumasa Anno. (Crowell, 1977.) In *Anno's Counting Book*—not to be confused with *Anno's Counting House* (1982)—the artist depicts simple arithmetic progression using common examples from daily life and seasonal change. In beautiful watercolors, he begins with a barren winter landscape capturing the concept of zero. Turn the pages, and the numbers increase as time passes and a town grows more complex. In a series of two-page spreads, children are invited to count the objects that they see and perhaps construct a rudimentary story. There are many books that aim to teach young children basic math concepts: *Anno's Counting Book* does it with panache. The book earned critical recognition from Boston Globe–Horn Book, the *New York Times*, and the American Library Association. (Ages 3–7.)

2. *Anno's Counting House.* By Mitsumasa Anno. (Philomel, 1982.) *Anno's Counting House* is the most plainly educational book in the Anno series, and readers may be disappointed to find that it is not as engaging as the author's other books featuring travel to cultural and historical landmarks. The objective here

is to teach basic math, as ten kids move from their old house to a new one with all their furnishings. Elementary addition and subtraction can be used to keep track of children coming and going. This concept picture book makes good use of cutaway windows to allow readers to peek inside the house. *Anno's Counting House* may not be the most inspired work of the world-renowned Japanese illustrator, but it is still preferable to many humdrum counting books that are even more didactic. (Ages 4–8.)

3. *Letter Lunch*. By Elisa Gutiérrez. (Owlkids Books, 2014.) Littered with letters but with nary a word, Canadian illustrator and graphic designer Elisa Gutiérrez's clever story features a hungry brother and sister who hunt for edible letters of the alphabet to make a meal. Skillfully using collage in a comic book style, she shows the boy and girl looking in their backyard and the forest for tasty fonts and sizes. Letters are everywhere, but when the boy and girl visit the local market, they find them conveniently arranged and sorted. At home, the foragers put the letters, all consonants, in a salad bowl and realize that they need some vowels, kept in the spice rack, to make the meal complete. At first glance, *Letter Lunch* looks like a book for kids just learning the alphabet, but decoding the pictures will challenge some elementary school–age children. (Ages 3–8.)

4. *The Numbers*. By Monique Felix. (Creative Education, 1992.) Who knew what could happen when mice get magically trapped inside a book! Monique Felix's *The Numbers* takes its place alongside *The Alphabet* (1992), *The Boat* (1993), *The Colors* (1991), *The House* (1993), *The Opposites* (1993), *The Plane* (1995), *The Wind* (2012), and *The Valentine* (2013) as a concept book about a group of mice chewing the numbers one through ten out of blank sheets of paper. The counting lesson begins when a little rodent chews a hole, adding numbers and joined by more mice as it spreads deeper into the book. The facial expressions of the mice set *The Numbers* and Felix's other books apart from comparable educational books for the youngest set. (Ages 2–5.)

5. *Up to Ten and Down Again.* By Lisa Campbell Ernst. (Lothrop, Lee & Shepard Books, 1986.) Lisa Campbell Ernst introduces basic counting skills in a picture book that looks like a photo album. As a single duck enjoys paddling across a pond, he observes two cars filled with three dogs, four boys, and five girls arriving for a picnic. In a metanarrative twist, the duck steps outside the pictures and watches the group have fun playing with balls, sailing toy boats, and eating packed lunches. When ten clouds arrive bringing rain and wind, the group departs, while the duck reenters the picture and is joined by nine other ducks. *Up to Ten and Down Again* provides plenty of opportunities to strengthen number skills by counting backward and forward. The objects in this rudimentary story also appear as items to be counted in boxes located at the top or bottom of the pages. (Ages 3–7.)

6. *Anno's Alphabet: An Adventure in Imagination.* By Mitsumasa Anno. (Crowell, 1975.) Parents looking for a straightforward guide to teaching the alphabet to prereaders will be disappointed with *Anno's Alphabet.* Letters of the alphabet are drawn like crafted pieces of wood, many employing visual twists that older children and adults will appreciate more than kids who are learning the basics. While the objects to which the letters apply are imaginative, they are sometimes too difficult for beginners. As with most of Mitsumasa Anno's books, the most captivating feature is finding his hidden objects, which are contained in the detailed page borders. Anno is a master illustrator who routinely challenges his young audiences with advanced material, but this time his intricate artistry and sophistication are somewhat counterproductive. (Ages 6–9.)

7. *1, 2, 3 to the Zoo.* By Eric Carle. (Puffin, 1998.) First published in 1968, this title still ranks among the best concept books for introducing numbers and counting. This board book, like earlier editions, succeeds because of its whimsical pictures of animals riding on a zoo train with an engine and boxcars. As the procession passes by, each cheerfully illustrated car has one animal more then the previous car. The pages have large clear numbers to accompany the train that begins with one elephant and ends with ten birds. As an added bonus, each animal page has a little mouse for toddlers and preschoolers to find. The book concludes with a view of the entire zoo. (Ages 2–5.)

8. *Alphabet City.* By Stephen T. Johnson. (Viking, 1995.) Pastel and watercolor paintings so realistic that they can pass as photographs create the letters of the alphabet in this superb urban art catalog. With twenty-six studies in all, there is one inspired letter per page, including a simple construction sawhorse forming an A, the neck of a lamppost fashioning a G, a building's fire escape creating a Z, and so forth. Wordless but not letterless, this Caldecott Honor book may leave some parents wondering about its intended audience. The alphabetic theme is a matter for preschoolers, but its artful illustrations are sometimes too sophisticated for this young cohort to decipher. This is one alphabet book that can actually deliver on the promise of offering something for all ages. (Ages 3+.)

9. *Mouse Letters: A Very First Alphabet Book.* By Jim Arnosky. (Clarion Books, 1999.) This companion to Jim Arnosky's *Mouse Numbers: A Very First Counting Book* (1999) teaches the alphabet by showing the comic attempts of a mouse to construct individual letters entirely out of sticks or twigs. The hapless but persevering little creature struggles with his building materials until he brings his project to a successful

end. The mouse's many mishaps will keep children engaged, as they see him form the letters *U* and *V* by hanging perilously in a chasm or observe him crash to the ground while sleeping on the horizontal rung of the letter *H*. Arnosky is best known for his nature books for children, including *All about Alligators* (2008), *All about Deer* (1996), and *Tooth and Claw: The Wild World of Big Predators* (2014). (Ages 1–4.)

10. *Picture a Letter.* By Brad Sneed. (Dial Books, 2002.) This alphabet book is filled with stunning illustrations of letter-coded objects, people, and places, as well as hunt-and-seek challenges. A quick look at the *A* page discloses an acrobat, airplane, and alligator; *C* highlights a caterpillar, camel, castle, and cactus; *H* features hippos, hydrants, helicopters, hula dancers, and haystacks. Tiny mice are embedded in pictures throughout the book; one mouse has a cart full of letters that he lines up and playfully illustrates, for example, by taking a nap for the letter *N*. Both children and adults will be entertained by the inventive illustrations and the running humor of the mice's antics. (Ages 3–6.)

11. *Mouse Numbers: A Very First Counting Book.* By Jim Arnosky. (Clarion Books, 1999.) Preschool books that teach basic counting are hugely important to parents and teachers, and this one stands out in a genre that has plenty of good choices. This small-format book tells the story of a mouse's trip to the beach and back home again, which introduces youngsters to the idea of counting forward and backward based on objects encountered in the environment. The umbrella-toting hero of this little adventure counts things along his way until a fish with ten teeth frightens him, sending him back home. Jim Arnosky has an earlier title, *Mouse Numbers and Letters* (1982), which also involves traveling to the beach, counting objects from one to ten, and using twigs to construct the letters of the alphabet. (Ages 2–5.)

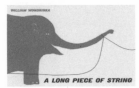

12. *A Long Piece of String.* By William Wondriska. (Chronicle Books, 2010.) First published in 1963, this classic alphabet book is elegant in its simplicity, showing a lengthy piece of string going from page to page, tying together twenty-six images in alphabetical order. The book is not only wordless but letterless, and some youngsters may miss the connection until it is pointed out. The real fun begins as they recognize the sequencing, observing that the image of a house precedes the picture of an ice-cream cone, just as a key precedes a leaf, and so forth. From alligator to zipper, the drawings are all done in black and reddish orange and are strikingly bold. Children with prior knowledge of the ABCs will get the most out of this unique and creative letter book. (Ages 3–7.)

13. *Albert B. Cub and Zebra: An Alphabet Storybook.* By Anne F. Rockwell. (Crowell, 1977.) Albert B. Cub and Zebra are pictured on the book cover, the plump bear sitting atop the banded and cheery quadruped Zebra. When Zebra goes missing, his furry friend journeys around the world and through the alphabet to find him. This alphabetic trip is packed with objects and activities illustrative of each letter, which sets the book apart from much simpler alphabet books that typically show fewer images per page. Each letter is clearly shown in upper and lower cases, and the written account of the bear's journey is included at the back of the book. *Albert B. Cub and Zebra* is an excellent choice for preschoolers ready to move on to more complex picture books requiring more thought and analysis. (Ages 3–6.)

14. *Alphabet House.* By Nancy Elizabeth Wallace. (Two Lions, 2005.) Using three-dimensional cut-paper illustrations, Nancy Elizabeth Wallace has fabricated a house inhabited by a large family of bunnies who need help finding objects starting with the letters *A* to *Z*. On each page, some member of the extended family—grandma, grandpa, mom, dad, or one of five children—is surrounded by mostly familiar examples of objects beginning with the corresponding letter, the point being for readers to name as many letters as they can. Open the book to any page, and pre-schoolers will see depictions of daily activities, with uppercase and lowercase letters situated in a page corner. To make sure nothing is missed, there is a handy answer key at the back of the book. (Ages 2–5.)

15. *City by Numbers.* By Stephen T. Johnson. (Puffin, 2003.) With splendid photorealistic paintings of New York City, Stephen T. Johnson's concept book does for numbers what his *Alphabet City* (1995) does for letters. The difference in this impressive companion volume is that young readers must find the numbers zero through twenty-one hidden in plain sight. For example, the number two can be found in peeling paint, three can be seen in a wrought iron gate, fifteen is camouflaged in cracked mortar, and twenty-one emerges from the lighted windows in a skyscraper. Parents will welcome *City by Numbers* as a tool for teaching counting. But its biggest contribution is to promote awareness and appreciation of the rich trea-sures found in the details of urban infrastructure and architecture. (Ages 4–8.)

16. *Abstract Alphabet: A Book of Animals.* By Paul Cox. (Chronicle Books, 2001.) In this unique word-game book, colorful abstract shapes are substituted for letters of the alphabet, and children are challenged to decipher words to figure out the names of animals. Amateur cryptographers and junior semioticians will be aided in their work by the fact that there are twenty-six different letter groupings conveniently arranged in alphabetical order. Once kids determine that the letter *B* is always represented by a pale blue circle and that *G* resembles a lime green boomerang, and so forth, the pieces of the puzzle will fall into place. There is no chance of getting stumped because there is a foldout key showing the matchups between the shapes and letters. Children will be captivated by the problem solving and enlightened by the knowl-

edge that the alphabet is not the only possible symbol system. (Ages 6–10.)

17. *The Alphabet Parade.* By Seymour Chwast. (Harcourt Brace Jovanovich, 1991.) In a cheerful procession of letters, children will enjoy finding over three hundred items from *A* to *Z*. Interesting twists will captivate and challenge preschoolers and beginning readers, making children feel that they are part of the continuous line of parade spectators shown at the bottoms of the pages. Some of the illustrations may actually be too challenging for the younger set, so it helps that Seymour Chwast has included a word list at the end of the book. With Martin Moskof, Chwast created another minimal-text title called *Still Another Number Book* (2013) that teaches counting from one to ten. (Ages 3–7.)

18. *Animal Alphabet.* By Bert Kitchen. (Dial Books, 1984.) This beautifully designed book shows each capital letter of the alphabet along with an appropriately named animal interacting with it in some way. On the book's cover, the trunk of a realistically drawn elephant is wrapped around the letter *E*. Inside the book, the horn of a rhinoceros pierces the letter *R*, a snail slithers on the curve of the letter *S*, and the feet of an umbrella bird are attached to the letter *U*. From armadillo to zebra, the animals, along with their oversize letters, are rich in detail and texture, all set against a white background. The names of the animals are listed in the back of the book. Bert Kitchen achieves the same effect with *Animal Numbers* (1987). (Ages 2–5.)

CHAPTER 5

Best at Bedtime

Are the wordless books a response of sorts to a timely longing for more and better chances to sit quietly with overscheduled children, switch off screen devices, and, with a picture book in hand to get things started, enjoy an old-fashioned conversation?

—Leonard S. Marcus

1. *Sunshine*. By Jan Ormerod. (Frances Lincoln Children's Books, 2009.) First published in 1981, this Mother Goose Award–winning book is about a little girl starting her morning routine. Waking up as rays of sunshine flood her bedroom, she starts her day by having breakfast and crawling into bed with her parents while they drink coffee and read the newspaper. After a leisurely start, the family dashes out the door, with the girl wearing her shoes on the wrong feet. *Sunshine* was the first of over fifty books by the Australian illustrator known for her ability to tell uncluttered stories where people can recognize priceless moments from their own lives. *Sunshine* was also honored as an Australian Picture Book of the Year. (Ages 3–7.)

2. *Moonlight*. By Jan Ormerod. (Frances Lincoln Children's Books, 2004.) This companion to *Sunshine* (2009), which depicts a girl and her family going through their morning routine, shows the same family getting ready for bed. After they eat

31

and wash up following their evening meal, they embark on a nightly ritual that will be familiar to many children, including a bath, a goodnight to toys, a bedtime story, a hug and kiss, a last-minute glass of water, and exhausted parents falling asleep before their child. In contrast to the abundance of wordless books that find entertainment only in the surreal, Jan Ormerod sheds her light on the rhythms of everyday reality. (Ages 3–7.)

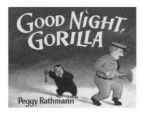

3. *Tabby: A Story in Pictures.* By Aliki. (HarperCollins, 1995.) When a little girl and her dad visit an animal shelter, they decide to adopt a wide-eyed kitten. In images as tender as they are colorful, Aliki shows the tabby pass through the seasons of her first year with her new family, culminating with the celebration of her birthday. The lucky pet has a warm basket near the girl's bed, ample milk to drink, and constant entertainment from her owner, whom she watches build a snowman or play in the garden. When a kitten moves in next door, Tabby gets a new playmate. Aliki Brandenberg, a recipient of the Pennsylvania School Librarians' Association Award, is author and illustrator of many children's books. (Ages 2–6.)

4. *Good Night, Gorilla.* By Peggy Rathmann. (Putnam Juvenile, 1996.) While a sleepy zookeeper says good night to his animals, he doesn't notice that the naughty gorilla has stolen the keys from his back pocket. In this endearing board book, the ape releases all the animals from their cages, and they form a parade line to follow the man home. Creatures large and small enter his dwelling to sleep, and the gorilla snuggles up next to the zookeeper's wife. The still unobservant man doesn't even notice his wife gently leading the adorable crowd back where they belong. The crafty gorilla, however, still has the keys and amusingly returns to the comfortable little house to snooze again. (Ages 2–6.)

5. *Breakfast for Jack.* By Pat Schories. (Boyds Mills Press, 2004.) Jack is a winning orange-and-white terrier who belongs to a family in such a rush that they have fed themselves and the cat but forgotten him! With enjoyably retro pastels, Pat Schories nicely captures the frenetic activity of a family getting ready for school and work. Poor Jack tries to draw attention to his empty food bowl—and the cat's full one—as everyone hurries to eat breakfast, get dressed, and leave for the day. Fortunately, the redheaded, freckle-faced boy stops on the front walk and remembers to feed the bewildered mutt. Kids will feel sorry for the perky canine, while parents may see an opportunity for a conversation about family responsibilities. (Ages 2–6.)

6. *The Angel and the Soldier Boy.* By Peter Collington. (Knopf Books for Young Readers, 1987.) After hearing about pirates in a bedtime story, tiny buccaneers who live in a model ship rob a little girl's piggy bank while she sleeps with her little wooden soldier boy and angel. The pirates steal a silver coin, but the soldier gives chase and is captured. Soon the angel doll wakes up and comes to his rescue, facing a perilously close encounter with the family cat before they return the booty together. Drawn with colored pencil and soft pastels, this adventure book is well suited as a bedtime story. *The Angel and the Soldier Boy* has received awards, been made into a movie, and inspired an album of the same name by Clannad, an Irish folk group. (Ages 4–8.)

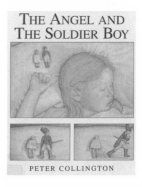

7. *The Wind.* By Monique Felix. (Creative Editions, 2012.) Swiss artist Monique Felix's story of a curious and adorable little mouse shows him eating his way through a book and getting trapped there until he notices wind blowing through the hole. Inspired by the sight of a hawk, airplane, and helicopter, he creatively turns blank sheets of paper into a pinwheel attached to his tail, leveraging the wind's power. The mouse manages to escape from the book into the sky using

this whirligig invention. Children will not be blown away by this title, but they will find enough appeal to want to move on to the series of books featuring Felix's book-gnawing mice. (Ages 3–5.)

8. *Jacko.* By John S. Goodall. (Harcourt Children's Books, 1972.) John S. Goodall employs his usual style of alternating full and half pages in an old-time English story set in a seaport town featuring a monkey named Jacko, who escapes from his organ-grinder master. The chimp stows away on a ship and hides in a treasure chest in the captain's cabin. When Jacko gets out of the chest, he frees a parrot from its cage. After pirates attack their vessel, the two go aboard the pirate ship, traveling to a tropical island where Jacko reunites with his mother and the bird makes a new friend. Children will admire the monkey's gumption and will be heartened that his courage brought such a just reward. (Ages 5–8.)

9. *Good Night, Garden Gnome.* By Jamichael Henterly. (Dial, 2001.) For parents looking for a tranquil read like *Good Night, Moon* (1984), *Good Night, Garden Gnome* will not fit the bill. The title is derivative, but the simple story is not. A little girl leaves a bearded garden statuette outside, where he protects his territory, feeds the rabbits and birds, repels predators, and even rescues a stuffed toy that belongs to her. The book reaches its apex when the vigilant and slightly scary gnome is almost buried by a dog. Children will love this bedtime adventure, not because it will put them to sleep but because it will inspire them to imagine the strange nocturnal world that exists in their own backyards. (Ages 4–7.)

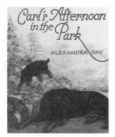

10. *Carl's Afternoon in the Park.* By Alexandra Day. (Farrar, Straus & Giroux, 1991.) America's most beloved Rottweiler is babysitting again, but this time he is responsible for a baby and a puppy. While mother takes tea with a friend, the threesome ramble through the park, visiting a children's zoo, riding a merry-go-round, romping in a flowerbed, and enjoying ice cream together. Carl and the baby even stop to pose for painters, who do portraits of them in wildly different styles. Naturally, the dog dutifully deposits his charges back at their point of origin just before mom returns from teatime. Lush park images provide the perfect backdrop for this afternoon adventure, while the board pages radiate energy and warmth. (Ages 2–5.)

11. *Just in Passing.* By Susan Bonners. (Lothrop, Lee & Shepard Books, 1989.) Beautiful watercolor illustrations tell the story of how truly infectious yawns are as they pass from one person to another. Starting with a sleepy baby being held by her mother on a sunny street, the cycle of yawns grows to include many people, including an older woman, a newspaper vendor, a window washer, a zookeeper, a cyclist, a farmer, a dog, a telephone repairperson, and a businessman, before returning to the original baby. Children will not be able to view this book without stifling a yawn—but not one of boredom. *Just in Passing* is just the kind of book that will resonate with young readers, becoming the perfect bedtime story. (Ages 4–8.)

12. *Flicks.* By Tomie DePaola. (Harcourt Brace Jovanovich, 1979.) Tomie DePaola has drawn attention to the often mentioned comparability of silent films to wordless books in a nifty little volume that shows children attending five short flicks, titled "Tooth Troubles," "The Birthday Cake," "Rhonda Rolls Along," "The New Baby," and "A Sleep-Time Saga." Children appear in silhouette at the bottom of the pages in the manner of a mock theater audience. The movies include one about a child intentionally trying to lose a tooth to get money from the tooth fairy and another about a girl having trouble blowing out her birthday candles. DePaola's attractive pastel illustrations create the atmosphere and mystique of old-time silent film. (Ages 4–8.)

13. *I Can't Sleep.* By Philippe Dupasquier. (Walker Books, 1999.) It's the middle of the night, and dad, who is an artist, can't sleep. Neither can his daughter or even the cat. One by one, the insomniac family members assemble in the kitchen for milk

and a snack and then go outside to look at the starry night. Returning to bed for a second time, this time they achieve REM sleep just before the sun rises. This warm family tale would be the perfect choice for bedtime reading—except for its suggestion that there are better things to do than sleep. Philippe Dupasquier was born in Switzerland, attended art school in France, and works as an illustrator in England. (Ages 3–7.)

14. *Sun's Up.* By Teryl Euvremer. (Crown Publishers, 1987.) Like everyone else, the sun sleeps at night and must wake up to go to work every morning. Depicted as a friendly anthropomorphized gentleman wearing a crown of golden tendrils, the sun starts his day by replacing his pajamas with work clothes, having breakfast, combing his hairlike strands, and heading to work. He spends the day (made possible by him) moving across the sky, warming and lighting the way for country folk engaged in their parallel daily pursuits. As time progresses, he shifts from bright yellow to dark orange. When the sun's shift is over, he is replaced by the moon, depicted as a pale woman with her own job to do. (Ages 3–7.)

15. *Snow Sounds: An Onomatopoeic Story.* By David A. Johnson. (Houghton Mifflin, 2006.) After fluffy white snow has accumulated during the night, a boy awakens to this wintery blanket and readies himself for school. A snowplow clears the road to his country house, dad uses his snow blower on the driveway, and the boy uses a shovel to clear the walk. Silent, except for descriptive sound words, David A. Johnson's book imparts elegance to the seemingly mundane activity of snow removal with his hazy, glowing watercolors. From the boy's gentle "snore" to a bus's loud "honk," young children will enjoy listening to and imitating the familiar sounds that punctuate the predawn quiet in this story set just days before Christmas. (Ages 3–8.)

16. *Lights Out.* By Arthur Geisert. (Houghton Mifflin, 2005.) When parents tell a little piglet that it's time for bed and lights out, his fear of the dark becomes the mother of invention. Young folk will eagerly follow the process of how he gets his light to delay turning off on its own by engineering a series Rube Goldberg contraptions. Technologically minded children will be fascinated less by the story line than by the ingenious chain of events gradually leading to switched-off lights. In his time-delaying invention, the piglet creatively employs scissors, dominoes, tricycles, bowling balls, baseball bats, and more in a complex series of movements that span the roof, walls, backyard, and basement of his home. Arthur Geisert's meticulous artwork is likely to inspire would-be techies to attempt their own elaborate combinations of force and motion, just for the fun of it. (Ages 6–10.)

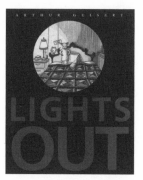

17. *The Chimp and the Clown.* By Ruth Carroll. (H. Z. Walck, 1968.) Dynamic colored drawings tell the story of a chimp who becomes tired of a circus parade and runs away from his clown owner. The clown pursues the mischievous chimp as he climbs up a tree and goes from adventure to adventure, including being thrown out of a zoo, climbing into a baby carriage with an infant, and overturning a boat, until the clown finally rescues him from the water. Ruth Carroll's pencil drawings are not something out of the typical Disney sketchbook. Her circus performers are a little creepier than is usual in modern books for young children, but they are also exciting and will keep the audience engaged. Carroll is creator of *What Whiskers Did* (1932), the first wordless picture book for children. (Ages 4–8.)

18. *Man's Work!* By Annie Kubler. (Child's Play International, 1999.) The title of this board book naturally raises the worry that it might be a primer in sex-role stereotyping, filled with images of handymen, soldiers, policemen, and firemen, all operating heavy equipment and riding around in trucks. Instead, it is quite the opposite. A cheerful dad and his

small son are pictured performing everyday activities such as ironing, vacuuming, dusting, scrubbing the floor, polishing furniture, and cleaning the bathtub. The complete absence of traditional male activities will be disconcerting to some readers, but most parents will definitely want to share *Man's Work!* with their children, if only to gauge how well it reflects the actual distribution of labor in their own homes. (Ages 2–6.)

19. *Flashlight.* By Lizi Boyd. (Chronicle, 2014.) This exploration of the night focuses on the simple appeal of a flashlight, as a child ventures out of her tent and into the darkness with the device in hand. Mice, skunks, fish, a fox, and a deer, along with apples and tiny plants, are captured in cones of light that reveal their colors. When the flashlight is dropped, a raccoon retrieves it and shines its light on the child. The book also has cut-out holes providing sneak peeks of what is to come. Parents might want to add an element of additional fun to this excellent bedtime story by reading it under a blanket with their child, illuminated only by the glow of a flashlight. (Ages 3–7.)

20. *The Spring Hat.* By Madelaine Gill. (Simon & Schuster Books for Young Readers, 1993.) When mother bunny and her three playful offspring go for a spring picnic by the river, mother takes a snooze, and the little bunnies use her straw hat as a do-it-yourself Frisbee. Much to mom's displeasure, they lose the hat in the water. With some help, the bunnies make things right by fashioning a new head covering that is a wreath of spring flowers. Readers, seeing the perturbed expression on mother's face, might feel the bunnies' discomfort over this misdeed, but they will not see much in the expressions of the young bunnies who are drawn alike, showing little convincing emotion. Madelaine Gill's pastel illustrations are pleasant but dull. (Ages 3–6.)

21. *Blackout.* By John Rocco. (Disney-Hyperion, 2011.) When the lights go out one summer night in the city, a family first uses flashlights and candles to light its apartment and then goes up on the roof to escape the heat and gaze at the bright stars. Down below the whole neighborhood comes alive and is out on the street having fun. The family members play a board game together, something they were too busy to do when the lights were on. When the power comes back on, the family decides to continue playing a game by candlelight. Readers of all ages will be reminded that there are simple pleasures that do not require electricity, and there are benefits to taking a break from phones and computers. Rocco's rich illustrations earned *Blackout* a Caldecott Honor. (Ages 4–8.)

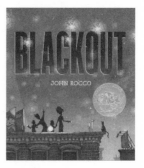

22. *Wow! City!* By Robert Neubecker. (Disney-Hyperion, 2004.) "Wow!" is the operative word in this story about Izzy the toddler's first exciting exposure to vibrant, larger-than-life New York City. Transported around town by her dad, she expresses her exuberance in two-word chunks such as "Wow! Taxi!" "Wow! Skyscrapers!" "Wow! Tunnel!" and "Wow! Fire engine!" Readers will love finding the father and daughter in busy scenes that demonstrate the grandeur of a big city as it seems to a child. Robert Neubecker's eye-popping, two-page spreads do such a masterful job of capturing the hustle and bustle of urban life that young readers will also be exclaiming, "Wow! City!" The story is based on Neubecker's daughter's actual visit to the Big Apple. (Ages 2–7.)

23. *A Growling Place.* By Thomas Aquinas Maguire. (Simply Read Books, 2007.) In this bedtime adventure reminiscent of *Where the Wild Things Are* (1963), Thomas Aquinas Maguire tells the tale of a little girl named Aril who follows her teddy bear to a growling place—that is, a lair of actual bears. The bears try to bully her, and when she stands up to them, they

show remorse. The story concludes with Aril sleeping in bed, with teddy bears assembled in a corner of her bedroom. Unlike many picture books, this spare-text title is divided into chapters, with its table of contents comprising emphasized words from the few sentences in the book. Maguire's amazing dreamscapes are done in muted colors, making Aril stand out in her bright pink dress. Maguire got his professional start thinking about the imagination of children as a toy designer for Fisher-Price and Lego. (Ages 4–8.)

24. *Snow Day.* By Daniel Peddle. (Doubleday, 2000.) Minimally illustrated, this radiant series of watercolors documents the brief and glorious life of a snowman. Readers are introduced to the book's stark simplicity by its plain white cover showing only a close-up of the dark eyes and carrot nose of the main character. The inside illustrations show a child in a snowsuit constructing a classic snowman out of three large snowballs, using sticks for arms, inserting coal for eyes and buttons, and basking in the early morning light. As shadows lengthen and night falls, the snowman reigns over his winter kingdom, before meeting his expected downfall the next day when he must face the persistent warm sun. (Ages 3–5.)

CHAPTER 6

Animals Aplenty

Some people talk to animals. Not many listen though. That's the problem.

—A. A. Milne

1. *Welcome to the Zoo.* By Alison Jay. (Dial Books for Young Readers, 2008.) Alison Jay leads readers on a tour through a whimsical menagerie and role reversal that allows animals to observe humans behaving in something like their natural habitat, with everyone freely interacting without cages. Animals level the playing field by sometimes acting like humans, with some of them sporting sunglasses, reading the newspaper, and buying ice cream. The illustrations are done with oil paint and a burnished, crackling varnish that makes the pictures look quaint and old world. Kids will enjoy seeing the usual caste of zoo characters—hippos, monkeys, giraffes, penguins, bears, and tigers—in a new light, casually mingling with people without concern that the creatures might run away or eat someone. (Ages 4–8.)

2. *Hug.* By Jez Alborough. (Candlewick Press, 2002.) Bobo, a needy little chimp, searches the jungle asking one animal after another for a hug, but nothing seems to satisfy his longing. He witnesses tender parent-child signs of affection in chameleons, giraffes, pythons, lions, hippos, and more but does not get what

41

he needs, making him cry. His tears go away when his mom arrives, and young readers will recognize that it wasn't just any hug that the tiny monkey needed but the embrace of his parent. This simple board book uses only three words—"HUG," "BOBO," and "MOMMY"—and they are more than enough to convey the strong need for security and parental love that all children have. (Ages 2–5.)

3. *Fish on a Walk.* By Eva Muggenthaler. (Enchanted Lion Books, 2011.) Children will have to go the extra mile in teasing out narratives in this nearly wordless picture book of surrealistic animals in offbeat settings with text that if removed would not be missed. For each of the bright and detailed illustrations, Eva Muggenthaler has included pairings of words or phrases at the bottom of her apparently unrelated spreads, which are usually, but not always, opposites. Here are a few: "Scared–Brave," "Ready for Fun–Ready for Bed," "Cranky–Kind," "Jealous–Accepting," and "Tricky–Truthful." Her animal characters include hedgehogs on the beach, an elephant on a teeter-totter, ants with shopping bags, and goats on a toboggan. Muggenthaler is one of Germany's most popular artists. (Ages 6–9.)

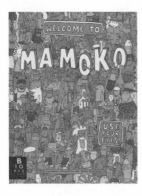

4. *Welcome to Mamoko.* By Aleksandra Mizielińska and Daniel Mizieliński. (Big Picture Press, 2013.) First published in Poland, this densely illustrated, sixteen-page board book is an interwoven series of adventures featuring quirky animal characters. The trick is to locate each of a cast of characters and to follow them from page to page to see what they are up to as they travel to a carnival in the town of Mamoko. The book's first page lists and briefly describes the zany characters, with names such as Mrs. Full-Wool, Pamela Snout, Miss Chubb, Vincent Brisk, Edwin Drench, and Cecily Beak. Each page is packed with attention-grabbing curiosities and mini-dramas that children will want to return to many times. (Ages 5–8.)

5. *We Hide, You Seek*. By Jose Aruego and Ariane Dewey. (Greenwillow Books, 1979.) Jose Aruego and Ariane Dewey have created an enjoyable book involving jungle animals hiding in their natural habitats, introducing the notion of camouflage and serving as a primer on the varieties of East African wildlife and their different ecological niches. The vehicle for this education in disguise is a red rhinoceros playing a game of hide-and-seek. He clumsily moves from animal to animal, doing a good job of seeking them out in desert, swamp, river, and plain locations. When it is his turn to hide, the rhino cleverly finds perfect cover blending in with other red horned behemoths of his own kind. There is a handy guide to the different species in the endpapers. (Ages 4–8.)

6. *Red Hat*. By Lita Judge. (Atheneum Books for Young Readers, 2013.) In this fair-weather sequel to *Red Sled* (2011), Lita Judge again uses onomatopoeia to convey the joyous romp of a troop of baby animals who pilfer a girl's knitted hat. The action starts when a bear cub steals a red hat hanging out on a clothesline to dry. The hat slowly unravels as it wildly exchanges hands several times. Except for the occasional high-spirited animal sound effects—"Hiii-ya," "Wow-za," "Yoo-ha," "Shwoop," "Doot-do-doo"—the book is wordless, but it certainly is not mute, as young readers will feel as though they can actually hear the playful noises coming from bunnies, raccoons, and other forest creatures. (Ages 2–6.)

7. *Hot on the Scent*. By Bente Bech and Peter Lind. (Gareth Stevens, 1992.) When Father Mouse goes into the woods to gather acorns, he smells something so irresistibly yummy that he risks life and limb to follow the sweet odor. After gnawing a tree down to cross a gorge, he is confronted by a dragonfly, chased by a mole after falling into its underground chambers, almost impaled by a farmer's spade, attacked by a hawk, pursued by a vicious cat, and caught in a spider's web, before he finally

arrives home to discover the origin of the enticing aroma. His wife has made pancakes, which she and the children have kept in a tall stack while patiently awaiting his arrival. (Ages 4–8.)

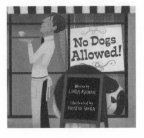

8. *No Dogs Allowed!* By Linda Ashman and Kristin Sorra. (Sterling Children's Books, 2011.) When a boy and his dog approach Alberto's new restaurant, the owner quickly changes his chalkboard message from "Welcome" to "No Dogs Allowed." As a succession of customers arrive with increasingly strange pets—a cat, rabbit, kangaroo, armadillo, elephant, pig, and monkey—Alberto expands his exclusionary policy to "No One with Fur, Feathers, Shells, Scales, or Trunks Allowed," and they all join the boy at the town fountain where the group buys lemonade and ice cream from a street vendor. Faced with the loss of business, Alberto completely reverses course, renaming his establishment "All Critters Bistro" with "Everyone Allowed." Kids will cheer the social message, while some parents and teachers may view the story as a parable about the self-correcting power of the marketplace. (Ages 3–8.)

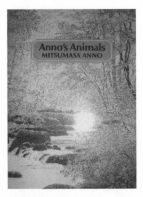

9. *Anno's Animals.* By Mitsumasa Anno. (Collins, 1979.) Mitsumasa Anno challenges children to go on a treasure hunt looking for animals hidden in lush foliage. To find the creatures embedded in the woodland scenes, readers will need to view the book at different angles to locate all the skillfully camouflaged animals, birds, and people. Like Anno's other books, this one is dense with imagery and no quick read. It should be approached like a leisurely walk in the woods, with time taken to soak in the pleasures that come from being an alert observer. Anno, a Japanese illustrator known for his mastery of wordless picture books, is a recipient of the international Hans Christian Andersen Medal, acknowledging his enduring contribution to children's books. (Ages 4–8.)

10. *Who?* By Leo Lionni. (Pantheon, 1983.) Intended for toddlers and slightly older kids, this wordless book essentially asks, Who is the animal on this page? *Who?* introduces the world of animals by having small mice meet them, in torn-paper images that include squirrels, turtles, rabbits, hens, owls, and porcupines. Leo Lionni's bold and simple illustrations make this title a wise choice for a child's first exposure to books. The 2014 board book edition of *Who?* contains some text. Lionni has received four Caldecott Honors for *Frederick* (1973), *Swimmy* (1973), *Alexander and the Wind-Up Mouse* (1974), and *Inch by Inch* (1995). The Italian artist was the first to use collage as the medium for illustrating children's books. (Ages 2–5.)

11. *My Friend Rabbit.* By Eric Rohmann. (Square Fish, 2007.) Winner of the Caldecott Medal, *My Friend Rabbit* is a minimal-text tale of a rabbit who gets his friend mouse's toy airplane stuck in a tree. Rabbit comes up with a plan to retrieve it by stacking several animals on top of one another, using an elephant, rhino, bear, crocodile, and hippo. The pile of animals comes tumbling down, producing havoc and annoyance with the well-intentioned but trouble-prone rabbit. The airplane is freed by the rumpus, and the mouse uses it to rescue his best buddy from the angry menagerie. Children will marvel at Rabbit's ingenuity and take pleasure in examining the range of comical facial expressions. *My Friend Rabbit* was made into an animated PBS series. (Ages 4–8.)

12. *Hippo! No, Rhino!* By Jeff Newman. (Little, Brown, 2006.) Little kids might be forgiven for confusing the names of extra-large African jungle animals, but adults should know better. When zookeeper Randy mistakenly places a hippo sign in front of the rhino enclosure, this naturally rubs the bright blue beast the wrong way. The rhino becomes increasingly distraught when people pass by and agree with this outrageous inaccuracy, forcing him to

loudly announce again and again that he is no hippo. Finally, an observant boy comes to the rescue by finding the right sign, lifting the indignant behemoth out of his funk. The only text in these appealing pictures using supersaturated hues is found in a few signs and speech balloons. (Ages 3–7.)

HANIMALS

13. *Hanimals.* By Mario Mariotti. (Green Tiger Press, 1984.) *Hanimals* is a series of colorfully painted human hands photographed in unusual positions and shapes, creating an exceedingly clever group of animals. Often with the aid of a marble employed as an eye, the pictures are striking depictions that most preschoolers will delight in and will certainly want to try themselves as an art project. On the book cover, readers will see a black-and-white-striped zebra head, while inside there are many equally imaginative animals, including ducks, chickens, doves, octopuses, giraffes, elephants, and even fanged snakes. Mario Mariotti's companion books are *Humands* (1982), *Humages* (1984), and *Hanimations* (1989). (Ages 4–9.)

14. *Tall.* By Jez Alborough. (Candlewick Press, 2005.) With minimal text and expressive illustrations, Jez Alborough shows a tiny chimp's attempt to become tall by climbing on top of a succession of larger animals. Bobo, the monkey who made his debut in *Hug* (2001), begins his quest for grown-up ascendancy when he scales a rock, then moves on to the heads and shoulders of a lion cub, baby elephant, and giraffe, before taking a tumble and being rescued by his mother. This story of a little monkey in a big jungle will win the hearts of young readers of small stature who will understand his eagerness to loom larger in an oversize world. (Ages 1–3.)

CHAPTER 7

Christmas Cheer

The holiest holidays are those
Kept by ourselves in silence and apart;
The secret anniversaries of the heart.

—Henry Wadsworth Longfellow

1. *A Small Miracle.* By Peter Collington. (Dragonfly Books, 2011.) A poor old woman who lives
alone in a trailer plays an accordion on the street for
money. Forced to sell her beloved musical instru-
ment for cash, she is robbed of her last money by
a thief who steals the poor box from a church and
vandalizes its nativity scene. The elderly woman
manages to recover the church's money from the
masked bandit and restore the broken nativity
scene. But departing the church, she passes out in
the snow. Seeing her distress, the nativity figures
spring to life and carry her home. They buy food,
build a fire, erect a Christmas tree, and bring back
her accordion. *A Small Miracle* is the perfect Christmas story, but its touching message of kindness and
selflessness make it an appropriate choice for any
season. (Ages 4–11.)

2. *Peter Spier's Christmas!* By Peter Spier. (Doubleday, 1983.) In the most idyllic and well-to-do home setting, two parents and their three children lovingly celebrate every aspect of Christmas. There is no hint of want or discord as this perfectly picturesque family shops for gifts, visits the store Santa, mails holiday cards, selects a tree, decorates the house, bakes cookies, puts up the nativity scene, attends church, welcomes relatives, consumes the Christmas feast, and happily cleans up, with mom and dad stealing a kiss under the mistletoe. Peter Spier's charmingly nostalgic picture book is both the distilled essence of all that is thought to be good and pure about Christmas and an ideal that may strike some readers as almost too sugary and sentimental. (Ages 4–8.)

3. *Small, Medium & Large.* By Jane Monroe Donovan. (Sleeping Bear Press, 2010.) A girl writes two short letters to Santa Claus. In the first, she says that she doesn't want any toys for Christmas, and in the second she indicates a longing for something more meaningful. Her wish comes true when on Christmas morning she finds under the tree small, medium, and large boxes containing three new friends—a cat, a dog, and a pony—with whom she can share holiday cheer. The foursome have a jolly time baking cookies, making snow angels, having a snowball fight, sitting by the fire, and snuggling in bed. This cozy story would make the perfect holiday gift. Jane Monroe Donovan is author of *Winter's Gift* (2004), another charming Christmas picture book. (Ages 4–8.)

4. *Silent Night.* By Sandy Turner. (Atheneum, 2001.) With minimal text consisting of dog sounds, Sandy Turner has come up with a new angle on the supposedly quiet hours of darkness that precede Christmas Day. In scenes that may remind readers of the unheeded dog barks that are a staple of science fiction films, parents don't have a clue why their terrier is constantly yapping and woofing as they get ready for Christmas and go to bed. It never occurs to mom, dad, and the kids that Santa Claus is paying them a visit and that their dog is the only one who can see him. The perceptive and frustrated pooch even takes a bite out of Santa's pants, leaving a visible bright red swatch behind that gets whisked up the chimney in the morning. But the square of cloth is not lost. There is a piece of red felt smartly pasted in the endpapers, adding a nice touch to the book's other memorable features. (Ages 4–8.)

5. *The Christmas Gift.* By Emily Arnold McCully. (StarWalk Kids Media, 2012.) With pictures that are rich in detail and full of Christmas cheer, Emily Arnold McCully begins her story with a mouse family engaged in familiar holiday morning chaos, opening gifts in front of a decorated tree, with wrapping paper everywhere. Amid the hustle and bustle of trumpets, xylophones, and other toys, a little mouse only has eyes for a remote-controlled airplane, a gift so singularly superior that it is taken along on a visit to Grandma and Grandpa's house. When this new toy is broken, so is the mouse's heart, until Grandma goes up into the attic and retrieves an old train set to console her. First published in 1988, *The Christmas Gift* is a must addition to every family library. (Ages 3–6.)

6. *Carl's Christmas.* By Alexandra Day. (Farrar, Straus & Giroux, 1990.) This gorgeous addition to the Carl series will have fans of the faithful babysitting Rottweiler eager to find out what he will do this time to pull the wool over the eyes of his owners. "We're going to Grandma's and then to church. Take good care of the baby, Carl," are the only words in this otherwise text-free book, setting the stage for a special Christmas Eve adventure. When the parents leave, Carl and his young ward travel around town, spreading yuletide cheer, joining some holiday carolers, and donating a basket to the poor. Back at home, the amazing dog helps Santa distribute gifts and puts the baby to bed. As far as returning mom and dad know, not a creature was stirring, not even a mouse. (Ages 2–5.)

7. *The Christmas We Moved to the Barn.* By Cooper Edens and Alexandra Day. (HarperCollins, 1997.) When a mom and her two daughters receive news that they are being evicted from their home on Christmas Eve, a menagerie of supportive pets help them haul their belongings over a snowy landscape into an abandoned barn. Dogs and cats, parrots and ponies are among the twelve animals who go back and forth over wintery fields, clean the place up, hang the family's stockings, and put up a tree. In this warm and whimsical nod to the original Christmas tale, this homeless family makes the best of a difficult situation, succeeding in celebrating the holiday in a modest shelter, abundant with love. (Ages 3–7.)

8. *The Snowy Path: A Christmas Journey.* By Lark Carrier. (Picture Book Studio, 1989.) A lone girl follows the tracks of animals in a snowy forest at twilight, with each page of snow prints leading to a die-cut flap, which when flipped reveals who made the tracks, pointing to a dog, rabbit, mouse, deer, skunk, bear, turkey, and finally Santa and his reindeer. Under a starry sky, the girl and animals complete their journey by watching in awe as Santa and his sleigh race up a wintery slope, magically ascending into the air. *The Snowy Path*, wordless except for two introductory paragraphs, will stimulate children to make meaning of the muted watercolor scenes by verbalizing their own Christmas stories. (Ages 4–8.)

9. *Don't Forget Me, Santa Claus.* By Virginia Mayo. (Barrons Juveniles, 1993.) The cover of this holiday offering shows a shocked and despondent toddler kneeling in the snow wearing striped pajamas and holding an empty red stocking. Sadly, Santa forgot to fill it with Christmas goodies, so the little guy stows away on the magic sleigh for an exciting trip to the North Pole to get his just reward. When the jolly old elf discovers his passenger, he gives the child a tour, allows him his choice of toys, and even lets him wear the Santa outfit on the trip back home. The toddler is still wearing Santa's cap when he awakens on Christmas morning. (Ages 2–6.)

10. *How Santa Claus Had a Long and Difficult Journey Delivering His Presents.* By Fernando Krahn. (Dell Publishing, 1988.) Wordless, except for its wordy title, Fernando Krahn's book is a variation on the familiar theme of a Christmas that almost didn't come to pass. After a bear awakens Santa, the old gentleman dresses and packs the sleigh, but when the harness breaks, the reindeer fly off without him. The toys are unsuccessful in trying to get the jolly old elf airborne, but the blessed day is saved when passing angels miraculously fly Santa and his sleigh to the reindeer waiting for him on a rooftop. *How Santa Claus Had a Long and Difficult Journey Delivering His Presents* is not exactly *How the Grinch Stole Christmas* (1957) or *Rudolph the Red-Nosed Reindeer* (2001), but it will easily pass muster with young children who will never grow tired of contemplating the catastrophic possibility of a Christmas without Santa's toys. (Ages 4–8.)

11. *An Edwardian Christmas.* By John S. Goodall. (Atheneum, 1981.) This tastefully illustrated picture book portrays Christmas festivities on an English country estate overflowing with all the accoutrements of wealth and privilege, including servants, elegant clothing, and extravagant parties. Family preparations and holiday celebrations of this bygone era are depicted in classic style with beautiful paintings reminiscent of the set for *Downton Abbey*. John S. Goodall is clearly committed to evoking nostalgia for the genteel sensibilities of traditional upper-class life, having also created *An Edwardian Summer* (1976), *An Edwardian Holiday* (1979), *An Edwardian Season* (1980), and *Edwardian Entertainments* (1982). Many of Goodall's other titles also feature class-based, Victorian-style imagery. (Ages 4–8.)

CHAPTER 8

Character Values

We don't see things as they are; we see them as we are.

—Anaïs Nin

1. *Changes, Changes.* By Pat Hutchins. (Aladdin Paperbacks, 1987.) A tiny wooden couple happily build a house of blocks until it catches on fire! They build a fire engine to extinguish the flames, and when the water creates a flood, they build a boat to sail away. The resourceful and persevering figurines also build a truck, a train, and in due course a new home. The book will teach children about the concept of change, conveying the message that when things go wrong, something new can be constructed out of what remains. Children will be inspired to use their imaginations, not just to play with blocks, but also to solve problems in a variety of situations. (Ages 2–6.)

2. *Four Hungry Kittens.* By Emily Arnold McCully. (StarWalk Kids Media, 2013.) A mama cat's hunt for a mouse leads her into a barn's grain room where she is inadvertently trapped inside. Waiting for their food, the four kittens get into mischief, two of them falling into a container full of milk. An alert dog comes to the rescue, scaring off a hawk, alerting the farmer to the milky mishap, and signaling that the mother cat needs to be released. Touchingly, the well-intentioned pooch even offers a bone to the kittens. The book ends with the mother cat delivering her prey to her hungry offspring but does not show them eating it. Children will realize that this is not a happy ending for everyone and will want to know what happens to the mouse. (Ages 3–6.)

3. *Inside Outside.* By Lizi Boyd. (Chronicle Books, 2013.) Featuring die-cut windows, *Inside Outside* shows a boy and his dog playing, with cutouts providing clues to the fun he has inside his house and outdoors during different seasons of the year. This productive boy is a whirlwind of activity. He makes snowmen, plants a garden, rakes leaves, puts on a puppet show, builds a tree house, and sails a boat in a little pool. Along the way, two mice share in the activities, and readers will enjoy locating them throughout the book. The nifty book cover has the homey look of a paper bag, adding to its appeal. Children looking for something to do will benefit from perusing this book and imitating the industriousness of its main character. (Ages 3–5.)

4. *A Day, a Dog.* By Gabrielle Vincent. (Front Street Press, 1999.) Minimalist charcoal illustrations tell the poignant and bleak story of a dog forced out of a car and abandoned by the side of the road. The poor dog tries to follow his owners, narrowly avoids being run over, and causes an auto accident. When he makes his way to another town, he meets a boy and perhaps finds a new home. Children will have nothing but sympathy for this forlorn creature and disgust for the dog-dumping family. This book could be used to discuss cruelty to animals or to explore the topic of personal responsibility. *A Day, a Dog* is a provocative book and deserving winner of the Parents' Choice Gold Award. (Ages 7–12.)

5. *Hank Finds an Egg.* By Rebecca Dudley. (Peter Pauper Press, 2013.) While strolling in the forest, Hank discovers an egg on the ground, finds its nest, and works very hard to return it to its proper home. Less clear is Hank's animal nature: he is either a hand-stitched bear or a monkey. In charming close-up photographs of painstakingly constructed

dioramas, Rebecca Dudley shows detailed, small-scale woodland settings modeled in clay, felt, and other materials. After several failed attempts to return the egg to its nest, Hank carefully hands the egg off to its hummingbird mother, who flies it to her treetop home. Children will love Hank, finding him adorably kind and unfailingly diligent. (Ages 3–8.)

6. *The Girl and the Bicycle.* By Mark Pett. (Simon & Schuster Books for Young Readers, 2014.) With old-time sepia-tinted drawings, Mark Pett tells the story of a girl who spots a shiny green bike in a store window and does yard work for a kindly neighborhood woman to earn the money to buy it. They work together through the seasons and form a tight bond. When the time comes to purchase the bicycle, the hard-working girl finds that her heart's desire has already been sold. Instead of acting sullen and disappointed, she uses her earnings to buy a tricycle for her little brother. In a concluding scene that older kids may anticipate, the girl is surprised to find that the bespectacled woman has already bought her the bike. Celebrating the virtues of hard work, persistence, and generosity, this touching retro-style picture book has the makings of a contemporary classic. (Ages 4–8.)

7. *The Red Scarf.* By Anne Villeneuve. (Tundra Books, 2010.) When a strange caped man leaves a red scarf behind in a taxi, the cab driver, a white mole named Turbin, is determined to return it to him. The responsible cabbie is soon engrossed in a world of circus performers, including a roller-skating polar bear, an agreeable lizard, a turbaned monkey, and a fearsome lion. Becoming part of the circus show, Turbin is swallowed by the lion and falls from a high wire into a trunk that is penetrated with swords. Unharmed by the adventure, the taxi-driving mole manages to return the scarf but leaves his hat behind.

Quebecois illustrator Anne Villeneuve first published *The Red Scarf* in French as *L'echarpe rouge*. Readers will find the book's cartoon art loosely energetic and expressive, with several scenes to a page. (Ages 4–8.)

8. *Early Birdy Gets the Worm.* By Bruce Lansky and Bill Bolton. (Meadowbrook, 2014.) Big, easy-to-follow illustrations welcome children to participate in this lesson about birds waking up and taking care of themselves. After seeing his mother tug a worm from the ground, a little bird tries to do the same thing himself. When he mistakenly goes after a mouse's pink tail, he learns that the process is not as easy as it seems. Parents will like imparting the message that if you wake up and get to work early, you are more likely to succeed, but in the end this little bird's success relies not on his diligence but on his mother's ability to get him a worm. *Early Birdy Gets the Worm* received a Mom's Choice Awards for excellent family-friendly products and media. Preschoolers who enjoyed *Early Birdy Gets the Worm* will be eager to read *Polar Brrr's Big Adventure* (2014) and *Monkey See, Monkey Do* (2014). (Ages 2–6.)

9. *Noah: A Wordless Picture Book.* By Mark Ludy. (Plough Publishing, 2014.) *Noah* is advertised as a biblically faithful account of the end of the world, a claim that will have strong appeal to a fundamentalist readership. This visual retelling of one of the world's greatest stories focuses on Noah's faithfulness to God, his relationship with his family, and the building of the ark. Ludy's playful, cartoonish illustrations will make this graphic novel accessible to a young audience, as he treads lightly on the wickedness of humankind that causes God's wrath and the catastrophic flood. Ludy's inclusion of dinosaurs, extinct millions of years before the evolution of humans, is sure to increase the skepticism of parents who are mindful of the vast geological record. (Ages 3–8.)

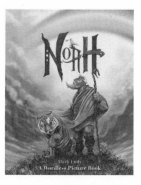

10. *Coming Home.* By Greg Ruth. (Feiwel & Friends, 2014.) *Coming Home* is a tribute to soldiers who fight for their country and to the loved ones who eagerly await their return. In this almost wordless book, a young boy anxiously scans an airport crowd looking for his returning parent. Amid other joyful homecomings of military personnel, the boy locates his uniformed mother and leaps into her arms. The illustrations are realistic, capturing a range of emotions from tension and anticipation to absolute joy. Seeing parents reunited with their children packs an emotional wallop, and Greg Ruth accomplishes this without becoming too maudlin. This patriotic story will be useful in assuaging the fears of children whose parents serve in the armed forces. (Ages 3–7.)

CHAPTER 9

Fabulous Friendships

What sort of relationship do you want to be in? What sort of partnership will push you to be your best, freest, happiest self?

—Courtney E. Martin

1. *Flora and the Flamingo.* By Molly Idle. (Chronicle Books, 2013.) This is a whimsical story of a graceful flamingo and an awkward girl who learn to dance together in almost perfect harmony. Flora, dressed in a pink bathing suit and bathing cap, lacks the elegance of her initially standoffish teacher, but the flamingo warms up to the point where they finally succeed in synchronizing their movements. Fold-down flaps add to the fun as new insights are revealed about this unlikely pair. The book climaxes with bird and girl doing a cannonball together into a swimming pool. Abundant emotional chemistry and lean illustrations combine to make *Flora and the Flamingo* a deserving recipient of the Caldecott Medal. (Ages 3–6.)

2. *Do You Want to Be My Friend?* By Eric Carle. (HarperFestival, 1995.) First published in 1971, this simple board book, illustrated with brilliant collages, follows a lonely mouse's patient search for companionship. The little gray creature meets many animals, including a seal, giraffe, fox, alligator, and hippopotamus, inquiring, "Do you want to be my

friend?" Finally, he meets a mouse who does. The green border that appears throughout brings the book to a dramatic finish. Eric Carle's classic book seems the perfect choice for a prereader, but parents and teachers will want to ensure that the book does not impart the message that friendship is possible only with animals of one's own kind. (Ages 2–6.)

3. *Bluebird.* By Bob Staake. (Schwartz & Wade Books, 2013.) The topics of bullying and death are explored in this poignant story of a young boy and the friendship he develops with a lively bluebird. The boy's lonely existence in a metropolis is enlivened when a bluebird begins following him. They share a treat, sail a boat in a pond, and play hide-and-seek before entering a dark forest, where a gang of bullies accost them. Shockingly, the bird is killed protecting the boy from injury. The boy cradles his fallen friend, and the two are magically lifted toward the sky by a flock of birds. The bluebird comes back to life and ascends into the clouds, while the boy waves good-bye. *Bluebird* is a beautiful fable that will prompt many conversations about cruelty, friendship, and sacrifice. (Ages 4–8.)

4. *Clown.* By Quentin Blake. (Henry Holt, 1998.) When a toy clown is thrown into the trash with some stuffed animal friends, he escapes and tries to find a home for his fellow discarded toys. After experiencing some rude treatment, the clown is tossed through the window of a shabby apartment. Paint is peeling off the walls, unwashed dishes are scattered about, and a young mother is caring for a crying baby. The clown lifts the family's spirit by juggling and makes himself useful by cleaning up and changing the baby. In return, they all set out to rescue the cast-off toys. When the grandmother arrives, she sees a happy domestic scene. This charming story may inspire families who throw away still-useful toys to rethink their wasteful ways. Quentin Blake is best known for illustrating books written by Roald Dahl, including *The BFG* (1982), *The Witches* (1983), and *Matilda* (1988). (Ages 3–8.)

5. *Owly & Wormy, Friends All Aflutter!* By Andy Runton. (Atheneum Books for Young Readers, 2011.) Graphic novelist Andy Runton takes aim at a young audience in this cheerful story involving metamorphosis. In this picture book, Owly and Wormy want butterflies and learn from a raccoon florist that planting milkweed is a good way to attract the beautiful insects. When the plant becomes home to not-so-beautiful caterpillars, the two are at first disappointed but then become friends with their new playmates. Owly and Wormy are puzzled when their buddies disappear and must wait a long time before learning what has become of them. Older children will figure out what is going on, but many toddlers and preschoolers will be surprised by the monarchs and amazed by the knowledge of their transformation. (Ages 3–6.)

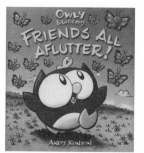

6. *Chicken and Cat.* By Sara Varon. (Scholastic Press, 2006.) When Cat goes to visit Chicken in New York City, he is not happy with what he finds. He misses his country greenery and is disheartened by the urban blight. To perk things up, the big-eyed buddies ride bikes in Central Park, eat ice cream, and hop the train to Coney Island, taking in its beaches. But seeing what the city has to offer is still not enough for the cute but parochial feline. Chicken improves his companion's mood by planting a colorful vegetable and flower garden in a vacant lot outside Chicken's apartment window. Children of all ages will find Sara Varon's quiet characters sweetly innocent and very appealing. (Ages 4–8.)

7. *Chicken and Cat Clean Up.* By Sara Varon. (Scholastic Press, 2009.) In this welcome sequel to *Chicken and Cat* (2006), Cat has overcome his aversion to life in the city and has been hired by Chicken to work for him in a housekeeping business. Cat is not well suited for this career and makes lots of mistakes, causing distress to both pals. However, Cat proves his worth in a way that is true to his nature

when he catches a purse-snatching mouse. Now a hero, not a hapless failure, Cat becomes Chicken's equal partner in a new business that includes housekeeping and mouse-catching services. Varon's bright and simple illustrations are a joy to behold. Her clean imagery and endearing characters will leave children hoping for more books about this adorable twosome. (Ages 4–8.)

8. *The Boys*. By Jeff Newman. (Simon & Schuster Books for Young Readers, 2010.) A new boy to the neighborhood is too shy to play baseball with the other kids until a group of four old men intervene and give him the confidence to get involved. Day after day the quiet lad shows up at the city park, looking increasingly more like an old geezer than a vigorous youngster. The elderly gentlemen know the boy wants to do more than just feed the pigeons, so one day they leave their park bench and give him a demonstration of how to ride bikes, frolic on the jungle gym, and play baseball. After playing along with the men and receiving their comical instruction on how to be a kid, the boy finds the courage to engage with his peers. (Ages 4–8.)

9. *Peep!* By Kevin Luthardt. (Peachtree Publishers, 2012.) This nearly wordless picture book cheerfully begins with a whistling boy walking along a sidewalk. He spots an egg, watches it crack open, and sees a cute yellow duckling emerge. The bird "peeps," and despite efforts to get him to stay put, the imprinted duckling follows the boy home. They become fast friends, watching TV together, attending soccer matches, and even making an appearance at school for show-and-tell. When autumn comes, the duckling sees a flock of ducks flying south. Its "peep" matures into a "quack," and the boy must set it free. But all is not lost. In the final picture, the boy hears a "mew" and finds a new pet kitten. (Ages 4–7.)

10. *An Ocean World.* By Peter Sís. (Greenwillow Books, 1992.) This poignant book is about a whale that readers first see as a baby calf in a small inflatable pool. Raised in lonely captivity, he gradually outgrows different tanks and in adulthood is finally released into the open sea. But he has never seen another member of his own species and is puzzled and curious when he comes face to face with several gargantuan objects that might be of his own kind. He has funny encounters with a blimp, a submarine, a cloud, a school of fish, a shipwreck, and a polluting barge that dumps trash on the beleaguered wanderer. When another whale finally appears on the horizon, it becomes love at first sight. The two whales are pictured on the back cover making a rainbow. (Ages 4–8.)

11. *The Farmer and the Clown.* By Marla Frazee. (Beach Lane Books, 2014.) When a child clown gets bumped off a fast-moving train, a scowling, lonely farmer reluctantly rescues him and babysits for a day until the clown's family comes back for him. The pair is a study in contrasts, the child dressed all in red and yellow with a painted-on smile and the hunched over farmer in black overalls with a gloomy, bearded face. But the unlikely pair bonds when the farmer takes the clown home. Once the little clown removes his cheerful makeup, his face is revealed to be quite sad, and the farmer does tricks to cheer him up, while the tiny comic helps out with chores. They even juggle eggs together! By the time the circus train returns, they have become real friends. *Kirkus Reviews* selected *The Farmer and the Clown* as one of the year's best books to start a conversation. (Ages 3–9.)

12. *Little Bird.* By Germano Zullo and Albertine. (Enchanted Lion Books, 2012.) The Swiss team of Germano Zullo and Albertine has created a delightful visual narrative about a man in overalls who helps a bird to fly. When the man drives his truck to the edge of a cliff, he releases a flock of birds, but a tiny fearful one stays behind. He sits with his little friend, shares a sandwich, and encourages the

bird to fly by comically flapping his arms. The bird finally takes flight, and the truck driver departs, but he gets an unexpected reward when the flock returns to carry him up to the sky to fly like them. *Little Bird* includes a few unnecessary remarks, such as "Most of the time we don't notice the small things" and "There are no greater treasures than the little things," to support its simple, color-saturated illustrations. (Ages 5–10.)

13. *The Secret of Love.* By Sarah Emmanuelle Burg. (Penguin Young Readers Group, 2006.) The French artist uses minimal charcoal pencil to show a boy and girl strolling hand in hand. When they both reach for a red heart-shaped flower, they fight about its ownership, tear the flower apart, and go their separate ways. But soon they miss one another and each decides to resolve their differences by giving the other the same gift, seeds to be planted and nurtured into a field of flourishing red flowers. *The Secret of Love* has a simple message about hurt feelings, reconciliation, and the fragility of relationships that preschoolers will be able to grasp but which might have greater meaning for older children. (Ages 4–9.)

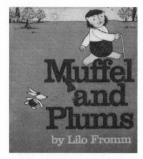

14. *Muffel and Plums.* By Lilo Fromm. (Macmillan, 1972.) Originally published in Germany, the book consists of nine short stories involving a stuffed toy lion and a small clumsy character that is either a rabbit or a piglet. This low-key friendship resembles the comfortable relationship described in Arnold Lobel's famous *Frog and Toad Are Friends* (1970), and the little maladroit creature, Plums, is reminiscent of Piglet from A. A. Milne's classic Winnie the Pooh series. Muffle and Plums share a home together and mostly engage in everyday activities such as riding bicycles, having picnics, and catching butterflies. Sketched in black and white, these dissimilar friends are excellent models of warm and enduring companionship. (Ages 3–6.)

15. *Good News, Bad News.* By Jeff Mack. (Chronicle Books, 2012.) Using only four words but many energetic cartoon illustrations, Jeff Mack has created a book about two friends who are polar opposites. Bunny sees only the positive, while Mouse sees only the negative, and the temperaments of this odd couple are on full display when they go on a picnic. The sunny rabbit offers good news in the form of a picnic basket, but the glass-half-empty rodent sees only the possibility of rain. When raindrops begin to fall and optimistic Bunny offers the good news of an umbrella, a strong gust of wind propels umbrella-holding Mouse into a tree. Kids will laugh at the slapstick comedy, but world-weary parents might see the roots of political dysfunction foreshadowed in these sharply different dispositions. (Ages 3–7.)

16. *Pssst! Doggie—.* By Ezra Jack Keats. (Franklin Watts, 1973.) In children's literature, cats and dogs are typically antagonists, but in this almost wordless book, Ezra Jack Keats shows them pairing up to produce surprising results. On the book's cover, a cat is shown approaching a sleeping dog, presumably waking the shaggy mutt with "Pssst! Doggie!" Inside, readers will find that the cat has asked him to dance, and the pair is pictured wearing costumes and dancing from country to country. Children will enjoy the funny antics of this supple cat and stout dog and will perhaps imagine that they hear the same music that accompanies their movement across the dance floor. Keats is best known for his book *The Snowy Day* (1962), which won the Caldecott Medal and introduced African Americans into a genre that had been dominated by white characters. (Ages 4–8.)

17. *Kitten for a Day.* By Ezra Jack Keats. (Perfection Learning, 2008.) This nearly text-free story, originally published in 1974, shows what happens when a friendly puppy temporarily joins a litter of kittens. The floppy-eared puppy is clumsy and confused as he spills milk, bumps his head, chases a mouse, and frolics with the four energetic felines, never quite able to fit in. When his mother calls the little hound dog

back from his new friends, he says, "Next time, let's all be puppies!" Keats's sweet story about carefree baby animals is a perfect choice for preschoolers. Its messages about the joyfulness of play, the acceptance of differences, and the importance of self-discovery strike just the right note. (Ages 2–7.)

18. *Mighty Mizzling Mouse and the Red Cabbage House.* By Friso Henstra. (Little, Brown, 1984.) This sequel to *Mighty Mizzling Mouse* (1983) involves the determined efforts of a mouse to build a house and impress his girlfriend. She, dressed in a yellow skirt with purple polka dots and matching shoes, picks out a large red cabbage that Mighty skillfully dispatches with a large axe. With the aid of a frog associate with a saw, the resourceful rodent transforms the cabbage into an impressive house. But the couple's happiness is short lived. While Mighty (who wears nothing but turquoise sneakers) is giving flowers to his lady friend, a villainous rabbit appears and destroys their house. It is obvious that the girl blames Mighty for this misfortune, but he seems undaunted, marching off with his axe to begin again. (Ages 4–8.)

19. *Yo! Yes?* By Chris Raschka. (Scholastic, 2007.) *Yo! Yes?* This is a Caldecott Honor book about isolated boys, one African American, one Caucasian, who meet on the street and become friends. This short story shows the two boys getting acquainted with two-word monosyllabic exchanges such as "What's up?" and "Not much," but the important aspects of their delicate emerging relationship are transmitted nonverbally. One of the boys is shy and the other outgoing, but their temperamental differences are overcome, making their encounter kindly rather than combative. The book reads like a simple two-character production set on a stage without scenery or props, just two kids expressing a range of emotion and succeeding in bridging a divide. (Ages 4–8.)

20. *Ball.* By Mary Sullivan. (Houghton Mifflin Harcourt Books for Children, 2013.) Mary Sullivan's award-winning book is about the single-minded fascination that dogs have for balls. Except perhaps for a Frisbee, no toy is so able to unleash the primal canine urge to play catch. When his owner and usual playmate leaves for school, the dog dreams of finding a partner for his favorite pastime. Having failed to interest the mother of the household and the family cat, and after abandoning a one-sided game of catch, he imagines flying through space, chasing the bright red ball, and having a cake decorated with his beloved sphere. Readers will feel the dog's bliss when his master returns and he is once again able to do what his heart most desires. (Ages 4–8.)

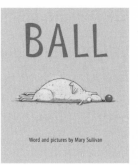

CHAPTER 10

Comedy Capers

Some stories are best told without words.

—Suzy Lee

1. *Where's Walrus?* By Stephen Savage. (Scholastic Press, 2011.) While everyone else in the zoo is asleep, a sly and adventurous walrus escapes and leads the zookeeper on a lively chase through the city. The recurring comic gag is that the walrus continues to avoid detection by hiding in plain sight: among businessmen at a lunch counter, with mannequins in a department store window, with firemen spraying a burning building, with artists painting in the park, and even in a chorus line of dancers. The walrus's silly blending into each scene comes to an end when he distinguishes himself by winning a diving competition. When the walrus returns to the zoo, readers see that the zookeeper has wisely refurbished it with a diving pool. Kids will love the seek-and-find format of this charming book. (Ages 3–7.)

2. *Oops*. By Mercer Mayer. (Puffin Books, 1978.) *Oops* chronicles a series of silly pratfalls involving a large lady hippopotamus. Swatting at a fly at a dinosaur exhibit, she destroys one of the skeletons, and when she picks up a flower on the railroad tracks, the speeding locomotive, not the hippo, bares the brunt of their collision. When she selects a grape-fruit from an outdoor stand, a bunch of them spill to the ground. When she enters a shop full of fine china, there is really no question about what will happen. Clumsy and oblivious to her surroundings, the endearing creature brings havoc everywhere she goes. Children will appreciate the simple humor and cartoonish drawings. (Ages 3–7.)

3. *Hocus Pocus.* By Sylvie Desrosiers and Rémy Simard. (Kids Can Press, 2011.) Hocus Pocus is a mischievous blue rabbit who lives in a magician's top hat. When the magician arrives home one day with a shopping bag full of food, the bunny spots some carrots and decides to go after them. But to get to the inviting orange veggies, he must first sneak by the magician's sleeping pet dog. The canine awakens, and the two engage in a battle of wits that goes to the clever rabbit, ending with the chagrined mutt being locked outside. This funny contest is drawn in the style of a colorful old cartoon, with lots of action and movement. Young children will identify with the cute bunny as he triumphs over the larger animal. (Ages 3–7.)

4. *Follow Carl!* By Alexandra Day. (Farrar, Straus & Giroux, 1998.) In this series book, gentle dog babysitter Carl leads the neighborhood children in a game of follow the leader and has them doing canine things such as carrying sticks in their mouths, begging for treats at a bakery, and barking at squirrels in a tree! This lively adventure, done with impressionistic watercolors and set in a suburban fall landscape, includes kids riding on the Rottweiler's back, visiting a croquet court, and hopping over a stream. As is always the case in the Carl stories, the big black dog and his toddler companion are innocently back where they belong before the mother returns. (Ages 3–6.)

5. *Jack Wants a Snack.* By Pat Schories. (Boyds Mills Press, 2008.) In this fourth book in the series about an always hungry and curious dog, Jack finds that the girl in his family is having a tea party with popcorn, and he hasn't been invited. She gives him one measly piece, reserving the batch for her dolls and stuffed animals, but he wants a more ample snack. Meanwhile, a gutsy chipmunk crashes the party, and the dog and girl give chase. She tries to trap the unwelcome rodent in a box but ends up catching Jack instead! The Bank Street College of Education designated *Jack Wants a Snack* as one of its best children's books of the year. (Ages 2–6.)

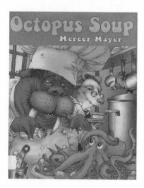

6. *Once upon a Banana.* By Jennifer Armstrong and David Small. (Simon & Schuster / Paula Wiseman Books, 2006.) A wide-eyed monkey runs away from his juggler partner toward a fruit stand full of bananas, starting a domino effect chain of events as the juggler chases down the chimp. This slapstick comedy takes off when the monkey steals a banana, tossing the peel on the sidewalk, setting off a chaotic succession of toppling people. A dismounted biker slips on the peel, causing a ladder to tremble, knocking off the painter, who falls into a passing shopping cart, which knocks down a barber pole, pulling dog leashes out of an owner's hand, and so forth. There is mayhem in every image and even a few sly appearances of Laurel and Hardy. Although the book is technically wordless, each picture contains a cleverly rhyming street sign, such as "One-Way Street No Bare Feet." (Ages 4–8.)

7. *Octopus Soup.* By Mercer Mayer. (Marshall Cavendish Children, 2011.) This humorous misadventure begins when a little green octopus leaves his undersea home, climbs the anchor line of a boat, and sneaks into the fisherman's basket. When they get ashore, the startled fisherman flings the little creature onto the head of a frog dining in a restaurant, who sweeps him into a water pitcher in the eatery, within reach of the walrus chef with an ominous meat cleaver. To avoid becoming a menu item, the eight-legger runs for his life, comically pursued through the town by the chef and other animals. The terrified octopus finally makes it back to his aquatic sanctuary and the protection of his mother. (Ages 4–8.)

8. *Hello, Mr. Hulot.* By David Merveille. (NorthSouth, 2013.) Mr. Hulot is a naive and absent-minded iconic character in the tradition of Charlie Chaplin, Walter Mitty, and Mr. Bean, made famous in a series of French films in the 1950s and 1960s. In twenty-two comedy vignettes, David Merveille captures the essence of this pipe-smoking, umbrella-toting, would-be hero, as he silently struggles with the most basic features of modern existence. When he bends over to smell a flower, he accidentally flashes someone the moon. When walking on a crosswalk, he imagines himself leaping over a series of crevasses, and while purchasing a snow globe, Mr. Hulot somehow creates a real snow storm. There is a lot of sophistication built into this entertaining title, and some visual jokes may require explanation to young children. (Ages 5–9.)

9. *Look What I Can Do.* By Jose Aruego. (Aladdin Books, 1988.) When one water buffalo challenges another to a friendly look-what-I-can-do contest, they romp through the jungle, each trying to one-up the other. The competitive show-offs, showcased in large double-paged spreads, create havoc for other animals along the way. After a series of exhausting follow-the-leader maneuvers, the two large creatures are left breathlessly crawling out of the river, only to be taunted by the arrival of another pretentious beast. The posturing of these funny buffalo not only mimics rituals in the animal kingdom but also sheds light on the inflated male ego. This minimal-text title was originally published in 1971. (Ages 3–8.)

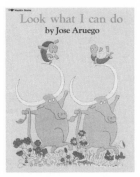

10. *Red Sled.* By Lita Judge. (Atheneum Books for Young Readers, 2011.) When a little girl leaves her sled on the front porch of her cabin, mountain animals take it for a nocturnal joy ride. Led by an inquisitive bear and joined by a mouse, rabbit, moose, opossum, raccoon, and porcupine, the animals joyously zoom over the winter terrain, comically chang-

ing positions for every turn. Lita Judge has included a few onomatopoeic phrases, such as "scrunch scrinch scrunch" to convey the sound of the bear walking on snow and "gadung gadung gadung" to signify the sound the sled makes going down the hill. The most outstanding feature of these high-energy romps is the innocent delight of the woodland creatures. The animal gang returns the borrowed sled, leaving the girl to puzzle the next morning over the paw prints in the snow. (Ages 2–6.)

11. *Rosie's Walk.* By Pat Hutchins. (Red Fox, 2010.) When Rosie the plump hen decides to leave her chicken coop for a stroll around the farmyard, an ill-fated fox keeps messing up his opportunities to catch her. Rosie doesn't know he is on her tail, but she still leads him into one mishap after another. First published in 1968, this spare-text classic is the quintessential bumbling-hero narrative. Rosie remains blissfully clueless, yet stymies the predator at every turn. The fox is finally chased off by a swarm of bees, while the oblivious chicken goes safely home. Kids will love this tongue-in-cheek story and may even feel sympathy for the unlucky fox. (Ages 2–7.)

12. *The Bear and the Fly.* By Paula Winter. (Crown Publishers, 1976.) A mother bear gently holds her wine glass, while her husband and daughter politely spoon food into their mouths, and a pooch expectantly waits for a scrap of food from the tranquil family meal. All is well with the furry family until a fly buzzes in and destabilizes this civilized setting. Father bear goes berserk, relentlessly pursuing the bug with a swatter, knocking his family unconscious, and destroying the room furniture until he falls from a chair he has stacked on top of the table. Oblivious to the destruction in his wake, the fly proceeds out the window. Children will adore the pandemonium and wonder if this could be the same family of Goldilocks fame having a bad day. *The Bear and the Fly* was named a Best Illustrated Children's Book by the *New York Times*. (Ages 3–6.)

13. *April Fools.* By Fernando Krahn. (E. P. Dutton, 1974.) This story centers on two mischievous boys who mastermind an April Fools' Day prank played on the citizens of their community. Celebrated Chilean cartoonist Fernando Krahn's picture book shows them secretly constructing the neck and head of a dragon-like creature that mysteriously pops up all over town. First having it appear on roofs and in windows, the boys tow it across a lake, creating both alarm and excitement among the townsfolk. The two are forced to reveal their trick when they get lost in a forest and have to lift their creation above the trees to attract rescuers. Kids will love the shenanigans, while parents will find the book a perfect introduction to the tricksters' annual holiday. (Ages 4–7.)

14. *Naughty Nancy Goes to School.* By John S. Goodall. (Atheneum, 1985.) Naughty Nancy made her first appearance in *Naughty Nancy: The Bad Bridesmaid* (1975), where the unruly Victorian mouse creates havoc at her sister's wedding. This time the tiny wrecking ball doesn't want to go to school, and once there she is unable or unwilling to stay in her seat. Her fellow students find her antics funny, especially when she mocks the teacher behind the teacher's back or throws a ball onto the schoolhouse roof. On a field trip to the beach, Nancy again makes herself a nuisance but is redeemed when she heroically rescues a rafter and gets a trophy for her selfless act. (Ages 4–8.)

15. *Hiccup.* By Mercer Mayer. (Dial, 1976.) In Mercer Mayer's *Ah-choo* (1976), the topic is sneezing hippos. In this sequel, the problem is the hiccups, specifically Mr. Hippo's attempts to cure his coy lady friend of her funny but involuntary guttural malfunctions as they go for a romantic boat ride and a picnic. He tries dousing her with water, bopping her on the head, and shouting "Boo," all to no avail. The tables turn when he starts hiccupping and she gets to administer her own cures. Looking ahead to the future, parents might want to suggest that their kids remember *Hiccup*, earmarking it as the definitive guide on how not to act on a date. (Ages 4–7.)

16. *Hocus Pocus Takes the Train.* By Sylvie Desrosiers and Rémy Simard. (Kids Can Press, 2013.) Children who liked the fast-paced action and gamesmanship of *Hocus Pocus* (2011) will love *Hocus Pocus Takes the Train*, because it involves another battle of wits between the heroic blue bunny protagonist and the magician's devious dog. In this exciting sequel, the rabbit gets separated from the magician, who is boarding a train. Hocus Pocus befriends a purple stuffed rabbit mistakenly left behind at the station, and together they pursue the train on a makeshift surfboard, repeatedly having to outwit the canine nemesis. The book ends on a triumphant note with Hocus Pocus back in his magic hat, the stuffed bunny back with his toddler owner, and the meddlesome mutt back in the doghouse. (Ages 3–7.)

17. *Ah-choo.* By Mercer Mayer. (Dial, 1976.) Mercer Mayer's small-format book features large-size animals who sneeze with catastrophic results. When a mouse gives an elephant a bouquet of posies, he sneezes so hard that he knocks down his house. When he lands in jail, his sneezing destroys the jailhouse. An equally allergic lady hippo gets into the act when the hippo jailer offers her aromatic flowers and her sneeze blows him away, while the elephant winningly offers her his handkerchief. The expressive black line drawings look a little old fashioned, but they will produce bursts of laughter that won't blow the house down but will keep the kids entertained. (Ages 4–8.)

18. *Mister O.* By Lewis Trondheim. (NBM / Nantier, Beall, Minoustchine, 2004.) There are echoes of Charlie Brown and Wile E. Coyote in Lewis Trondheim's sixty paneled doodles about Mister O, a hapless little stick figure who tries repeatedly to jump a chasm. This silly, barely rendered character is shown watching others traverse a canyon using all manner of conveyance—jumping, flying, springing, and using grappling hooks—but everything Mister O tries ends in disaster, landing him in the bottom of a pit. French cartoonist Trondheim is an awarding-winning artist, but his talents are not on full display in this story of a character drawn as a circle. Perhaps he is simply tapping into an existential vein of frustration for which there will always be an audience. (Ages 7–12.)

19. *Paddy Pork's Holiday.* By John S. Goodall. (Atheneum, 1973.) Paddy sets out on a summer camping trip in the English countryside, but things go haywire for the lively pig when his tent is blown away, he climbs a tree and falls into a coal car of a moving train, his clothing is taken by dogs while he is swimming in a pond, and, when donning a scarecrow's tuxedo, he is mistaken for a master pianist, even making an appearance on a concert stage. Things return to normal when he joins a traveling family that takes him home with them. In John S. Goodall's customary fashion, the book has the unusual feature of half-pages inserted between each set of full pages. (Ages 4–8.)

20. *The Marvelous Misadventures of Fun-Boy.* By Ralph Cosentino. (Viking, 2006.) This batch of twelve large-format comic stories is perfect for preschoolers and early school-age audiences. In one episode, Fun-Boy repeatedly visits the same house wearing the same Halloween mask until the home owner finally catches on and gives him an old shoe. In another adventure, Fun-Boy rushes to douse a raging fire in his yard that turns out to be his dad's barbecue grill. In still another tale he reads a book about building a robot that immediately attacks him! Kids will enjoy these little mishaps, particularly the slightly disgusting one involving Fun-Boy climbing to the top of a slide, where he slips on a sticky dollop of bird poop and tumbles down. (Ages 3–7.)

21. *Sunday Love.* By Alison Paul. (HMH Books for Young Readers, 2010.) Designed as the perfect holiday gift, this graphic novel is about a prisoner who is sick of jailhouse food and breaks out on Valentine's Day to attain his one true love, ice cream. Bruno, a slapstick burglar, escapes from the big house by digging a tunnel with a spoon. Dragging a ball and

chain, he is pursued by constables, has crazy encounters with a soccer team, a group of nuns, and kitchen workers, and even goes through a bullfighting arena. Illustrated entirely in red, white, and black, the action-packed romp lands Bruno back in jail, but not until he reaches an ice-cream parlor, which reveals the object of his affection. (Ages 4–8.)

22. *Paddy Pork: Odd Jobs.* By John S. Goodall. (Atheneum, 1983.) Master watercolorist John S. Goodall casts his beloved pig protagonist as a hapless handyman who is willing to try his hand at just about any job but always ends up with comically disastrous results. Paddy fails at being a window washer, breaks the village pump, wallpapers over a doorway, falls from a roof, and makes a mess of everything he touches. The persistent porcine worker, on the run from one angry employer after another, finally redeems himself by performing the heroic job of finding a missing baby in a toolshed. Goodall fans will root for Paddy as he struggles to make his way in this quaint English country village, interacting with anthropomorphic animals that are oddly yet stylishly dressed. (Ages 4–8.)

23. *The Great Escape.* By Philippe Dupasquier. (Houghton Mifflin, 1988.) In this action-packed, slapstick adventure reminiscent of the Keystone Cops, a clever prisoner breaks out of jail and leads the inept police on a wild chase through a department store, museum, wedding ceremony, restaurant, circus, and film set, into tunnels, and over rooftops, creating chaos along the way. Drawn in cartoon form, the vigorous pursuit ends when the prisoner goes through a sewer pipe that leads him back inside the prison. When he is back in his cell, the jailbird inadvertently breaks a bar in his window, and the chase is on again. This fast-paced story will capture the attention of even the least bookish children. (Ages 4–8.)

24. *The Rabbits Are Coming!* By Kathleen Bullock. (Simon & Schuster Books for Young Readers, 1991.) Children will love narrating this story of twenty happy bunnies, each with a colorful balloon, invading a house to the astonishment of its human inhabitants. Receiving the helium inflatables from their mother, they travel to the house, enter an open window, and raise a ruckus. They taste dough in the kitchen where father is cooking, they enter the bathroom where grandfather is getting ready for a bath, and they play with the children's toys. The family is bemused by this carefree romp and can do nothing but stare as the rabbits depart, floating over a lake back to their tree-trunk home. (Ages 3–6.)

25. *Dancing Boy.* By Ronald Himler. (Star Bright Books, 2005.) Parents know, but seldom advertise, that most small children love to get naked and often have the run of the house. These natural born streakers, normally confined to the home, will beam with enjoyment at this story about a boy who gets to break the rules of American society by dancing in the buff all through the town. What's more, he gets other kids to shed their clothes and join him in a free-spirited romp, unnoticed by grown-ups. When the boy gets to the edge of town, his followers put on their clothes and return to what they were doing. The book is innocent fun—the nudity is not that revealing—but there is always the fear that a book like *Dancing Boy* will end up on some list of banned books on the pretext that it sends the wrong message. (Ages 3–7.)

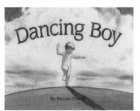

26. *Splat! Starring the Vole Brothers.* By Roslyn Schwartz. (Owlkids Books, 2014.) This nearly wordless, completely lowbrow story about two of Canada's favorite rodents features enough potty humor to satisfy even the silliest preschooler. When two brothers are out walking, they look up and see a pigeon that deposits white bird poo on one of their heads. The unaffected brother finds this terribly funny, so

the splatted brother throws some of the excrement in his face. Yes, his face! The newly splatted brother returns fire, misses the mark, and ends up giving the pigeon a taste of its own medicine. This irreverent slapstick comedy is not morally uplifting, and it won't be shelved with great classics of literary culture, but there is a good chance that it will be your kid's favorite book. Children will be eager to read Roslyn Schwartz's *The Vole Brothers* (2011) and *The Complete Adventures of the Mole Sisters* (2004). (Ages 3–7.)

27. *Carl's Snowy Afternoon*. By Alexandra Day. (Farrar, Straus & Giroux, 2009.) Carl the Rottweiler and Madeline the toddler are back for another almost text-free and completely carefree adventure requiring them to sneak away unbeknownst to their caregivers. Mom and dad are headed to a pond party and, unlike in prior books in the series, have actually hired a human babysitter, who is more interested in watching television than doing her job. So the dog and girl have no problem exiting the house through the doggy door to covertly visit the pond party themselves. Along the way, the sly duo romps in the snow, helps build a snowman, goes sledding, has a couple of hot dogs, and gets home just in time to keep the girl's parents in the dark about their chronic sneakiness. (Ages 3–8.)

28. *The Train*. By Witold Generowicz. (Dial, 1982.) *The Train* advertises on its cover that it is about an "amazing train chase that unfolds into one of the longest books in the world." The claim is technically true, but the catch is that it is an accordion-fold book. The train chase involves two robbers who jump aboard a train and are pursued from car to car, passing a continuous stream of strange and humorous cargo. Witold Generowicz's novel book is full of clever visual gags, but it requires a lot of space to handle and display, making it a real challenge for parents tempted to use it for bedtime reading. The Children's Book Council of Australia recognized *The Train* as one of its most highly commended titles. (Ages 4–8.)

29. *Who's Seen the Scissors?* By Fernando Krahn. (Dutton, 1975.) Children are often warned against running with scissors, but what if the scissors had a mind to run away on their own? This is the premise of Fernando Krahn's amusing narrative about a tailor's red shears, which fly off, clipping their way around town in an unexplained but silly romp that will leave children in stiches. The mischievous cutter runs riot in a spree that includes snipping a girl's hair, a man's tie, a newspaper clipping, the heads of flowers, and the reins of a horse. When the rampaging scissors return, the tailor wisely confines them to a cage. The drawings are in black and white, except for the scissors and its path, which are shown in red. (Ages 4–8.)

30. *Bang.* By Leo Timmers. (Gecko Press, 2013.) Comedic multivehicle collisions are the essence of this silly story involving distracted deer, pig, giraffe, and alligator drivers who can't stop in time, sending their cargo flying. Of course, no one is injured in these cartoon mishaps, but that doesn't prevent the drivers from expressing themselves in the most funny and exaggerated ways. Children will want to shout out the book's only word, "Bang," every time a car crashes, sending books, chickens, clothing, tires, and fish through the air. *Bang* is not exactly a cautionary tale about the need to pay attention to the road, as the sequence of fender benders starts with a deer who is reading a book while driving. (Ages 4–8.)

31. *Uh-oh!* By Mary Newell DePalma. (Eerdmans Books for Young Readers, 2011.) "Uh-oh!" is just what children will say as they follow a young green dinosaur from one entertaining mishap to another. Bright watercolors depict the lighthearted mayhem of a little terror who knocks over his sibling's blocks, topples a house plant, spilling its dirt, dumps a container of milk on the floor, causes the dishwasher to overflow, and manages to get bubble gum everywhere. The disasters are all accidental, but he

still must help clean up his messes and spends some time on the time-out chair. *Uh-oh!* is Mary Newell DePalma's twentieth book. Fans of her work should read *Bow, Wow Wiggle-Waggle* (2012) and *Two Little Birds* (2014). (Ages 3–8.)

32. *Yum! Yuck! A Foldout Book of People Sounds.* By Linda Sue Park, Julia Durango, and Sue Ramá. (Charlesbridge, 2005.) Paradoxically, this mostly wordless book celebrates the diversity of language. In a bustling market, children enjoy ice cream, expressing their pleasure in different languages, with kids saying, "Nam-nam!" in Danish, "Bah-bah!" in Farsi, "Geshmark!" in Yiddish, and "Leckah!" in German. Lifting the flap reveals English-speaking youngsters expressing their epicurean delight with "Yum!" When a dog overturns a spice cart, spilling pepper on the children's tasty treats, their exclamations now express shock and disappointment, spoken as "Oh-gah!" in Yoruba, "Oy!" in Polish, "Oo-wah!" in Japanese, and "Yikes!" in English. The English translations are always hidden under the fold, giving young Anglo readers a chance to guess the sound. Children may conclude that beneath the veneer of language and custom, people feel the same way. (Ages 3–6.)

33. *Mister I.* By Lewis Trondheim. (NBM Publishing, 2007.) *Mister I* is a collection of minimalist doodle-like gags arranged in tiny panels that together resemble pages of quirky postage stamps. This thirty-two-page sequel to *Mister O* (2004) shows a hapless hero shaped liked a sausage going from one disaster to another, trying to get food and always turning up dead. The repetitiousness of the small panels and the recurrence of the same theme probably will not engage young readers for very long and will leave older kids either chuckling or puzzling about the point of these bleak little comics. Lewis Trondheim is creator of *A.L.I.E.E.E.N.: Archives of Lost Issues and Earthly Editions of Extraterrestrial Novelties* (2006), a wordless graphic novel for teenagers. (Ages 8–12.)

34. *Stick Man's Really Bad Day.* By Steve Mockus. (Chronicle Books, 2012.) Real and imagined cautionary signs from all over the world remind us of how dangerous and unpleasant life can be for an almost universally recognized icon. Readers will observe him engulfed in flames, picking up dog waste, being attacked by an alligator, and falling down on a slippery surface, all in a day's work. Narrating in safety signs, Steve Mockus follows Stick Man from the time he wakes up to the time he goes to bed as he stumbles into one hazard after another. At least one thing goes his way, as one illustration suggests that he has fallen in love. Tweens and teens will find the daily disasters of Stick Man so bad as to be hilarious. (Ages 8+.)

CHAPTER 11

Acts of Kindness

Though we travel the world over to find the beautiful, we must carry it with us, or we find it not.

—Ralph Waldo Emerson

1. *South*. By Patrick McDonnell. (Little, Brown Books for Young Readers, 2008.) In *South* Patrick McDonnell, creator of the comic strip *Mutts*, features a kindly cat named Mooch, one of his regular strip characters. This feline protagonist comes to the aid of a little bird who has gotten separated from his flock, which left the slumbering bird behind on its way south for the winter. Panic-stricken and weeping, the tiny bird is befriended by Good Samaritan Mooch, who decides to carry him until he is reunited with his feathered friends. This tender story, done in watercolors, will particularly resonate with children who have ever felt lost or abandoned. Patrick McDonnell is best recognized for the Caldecott Medal he earned for *Me . . . Jane* (2011) and his *New York Times* best seller *Hug Time* (2007). (Ages 3–6.)

2. *The Hunter and the Animals: A Wordless Picture Book*. By Tomie DePaola. (Holiday House, 1981.) A hunter's plan to kill animals is thwarted by the wildlife, which warn each other and hide in the forest. When he can't find any prey, the discouraged sportsman falls asleep. Awaking confused, he starts to cry, and the animals, feeling pity for him, show him the way home. The hunter decides to give up this violent sport and becomes friends with the woodland creatures. Parents looking for small antidotes to our gun-saturated culture will be pleased to share this gentle story. Painted in the style of Hungarian folk art, Tomie DePaola's appealing illustrations will have children returning to the book often, each time finding a new animal in hiding. (Ages 5–9.)

3. *A Circle of Friends.* By Giora Carmi. (Star Bright Books, 2006.) This "pay-it-forward" picture book begins with a boy buying a muffin at a bakery. On his way home, he anonymously shares most of it with a homeless man sleeping on a park bench, an action that sparks more good deeds. When the man wakes up, he eats some of the food but shares a few crumbs with the birds. A small bird asks for more, receives a seed from the man's pocket, and deposits it in a window box outside the generous boy's home. The last picture shows the boy admiring the magnificent sunflower that has grown from the seed of his original act of kindness. (Ages 4–8.)

4. *Fox's Garden.* By Princesse Camcam. (Enchanted Lion Books, 2014.) After being repelled by adults on a cold winter's night, a fox finds shelter in a small greenhouse. When a little boy spots the fox, he sneaks her a basket of food, finding her vulnerable and busy suckling her four newborns. For his act of compassion, the boy receives an unexpected thank-you from the mother fox and her offspring in the form of a bouquet of flowers delivered to his bedroom. Princesse Camcam's images have an attractive warmth and depth deriving from her method of photographing cut-paper dioramas. This tribute to kindness and generosity, the best of the Stories without Words series, will touch the emotions of children and adults. (Ages 3–8.)

5. *Fly, Little Bird.* By Tina Burke. (Kane/Miller, 2006.) When a little girl and her puppy are out gathering flowers, they find a tiny green parrot. The girl picks up the bird and encourages it to fly, but it tumbles to the ground, too young and afraid to take flight. They take the fledgling home where the girl feeds it, reads to it, paints its picture, and makes a place for it to sleep. The bird soon begins to fly, and the girl awakes the next morning to find it missing. She goes outside and spots the parrot happily singing and cavorting with other birds. This simple story of making friends and learning to let them go will be a helpful book for toddlers and preschoolers who must deal with the same issues. (Ages 2–6.)

6. *Amanda's Butterfly.* By Nick Butterworth. (Collins, 1991.) After reading a book about butterflies, Amanda, net in hand, goes into her yard in search of them. Rain forces her to seek shelter in a garden tool shed, where she discovers a tiny fairy with a tear in its gossamer wing. Amanda rummages through the shed looking for a way to help with no success, then runs into the house for a roll of tape. After she mends the broken wing, the girl and the barefoot little sprite shake hands. The thankful fairy flies away as Amanda brims with satisfaction. *Amanda's Butterfly* is a charming and sensitive fantasy that evokes the best angels in our nature. (Ages 3–7.)

7. *The Good Bird.* By Peter Wezel. (Harper & Row, 1964.) Originally published in Switzerland under the title of *Der gute Vogel Nepomuk*, Peter Wezel's plain and simple tale starts when a pink bird flies by a house, spotting a sparkling orange fish inside a fishbowl. It is cross-species love at first sight when he leaves and returns with the gift of a worm for this apparently lonely and hungry aquatic creature. The fish is at first afraid of the bird's intentions, but the bird roosts by the bowl all night, and the fear dissipates. Wezel's bright crayon colors and modest sketches are rendered with a deliberate childlike naiveté, which will work quite well with his intended preschool audience. *The Good Bird* is a good choice for children in need of stories about kindness, sharing, and friendship. (Ages 2–5.)

8. *The Special String.* By Harald Bakken and Mischa Richter. (Prentice Hall, 1981.) As a barefoot farmer boy with a straw hat rolls up a ball of string, the ball grows bigger and bigger. Along his way, he encounters people who can benefit from a part of his accumulating cord. He breaks off a bit to help a woman repair a clothesline; he assists a lion tamer whose pants have fallen down; he gives part of the string to a boy whose chickens are escaping from their coop; and he contributes to making a lasso and a tightrope. Eventually, he finds a barefoot girl collecting the string from the opposite direction, and they decide to go fishing. The cartoon drawings are black and white except for the red string. (Ages 4–8.)

9. *Boom Boom.* By Sarvinder Naberhaus and Margaret Chodos-Irvine. (Beach Lane Books, 2014.) A little boy covers his ears and closes his eyes while a diverse group of children crowd at a window gaping at lightning. He is off by himself, terrified by the storm, and after it passes, a girl schoolmate sympathetically takes his hand when the class goes outside. They have fun splashing in puddles, and the book shows their friendship grow along with the change in seasons. There are bright and cheerful pictures of the boy and girl blowing dandelions, observing bees, playing in the leaves, and capturing snowflakes. Each spread is accompanied by onomatopoeic pairings such as "Boom Boom," "Splash Splash," "Buzz Buzz," and "Crunch Crunch." Youngsters will be touched by the message of friendship and belonging, become conversant with seasonal change, and learn sixteen new words, each repeated twice. (Ages 2–7.)

10. *The Lion and the Bird.* By Marianne Dubuc. (Enchanted Lion Books, 2014.) A lion generously decides to care for an injured bird that has been left behind by its migrating flock. In this quietly affectionate, minimal-text book, the unlikely companions forge a strong bond as they spend the winter together in the lion's comfortable cottage. The little bird sleeps in the lion's slipper by the fire, and the two of them have fun ice fishing and tobogganing. When the fully recovered bird rejoins his flock in the spring, the melancholy lion occupies his time tending his garden, fishing, and reading. Children will be overjoyed when the bird decides to forgo his annual trip south to spend another winter with his special friend. (Ages 4–8.)

CHAPTER 12

Lost and Found

> One of the best things about paintings is their silence—
> which prompts reflection and random reverie.
>
> —Mark Stevens

1. *A Ball for Daisy.* By Chris Raschka. (Schwartz &
Wade Books, 2011.) Daisy, an energetic little black-
and-white dog, could not be happier with her new
big red ball. Her delight is evident as she plays with it,
cuddles with it, and takes it to the park with her human
owner. But when a big brown dog arrives and joins the
play, things go horribly wrong when the interloper bites
down too hard and destroys the cherished ball. Daisy's
despondence turns to glee when she returns to the park
and is given a new blue ball by the bigger canine to re-
place her old toy. Children will love this book for its impressionistic watercolor illustrations and for its satisfying
conclusion. *A Ball for Daisy* will appeal to kids who have
experienced the joy of possessing something special and
then suffered the anguish of losing it. (Ages 3–7.)

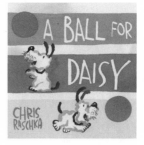

2. *Daisy Gets Lost.* By Chris Raschka. (Schwartz &
Wade Books, 2013.) Fear is again the theme of this
endearing Daisy the dog book. But instead of a beloved toy, as in *A Ball for Daisy* (2011), this time it is
Daisy that gets lost. The pup still likes to play with
her ball in the park, but in this escapade she chases
a squirrel too far into the scary woods. Chris Rasch-

ka's art proficiently captures the energy, movement, and emotional wallop of Daisy's distress, as she finds herself alone in dark, unfamiliar territory, while her worried owner looks for her. The frantic pooch and relieved master are joyfully reunited with the same affection that made the first Daisy book such a success. (Ages 3–7.)

3. *School.* By Emily Arnold McCully. (Harper & Row, 1987.) Mouse parents prepare breakfast for their nine children in a comfortable kitchen packed with all the stuff the mice will need for school. After eight of them go on their way, the littlest one, not yet old enough for school, decides to follow her brothers and sisters to see what is going on. The teacher welcomes the inquisitive youngster and puts her to work, but by the time her worried mother arrives to retrieve her lost daughter, the preschooler is ready to go home. *School* was reissued in 2005 in a larger format with unnecessary text. Emily Arnold McCully won the Caldecott Medal for *Mirette on the High Wire* (1992). (Ages 2–5.)

4. *Have You Seen My Duckling?* By Nancy Tafuri. (Greenwillow Books, 1984.) Nancy Tafuri's award-winning book successfully executes the popular picture book strategy of inviting children to search pages for a partially concealed central character. When an independent and adventurous duckling separates from the brood, the mother duck searches for her lost offspring throughout the pond, querying animals as to whether they have seen the wayward bird. She approaches a turtle, a crane, a beaver, a fish, and other pond inhabitants in brightly colored scenes that show both the worried parent and the baby duckling hiding somewhere in the frame. Eventually the lost duckling finds her way back to her mother and her seven brothers and sisters. This beautifully rendered title is the perfect choice for preschoolers looking to read a book on their own. (Ages 2–7.)

5. *Beaver Is Lost.* By Elisha Cooper. (Schwartz & Wade Books, 2010.) Beaver goes missing when he jumps on a log floating down the river. Preoccupied with his wood gnawing, he doesn't realize that he has made his way to a lumber camp, where a crane deposits him and his log onto a city-bound truck. Our semiaquatic hero encounters many challenges in this strange environment, including busy streets, threatening dogs, and even a zoo crocodile. He finds refuge in the smelly city sewer before a fellow member of the rodent family shows him the way to the river. After a long swim, the beaver makes it safely home. This exciting adventure contains only four words, "Beaver is lost," upon his arrival in the city, and "Home," when he completes his journey upstream. (Ages 3–7.)

6. *Where's My Monkey?* By Dieter Schubert. (Dial Books for Young Readers, 1987.) A little boy loses his special stuffed monkey while bicycling with his mother in a rainstorm. When mother and son return to look for the beloved toy, a family of mice has already dragged him into their tree-hollow home. The monkey is passed on to a hedgehog family, which takes him outdoors, then to a magpie, who takes him to its nest and drops him in a pond. The stuffed animal is finally rescued by a toymaker who fishes him out of the water, makes necessary repairs, and puts him on display in his store window. Spotting the cherished monkey while shopping with his mother, the boy joyously reunites with his long lost friend. (Ages 3–6.)

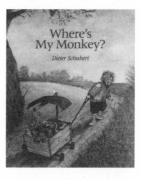

7. *Catch That Cat!* By Fernando Krahn. (Dutton, 1978.) The Chilean cartoonist begins his story with a boy spotting his runaway cat while gazing out at a harbor. He chases the agile pet through city streets, past a fruit cart, and across a busy street, where it ventures onto a ship dock and into a crate bound for Singapore. The boy follows the cat into the large container, which is loaded onto a cargo ship named

Catalina. The ship sets sail with the two stowaways on board. The boy and the feline are discovered, get into some serious trouble, and are sent home. There is a particularly good picture of a hairy sailor reprimanding the frightened boy, holding him in the air by his suspenders. Fernando Krahn does *Catch That Cat!* in shaded black-and-white pencil sketches, ably rendering all the action of this accidental adventure. (Ages 4–7.)

8. *The Zoo.* By Suzy Lee. (Kane/Miller, 2007.) Originally published in South Korea in 2004, this is a slight-text story about a mother and father going into panic mode when their little girl wanders off during a visit to the zoo. While the parents, depicted in a somber palette, are realizing their worst fear, the girl plays with brightly colored zoo animals. The two opposite experiences of the zoo visit are run side by side, until the girl is finally found sleeping on a bench. "I love the zoo. It's very exciting. Mom and dad think so, too," the girl concludes, oblivious to her parents' fright and fatigue. The National Council of Teachers of English designated *The Zoo* a Notable Children's Book in the Language Arts. (Ages 4–8.)

9. *Where's Al?* By Byron Barton. (Clarion, 1972.) Vibrantly hued pictures show a boy and his lost dog, Al, as their paths cross in a busy city. The black-and-white spotted puppy gets lost when he chases a stick. Pictures show him around town pursuing a cat in front of a food market, knocking over fruits and vegetables, and going through the garbage, while the boy traces Al's steps, posts notices, and speaks to vendors. The parallel travels of the two are shown on opposite pages until they finally find each other. The few words in this simple adventure appear in cartoon-style bubbles containing the searching boy's speech. (Ages 4–8.)

10. *Crocodile and Pierrot.* By Russell Hoban and Sylvie Selig. (Charles Scribner's Sons, 1975.) Pierrot the clown steals a doll baby from a sleeping crocodile. When the croc realizes his toy is missing, he follows the clown and doll through a series of scenes, with objects and people along the way identified with word labels. The crocodile pursues his prey through a variety of colorful places—park, country, beach, street, and bridge—finally recovering the stolen doll at an outdoor wedding. Children might be expecting some form of retribution, such as the big lizard making a meal of the naughty clown, but the two decide to share the doll. It is not clear why the protagonists act the way they do, why the objects and people are labeled, or how the objects are related to the story. (Ages 4–8.)

11. *Picnic.* By Emily Arnold McCully. (Harper & Row, 1984.) In this energetic adventure, a family of mice packs a picnic basket and loads it into red pickup truck for an outing near a pond. When one of its smallest members bounces off the back of the vehicle as it is in transit, the family unknowingly proceeds on its way. When the family recognizes that the little mouse is missing, they are more worried than he is, but all are soon reunited. Families who have ever lost track of a little one, even for a short time, will relate to the mouse family's feeling of alarm. The 2003 edition of *Picnic* includes some text. (Ages 2–5.)

CHAPTER 13

Gala Gatherings

I do wordless books because I am attempting to activate minds.

—Tana Hoban

1. *The Crocodile Blues.* By Coleman Polhemus. (Candlewick Press, 2007.) A man and his pet cockatoo bring an egg to their apartment and put it in the refrigerator. In the middle of the night, cracking sounds awaken them, and when they investigate, they discover that a smiling crocodile has hatched! The two make a swift retreat and set up housekeeping in a safer location. But then they receive an invitation to attend a party at their old digs. When the man and bird return, they find that their abode has been converted into a swinging nightclub and that the squatting crocodile is actually more of a buddy than a beast. Children will enjoy the cartoonish characters and the foldout pages. (Ages 4–8.)

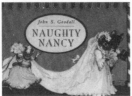

2. *Naughty Nancy.* By John S. Goodall. (Margaret K. McElderry, 1999.) Nancy is a bold little mouse dressed in pink ruffles who creates chaos at her sister's wedding. She is the bridesmaid in the ceremony, causing disruption and mischief at every turn. Her antics include riding on the bride's train, sitting on the wedding cake, hiding in her sister's going-away trunk, and becoming an uninvited guest on the couple's honeymoon. Nancy is irrepressibly hyperactive and out of control but still cute and endearing. This book was first published in 1975 under the title *Naughty Nancy: The Bad Bridesmaid* and was the inspiration for another amusing title, *Naughty Nancy Goes to School* (1985). (Ages 4–8.)

3. *Carl's Birthday.* By Alexandra Day. (Farrar, Straus & Giroux, 1997.) Those who follow the adventures of clever dog Carl and mischievous Madeleine, the girl whom he is always babysitting, will know that Carl's owner never outsmarts him, and this episode is no exception. In this sturdy board book, mother is planning a surprise birthday party for the resourceful Rottweiler and thinks that he and her daughter are out of the picture taking a nap at a neighbor's house. But these two never sleep! True to form, they are sneaking around, peeking at gifts, and even sampling the food and punch. The secretive pair scurry back just in time to complete their ruse, and, as always, mom is none the wiser. (Ages 2–5.)

4. *Shrewbettina's Birthday.* By John S. Goodall. (Margaret K. McElderry, 1998.) This little gem, originally published in 1970, follows the special day of a bright-eyed birthday-girl shrew in the English countryside. Illustrated in Victorian style, this diminutive book begins with little Shrewbettina asleep in her comfy four-post bed, until the chiming of an old-fashioned clock awakens her. When she travels to the market, a masked thief grabs her purse. But he is intercepted by a gentlemanly mouse dressed in red, who then escorts the shrew to her destination. The story ends festively, complete with beverages and a birthday cake, presided over by the heroic gentleman seated at the head of the table, with Shrewbettina slicing the cake. (Ages 4–8.)

5. *A Special Birthday.* By Symeon Shimin. (McGraw-Hill, 1976.) A loving father plans a unique surprise for his little girl to greet her when she awakens on her birthday. While the family cat watches, the father strings a tangle of ribbon through the house that leads the lucky girl to her presents and finally to her dad's warm embrace. Children and parents will like Symeon Shimin's use of warm colors to realistically render this touching occasion. Shimin, a Russian-born artist, has illustrated over fifty books and was once commissioned to paint a mural at the US Department of Justice in Washington, DC. He has collaborated with many great writers, including Isaac Asimov, Virginia Hamilton, and Madeleine L'Engle. (Ages 4–8.)

6. *A Birthday Wish.* By Ed Emberley. (Little, Brown, 1977.) The book begins with a mouse snatching cheese from a trap and then using it with a candle to fashion a cheese birthday cake present for another mouse. Once this guest-of-honor mouse blows out the candle on his cheesy gift, his birthday wish is granted in a roundabout way. After blowing a party hat out the window and triggering a chain of events that include the slapstick involvement of a woodpecker, frog, fox, rabbit, and turtle, the mouse finally gets what he really wanted: strawberry ice cream. Ed Emberley has illustrated eighty children's books, with *A Birthday Wish* being his first. The Caldecott-winning artist is best recognized for his many books on teaching children to draw. (Ages 4–8.)

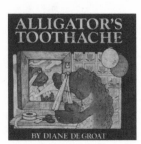

7. *Alligator's Toothache.* By Diane de Groat. (Crown, 1977.) While he is getting ready for a party, Alligator gets a painful toothache and goes to bed. His friends summon a dentist, but the big lizard is afraid and refuses to see him. Eventually his friends trick him by smuggling the dentist into his room on a lidded serving tray. When the tooth is removed, the party goes on as planned. Parents should know the book is intended only as entertainment; it is not a remedy for overcoming fears of the dentist. Fans of *Alligator's Toothache* might enjoy *Doctor De Soto* (1982), a story with text and pictures about a mouse dentist who helps a fox with a toothache despite knowing that he risks being eaten. (Ages 4–8.)

8. *Foxly's Feast.* By Owen Davey. (Templar, 2010.) Featuring pleasing retro-style artwork, this is a story about the power of preconceptions. A hungry fox sets out to satisfy his well-known appetite. Cruising the countryside to assemble his feast, he encounters many animals—chickens, mice, ducks, rabbits, sheep, owls—who readers will worry are in imminent danger, but they will be wrong. The feast that the busy-tailed protagonist has in mind requires that the animals join him as his guests, not as his meal. Owen Davey is sly as a fox in crafting a tale that will open children's eyes to the idea of stereotypes and their power to make us establish narratives in advance of knowing the facts. (Ages 3–7.)

CHAPTER 14

Pet Mischief

I am fond of pigs. Dogs look up to us. Cats look down on us. Pigs treat us as equals.

—Winston Churchill

1. *Good Dog, Carl.* By Alexandra Day. (Little Simon, 1996.) This classic is the first in the popular series of illustration-only picture books about a lovable, babysitting canine named Carl and Madeleine, the toddler girl he takes care of. As soon as mother leaves her daughter alone with this unbelievably capable Rottweiler, things go sideways right away. Madeleine slides out of her crib and onto the dog's back, and they get into one mishap after another, including swimming in the fish tank and sliding down the laundry chute. Before mom returns home, the dog dutifully cleans up the house and is rewarded with "Good dog, Carl." First published in 1985, this board book produces both youthful glee and perhaps parental horror at the thought of anyone leaving a baby alone in the care of a large animal. (Ages 2–5.)

2. *Frog Goes to Dinner.* By Mercer Mayer. (Dial, 2003.) Many parents and grandparents will have fond memories of this comedic classic originally published in 1974, as part of the series that began with *A Boy, a Dog, and a Frog* (1967), and will be eager to share it with a new generation. In this book, the dog stays home when the family goes out to a nice restaurant, while the boy's pet frog mischievously stows away in his jacket pocket and then jumps out, wreaking havoc with the other diners. Embarrassed and angry, the family is kicked out of the eating establishment. Mercer Mayer does an excellent job capturing their emotions and facial expressions in his black-and-white illustrations. Children will love the frog's antics and will want to read all the books in the series. (Ages 3–7.)

3. *Frog, Where Are You?* By Mercer Mayer. (Dial, 2003.) During the night, a boy's pet frog escapes from his jar and jumps out the bedroom window. The boy and his dog look everywhere for the missing amphibian and suffer a few misadventures along the way. The boy calls down a hole and is bitten on the nose by a gopher, while the dog stirs up a hornet's nest. After an encounter with an angry owl, the boy and dog climb on a deer's antlers, mistaking them for tree branches, and are thrown by the large animal over a cliff, splashing down safely in a pond. Hearing a sound, they locate their frog, who has rejoined his frog family, which includes some baby frogs, not tadpoles. This sequel to *A Boy, a Dog, and a Frog* ends with the boy taking one of the little frogs home for a new pet. (Ages 3–7.)

4. *Frog on His Own.* By Mercer Mayer. (Dial, 2003.) Readers looking for visual humor will not be disappointed by this title in the beloved series. During a walk in the park with his mammalian companions, the frog jumps out of his pail and gets into a lot of trouble. True to his mischievous nature, he disrupts a couple's picnic, he sinks a child's sailboat, he is stung on the tongue by a bee when he tries to eat it, and he hops into a baby's stroller, drinking from the baby's bottle, until he is chased away by a cat. Tired from his misadventures, the frog happily reunites with his group. (Ages 3–7.)

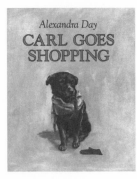

5. *Carl Goes Shopping*. By Alexandra Day. (Farrar, Straus & Giroux, 1992.) The naughty but faithful Rottweiler and his baby sidekick are at it again in this fun title in the Carl series. In this installment, mom, dog, and baby are shopping when mom asks Carl to babysit, leaving the duo unattended in a busy department store. Exiting her buggy, the tyke hops on the dog's back, and they go on a grand romp through the store, returning to their original spot just before the trusting and gullible mother returns. The mischievous twosome make plenty of stops, the most memorable of which has them using a video camera to get themselves projected on multiple TV screens in the store. (Ages 3–6.)

6. *Carl's Masquerade*. By Alexandra Day. (Farrar, Straus & Giroux, 1992.) The world's slyest yet most trustworthy Rottweiler and Madeleine are at it again! Unbeknownst to mom and dad, Carl and the little kid decide to follow them to a masquerade party. The mischievous twosome gain admittance to the costume ball with no trouble, as they are taken to be creatively garbed as a horse and rider. Mingling with guests but avoiding the partying parents, they fit right in with evening's games and dancing. Carl and his young charge manage to get home just in time to avoid blowing the whistle on their secret adventure. This lushly illustrated board book will tickle preschoolers, while adults might think that a call to Child Protective Services might finally be in order. (Ages 2–5.)

7. *Jack and the Missing Piece*. By Pat Schories. (Boyds Mills Press, 2004.) After Jack continually knocks down block towers constructed by his boy owner, the dog is blamed when one of the decorative blocks goes missing. But is the lovable, red-spotted pup really the culprit? After all, he did have easy access to and has a track record of messing with the building set. However, Jack redeems himself through some basic detective work, discovering that the cat is to blame. The boy hugs and apologizes to Jack, as a new block structure invites the perky pooch to resume his fun and mischief. The book would be a good conversation starter about the tendency to jump to conclusions without considering all the possibilities. (Ages 2–6.)

8. *Carl's Summer Vacation.* By Alexandra Day. (Farrar, Straus & Giroux, 2008.) Fans of sweet Madeleine and her large canine companion, Carl, know that when they are supposed to be napping, they never do! In this adventure, set at the family lake cottage, the toddler and Rottweiler surreptitiously go canoeing, visit a playground, eat blackberries, have an encounter with a skunk, and poach food from someone else's picnic. In the evening, easily duped mom and dad wonder why the lovable twosome is so tired. (If these parents ever wise up, it will spoil all the fun.) As usual, Alexandra Day's watercolors are lush and beautiful, providing a visual feast that could be enjoyed even if the images did not tell an amusing story. (Ages 2–6.)

9. *Carl Makes a Scrapbook.* By Alexandra Day. (Farrar, Straus & Giroux, 1994.) In gorgeously realized paintings, Alexandra Day brings her usual old-fashioned vibe to Carl and Madeleine's decision to update the family album. With mother outside gardening, the dog and the tiny girl are supposed to be watching a video, but they have more ambitious plans. The left side of the scrapbook has mom's pictures, while the right side is empty, allowing Carl to glue in some of his favorite snapshots and mementoes, including material that Carl aficionados will recognize from earlier books in the series. In a slight twist on Day's winning formula, the stealthy activities of mischievous Rottweiler and toddler may finally be detected as Carl is covered with gluey bits when mother returns. (Ages 3–8.)

10. *10 Minutes till Bedtime.* By Peggy Rathmann. (Puffin, 2004.) Caldecott-winning artist Peggy Rathmann has created a book that succeeds as an introduction to counting, as an overview of bedtime rituals, and especially as a madcap tour of a family home initiated by a boy's entrepreneurial pet hamster. When dad announces that it is ten minutes to bedtime and starts counting down the minutes, a small army of hilarious hamsters arrives to witness a boy's preparation for bed. More and more curious rodents invade the premises as the boy has a snack, puts away toys, takes a bath, brushes his teeth, and jumps into bed. The multitude of furry creatures vanishes when father arrives for a good night kiss. Rathmann is author of the acclaimed *Officer Buckle and Gloria* (1995) and *Goodnight Gorilla* (1993), both of which make appearances in this perfect bedtime book. (Ages 3–8.)

CHAPTER 15

Aquatic Adventures

Live in the sunshine, swim the sea, drink the wild air.

—Ralph Waldo Emerson

1. *Wave*. By Suzy Lee. (Chronicle Books, 2008.) This evocative book of untroubled childhood joy and adventure shows a little girl's first encounter with waves on a beach. Disarmingly simple and sketched in charcoal and acrylic, Suzy Lee shows the girl first being afraid of the waves, and then a large one crashes over her. But the drenched girl is undaunted by the vibrant blue ocean. As a flock of seagulls flies overhead, she grows increasingly bold, dancing in and out of the splashing surf, gauging its rhythm, and discovering the beach's many hidden treasures. When her mother comes to call it a day, the girl waves a sweet, secret good-bye to her exciting new friend. (Ages 3–8.)

2. *A Boy, a Dog, and a Frog*. By Mercer Mayer. (Dial, 2003.) Originally published in 1967, this wordless classic chronicles a boy and dog's unsuccessful attempts to trap a wily frog in a pond. With simple black-and-white illustrations, Mercer Mayer shows that the would-be captors, armed with a pail and net, are no competition for the smiling frog. After a number of clumsy moves, the boy and dog land in the water, and they return home from their swampy adventure needing a bath. The frog, who had enjoyed

being pursued, now misses their company. Following their muddy footprints, he hops to their home and joins them in the tub! This lighthearted tale, the first book in a popular series, is perfect for preschoolers and emergent readers. (Ages 3–7.)

3. *Dinosaur!* By Peter Sis. (Greenwillow Books, 2005.) Toy dinosaur in hand, a little boy gets into his bathtub and sees it erupt into a prehistoric swimming pool! One by one, dinosaurs pop out of the bath water, each one bigger than the last, and the amazed boy finds himself in a vast desert landscape with live volcanoes and ancient lizards of all kinds. In the final spread, he is back in the overflowing tub, smiling and waving good-bye to the beasts, his mom getting ready to scoop him up and towel him dry. For those who would add an educative element to this time-traveling adventure, the endpapers include a guide to different dinosaur species. (Ages 2–6.)

4. *A Boy, a Dog, a Frog, and a Friend.* By Mercer and Marianna Mayer. (Puffin Books, 1993.) The protagonists of the A Boy, a Dog, and a Frog series visit a pond to do some fishing. But when a playful turtle bites on their fishing line, the boy is pulled into the drink, with his pals following close behind. When the turtle takes off with the fishing pole, the dog goes after him and gets bitten on the paw. After a struggle in the water, the group is shocked to see the shelled reptile floating on his back, apparently dead! While the boy digs a hole for a proper burial, the uninjured turtle opens his eyes and all is well, and a new friend is added to the fold. This black-and-white illustrated classic was originally published in 1971. (Ages 3–7.)

5. *The Tree House.* By Marije Tolman and Ronald Tolman. (Lemniscaat, 2010.) The Tolmans, a Dutch daughter-father artistic team, won Italy's prestigious BolognaRagazzi Award for the illustration of their story about a polar bear who swims to a special tree house. The white furry animal is joined by a brown bear who arrives by boat at this structure located in a tall tree standing alone in the water. They read books and are joined by flamingoes, peacocks, owls, panda bears, and others who swing from the branches and find interesting ways to pass the time. Oversize and done in deep colors, *The Tree House* is about a wonderful sanctuary embedded in nature, a leisurely haven where different species interact in quiet harmony. Children will be comforted by the tree house's welcoming atmosphere and hope one day to visit such a place themselves. (Ages 3–5.)

6. *Peter Spier's Rain.* By Peter Spier. (Doubleday, 1982.) A rainy summer day is the perfect occasion for a brother and sister to romp in their backyard and neighborhood. Slipping in puddles, standing in running water by the curb, making muddy footprints, and observing droplets in a spider's web, two children explore a world that is both familiar and altogether fresh and new. When they return home to a warm bath and a meal, the siblings look forward to the possibilities of a new day. There is a beauty and sensual wonder contained in a child's experience of a rain-soaked day. For kids that are experiencing it for the first time and for adults who have fond memories, Peter Spier gets it just right. (Ages 4–8.)

7. *The Treasure Bath.* By Dan Andreasen. (Henry Holt, 2009.) A boy gets messy while helping his mom make a chocolate cake and takes a bath. Beneath the suds he discovers a magical world with sea creatures, a map, and a sunken treasure chest. As a grinning whale looks on and an eel holds him tight, a peppy orange octopus scrubs the boy clean. On his return to dry land, where his mom waits with his pajamas, he gladly joins her for a piece of that cake fresh out of the oven and a glass of milk. Children will look forward to their next trip to the tub knowing that it holds the possibility of an undersea adventure. (Ages 2–6.)

8. *Hogwash*. By Arthur Geisert. (HMH Books for Young Readers, 2008.) For little piggies who love to get dirty, mama pig has a new way of cleaning them up. It's a kind of car wash for pigs, a huge intricate hogwash contraption that soaps and scrubs them in assembly-line fashion and even dries their clothes. The piglets not only wallow in the mud but go to an abandoned paint factory and make matters much worse. Mother pig is not pleased with this situation, but young readers will love it. Her inventive technological fix will fascinate children, particularly those who have seen the swinging brushes and rotating jets of soap in a real car wash. Kids will want to spend extra time studying this mechanical marvel and wondering if their own bath time could benefit from some motorized streamlining. (Ages 4–8.)

9. *Paddy Under Water*. By John S. Goodall. (Atheneum, 1984.) This little gem will happily surprise fans of the Paddy Pork series. They will recognize the same delicate artwork but will find the book different from the author's usual bucolic or Edwardian-themed creations because of its more unconventional setting. In this small book, the iconic pig goes scuba diving and encounters several sea creatures, including a baby sea monster that he rescues from an octopus. After Paddy meets King Neptune, mermaids guide him to a sunken ship with a treasure chest. John S. Goodall does an excellent job with the underwater scenes, crafting his signature watercolors in shades of green and blue. Children might see the gentleman pig in a different light after reading this adventure. (Ages 4–8.)

10. *Beach Day*. By Helen Oxenbury. (Dial Very First Books, 1991.) This board book about a round-faced, red-cheeked toddler at the shore is filled with sandcastles, splashing seawater, seashells, plastic buckets, ice-cream cones, and interactions with his parents. In simple two-page spreads, the cheerful boy is shown playing contentedly on the sandy beach, using his shovel to dig and clearly enjoying a sunny day. Helen Oxenbury is an acclaimed British illustrator known for her pioneering work on board books, including *Dressing* (1981), *Family* (1981), *Friends* (1981), and many other titles aimed at the youngest children. In 2004 she published the first American edition of *The Helen Oxenbury Nursery Collection*, an anthology of favorite stories. (Ages 2–4.)

11. *Ship Ahoy!* By Peter Sis. (Greenwillow Books, 1999.) A boy sitting on a living room couch imagines that it becomes a succession of vessels and that he is the captain of a sailboat, canoe, ship, submarine, pirate ship, and ocean liner. As he pilots this collection of boats, he dresses accordingly, wearing a baseball hat for the sailboat, a buccaneer's scarf for the pirate vessel, and so forth. When his mother enters the room with a vacuum cleaner, his inventiveness reaches a crescendo as he conjures up an image of an angry sea monster. In the final scene, he and his mother read a book about boats while sitting on a blue rug that he had earlier imagined as the blue ocean. (Ages 3–7.)

12. *Mudkin.* By Stephen Gammell. (Carolrhoda Books, 2011.) Stephen Gammell, a Caldecott-winning artist, is in top form in this fantasy about playing in the mud on a rainy day. Almost wordless and always whimsical, this lively story is about a girl who rushes outside after a rain shower and is greeted by Mudkin, a little creature with an onion-shaped head. He invites her to become queen of the mudkins, she accepts, and they embark on a mud-splattered adventure. The girl wears a crown and robe as they romp around the yard, complete with a carriage and a castle, surrounded by her admiring mudkin subjects. This mucky, gloopy, blotchy masterpiece comes to an end when the rain returns, washing everything away but the girl's inventive imagination. (Ages 4–8.)

13. *Rolling Downhill.* By Ruth Carroll. (H. Z. Walck, 1973.) In this simple story from the creator of *What Whiskers Did* (1932), a rambunctious puppy and an energetic kitty get entangled with a ball of yarn and enjoy rolling in the grass near their cabin in the mountains. As the title suggests, they tumble downhill, which qualifies as the rising action in the plot of this rather thin offering. The frolicking friends then fall into a pond, where they are helped by fish and a turtle. After encountering other animals, they return home, the weary dog taking a nap, while the cat plans more activity. Preschoolers will like this quick read but are not likely to return to it for a second look. (Ages 2–5.)

14. *Ocean Whisper / Susurro del océano.* By Dennis Rockhill. (Raven Tree Press, 2008.) Preceded by an introductory poem printed in both English and Spanish, pictures tell the story of a boy's dream about becoming a whale, inspired by a poster, seashell, and fishbowl in his room. As the book develops, the boy and his room are transformed as the sea comes to life and he cavorts with whales in a deep blue and green ocean landscape. The perfectly realized illustrations are striking, creating a fantastic atmosphere, with all evidence of the ocean gone when he wakes from his undersea adventure. *Ocean Whisper / Susurro del océano* is an interesting contrast and companion to *Polar Slumber / Sueño polar* (2004). (Ages 4–8.)

15. *What If?* By Laura Vaccaro Seeger. (Roaring Brook Press, 2010.) This innovative Bank Street Best Children's Book is similar to the choose-your-own-ending adventure books that are popular with middle schoolers. Laura Vaccaro Seeger plays out three different scenarios with three different emotional outcomes, all involving a boy who kicks a beach ball to seals playing in the ocean. Children get to choose the ending that makes the most sense. In the first two cases, a different seal is left out of the action, while in the third scenario all the seals play together joyfully and no one is excluded. *What If?* is a good primer on emotional intelligence and a clear demonstration that actions have consequences. (Ages 3–7.)

16. *The Happy Dog.* By Hideyuki Tanaka. (Atheneum, 1983.) A small, white, shaggy dog who walks on two legs stars in three slight misadventures. First, while playing baseball, she soils a newly washed sheet hung out to dry and bungles the attempt to clean it. Second, she goes for a rainy-day walk, splashes in puddles, loses her boots in the mud, gets thoroughly wet, and shakes herself off, doggy style. Third, the little dog plays with a big red balloon. She blows it up, lets it fly into the sky, loses it on the limb of a tree, and must climb the tree to fetch it. These simple, easy-to-follow vignettes will connect with preschoolers who encounter the same types of challenges as the playful dog. (Ages 3–6.)

17. *Out of the Blue.* By Alison Jay. (Barefoot Books, 2014.) The book begins with a young lighthouse-dwelling boy quietly spending time at the beach. He meets a girl who joins him in his beachcombing until they are threatened by a coming storm. When a large octopus is washed ashore out of the blue, the poor animal is entangled in fishing line, spilling tears of fear and sorrow over its sorry state. With the aid of a coalition of creatures, including dolphins, whales, seals, and humans, the boy and girl lead the effort to rescue him. This handsome book, with illustrations magnificently painted in oil and crackling varnish, effectively combines adventure, compassion, and a little humor, as the assembled creatures struggle to pull the giant octopus back into the sea. Alison Jay has included helpful endnotes on tide pools, marine animals, and lighthouses. (Ages 3–8.)

18. *(Mostly) Wordless.* By Jed Alexander. (Alternative Comics, 2014.) The main attraction of this wonderful collection of eight stories is "Ella and the Pirates," featuring three kids who journey across the ocean, have sword fights with pirates, and find buried treasure. Jed Alexander's other vignettes are much shorter, including "Midnight Snack" about a

runaway nose and mustache, "Rainy Day" about a boy and his umbrella, displayed on the book cover, and "Jack Be Nimble," an illustrated nursery rhyme featuring an athletic mouse. Alexander's paintings are realistic and rendered with a dry-brush technique. The book project got its start from a successful Kickstarter campaign, with the artist initially making copies of "Ella and the Pirates" by hand. (Ages 3–6.)

CHAPTER 16

Wonders of Nature

> I like physics, but I love cartoons.
>
> —Stephen Hawking

1. *Clementina's Cactus*. By Ezra Jack Keats. (Viking Juvenile, 1999.) While walking in the desert, little Clementina and her dad discover a shriveled cactus all by itself. The girl is interested in the spiny plant and spends some time studying it, but a rainstorm forces them to head home. They rush back the next morning and are pleased to find that the little cactus has spectacularly bloomed flowers. Ezra Jack Keats's stunning artwork shows the coolness of the moonlit night and the warm rich hues of the sunlit desert. Keats wrote and illustrated twenty-two children's books, with *Clementina's Cactus* being his only wordless title. He is recognized for the role he played in introducing multiculturalism into children's literature. (Ages 3–8.)

2. *Gem*. By Holly Hobbie. (Little, Brown, 2012.) Almost wordless, except for brief correspondence between a girl and her grandmother at the book's beginning and end, this visual biography of a toad named Gem would make a fine addition to a school or family library. The toad's emergence from hibernation and his survival in sometimes perilous circumstances are realistically depicted. Gem is almost hit by a car and nearly eaten by a hawk but manages

to mate and raise a family. Fortunately, Gem is not taken as a pet, as it is clear that from the pictures and letters that "toads are not pets. They want to be free, like everything else." Holly Hobbie's graceful ink-and-watercolor illustrations capture the wonder of nature. (Ages 2–6.)

3. *Flood.* By Alvaro F. Villa. (Picture Window Books, 2013.) Beautifully illustrated, *Flood* is the dramatic story of a family trying to save its house from terrible destruction. A picturesque scene of lush green grass and children playing gives way to ominous storm clouds, pouring rain, and scenes of nervous anticipation. When sandbags are unable to hold back the floodwaters, the family is forced to flee to a motel. One shocking spread shows the interior of the house churning with floodwater, the family's furnishings now in ruins. The family's home is destroyed, but children will see a new home rebuilt and learn that life goes on even after disaster. With superstorms and hurricanes becoming more common, this book could help prepare children to understand some of the consequences of climate change. (Ages 6–9.)

4. *In the Woods.* By Ermanno Cristini, Luigi Puricelli, and Renato Pegoraro. (Scholastic, 1990.) *In the Woods* is a handsomely illustrated nature study and a companion to Ermanno Cristini and Luigi Puricelli's two other lavish explorations of ecological niches, *In My Garden* (1985) and *In the Pond* (1984). Operating as a panoramic mural, each page of *In the Woods* continues from the preceding page, showing the abundance of life on the floor of the forest. The Italian illustrators proceed by showing part of an animal and modestly challenging readers to figure out the whole, as when they show only the talons of a hawk preparing to attack a rabbit. This visual treat is a tribute to the unspoiled beauty of forest life that will motivate youngsters to explore the woods to find treasures of their own. (Ages 4–8.)

5. *The Apple and the Butterfly.* By Iela Mari and Enzo Mari. (Price Stern Sloan, 2013.) Originally published in Italy under the title *The Apple and the Moth* (1969), this work reveals the life cycle of a caterpillar in bold and simple graphic pictures. Children see a stark green apple on the book's cover, followed by an equally bare red apple on the title page. A cut-out view of the fruit shows seeds inside and a red spot from which a caterpillar emerges, exiting the apple. In a series of double pages, the worm settles on a branch and spins a cocoon that undergoes the process of metamorphosis, finally becoming a butterfly. The natural process is set to repeat when the beautiful winged creature flies off to lay its eggs in another flowering apple tree. This glimpse of the birth and development of an insect will make a fine addition to a preschool science library. (Ages 3–5.)

6. *Island Dog.* By Rebecca Goodale. (Two Dog Press, 1999.) This day in the life of an adventurous dog shows him swimming, chasing seagulls, snoozing on sea rocks, rolling in the sand, and cavorting about the island before returning for the evening to the lighthouse where he resides with his human family. This gentle visual narrative is set on a sunny Maine coastal isle and has picturesque panoramic views made even more interesting through the use of gatefolds. Children will be most excited when another dog enters the picture, but all the illustrations will keep children engaged. Anyone who has ever owned a dog or romped with one at the beach will appreciate the spot-on portrayal of this scenic and leisurely profile. (Ages 5–8.)

7. *Dreams.* By Peter Spier. (Doubleday, 1986.) Peter Spier shows expected sensitivity to the force of visual interpretation in this book about two children watching cloud formations, as they ascribe meaning to them in fanciful ways. A boy, a girl, and a dog play leisurely in a flowery green meadow as a parade of cloud shapes—animals, ships, trains, fish, knights,

and dragons—pass by. Spier's book is a tribute to the wonders of nature, the power of imagination, and the tender innocence of childhood. The only words in this otherwise text-free title appear at the end, offering the suggestion that children should dream when they gaze into the sky. (Ages 4–8.)

8. *Circle of Seasons.* By Gerda Muller. (Duttons Children's Books, 1995.) In this book first published in the Netherlands, Gerda Muller uses heartwarming illustrations and spare text to celebrate the joys and passage of each season. Children are featured enjoying outdoor activities such as planting a garden, going to the beach, playing in leaves, and building a snowman. With two wordless spreads for each of the four seasons, this book is designed for leisurely examination, and time should be set aside to take in the lush details and appreciate its wholesome message of family togetherness. Muller makes a point of emphasizing that while the seasons are distinct, they still form a circle, constituting the connecting thread of how we mark time. (Ages 3–7.)

CHAPTER 17

Rural Rewards

No two persons ever read the same book.

—Edmund Wilson

1. *Pancakes for Breakfast.* By Tomie DePaola. (Harcourt, Brace, Jovanovich, 1978.) An endearing old woman who lives on a farm wants to make pancakes, but she faces obstacles gathering the ingredients. She must leave her house to collect the eggs from her chickens and exit again to milk the cows and churn the cream into butter. When she goes to borrow syrup from a friend, her mischievous dog and cat break the eggs, spill the ingredients, and ruin her meal. This patient and determined lady finally gets the breakfast she wants when she catches a whiff of her neighbor's pancakes and invites herself to join the morning repast. *Pancakes for Breakfast* is wordless but for one thing: it includes a recipe for pancakes. (Ages 4–7.)

2. *Thunderstorm.* By Arthur Geisert. (Enchanted Lion Books, 2013.) Arthur Geisert's meticulous artwork follows the progress of a powerful thunderstorm from late morning to late afternoon as it moves through farm country. His account captures not only the subtle and profound changes in atmospheric events but also people's reactions to them. A rural family gets ready for the storm by loading bales of hay and bringing in the laundry. Cutaway views

show rabbit burrows, fox dens, and the insides of buildings. There are stunning watercolors of damaging flash floods, strong winds, and lightning strikes. After the storm, the community comes together to clean up and rebuild. Minimal text in the form of a timeline accompanies the pictures. (Ages 4–8.)

3. *Early Morning in the Barn*. By Nancy Tafuri. (Greenwillow Books, 1983.) In this spare-text picture book, a rooster crows and awakens the barnyard animals. Three chicks scurry around as the sun rises, and each creature makes its own distinctive sound, with the words for the sounds printed on the emitting animal. Nancy Tafuri brings early morning to life in large, two-page spreads that show animals in motion—the cat, for example, chases a mouse until it escapes into a hole. Toddlers will like the book, especially the animal noises that they already know themselves or can mimic from mom or dad. The only readers who might not be in love with this simple title are artistic purists, who might question the need to print the words "moo," "meow," "cheep," and "cock-a-doodle-doo" in illustrations that speak for themselves. (Ages 1–3.)

4. *Our House on the Hill*. By Philippe Dupasquier. (Viking Kestrel, 1988.) Small details loom large in Philippe Dupasquier's depiction of the seasonal activities of a family living an ordinary life. The month-by-month chronicle shows a country house on a hill in a peaceful setting of pastures, lakes, and trees. The two-story house and its beautiful surroundings are pictured in aerial-perspective two-page spreads, with smaller shots of family happenings. The scenes of bed sheets drying, snow sledding, kite flying, hot dog roasting, cow chasing, and birthday celebrating are all unexpectedly interesting because they are quite commonplace staples of rural existence. Parents can use the book to discuss family life and teach the months of the year. (Ages 3–8.)

5. *The Story of a Farm.* By John S. Goodall. (Margaret K. McElderry, 1989.) John S. Goodall's visual history of the English farm begins in the Middle Ages and, after several permutations, ends with a contemporary farm using modern technology. He uses vivid water-colors to depict rustic daily routines, seasonal celebra-tions, and the relationship of the farm to a nearby town. The quaint images provide an especially good overview of architectural changes over time. With its depictions of England's genteel country life and agriculture, Goodall does a masterful job of showing the inexorable unfolding of social history on a small scale. The artist uses his usual half-page inserts to break up the flow of the larger double-page spreads. (Ages 5–9.)

6. *The Chicken's Child.* By Margaret A. Hartelius. (Doubleday, 1975.) When a chicken finds an egg near a stream without a nest, she takes it home and hatches it. The baby turns out to be a cute green al-ligator, who becomes less cute as he grows larger and more insatiable in his appetite, devouring the farmer's tractor, stepladder, pumpkins, pies, and washtub. The farmer finally banishes him from the property, but the big lizard redeems himself by rescuing his dear foster mother from the clutches of a fox. As a reward for saving the day, the farmer welcomes the alligator back and serves him a few stacks of pancakes. Margaret A. Hartelius's gray-and-green cartoon il-lustrations are warmly expressive and will appeal to young readers. (Ages 4–8.)

7. *Wings.* By Shinsuke Tanaka. (Purple Bear Books, 2006.) An elderly farmer riding his bike down a country lane finds a box with an adorable puppy inside. No common canine, the puppy has wings. The farmer, his wife, and a regular wingless dog already in residence welcome the sweet little mutt into their home and hearts. When the puppy grows larger, he takes the farmer on a flight over the local

village, which creates havoc and pushback from the townies. The farmer decides to end the flights, taking away what is truly special about the dog by tying back his wings. Then, when the dogs are playing, the restrained dog is killed in a traffic accident. The sadness of this unjust and touching denouement is only slightly diminished by the subsequent birth of a litter of wingless puppies. (Ages 4–8.)

8. *Oink.* By Arthur Geisert. (HMH Books for Young Readers, 1991.) In this single-word book, eight piglets are awakened at dawn by mother pig and spend their day oinking, eating, and splashing around in a muddy water hole until it is time for everyone's nap. While the sow sleeps, her piglets sneak away and get into some mischief. They climb a haystack and launch themselves into a tree to eat apples, shouting, "Oink," as they fly through the air. Mother pig is dismayed when jarred from her nap by all the commotion. Arthur Geisert fans will recognize the same fine black-and-white etching style that he used in *Pigs from A to Z* (1986). This playful porcine family also stars in the sequel *Oink Oink* (1993). (Ages 5–8.)

9. *Moo!* By David LaRochelle and Mike Wohnoutka. (Walker Books for Young Readers, 2013.) Cartoon pictures tell the hilarious story of a cow who takes a red sports car, which a farmer has put up for sale, for a wild jaunt through the country. In short order, the car careens out of control, goes over a cliff, and crushes a police car. When sent back to the farm, the cow unsuccessfully tries to shift the blame to someone else. Preschoolers who warm to the antics of David LaRochelle and Mike Wohnoutka's mischievous cow should consider reading the joy-riding classics *Duck on a Bike* (2002) by David Shannon and *Sheep in a Jeep* (1986) by Nancy E. Shaw and Margot Apple. (Ages 2–6.)

10. *Oink Oink.* By Arthur Geisert. (HMH Books for Young Readers, 1993.) In this sequel to *Oink* (1991), Arthur Geisert doubles the fun (and the words in the book title) in another pleasing adventure starring his little piggy octet. As in the earlier almost-text-free title, children will see that the lowly word "oink" can have many meanings, as the eight small porkers sneak into a farmer's field, pick ears of corn, and swim to a tiny island to chow down on their stolen goodies. The mischievous littermates lead their irate mother on quite a chase before she guides them home, cleverly keeping them from going on another wild romp. Geisert's animated drawings are done in black and gray with just enough muted pink to keep them interesting. (Ages 5–8.)

CHAPTER 18

Creative Journeys

The moment you doubt whether you can fly, you cease forever to be able to do it.

—J. M. Barrie

1. *Journey*. By Aaron Becker. (Candlewick Press, 2013.) In homage to Crockett Johnson's *Harold and the Purple Crayon* (1955), Aaron Becker's Caldecott Honor book follows a girl who uses a red crayon to draw herself a door on her bedroom wall to escape her sepia-toned existence and enter lush fantasy worlds. She travels through a mystical green forest, coming to an intricate castle and canal system where she finds a caged purple-plumed bird. The brave girl rescues the bird and returns home to find a boy with a purple crayon who had been looking for his winged creation. The youngsters team up and depart together on a red-and-purple tandem bicycle. *Journey* is an exercise of pure imagination that will inspire many readings. (Ages 4–8.)

2. *Trainstop*. By Barbara Lehman. (Houghton Mifflin, 2008.) Daydreaming children going to magical places is a staple of many wordless books, and Barbara Lehman successfully explores this theme with a girl going on an unusual train ride with her parents. In clean and simple illustrations, the colorfully outfitted girl leaves her drab world to hop off the train at an unscheduled stop. She enters a lush Lilliputian countryside, is greeted by a band of tiny folk, and rescues an aviator who has crashed his airplane into a fruit tree. After she reboards the train and returns home, the girl gets a surprise visit from her new friends, again mixing the real with the imaginary. This comfortably fantastical tale deserves an honored place alongside Lehman's other text-free treasures. (Ages 4–8.)

3. *The Secret Box.* By Barbara Lehman. (Houghton Mifflin, 2011.) Three boys find a box with a treasure map hidden long ago by a bespectacled boy beneath the floorboards of his boarding school. Focusing on modes of transportation, Barbara Lehman shows the passage of time from a farming community to a booming cityscape. The box holds memorabilia such as photos, tokens, ticket stubs, and a postcard, providing clues for the youngsters to travel to a mysterious secret location. The children wander through a city and go through a tunnel, finding their way to a boardwalk amusement park where kids of different times, including the bespectacled boy, are having fun. Children will wonder whether they would choose to remain in this timeless place or continue to grow up. (Ages 4–8.)

4. *Sea of Dreams.* By Dennis Nolan. (Roaring Brook Press, 2011.) A young girl builds a splendid sandcastle on the beach, abandoning it to inevitable destruction by the incoming tide as the sun goes down. But something quite remarkable occurs when a light comes on in the castle and eight tiny people run for their lives from the encroaching waves. Escaping by boat, the miniscule refugee family sets out on a fantastical journey to find a new home. During the rough ocean voyage, a boy is thrown overboard and is fortunate to be rescued by a teeny

mermaid. Oblivious to the life-and-death drama that has occurred, the beach girl returns the following day to build another sandcastle. This special title was named to *Publishers Weekly*'s annual list of best children's books. (Ages 4–8.)

5. *The Umbrella*. By Ingrid and Dieter Schubert. (Lemniscaat USA, 2011.) Wasting no time, the Schuberts, a Dutch wife-and-husband team, begin *The Umbrella* on the book's endpapers, showing a little black dog's discovery of a red umbrella on a windy fall day. The umbrella catches the wind and pulls him into the clouds and around the world on an incredible trip. He rides ocean waves, crosses deserts, goes to the North Pole, and visits jungles, using the umbrella to defend himself from hungry alligators. This exciting book concludes just as abruptly as it begins, with the dog returning to his original location, passing along the umbrella to the next globetrotting adventurer. Parents can use this canine journey as an introduction to Earth's diverse climate and geography. (Ages 4–8.)

6. *The Giant Seed*. By Arthur Geisert. (Enchanted Lion Books, 2012.) The same community of pigs made famous in *Ice* (2011) benefit from the arrival of a giant dandelion seedpod on their island, as well as from the foresight of the porkers who plant and tend to it. As their island faces catastrophe when a volcano is about to erupt, a giant flower blooms, producing huge seedlings. The lucky pigs calmly pack their belongings and escape the lava raining down on them, catching rides on these airborne tufts, which carry them to safety. Their old home having been blown to smithereens, the survivors look forward to rebuilding in a lush green paradise. Arthur Geisert fans will love the book's inventive story line and intricate artistry and will hope that he continues to create more stories to challenge the resourceful pigs. (Ages 4–8.)

7. *The Island.* By Marije Tolman and Ronald Tolman. (Lemniscaat USA, 2012.) This beautifully dreamy art book follows a polar bear who climbs aboard a cloud, travels to exotic islands, and intermingles with intriguing animals. Every new island represents a new world of possibility and wonderment. Whether swimming with dolphins, riding on hippos, or visiting a violin-playing raccoon, this mellow bear is on a spiritual quest for peace and tranquility, perhaps finding it at the conclusion while gazing up at the stars. *The Island* is a tribute to the beauty and magnificence of creation, but it is not a traditional narrative. Adults may have more success than children in appreciating the book's artistry and finding its deeper meaning. (Ages 4–8.)

8. *Draw!* By Raúl Colón. (Simon & Schuster, 2014.) A sick boy stuck alone in his bedroom because of illness is reading a book about Africa and begins to draw. Along with his easel, sketchpad, and pencil, he is imaginatively transported on an African safari, where he sketches elephants, zebras, giraffes, lions, water buffalos, and hippos, which generally turn out to be cooperative subjects. Danger erupts when a huge rhino charges, and the boy just barely manages to get out of the way of the oncoming beast. The book's best moment is when baboons steal the boy's art supplies and draw him! *Draw!* concludes with the young artist back in his room with his new sketches, which he later shares with schoolmates. (Ages 4–8.)

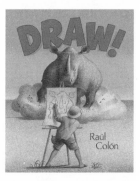

9. *The Bored Book.* By David Michael Slater and Doug Keith. (Simply Read Books, 2009.) While visiting their grandfather, two bored and irritable siblings lament the absence of television, computers, and video games. Revealing a hidden staircase, the old man sends them to the dusty attic where they find a special book that opens up into a giant map, leading them into adventures involving the Abominable Snowman, whales, pirates, knights, a dragon, and more. When they emerge from this mysterious vol-

ume, they return to their grandfather, who recognizes the literary nature of their encounters. He sets them to reading *Treasure Island* (2005) and other classics, and they become converts to the society of readers who are bored no more. (Ages 5–10.)

10. *Hot Air: The (Mostly) True Story of the First Hot-Air Balloon Ride.* By Marjorie Priceman. (Atheneum Books for Young Readers, 2005.) This almost word-less story of the world's first hot-air balloon flight in 1783 is told from the point of view of the frightened barnyard animals who were its first travelers. Wit-nessed by such luminaries as Marie Antoinette and Benjamin Franklin, the historic ballooning event shows a wide-eyed duck, sheep, and rooster ascending into the sky and having amusing and dangerous en-counters with a flock of birds, a clothesline, a church spire, and a boy's bow and arrow. The endpapers contain solid historical information on the event, but Marjorie Priceman's unique take on the story is price-less: she claims she heard it "from a duck, who heard it from a sheep, who heard it from a rooster a long, long time ago." Children will enjoy this mostly accu-rate slapstick adventure and will wish that all history could be made this much fun. (Ages 4–8.)

11. *Quest.* By Aaron Becker. (Candlewick Press, 2014.) Aaron Becker, creator of Caldecott Honor–winning *Journey* (2013), delivers an even more exciting and visually lavish fantasy adventure sequel in *Quest*. This time his magic crayon-wielding girl and boy protago-nists go on a quest to save a king and his realm, after the ruler suddenly emerges from a hidden door in a city park, giving them a map, an orange crayon, and a holster for holding more colored drawing sticks. After soldiers apprehend the old man, our young heroes use the portal to enter a vast exotic kingdom and follow the map to collect the crayons needed to rescue him. Along the away, they use their artistic talents to solve problems, for instance, using drawing keys or scuba equipment. Becker plans another book featuring his artist adventurers. (Ages 4–8.)

CHAPTER 19

Dreamy Departures

Books may well be the only true magic.

—Alice Hoffman

1. *Wonder Bear*. By Tao Nyeu. (Dial, 2008.) Two children plant mysterious seeds, growing one of them into a flowering vine from which an enormous bear emerges wearing a magic top hat. The hat enables the big bear to amaze the boy and girl by producing acrobatic monkeys, bubbles in the shape of lions, and flying porpoises. These activities are part of a dream that concludes with the bear cuddling the children and tucking them safely into their garden bed. *Wonder Bear* is a collection of spectacular illustrations in brilliant palettes, nicely presented in an oversize format, but it is an enigmatic story. Children and parents will be delightfully challenged to impart meaning to this series of eye-popping pictures. (Ages 2–5.)

2. *Last Night*. By Hyewon Yum. (Farrar, Straus & Giroux, 2008.) *Last Night* is a story that invites comparison to Maurice Sendak's classic *Where the Wild Things Are* (1963). An unhappy girl holds a fork over her dinner, unwilling to eat, and is sent to her room. She falls asleep and enters a forest with her teddy bear, where they frolic with wild animals and eventually grow tired. When she wakes up from this

moonlit adventure in her own bedroom, the girl runs downstairs to hug her mother, and all is forgiven. This title earned South Korean artist Hyewon Yum the Golden Kite Award for Picture Book Illustration. Children will find the book cathartic and appreciate the message that every day represents a new chance to get things right. (Ages 3–7.)

3. *Little Star.* By Antonin Louchard. (Hyperion Books for Children, 2003.) A tiny red starfish on the ocean floor dreams of leaving home to join his celestial brethren in the night sky. When he washes up on a beach, a girl tucks the creature into her hair like a decorative flower, where he is grabbed by a seagull, who transports him upward into the heavens. Eventually falling back into the ocean, the star-shaped adventurer resumes his place at the bottom of the sea. Readers will wonder whether this is a no-place-like-home tale or something much more. Inspired by a poem about a starfish's dreams of becoming a star in the sky, this creative book provides an excellent vehicle for encouraging children to talk about their own dreams and aspirations. (Ages 3–6.)

4. *The Little Red Fish.* By Tae-Eun Yoo. (Dial, 2007.) In a book that contains both written and wordless pages, a young boy named JeJe goes to a magical library in the middle of the forest with his librarian grandfather. The boy's red fish accompanies them. When the lad falls asleep in the dark library, he awakens to find that the fish has mysteriously disappeared from his bowl and has somehow entered a book. JeJe follows the fish into the volume, catches hold of a passing flamingo's leg, rescues his companion from the ocean, and returns the little red fish to the safety of the library. Kids will enjoy the adventure, and parents will be attracted by the always popular theme about the imaginative power of books. Tae-Eun Yoo created this attractive cloth-bound book as her graduate thesis for New York City's School of Visual Arts. (Ages 4–8.)

5. *Little Pickle.* By Peter Collington. (E. P. Dutton, 1986.) An impish toddler named Little Pickle goes on a fantasy journey that involves trading places with her mother. The adventure begins when she falls asleep in her stroller and dreams that her mom has taken her place, with Little Pickle now pushing the baby carriage. With her parent snoozing, they take a train ride to the shore, where the little girl sets out to sea alone in a rubber raft. When Little Pickle falls asleep in the stormy ocean, she is rescued by tugboat sailors and brought back to her mother, who is still dozing. The book ends with the two switching back to their original roles, with mom again pushing the carriage. (Ages 2–5.)

6. *Polar Slumber / Sueño polar.* By Dennis Rockhill. (Raven Tree Press, 2004.) Wordless, except for an appended poem and instructions in English and Spanish, this story tells of a little girl who falls asleep and dreams about the polar snow bear she built in her backyard. After imagining a night spent in the company of the bear and other creatures, including an owl, a seal, and a wolf, she awakes in her bedroom, while footprints of the bear in the snow suggest that her little adventure might have really happened. The book is comparable to *The Snowman* (1978), the wordless classic about a boy who builds a snowman who comes to life, but it does not break new ground. Dennis Rockhill's artwork is first rate, but his instructions on how to use the book are unnecessary. (Ages 4–8.)

7. *The Midnight Circus.* By Peter Collington. (Knopf, 1992.) In this fantasy adventure, a boy goes to bed unhappy that his favorite toy, a shopkeeper's coin-operated mechanical horse, has been removed from outside the store near his apartment and replaced with a rocket ship. After reading a bedtime circus book, the boy dreams that he leaves his house and finds the horse, now alive, who takes him to a midnight circus. They are invited to become part of the

show, have a run-in with a scary gorilla, and are a big hit. When the show is over, they have cake and cookies and then return home. Happily, the boy's wish is fulfilled, and the mechanical horse is returned to its original spot. (Ages 4–7.)

8. *Three Little Dreams.* By Thomas Aquinas Maguire. (Simply Read Books, 2009.) This innovative follow-up to *A Growling Place* (2007), also a dream fantasy, consists of three unbound books titled "Of Night and of Flight," "Of Dragons and Drowse," and "Of Sleep and of Sheep." The stories in this boxed set of accordion-style books are illustrated in a dark and subdued palette that is perfect for the fantastical and whimsical scenes involving soaring birds, flying dragons, and floating sheep. Each book folds out to about a yard in length and, like actual dreams, does not have a conventional beginning and end. Children will enjoy their visit to Thomas Aquinas Maguire's dream world and be eager to move on to *The Wild Swans* (2012), adapted from the tale by Hans Christian Andersen. (Ages 4–8.)

9. *REM: Rapid Eye Movement.* By Istvan Banyai. (Viking, 1997.) Hungarian emigrant Istvan Banyai, who gained critical acclaim for the unusual perspectives showcased in *Zoom* (1995) and *Re-zoom* (1998), penetrates into a boy's deep, surrealistic dream state filled with imagery. Inspired by toys and a book near the boy, who has fallen asleep in his room, sense and nonsense collaborate, creating a strange world where a frog morphs into a prince and a snowman becomes a princess ballerina. Children who are in touch with their sleeping selves will recognize that this is the stuff that dreams are made of, as they see the imaginative sequence come to a close, with the boy waking up, brushing his teeth, and washing away the alternate reality that lives behind his rapid eye movements. (Ages 5–9.)

CHAPTER 20

Fashionable Favorites

Elegance isn't solely defined by what you wear. It's how you carry yourself, how you speak, what you read.

—Carolina Herrera

1. *Archie.* By Domenica More Gordon. (Bloomsbury USA Children's, 2012.) When Archie, a fashion-loving dog, gets his own sewing machine, his designs become the rage of London. His outfits are in demand among not just dogs but also their owners, most notably when he tailors matching clothing for owners and their pets. Archie really hits the big time when he is pictured selling one of his couture creations to the queen and her royal pets. Budding young fashion designers will be straining at the leash to own this humorous book, but it might leave some kids wondering how dogs can both be owners and pets. Recalling the cartoon precedent established by Walt Disney's Goofy and Pluto, parents and grandparents will be more nonchalant about dogs walking upright alongside dogs traveling on all fours. (Ages 3–6.)

2. *Sing, Pierrot, Sing: A Picture Book in Mime.* By Tomie DePaola. (Harcourt Children's Books, 1987.) The story is about a love triangle between the infatuated Pierrot, the fetching Columbine, and her handsome lover, Harlequin. When Pierrot composes a song for Columbine, he is stunned to find that his love is unrequited, as a crowd witnesses his balcony

serenade and laughs at his humiliation. Mortified and rejected, he goes off by himself to brood until some children welcome him back and show him some affection by listening to his song. Pierrot, Columbine, and Harlequin are classic stock characters of Renaissance origin, with Pierrot known for his trusting, naive, and foolish nature. Tomie DePaola is an author and illustrator best known for his award-winning picture book *Strega Nona* (1975). (Ages 5–9.)

3. *Sir Andrew.* By Paula Winter. (Random House, 1984.) Sir Andrew is a gentlemanly donkey with a bad case of narcissism, comically oblivious of everything but himself. Sporting a hat and watch fob, he strolls down the street admiring his reflection in a plate glass window, when he goes head over hooves into a large open cellar hole. He breaks his leg and is given a cast in the hospital. When released and back on the street, the elegant donkey chases his hat unaware of the mishaps he has caused and is poised to slip on a banana peel and take another dangerous fall. The notion of vanity may be lost on youngsters, who are developmentally self-centered, but they will still like the bedlam and humor surrounding this dapper Adonis. (Ages 4–8.)

4. *Lavinia's Cottage.* By John S. Goodall. (Margaret K. McElderry, 1983.) Soft pastel illustrations and pop-ups are the main attraction in this nostalgic look at a girl in a beautiful country cottage in Victorian England. Children will enjoy moving tabs and lifting flaps to open doors and make characters move. This languid sequence of pictures of artifacts of an almost forgotten time will probably interest some social historians. But the exploration of Victorian curiosities—closets, cabinets, stalls, stairways, sheds, courtyards, thatched roofs, parasols, and bustles—has limited appeal to small children who are looking for a more active story line. The only item of narrative interest is that Lavina appears to have the measles, but her visitors seem unworried that they will catch it. (Ages 5–9.)

5. *The Heartaches of a French Cat.* By Barbara Mc-
Clintock. (D. R. Godine, 1989.) Structured in the
manner of an all-feline theatrical production, this is a
sophisticated story of love, heartbreak, and triumph
set in nineteenth-century high-society France. When
Minette, a poor cat in the mold of Cinderella, runs
away with a handsome count, the romance doesn't
last very long before she must choose between the
count and a worthier suitor. The heroine finally realizes her dreams by choosing neither of these men and
instead writing a successful memoir. The *New York
Times*, *Entertainment Weekly*, and *Time* placed *The
Heartaches of a French Cat* on their annual lists of
outstanding books for children. (Ages 7–12.)

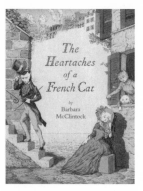

6. *An Edwardian Holiday.* By John S. Goodall. (Atheneum, 1979.) *An Edwardian Holiday* joins John S.
Goodall's other deeply sentimental and celebratory
Edwardian-period books, all focused on the quaint
niceties of a well-ordered, well-to-do British society.
In this installment, a girl and boy go on vacation to
the beach with their parents, see a Punch and Judy
show, go fishing, visit friends, and make a day trip
across the English Channel to France. Like the author's other pictorial essays of this bygone era, such
as *Edwardian Entertainments* (1982), *An Edwardian
Season* (1980), and *An Edwardian Summer* (1976),
An Edwardian Holiday is full of nostalgia but empty
of the action and narrative punch that children enjoy
in his Paddy Pork books. (Ages 4–8.)

7. *Paddy's New Hat.* By John S. Goodall. (Atheneum,
1980.) The plump protagonist of the Edwardian pig
series is proudly strutting down the promenade, when
a gust of wind blows his straw hat into a police re-
cruiting station. He signs up to become a policeman
and becomes involved with many mishaps, including
a traffic jam, but still manages to catch a burglar. The
book concludes with Paddy receiving a medal from a
royal couple. The dandified gentleman pig resumes
his walk, wearing his medal and a plume in his hat.

The pictures are painted with John S. Goodall's signature soft watercolors, and alternating full and half pages move the action along. (Ages 4–8.)

8. *Shrewbettina Goes to Work.* By John S. Goodall. (Atheneum, 1981.) Dressed in cumbersome layers of elegant, old-fashioned clothing, Shrewbettina decides to apply for a job as an assistant in a large store populated by a variety of very well-dressed animal shoppers. Anthropomorphized pigs, mice, and other furry creatures are made to look about the same size. The main action of this pop-up and pull-tab book involves Shrewbettina pursuing and capturing a purse thief who is a rat. This confident shrew made her first appearance in *Shrewbettina's Birthday* (1970), in which she is more a victim than a hero. In the earlier book, when a masked robber steals Shrewbettina's purse, a kindly gentleman mouse comes to her rescue and is rewarded with an invitation to her birthday party. (Ages 4–8.)

9. *Archie's Vacation.* By Domenica More Gordon. (Bloomsbury, 2014.) Originally released as *Archie's Holiday* (2013), this spare-text follow-up to *Archie* (2012) finds the well-tailored dog in need of a break from his clothing-design business. He readies himself for a seaside vacation, preparing for every possible contingency, until his overpacked suitcase explodes in a four-page foldout spread. As his little pet terrier looks on, the dapper dog comes up with a solution to his worries by filling his trench coat pockets and putting on layers of clothing, which finally enables him to keep his case from bursting open. Anyone who has ever gone overboard getting ready for a trip will appreciate Archie's anxiety. His worries include poor weather, overeating, and even jellyfish attacks. (Ages 3–6.)

CHAPTER 21

Fascinating Fantasies

Watch with glittering eyes the whole world around you because the greatest secrets are always hidden in the most unlikely places.

—Roald Dahl

1. *The Red Book.* By Barbara Lehman. (Houghton Mifflin, 2004.) In this fantasy adventure story, a young girl in a city finds a square red book in a snow bank, takes it to school, and opens it to find a boy on a tropical island beach. The boy discovers a duplicate book in the sand and uses it to see a panoramic view of a faraway city and the girl in a classroom. The children make a connection, opening a new world of experience and possibility. Composed as a series of detailed, paneled illustrations, Barbara Lehman's Caldecott Honor book is an exciting visual and conceptual treat. *The Red Book* conveys the powerful message that storybooks have the magical power to transport us anywhere. (Ages 4–8.)

2. *Time Flies.* By Eric Rohmann. (Crown, 1994.) When a bird enters a natural history exhibit in a museum, it finds that it has traveled back in time and is among actual living dinosaurs. A Tyrannosaurus rex swallows him, but the natural landscape dissolves back into a museum, and the bird flies free. Unusual visual perspectives and the suggestion

that dinosaurs were the evolutionary predecessors of contemporary avian life give the book special appeal. Eric Rohmann said he began the book with words, but as it took shape, "the words and images were saying the same thing. So I let the pictures talk by themselves." *Time Flies* earned Caldecott Honor status and was named a Best Children's Book by the *New York Times Book Review*. (Ages 3–7.)

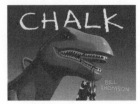

3. *Chalk*. By Bill Thomson. (Marshall Cavendish Children, 2010.) Three children dressed in rain gear find a bag of enchanted chalk at the playground, and their drawings come to life. The rain goes away when the first girl draws a sun, and butterflies magically materialize when a second girl draws the beautiful monarchs. The game takes a frightening turn when a boy draws a Tyrannosaurus rex, which ends up chasing them across the playground. With a combination of close-ups and distant perspectives, Bill Thomson's wonderfully expressive photo-style art makes the emotions of happiness, terror, and fear seem real. Fortunately, the kids are able to bring their intense problem to a satisfying end. Thomson's eye-catching dinosaur cover will grab the attention of children, while the sequence of visually exciting images inside will keep them on the edge of their seats. (Ages 4–8.)

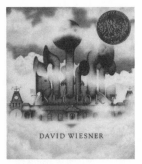

4. *Sector 7*. By David Wiesner. (Clarion Books, 1999.) David Wiesner, known for his mastery of wordless picture books, is at the peak of his creative powers in this critically acclaimed fantasy adventure that begins with a boy who likes to draw on a school trip to the Empire State Building. From atop the skyscraper, a fluffy and friendly cloud whisks him away to colossal, factorylike Sector 7, where clouds are made. When the young artist sketches some extraordinary cloud formations in the shape of fish, and the clouds eagerly assume these shapes, the stodgy cloud dispatchers are not amused. The boy is returned to the building just in time to rejoin his departing classmates. With stunning watercolor murals and picture panels, Wiesner's book overflows with whimsy and the allure of unconventional thinking. (Ages 5–9.)

5. *Mr. Wuffles!* By David Wiesner. (Clarion Books, 2013.) Mr. Wuffles is a black-and-white house cat who passes over his regular toys in favor of playing with a spaceship full of small green aliens from outer space. When the feline gets too rough with the spaceship, the tiny beings are forced to flee behind a house radiator, where they make friends with a ladybug and a bunch of ants. In one of the book's funniest scenes, the bugs and aliens immediately pose together for a group photo. In another sequence, the tiny creatures communicate in strange nonalphabetical speech bubbles in an area decorated with cave drawings of past insect-cat battles. With his claws deployed, a disappointed Mr. Wuffles looks on as the creatures escape and fly away. Count this Caldecott Honor book as another winner for the master of pictorial fantasy. (Ages 5–9.)

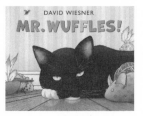

6. *Ice.* By Arthur Geisert. (Enchanted Lion Books, 2011.) Pigs don't like the heat, and they need plenty of water, so they leave their tropical island on an adventure in search of ice to relieve their distress. After examining a globe of the planet, the porcine community builds a balloon-powered airship and heads north to the Artic to capture an iceberg, an excellent source of cold, fresh water. Attaching a line to a huge iceberg, these can-do piggies tow it home, chop it into ice cubes, and put blocks of it in the community pool. This whimsical book could open the door to a serious discussion about global warming and the increasing scarcity of fresh water. *Ice* is formatted in the horizontal style common to all the books in the Stories without Words series. (Ages 4–10.)

7. *The Midnight Adventures of Kelly, Dot, and Esmeralda.* By John S. Goodall. (Margaret K. McElderry, 1999.) Originally published in 1972, this is the story of a koala bear named Kelly, a doll named Dot, and a mouse named Esmeralda, toys who come to life at midnight and get into deep trouble when they climb

into a picture on the wall of the nursery. When they fall out of a boat in this picturesque world, the three toys are invited to the home of a hedgehog to dry off and enjoy a meal. The beautiful pastoral scene takes an ugly turn when cat performers at a county fair capture dainty Esmeralda. Kelly and Dot come to the mouse's rescue, and they flee through the countryside, finding their way out of the painting and back to the nursery. (Ages 4–8.)

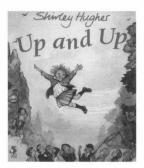

8. *Up and Up.* By Shirley Hughes. (Red Fox, 1991.) Originally published in 1979, this is the story of a young girl who watches birds and, more than anything else, wishes to join them in flight. She tries several strategies to get herself airborne, including homemade wings and balloons, but is completely stymied until a strange egg is delivered. The heroine eats some of the egg and begins to fly, much to the consternation of adults who do everything they can to catch her and coax her down as she soars through town. There is something deeply attractive in the childhood wish to fly like a bird, and this award-winning English illustrator and author has captured it in this imaginative story. (Ages 4–7.)

9. *Fossil.* By Bill Thomson. (Two Lions, 2013.) When a boy and his cocker spaniel go for a walk on the beach, the boy breaks open some rocks, unleashing prehistoric plants and animals! Picking up on the dinosaur theme from his successful picture book *Chalk* (2010), Bill Thomson's story brings to life an ancient fern, huge dragonfly, and scaly pterodactyl, with the flying reptile carrying away the boy's dog. Every page of this wordless wonder is filled with striking imagery. Realistic drawings rendered with photographic accuracy emphasize the boy's expressions of alarm as he tries to figure out how to get the extraordinary situation under control. The boy discovers that he can eliminate this antediluvian threat by smashing the fossilized rocks. (Ages 5–9.)

10. *The Surprise Picnic.* By John S. Goodall. (Atheneum, 1977.) Dressed in Victorian attire, a mother cat and her two kittens row to an island to have a pleasant picnic on a rocky beach. They lay the picnic out on what they think is a rock, but it turns out to be a tortoise that sprouts legs and goes into a nearby cave. The felines then get caught in a storm without their boat and are washed ashore in their picnic baskets and umbrella. They then use the latter to catch the wind and carry them up and away to safety and to teatime with the neighbors. Children will be surprised by the turn of events and by how the cats have dressed for their outing in ruffles and hoop dresses. (Ages 4–8.)

11. *The Self-Made Snowman.* By Fernando Krahn. (J. B. Lippincott, 1974.) *The Self-Made Snowman* begins on an unassuming note with mountain goats dislodging some snow from a ledge. But then the snow barrels down the hill, taking on a life of its own, finally accruing to the size and shape of a large snowman. This spontaneously formed winter figure makes a few stops along the way and is observed by curious woodland creatures. Somehow it ends up in a wagon and sails into town, becoming the centerpiece of a community celebration. Kids who have made their own snowman may be dubious about the origins of this one, but the book's story, rendered in black-and-white illustrations, is charming nonetheless. (Ages 4–8.)

12. *The 46 Little Men.* By Jan Mogensen. (Greenwillow Books, 1991.) Swedish illustrator Jan Mogensen's book chronicles the adventures of forty-six mischievous tiny men who live in a painting on the wall of a child's nursery. The book is wordless except for a list, included in the endpapers, of short descriptions of the elfin characters. These busy little imps climb out of the picture, explore the nursery, and set out to find the Island of Elves, where all the inhabitants turn out to be female. This playful and witty volume will provide hours of entertainment as readers scan the pages to find all forty-six elves, matching them up with their printed characterizations. (Ages 3–7.)

13. *Hunters of the Great Forest.* By Dennis Nolan. (Roaring Brook Press, 2014.) A troupe of tiny hunters, five men and two women, set out on an epic fairy tale journey to obtain a sumptuous prize. These brave insect-size adventurers travel over mountains and through forests with huge tree roots, encountering frightening dragonflies, toads, birds, chipmunks, and ants, to reach their ultimate goal, a girl sitting by a campfire roasting marshmallows. With some difficulty, they appropriate their prize from the bag of marshmallows and take it back to their village for a sweet feast. Dennis Nolan does an excellent job of showing readers a bug's-eye view of a world that seems quite dangerous and overwhelming to the intrepid hunters. (Ages 3–8.)

14. *The Wonder Ring: A Fantasy in Silhouette.* By Holden Wetherbee. (Doubleday, 1978.) Impressive hand-cut silhouettes tell the story of an ill-treated boy who shows kindness to a mysterious beggar, who rewards him with the gift of a magic ring. Exquisitely cut papers show the poor boy being criticized for not chopping enough wood and being sent to bed. He dreams of running away from home with his dog, slaying a giant, marrying a princess, and creating a palace. The book has an appendix with instructions on making silhouettes as well as a brief history of the art form. While the cut-paper images are well composed and lively, they will probably be of more interest to artists and illustrators than young children looking for a good story. (Ages 4–8.)

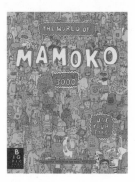

15. *The World of Mamoko in the Year 3000.* By Aleksandra Mizielińska and Daniel Mizieliński. (Big Picture Press, 2014.) In this second book in the Mamoko series, the settings are all in the future, filled with strange animals, robots, extraterrestrials, and clever details of a fully realized fantasy vision of the next millennium. The Polish illustrators have given the book a satisfying mixture of seek-and-find and a text-free narrative aided by an opening that lists thirty-two characters, inviting children to follow their progress and construct individual narratives. *The World of Mamoko in the Year 3000* is a fun read, but it could also be used to segue into a real discussion about what the future holds. Mamoko aficionados will want to investigate the history of this curious world in *The World of Mamoko in the Time of Dragons* (2014). (Ages 5–8.)

16. *Flying Jake.* By Lane Smith. (Macmillan, 1988.) In this winsome story, a boy named Jake suddenly attains the extraordinary power of flight when he follows his pet bird out the window and into the sky. Readers will appreciate what it is like to escape the confines of a cage and house as they vicariously soar over rooftops, trees, and people and into a bird's nest. Jake's adventure ends back in his bedroom, where he waits for the bird to return to his cage. But having experienced freedom, why should the bird return to being a pet? Some illustrations are displayed full-bleed, while others are crammed into too-small panels, sometimes as many as fourteen to a two-page spread. Lane Smith's offbeat, abstract style found a wider and more receptive audience in the illustrations he did for Jon Scieszka's *The True Story of the Three Little Pigs* (1989) and *The Stinky Cheese Man and Other Fairly Stupid Tales* (1992). (Ages 4–8.)

17. *The Flying Grandmother.* By Naomi Kojima. (Crowell, 1981.) A girl imagines that she has feathered wings and begins to fly. She decides to visit her stout grandmother, who happens to have an old pair of wings in a trunk, and with an assist from some birds, the two finally ascend into the night sky. They stop a bakery robbery, and after a misunderstanding with the bakery's owners, the girl and grandmother still manage to catch the thieves. One feature of *The Flying Grandmother*, illustrated in comic book style, is that the panels are numbered, from 1 to 132, which is strange because there is little risk that readers will get confused or lose their way in the sequence of pictures. Perhaps Naomi Kojima intended a little counting practice. (Ages 5–9.)

18. *Ben's Big Dig.* By Daniel Wakeman and Dirk Van Stralen. (Orca Book Publishers, 2005.) While visiting his grandmother, a prodigious baker of pies, Ben feels lonely and bored staying in the room that once belonged to his father. The boy creeps downstairs, finds a chest of mining equipment, and decides to embark on a midnight journey through the center of the planet. Wearing a lighted pit helmet and thick gloves and equipped with a shovel, the intrepid lad digs and digs until he accidentally hits water, requiring grandmother and her pies to come to his rescue. The deep blues of the comic book–style illustrations add just the right mood to this fantastical story. *Ben's Big Dig* is an inventive adventure that will immediately grab the attention of children and easily hold their interest through multiple readings. (Ages 4–9.)

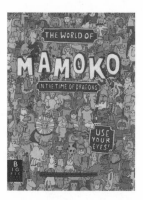

19. *The World of Mamoko in the Time of Dragons.* By Aleksandra Mizielińska and Daniel Mizieliński. (Big Picture Press, 2014.) Set in a mythological past, this richly illustrated book reads like a zany trip to a Renaissance fair. In this third installment in the Mamko series, Aleksandra Mizielińska and Daniel Mizieliński take readers on another seek-and-find journey that includes a royal banquet, maidens, courtiers, and a king being kidnapped by a dragon. As in previous books, the creators have provided a peculiar collection of twenty-six characters packed into pages of fun and adventure. Intricate spreads of medieval antics will keep readers enchanted as they follow the separate stories that develop for the characters first introduced inside the book's front cover. There is so much going on in this bygone world that readers will want to visit it often. (Ages 5–8.)

CHAPTER 22

Marvelous Mysteries

The job of the artist is always to deepen the mystery.

—Francis Bacon

1. *Tuesday.* By David Wiesner. (Clarion Books, 1997.) While people sleep, frogs magically rise into the air on their lily pads and fly through a suburban town. On a Tuesday under a full moon, this frog armada startles birds and spooks a dog as the frogs silently float around as if on flying carpets. There is no human protagonist in this story: these mysteriously airborne reptiles are on their own. Surreal and almost wordless, the voyage concludes when the sun begins to rise and the frogs come crashing to earth. In the final pages, David Wiesner forecasts the next Tuesday evening, this time showing the sky filling with pigs! Fellow artist Jerry Pinkney aptly described this graphically brilliant Caldecott winner as a masterpiece of visual storytelling. (Ages 5–9.)

2. *Free Fall.* By David Wiesner. (HarperCollins, 2008.) Originally published in 1988, this is a story of a boy who falls asleep while reading and finds himself on a magical adventure that includes dragons, castles, knights, wizards, and animated chess people in medieval garb. One picture shows the dreaming boy, dressed only in pajamas throughout his travels, as

Gulliver among the Lilliputians, while another shows him in a modern cityscape. The denouement shows him riding on a swan's back over an ocean and back to his bed. *Free Fall* is a wild and surreal journey with so many twists and turns that some young children may not be able to fathom it all. With stunning and always visually beguiling illustrations, this book earned David Wiesner his first Caldecott Honor. (Ages 4–8.)

3. *Rainstorm.* By Barbara Lehman. (Houghton Mifflin, 2007.) On a rainy day, a bored and lonely boy finds a mysterious key to a large trunk. Unlocking it, he climbs down a ladder to a basement that somehow connects to a faraway lighthouse on a bright and sunny island, reminiscent of the one featured in Barbara Lehman's *The Red Book*. He goes outside, makes friends, builds sandcastles, flies kites, and returns home at the end of the day to his stately mansion to dine alone. The next time it rains, the boy invites his island friends to traverse the secret passage and visit his home. This rainy-day story, done in attractive full-page illustrations and bright sequential panels, teaches children that melancholy can always be overcome with glorious imagination. (Ages 3–8.)

4. *The Grey Lady and the Strawberry Snatcher.* By Molly Bang. (Aladdin Paperbacks, 1996.) Young children will be enthralled and a little bit scared by an impish thief who follows an old woman from town and through the woods, attempting to steal her strawberries. In Molly Bang's mysterious book, this elusive lady buys her berries at a market and is then pursued by a long-fingered blue figure through a creepy swamp until he finds something he likes better. The wild pursuit includes catching a bus, swinging from a vine, and blending in with the surroundings. Children will find new points of interest every time they return to this surreal story of hide-and-seek. *The Grey Lady* is a Caldecott Honor book, an American Library Association Notable Children's Book, and a winner of the Boston Globe–Horn Book Award. (Ages 4–8.)

5. *Creepy Castle.* By John S. Goodall. (Atheneum, 1975.) Known for his Victorian and medieval themes, John S. Goodall, one of England's best-known illustrators, crafts an adventure story starring a fearless mouse, his lady mouse cohort, and a sinister rat who locks them in a scary castle. The hero battles dragons and bats in defense of his maiden companion and ends up pushing her out a window and into a moat, where they are paddled to safety by a frog on a lily pad. Meanwhile, the villainous rat, who is following them, gets what he deserves when he is dumped into the water before he is about to shoot a defenseless swan with an arrow. Kids will like the book's fairy tale quality and will of course root for the swashbuckling hero, who resembles Robin Hood. (Ages 4–8.)

6. *Where Is the Cake?* By Thé Tjong-Khing. (Abrams Books for Young Readers, 2007.) A dog couple pursues two rude mice who have stolen their cake from a table outside their cottage. In this seek-and-find adventure, they chase the black-clad thieves through a variety of changing and intricate landscapes—mountains, bamboo jungles, and streams—encountering other animals with their own narratives. A stork rescues a little pig who is falling off a cliff, a cat's hat is pilfered by monkeys, a bunny cries for her lost toy, and a chameleon sits on drying paint. *Where Is the Cake?* is worth many readings because every time the book is opened, some new drama or mischief will emerge that wasn't noticed before. Thé Tjong-Khing, one of Holland's most celebrated illustrators of children's books, was born in Java, Indonesia. (Ages 3–8.)

7. *The Surprise.* By Sylvia van Ommen. (Lemniscaat, 2007.) First published in 2004 under the Spanish title *La sorpresa*, this charming square book features a sheep making a series of unexplained moves that do not become clear until the surprise, a beautiful red sweater, is finally revealed. The book begins with the sheep checking herself out in a mirror. She then dyes her wool red, shears it off, and delivers it to a poodle at a spinning wheel, who turns it into yarn. After

knitting the yarn into a very long-necked sweater, the sheep presents this thoughtful gift to her giraffe friend. The European origins of this pleasant book are revealed in one tiny detail: the poodle is shown smoking a cigarette. (Ages 4–8.)

8. *Rooster's Revenge.* By Beatrice Rodriguez. (Enchanted Lion Books, 2011.) Following on the heels of *The Chicken Thief* (2010) and *Fox and Hen Together* (2011), *Rooster's Revenge* is the third book in Beatrice Rodriguez's text-free series. The rooster is still angry about losing a possible mate to the fox and sets out with his old pals, bear and rabbit, on a sea voyage. The trio's rowboat capsizes in a violent storm, and they are carried ashore by a group of turtles. The rooster takes possession of a glowing green egg in a mysterious cave that also has a large skeleton, bats, and slugs. After a long, surrealistic journey home, the egg hatches, leaving the rooster shocked and then happy to have a baby dragon to raise. The finish of this strange story is not revenge but a consolation prize for the jilted rooster. *Rooster's Revenge* was also released under the title *The Treasure Thief* (2001). (Ages 4–8.)

9. *The Mysteries of Harris Burdick.* By Chris Van Allsburg. (Houghton Mifflin, 1984.) *The Mysteries of Harris Burdick* comprises fourteen eerie and enigmatic black-and-white drawings, perhaps intended for creative writing exercises. Each mysterious drawing has a title and caption and can be considered in relationship to the others or as a stand-alone illustration. The pictures are both fantastical and realistic, designed to send young minds spinning, as with the image of a man attempting to beat something large under his carpet, a woman putting a knife into a pumpkin, or a nun sitting in a chair floating in a cathedral. In honor of this masterpiece, *The Chronicles of Harris Burdick* (2011) collects short stories by prominent authors, all inspired by this influential book. Chris Van Allsburg earned Caldecott Medals for *Jumanji* (1981) and *The Polar Express* (1985) and a Caldecott Honor for *The Garden of Abdul Gasazi* (1979). (Ages 5–9.)

10. *The Birthday Cake Mystery.* By Thé Tjong-Khing. (Gecko Press, 2012.) This unusual visual detective story is packed with characters, activities, and clues that leave a lot to the imagination. Anthropomorphized animals are getting ready for a birthday party, and readers are invited to follow their progress to figure out who is having the birthday and discern other issues revealed in twelve eventful two-page spreads. An adult dog in a Waldo-style striped shirt is trying to make the cake, a toddler is crying, a mother rabbit is having a picnic, monkeys are on the roof of a house, a fox and rabbit are digging a deep hole, and much, much more. To fully discern the artist's intentions, young children will want to visit *The Birthday Cake Mystery* a few times, with each viewing undoubtedly revealing some new and interesting detail. (Ages 4–8.)

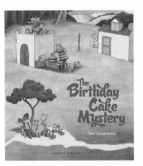

11. *Where Is the Cake Now?* By Thé Tjong-Khing. (Abrams Books for Young Readers, 2009.) This sequel to *Where Is the Cake?* (2007) follows a diverse group of cartoon animals traveling through the countryside looking for a place to have a picnic. Carrying two prized cakes on silver platters, they undergo many challenges and adventures and finally find the perfect location. But now the cakes are missing! Bedlam ensues as the creatures accuse each other of thievery. The group chases two suspicious-looking mice down a hill, but the crook turns out to be someone else. Children will have fun interpreting the mini-stories contained in the amply sized pages and going back to figure out how the theft was accomplished. (Ages 4–8.)

12. *One Scary Night.* By Antoine Guilloppé. (Milk & Cookies Press, 2004.) As a boy trudges through snow by himself at night through a cold and forbidding forest, a dark figure, perhaps a wolf, is clearly stalking him. Constructing his narrative in sharply contrasting black and white, Antoine Guilloppé skillfully builds suspense and tension, showing the predator getting closer and the frightened boy beginning to run. The beast pounces, but in a breathtaking twist, it is not a wolf at all but a friendly dog who has pushed the boy

out of the way of a large falling tree! Most children will be enormously relieved to see the two of them hug, while more savvy readers will have anticipated that this children's picture book would not end in a brutal mauling. (Ages 9–12.)

13. *Amanda and the Mysterious Carpet.* By Fernando Krahn. (Clarion Books, 1985.) A magic carpet takes a bossy little girl on a fanciful journey as it floats around the house and takes her for a ride. While she is reading a book of Arabian fairy tales at the kitchen table, a large package arrives containing the strange carpet. It takes flight, while she chases it about, angrily trying to command and control it. When she finally succeeds in boarding the elusive throw rug, it dumps her on the floor, but then she manages to use it as an elevator to gain access to treats stored in the top kitchen shelves. The mysterious carpet strands the imperious child on the roof of her home, where her annoyed mother must rescue her. (Ages 4–8.)

14. *Boat.* By Barbara Remington. (Doubleday, 1975.) As strange creatures look on, two bearded men use their umbrellas to sketch plans for a boat on a sandy beach. They pull tools from their umbrellas and start to work as the bright sun inexplicably begins to evaporate all the seawater. Faced with the dilemma of a boat with no water, the shipbuilders simply give up and walk away from the fully constructed vessel. Barbara Remington's story about a boat that is stuck in the sand with no place to go is an apt metaphor for this book because it will leave most readers high and dry. Remington is best known for her popular illustrations of J. R. R. Tolkien's novels *The Hobbit* (1965) and *The Lord of the Rings* trilogy (1965). (Ages 4–8.)

CHAPTER 23

Pictorial Perspectives

The eye sees only what the mind is prepared to comprehend.

—Henri Bergson

1. *Zoom.* By Istvan Banyai. (Viking, 1995.) "Zoom" is the operative word in this always surprising exploration of shifting visual perspective. In the manner of a camera lens, Istvan Banyai constantly zooms about, showing his subjects close up and far away, producing the effect that nothing is as it first appears. In one memorable series of pictures, a boy holding a magazine on a cruise ship transmutes into a ship poster on the side of a bus, then an image on a TV screen, and eventually a drawing on a postage stamp. On the last page, Banyai pulls away to show the Earth as a small dot in vast black space. The clever book will intrigue children with feats of artistic wonder. (Ages 5–8.)

2. *Re-zoom.* By Istvan Banyai. (Puffin Books, 1998.) The author of *Zoom* (1995) "re-zooms" his mission of visual surprise with another series of absorbing illustrations, each one farther away, that become details on subsequent pages. The book begins with cave art that, with the flip of a page, becomes a small part of a wristwatch, that, pulling back, appears on the arm of an archaeologist in a pyramid, that soon zooms out to become a movie poster, and so on,

143

until the continuing sequence turns out to be something that a boy is reading on the subway. Istvan Banyai is a master of spatial relationships, reminding us again that context and perspective make all the difference. (Ages 5–8.)

3. *Yellow Umbrella.* By Jae-Soo Lui. (Kane/Miller, 2002.) This rainy-day book, accompanied by delicate music on a compact disc, shows children holding umbrellas moving through city streets on their way to school. In this New York Times Best Illustrated Book, brightly colored umbrellas stand out from a drab and misty background, showing children walking over a bridge, going through a playground, descending steps, and passing other city sights. Originally produced in South Korea, this marriage of art and music is a rare experience that invites relaxation and contemplation. The music, composed by Dong Il Sheen, opens with the sound of falling rain and includes a song sung in Korean. (Ages 4–8.)

4. *The Other Side.* By Istvan Banyai. (Chronicle Books, 2005.) With varying visual perspectives as his theme, Istvan Banyai presents a series of everyday images, surprising us with what is on the other side. This challenging journey of sophisticated graphics depends on one page revealing part of a story, with a subsequent page revealing another point of view. In one set of images, for example, we see a boy looking out a jet's window, complemented by a boy viewing the same jet from the ground. The book also includes ongoing narratives that provide an additional sense of mystery and puzzlement, because some images appear to be unrelated to others. As with *Zoom* (1995) and *Re-zoom* (1998), children will be eager to keep turning pages to satisfy their curiosity and to learn what clever new trick Banyai has up his sleeve. (Ages 5–8.)

5. *Bee & Bird.* By Craig Frazier. (Roaring Brook Press, 2011.) No words are needed to tell this story because *Bee & Bird* is mostly an exercise in pictorial perspective. Bold geometric illustrations are the main attraction in this modest tale about a bumblebee and a red bird who go on an adventure of shifting visual viewpoints. Until they arrive at their final destination, a beehive, this strange duo will travel by truck, cow, sailboat, and bicycle basket. As the images zoom out, revealing more and more context, the bee remains comically perched on the bright-eyed bird's head. The book is full of surprises that will keep kids engaged in a manner similar to *Zoom* (1995) by Istvan Banyai. (Ages 2–6.)

6. *Topsy-Turvies: Pictures to Stretch the Imagination.* By Mitsumasa Anno. (Tuttle Publishing, 1970.) This playful companion to Mitsumasa Anno's *Upside Downers: Pictures to Stretch the Imagination* (1971) challenges readers' ideas about space and perspective in twenty-eight pages of mind-bending drawings. Strange and busy little men are seen going upstairs in order to go downstairs, impossibly walking on walls, and demonstrating that inside is outside. Children who have never seen optical illusions before will be dumfounded and will have hours of fun poring over what their eyes seem to be telling them. *Topsy-Turvies* was clearly influenced by the work of the great Dutch graphic artist M. C. Escher, known for his incredible perceptual constructions and explorations of spatial relationships. (Ages 5–9.)

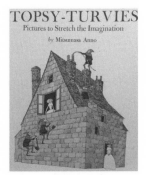

7. *Looking Down.* By Steve Jenkins. (Houghton Mifflin, 1995.) *Looking Down* is about gaining perspective. Steve Jenkins uses his trademark cut-paper collage illustrations to take his readers on an exciting journey that begins in outer space, showing the earth as a small blue-and-white ball in a black expanse, and ending in a backyard, showing a ladybug viewed through a boy's magnifying glass. The pictures zoom in progressively closer, first showing

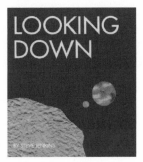

our planet from the perspective of the moon, then looking down to the North American coastline, then becoming an aerial view of a landscape scene with mountains, rivers, a town, and finally a house and a boy. *Looking Down* may provide some youngsters their first real sense of where they stand in the big picture, in relation to their planet and the vast universe. (Ages 4–8.)

8. *Invisible.* By Katja Kamm. (North-South Books, 2006.) In this whimsical book with no discernable story line, children go from page to page detecting things that were previously unseen and, conversely, have things suddenly become visible because they no longer match the background. The solid colors of the spread change with each succeeding spread, sometimes leaving heads and hands floating in space when their clothes disappear. Kids will love the book's irreverent humor, such as when a urinating dog appears, or when a chubby, bikini-clad woman pops up a few times, or when a child evidently becomes naked to blend in with the background, but some parents may be less delighted. (Ages 4–8.)

9. *Balloon Trip.* By Ronald Wegen. (Houghton Mifflin, 1981.) A father, daughter, and son go on a hot-air balloon trip in the company of other balloon enthusiasts. As the thrill-seeking family ascends from a meadow, readers will vicariously enjoy their dizzying view, which includes sightings of mom following them on the ground in a red truck. They drift over New York City, getting to see the harbor and the Statue of Liberty, and then land safely just before the arrival of a looming summer storm. Part of the fun of this exciting bird's-eye perspective of the beautiful landscape is spotting the red truck and imagining a worried parent trying to keep up with the free-floating airship. (Ages 4–8.)

10. *Take Another Look.* By Tana Hoban. (Greenwillow Books, 1981.) In this black-and-white photo concept book, similar in format to some of Tana Hoban's other books, the photographer uses a die-cut hole in pages to reveal a part of nine grainy subjects; when the pages are flipped, close-up shots of the objects are revealed. By viewing full-page photos with a variety of textures, young readers will learn that context counts, and things can be perceived in different ways. Hoban, a prolific designer of educational books, uses photos of common objects to teach fundamental concepts such as shape, color, size, letters, and numbers. Her work has been critically acclaimed and displayed in many exhibitions, including at the Museum of Modern Art. (Ages 3–7.)

11. *Travel.* By Yuichi Yokoyama. (PictureBox, 2008.) In *Travel*, Japanese manga artist Yuichi Yokoyama, known for his abstract geometry and originality, takes readers on a surreal and lengthy train ride through Japan. He pays close attention to detail in sequences that show multiple views of objects, but there is nothing resembling a plot except for passengers looking for their seats and then observing the passing scenery. This technically precise, avant-garde comic will appeal to some artists and novelty seekers, but it is not likely to satisfy children or adults hoping for a story, lesson, or puzzle to solve. Yuichi Yokoyama concludes his book with a commentary that pokes fun at the oddness of his own style, puzzling (like his readers) over his own intentions with certain drawings. (Ages 10+.)

12. *Oh!* By Josse Goffin. (Kalandraka, 2007.) In *Oh!*, originally published in 1991 by Belgian artist Josse Goffin, twelve foldout pictures situated in ample white space open to supply the reader with clever illustrations. When the flap is lifted, a simple coffee cup turns out to be an ocean liner, the toe of a shoe becomes a

dragon's tail, and a pointing hand is shown to be holding a crocodile balancing a teacup. This book is ideal for sharing with a group, with some members of the audience sure to call out the book's title as foldouts produce new surprises. Goffin has also created *Oh! Coloring Book* (1994), presenting images from his book in outline form ready to color. (Ages 3–6.)

13. *Graham Oakley's Magical Changes.* By Graham Oakley. (Atheneum, 1980.) Why do some books have the name of the author or illustrator in the title? Is it a marketing strategy or mere vanity that requires ostentation? It turns out that Graham Oakley does have something to be particularly satisfied with in this book, as it did receive a special citation award from the Boston Globe–Horn Book committee for its unusual horizontal page cuts, allowing the reader to mix and match different scenes, producing some surreal and funny combinations. This innovative book must have taken a lot of planning because each picture segment matches up perfectly, with strong vertical elements in the design. Oakley does deserve recognition for pushing the boundaries of book design, and readers would be wise to seek out his popular Church Mouse series. (Ages 5+.)

14. *Dots, Spots, Speckles, and Stripes.* By Tana Hoban. (Greenwillow Books, 1987.) While *Dots, Spots, Speckles, and Stripes* lacks the utility of some of her other childhood concept books, in it Hoban shares her keen photographic vision with young readers in a series of color photographs that explore the richness and diversity of patterns. This investigation of natural and man-made designs is arranged by theme. Children will notice the commonality between a peacock's spots and a spotted dress, the connection between a girl's freckled face and the speckles on a lobster, and much more. This catalog of dots, spots, speckles, and stripes as seen on faces, clothing, flowers, feathers, shells, and other places will make kids more visually aware and knowledgeable about patterns in their environment. (Ages 4–8.)

15. *Over, Under & Through.* By Tana Hoban. (Aladdin, 2008.) Tana Hoban employs well-composed black-and-white pictures and a few words to teach a lesson on spatial concepts appropriate for preschoolers and children who are a little older. Different word sets, such as "around," "across," "between," "against," and "behind," introduce each section, followed by photographs of children playing in an urban setting, effectively illustrating the positional relationships. Seeing children jumping over a fire hydrant, traveling through a pipe tunnel, or climbing on monkey bars as pictured on the cover, young readers will have enough material from everyday life to master twelve basic concepts. Hoban's book would be an excellent classroom resource and useful guide for children to physically demonstrate what they have learned. (Ages 3–6.)

16. *One, Two, Where's My Shoe?* By Tomi Ungerer. (Phaidon Press, 2014.) First issued in 1964, this vintage book challenges youngsters to find a pair of shoes hidden on each page. A schoolboy with a striped cap and tie is missing a shoe and exclaims, "One, two, where's my shoe," while readers can observe that it is hidden in the head of a dog. Other pictures show the shoes cleverly disguised as part of a locomotive, a scarecrow, a snake, and an old woman. On the last page, the same old-fashioned boy finds his shoe, announcing, "Three, four, on the floor." Tomi Ungerer was born in the Alsace region of France and lived there during the Nazi occupation before coming to the United States. (Ages 2–5.)

CHAPTER 24

Difficult Challenges

It's the children the world almost breaks who grow up to save it.

—Frank Warren

1. *One Frog Too Many.* By Mercer and Marianna Mayer. (Dial, 2003.) When a boy receives a gift of a little frog, his longtime frog companion resents the intruder and mistreats him. The larger frog bites and kicks the smaller one, making the creature cry, and the older pet is chastised for his rough behavior. Dressed as a pirate, the boy then leads the dog, turtle, and the two frogs to a pond where a raft is waiting. They cast off, intending to leave the large frog behind, but he hops aboard anyway, sending the tiny frog into the water. The group searches in vain for the little frog, and he turns up when they return home. The larger frog finally accepts the newcomer and decides to be nice to him. *One Frog Too Many* was originally issued in 1975. (Ages 3–7.)

2. *The Last Laugh.* By Jose Aruego and Ariane Dewey. (Dial, 2006.) Flicking his forked tongue and hissing all the way, a large snake goes around bullying several animals, but a duck does something wholly unexpected when he flies into the slithering reptile's mouth. This risky move replaces the snake's ominous hissing with silly quacking, attracting ridicule from fellow snakes and the unwanted attention of ducks. When the swallowed duck dislodges himself, he flies away with a flock of his own kind but gets the last laugh when he returns to sneak up on the serpent, delivering his own loud quack! Kids will love this karmic conclusion, and parents will like having a book to use as a conversation starter about bullying. (Ages 3–6.)

3. *Bear Despair.* By Gaetan Dorémus. (Enchanted Lion Books, 2012.) *Bear Despair* is an action-packed picture book that, while it will appeal to the preschool set, will be less popular with parents who prefer a milder approach to anger management. The activity begins with a sleeping bear awakened when a wolf steals his teddy. Despairing and angry at his loss, the bear eats the wolf, but not before the wolf hands the stuffed animal off to a lion, whom the bear then swallows in one gulp. With the bear growing in size with each succeeding conquest, this pattern continues with a vulture and elephant added to the contents of the bear's stomach. Events take a positive turn when a wise octopus returns the teddy to its owner. After dislodging the animals from his gut, the bear goes back to sleep. (Ages 4–7.)

4. *First Snow.* By Emily Arnold McCully. (Harper & Row, 1985.) The mouse family seen first in *Picnic* (1984) jumps aboard an old red pickup truck for a day of fun in winter's first snow. They try ice-skating, snowmouse building, and sledding, an activity that turns out to be a real challenge for the littlest mouse. After she conquers her fear, the pink-clad youngster wants to experience the thrill of going down the slope over and over again. Emily Arnold McCully's shift in perspective, from the fearful girl's view from the top of the mountain to her grandparents' view from the base, works very well. *First Snow* was republished in 2004 with brief text that does not add any new meaning to a story already well communicated through its art. (Ages 4–7.)

5. *The Wrong Side of the Bed.* By Edward Ardizzone. (Doubleday, 1970.) Things go from bad to worse for a pajama-clad little boy who literally gets up on the wrong side of the bed—the book cover showing him disgruntled and squeezed between his bed and the wall. When he arrives downstairs, his mother cleans him up, but this does not improve his foul mood. His subsequently awful day includes pulling his sister's hair, getting sent back to his room, running away, and finally apologizing to his mother. Many children will connect emotionally with this story and feel heartened by the knowledge that even the worst problem-filled day is not the end of the world. This book was also published in London as *Johnny's Bad Day* (1970). (Ages 3–8.)

6. *Coyote Run.* By Gaetan Dorémus. (Enchanted Lion Books, 2014.) This surprising story actually begins on the cover of the book with a coyote in the custody of a donkey sheriff. The action continues when the coyote escapes from jail, runs away, and is pursued by the lawman. When the rifle-toting sheriff catches up with his armed quarry, a standoff ensues. After a ladybug intervenes, the opponents lay down their weapons and even share a meal. In a strange twist, the sheriff and coyote join forces and run off together, chased by deputies. The pursuit of the two fugitives ends at the edge of a cliff, where ladybugs miraculously rescue the twosome, carrying them away. Gaetan Dorémus's reframing of the American Wild West cowboy drama is sure to create plenty of discussion and questions. (Ages 6–8.)

7. *Carl Goes to Daycare.* By Alexandra Day. (Farrar, Straus & Giroux, 1993.) Carl the Rottweiler ascends to a new level of resourcefulness and canine intelligence in this fifth book in the popular Carl series. In this episode, the world's most unlikely babysitter accompanies his charge to the daycare center. When the teacher accidentally gets locked outside, Carl decisively takes charge of the toddler class, follows the posted lesson plan, avoids an accident by preventing the water cooler from toppling, and generally shows that classroom management is yet another of his hidden talents. While the teacher tries in vain to reenter the building, the dog shows his expertise in keeping things from going sideways. Finally, the teacher holds up a sign at the window that reads, "Carl, open the door," which he does, just before his owner arrives to pick up her little tyke. (Ages 2–5.)

8. *Bobo's Dream.* By Martha Alexander. (Dial, 1970.) Bobo, a little dachshund, relaxes with his bone in the grass, while a young boy wearing a football helmet reads a book under a tree. A large dog comes by and steals Bobo's bone, and the boy gets it back for him. This episode prompts a doggy dream in which a grateful Bobo imagines that he is a huge dog able to return the favor for his master. In Bobo's reverie, bullies steal the boy's football, and the dachshund heroically retrieves it. When Bobo wakes up, the large thieving dog returns to make another pass at his bone, but this time the little dog gets some satisfaction by barking the intruder away. (Ages 4–8.)

9. *He's My Jumbo!* By Claude K. Dubois. (Viking Kestrel, 1990.) This story of young brother and sister bears explores the familiar world of sibling relationships, which are so important in children's lives. The little girl bear has a cherished stuffed elephant named Jumbo that her older brother covets. He steals Jumbo from his sleeping sister's bed but in the morning finds it back in her hands as she plays at feeding the elephant breakfast. Responding to his sadness, the girl decides to share Jumbo, and the story concludes with a group snuggle. Claude K. Dubois, a Belgian artist, has published a companion book, *Looking for Ginny* (1990), dealing with the same brother and sister arguing over a guinea pig. (Ages 3–7.)

10. *The Knight and the Dragon.* By Tomie DePaola. (Puffin Books, 1998.) This excellent book begins with the lines "Once upon a time, there was a knight in a castle who had never fought a dragon. And in a cave not too far away was a dragon who had never fought a knight." In this nearly wordless classic, Tomie DePaola plays on our expectations to produce a satisfying twist in a battle between age-old adversaries that never really materializes. These decidedly peaceable opponents reluctantly prepare for combat by reading books about it and hone their meager skills by practicing on dummies. When the big fight turns out to be a flop, a princess-librarian shows them another way to use their obviously relevant skills by working together to open a barbecue restaurant. (Ages 4–8.)

11. *Here Comes Alex Pumpernickel!* By Fernando Krahn. (Little, Brown, 1981.) During the course of a day, Alex goes through eight misadventures that stem from his desire to be helpful but lead to unfortunate predicaments. Fernando Krahn's framed strips are short vignettes depicting an active and resourceful boy who takes on more than he can handle as he tries to hang a picture, fix a pipe, swat a fly, and more. Each series includes a clock tracking the passage of time in Alex's problematic domestic world. Young children will identify with Alex's feeling of ineptitude as he does his best to meet life's little challenges. Krahn's sequel, *Sleep Tight, Alex Pumpernickel* (1982), focuses on the nocturnal adventures of this small boy. (Ages 3–7.)

12. *No, David!* By David Shannon. (Blue Sky Press, 1998.) This Caldecott-winning classic, a remake of a book David Shannon first made when he was five years old, is a catalog of his youthful naughtiness and perhaps a profile of the terrible twos. With minimal text, he depicts himself as a sharp-toothed, beastly little boy who threatens to pull over a hutch to get to a cookie jar, tramps mud all over the living room carpet, overflows the bathtub, runs naked down the street, loudly bangs pots and pans, plays with his food, breaks a vase, and picks his nose, finally being sentenced to a time-out in the corner. Unresponsive to the repeated "No, David!" rebukes, he finally calms down after his time in the corner, earning him a hug from his mother. (Ages 2–8.)

13. *Winterbird.* By Alfred Olschewski. (Houghton Mifflin, 1969.) *Winterbird* is a model of simplicity in this story of suspense and strength in numbers. Black-and-white sketches tell the story of a small bird walking on snow through the forest, unaware that he is being stalked by a cat, who in turn is being followed by a dog. When the cat finally reveals his intentions and leaps at the bird, the dog chases the cat up a tree, and thousands of birds come to the assistance of their vulnerable avian friend, while the cat and dog depart the scene. All that is left is their track patterns in the snowy landscape. This plain and simple sequence of pictures makes it a good choice for toddlers without a lot of experience with books. (Ages 2–5.)

14. *Flora and the Penguin.* By Molly Idle. (Chronicle Books, 2014.) As in *Flora and the Flamingo* (2013), a bird friend joins Flora in a graceful dance routine, this time wearing skates. When Flora straps on her skates and goes out on the ice, a penguin comes out of a hole and takes her hand. The duo leaps and glides in harmony, until a rift occurs, causing the penguin to dive back into the water. He returns with a fish for his human dance partner, which she tosses back, to the bird's annoyance. The story comes to a satisfying end when the two of them work together to capture the fish and happily skate away. Their little disagreement will give teachers and preschoolers plenty to discuss. Why did they have the falling out? Why did they get back together? (Ages 3–6.)

15. *Bedtime and New School.* By Anna Cunningham and Melanie Sharp. (Franklin Watts, 2011.) *Bedtime* and *New School*, two stories for preschoolers, acknowledge the reality of sometimes being afraid. The first deals with the almost universal fear of the dark that surfaces at bedtime, while the second covers the anxiety that comes with attending school for the first time. This two-story book, like others in the Talk a Story series, were explicitly created to encourage children to develop language skills by interpreting pictures in their own words. Kids will be eager to read other two-for-one books in the series, such as *Stormy Day and Snowy Day* (2011) and *Rocket Ship and The Planet* (2012). (Ages 3–5.)

16. *Mine!* By Shutta Crum and Patrice Barton. (Knopf Books for Young Readers, 2012.) What happens when a pair of grabby young siblings has to share a pile of toys? Add a lovable puppy to the mix, and watch the conflict and slapstick rivalry ensue. Shutta Crum and Patrice Barton's nearly wordless book—it uses only the words "mine" and "woof"—tells the perennial story of a toddler not wanting to share his stuff with a baby. Double-page spreads and a floor-level child's perspective show a toddler trying to hoard his possessions, uttering, "Mine," for each of them. When the baby tosses a toy bunny into the dog's water bowl, the mutt retrieves it, showering everyone with water and breaking the standoff. Touchingly, the happy baby manages to stand up, awkwardly walk over to hug his older brother, and say, "Mine!" (Ages 2–5.)

CHAPTER 25

Edifying Exploits

For some of us, books are as important as almost anything else on earth.

—Anne Lamott

1. *You Can't Take a Balloon into the Metropolitan Museum.* By Jacqueline Preiss Weitzman and Robin Preiss Glasser. (Dial Books for Young Readers, 1998.) In this elegant and well-planned story, a little girl and her grandmother visit New York's famous Metropolitan Museum of Art, but a guard makes the girl leave her yellow balloon outside, tied to a railing. While they are inside the museum, a curious pigeon loosens the string, sending the balloon and the pursuing guard on an uproarious trek through Manhattan, passing many city landmarks. Meanwhile, the girl and her grandmother view famous artworks that parallel the chaotic scenes created by the wayward balloon, delightfully hinting at the integral relationship between art and life. When the girl exits the Met, she gets her balloon back, happily unaware of the mayhem her toy created. (Ages 5–8.)

2. *Museum Trip*. By Barbara Lehman. (Houghton Mifflin, 2006.) The same boy who starred in *The Red Book* (2004) this time visits a museum with classmates, getting separated from the group and lost in a mystical world of labyrinths. Shrinking to diminutive dimensions, he enters six mazes before rejoining the tour wearing a gold medal of achievement, apparently for being able to glimpse some the museum's treasures. Barbara Lehman is a master illustrator, challenging older children to identify some of the skillful reproductions of famous paintings and sculptures she incorporates into the boy's journey. Her simple art and shifting perspectives will be a delight to all ages. *Museum Trip* is sure to arouse children's curiosity about museums and make them want to experience their wonders. (Ages 4–9.)

3. *The Boy, the Bear, the Baron, the Bard*. By Gregory Rogers. (Roaring Brook Press, 2004.) In this action-packed escapade, a current-day boy kicks his soccer ball into an old theater, travels through time, lands on none other than William Shakespeare, and disrupts a play on the stage of the renowned Globe Theater. The angry Bard chases the lad through seventeenth-century London in a comical trip that teams the boy up with a bear, releases a baron held prisoner in the Tower of London, and leads to Queen Elizabeth I. Gregory Rogers, an Australian artist, richly illustrates this slapstick adventure in full watercolor-and-ink panels. For young children, *The Boy, the Bear, the Baron, the Bard* provides a wonderful glimpse of Elizabethan London and an irreverent look at history's most esteemed playwright. (Ages 5–9.)

4. *Unspoken: A Story from the Underground Railroad*. By Henry Cole. (Scholastic Press, 2012.) While doing her farm chores during the Civil War, a young girl discovers a runaway slave hiding in the barn. In full-page sepia-tone drawings, reminiscent of a silent film, we observe the girl make a momentous moral choice, deciding to help the young hideaway by bringing him food. When slave hunters arrive and show her family a poster of the runaway, she says nothing, and the fugitive escapes. Henry Cole's beautifully rendered story brings a slice of history to life with haunting grace and compassion. *Unspoken* concludes with the girl watching the stars in the night sky, wondering about the runaway's fate and thankful for the handmade cornhusk doll he left as a token of thanks. (Ages 5–10.)

5. *Anno's U.S.A.* By Mitsumasa Anno. (Philomel, 1983.) This classic features the panoramic journey of a man on horseback traveling from the West to East Coast of the United States. As the scenery morphs from pioneer times to contemporary vistas and back again, this solo wanderer experiences changes not only in landscape but also in time periods. As always, Mitsumasa Anno's picture making is an education in cultural literacy, as he populates his drawings with notable figures from literature and history such as Tom Sawyer and Ben Franklin. Even the comedic duo of Laurel and Hardy make a cameo appearance as piano movers. As with his other text-free treasures, children and adults will spend many productive hours enjoying and learning from these detailed illustrations. (Ages 5–9.)

6. *The Yellow Balloon.* By Charlotte Dematons. (Front Street / Lemniscaat, 2003.) Following a tiny, errant yellow balloon around the world in various theme-based spreads, readers of all ages will find something to like about Charlotte Dematons's book. The journey contains hundreds of interesting literary, historical, and cultural details that will spark the imagination. There are references to Robinson Crusoe, UFOs, Mary Poppins, Santa Claus, the Great Wall of China, the African savanna, a man on a flying carpet, and the sinking *Titanic*. For every familiar image, dozens of other inventive illustrations demand even closer scrutiny. Dematons's

aerial perspectives and incredible juxtapositions will have special appeal for fans of Mitsumasa Anno's classic journey books. (Ages 5–10.)

7. *You Can't Take a Balloon into the Museum of Fine Arts.* By Jacqueline Preiss Weitzman and Robin Preiss Glasser. (Penguin Group, 2002.) In a continuation of the successful formula used in *You Can't Take a Balloon into the Metropolitan Museum* (1998) and *You Can't Take a Balloon into the National Gallery* (2000), this time children are barred from bringing a balloon into Boston's Museum of Fine Arts. Working its way loose from grandma's wrist, the balloon goes on a zany tour of historical landmarks that cleverly parallel what the kids are seeing in the museum. Causing chaos along the way, the balloon floats by the Paul Revere House, Fenway Park, Trinity Church, the Boston Common, Chinatown, and many other noteworthy sites. After reading this informative title, young readers will have no doubt about whether major museums will allow them to take balloons inside. (Ages 5–10.)

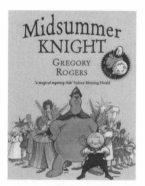

8. *Midsummer Knight.* By Gregory Rogers. (Allen & Unwin Children's Books, 2008.) In this mock-Shakespearean sequel to *The Boy, the Bear, the Baron, the Bard* (2004), Australian illustrator Gregory Rogers casts the same characters but has them play different roles in a world suggesting *A Midsummer Night's Dream.* The bear finds himself in an enchanted kingdom, where he is befriended by a young fairy, and both of them are thrown into a palace dungeon by a sinister William Shakespeare look-alike. This mustachioed villain also imprisons the king and queen, and the royals are freed after the bear has an intense swordfight with the royal usurper. Children will enjoy this story for its action, and adults will appreciate the literary references. (Ages 6–10.)

9. *The Hero of Little Street.* By Gregory Rogers. (Roaring Brook Press, 2012.) When chased by a gang of bullies, a boy ducks into the National Gallery. Suddenly, a painting (Jan van Eyck's *The Arnolfini Marriage*) comes to life, and a dog leaps out. Together they enter another painting (Jan Vermeer's *A Young Woman Seated at a Virginal*), transporting them through time and space to an exciting adventure in seventeenth-century Holland and back again. As with his previous books involving Shakespeare, young children will be engaged by the comedy and nonstop action but may be left behind by Gregory Roger's cultural erudition. The title of the book comes from Vermeer's *The Little Street* in Delft, Holland, a brick facade that art students will recognize in this stimulating romp. (Ages 5–9.)

10. *Anno's Britain.* By Mitsumasa Anno. (Philomel, 1982.) Mitsumasa Anno's man-on-horseback adventures are always an edifying experience, and *Anno's Britain* is no exception. Elaborate watercolors take readers on an information-rich journey through Scotland, Wales, and England in a montage of activities that could profitably take hours to fully digest. Although the book is designed for children, many adults in the United States will be challenged to identify the plethora of cultural and historical markers. The landmarks include Piccadilly Circus, Stonehenge, the Globe Theater, and Westminster Abbey, and the characters to spot include Robin Hood and Sherlock Holmes. The pictorial content is minutely detailed and richly evocative, a very wise investment of time. (Ages 6–12.)

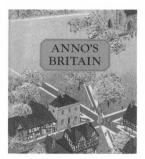

11. *Anno's Flea Market.* By Mitsumasa Anno. (Philomel Books, 1984.) Any of Mitsumasa Anno's books is a visual feast requiring careful viewing, and this one is no exception. In an apparent tribute to human history and commerce, two peasants are shown bringing their cart into a medieval European square. In this big open-air marketplace, countless objects and an overabundance of Anno's signature cultural and historical allusions are on display. There is a panorama

of people, clothing, toys, tools, musical instruments, kitchen utensils, weapons, farm implements, food displays, and more. In what amounts to a museum of cultural artifacts, children can spot popular characters such as Kermit the Frog and Santa Claus, parents will pick up on Popeye the Sailor Man, and grandparents will appreciate Charlie McCarthy, seated on the knee of ventriloquist Edgar Bergen. (Ages 4–10.)

12. *Anno's Spain.* By Mitsumasa Anno. (Philomel Books, 2004.) In *Anno's Spain*, the artist has supplied another superb travelogue through a country's heritage, scenery, architecture, and culture that is as educational as it is entertaining. In addition to viewing the obligatory references to Don Quixote, Roman aqueducts, and the running of the bulls, children will follow the rider on horseback through a host of landmarks and activities, including weddings, funerals, and shopping. The panoramic spreads are breathtakingly detailed and invariably whimsical, making them an excellent addition to any library, especially those that service Spanish-speaking populations. While Mitsumasa Anno's books are often recommended for young children, older students could profit from his encyclopedic knowledge and creative gifts. (Ages 5–9.)

13. *Holland.* By Charlotte Dematons. (Lemniscaat, 2013.) Selected as a New York Times Best Illustrated Book, *Holland* is a series of twenty-seven spreads of stunning landscapes and cityscapes that could be used as a travel guide to this culturally rich country. Of course there are tulips and windmills, but the book is much more ambitious, seeming to provide a cornucopia of all things Dutch. Kids will like the seek-and-find aspect of the book, which features several characters, including a gnome, that appear in every scene. For those who want more than breathtaking imagery, Charlotte Dematons and Jesse Goossens have authored *A Thousand Things about Holland* (2013), a companion volume to the picture book that provides more information on all the paintings. (Ages 4–8.)

14. *Anno's Italy.* By Mitsumasa Anno. (Collins, 1980.) *Anno's Italy* is another title from the distinguished Japanese artist. It too features a profusion of details about a country's landscape, architecture, and history, but the particulars that emerge most strongly have to do with Christian biblical themes. As in his other travelogues, Mitsumasa Anno shows a man on horseback going from place to place, and this book offers interesting portrayals of the piazzas of Venice, Rome, and Florence. Also pictured are scenes of Adam and Eve being expelled from the Garden of Eden, Mary and Joseph traveling, and Christ's birth and death. *Anno's Italy* is a rich and rewarding work of art and cultural history that offers something for everyone. (Ages 5–10.)

15. *Picturescape.* By Elisa Gutiérrez. (Simply Read Books, 2005.) On a field trip to the Vancouver Art Gallery, a young lad discovers wonderful pieces of art that, on examination, carry him to different locations. The boy is drawn in black and white but changes to color when he jumps into the vibrant paintings of Canada's Pacific Northwest, coastal Maritimes, and other scenic spots. He is shown visiting historic landmarks while flying on the wing of a bird, floating by balloon, and riding a bicycle. *Picturescape* is a tribute to twentieth-century Canadian art and a good introduction to one of the country's stars. Interested readers can sample the book by visiting http://www.picturescape.ca (Ages 5–11.)

16. *The Red Thread.* By Tord Nygren. (Farrar, Straus & Giroux, 1988.) Readers who love Mitsumasa Anno's journey books will be pleased to find Tord Nygren's *The Red Thread*. Like Anno, Nygren fills his pictures with fantastically detailed scenes rich in references to art and literature. The novelty is in the red string that begins on the book's front cover, winds its way through the pages and endpapers, and finally ends up on the back cover. Children are shown following this thread and finding all sorts of things, including trolls, a magic

garden, a circus, and easy-to-recognize characters such as Winnie the Pooh, Babar the Elephant, and Mona Lisa. Each reading will uncover more details, making the book a great investment of time and money. (Ages 4–8.)

17. *Dig, Drill, Dump, Fill.* By Tana Hoban. (Greenwillow Books, 1975.) Some children are absolutely fascinated by machines. Photographer Tana Hoban's introduction to some of the biggest construction machinery will definitely appeal to those preschoolers whose hearts are set aflutter by engines, appliances, contraptions, and devices. Hoban has supplied wonderfully instructive pictures of large dump trucks, earthmovers, mixers, backhoes, loaders, and cranes in sequences that demonstrate their use and purpose. For kids who need more information, each machine is briefly described in the back of the book. The black-and-white photographs are exceedingly sharp, nicely composed, and large enough to satisfy critics large and small. Don't be surprised if this prompts a trip to a construction site to experience the actual machines. (Ages 3–8.)

18. *The Story of a Castle.* By John S. Goodall. (Margaret K. McElderry, 1986.) *The Story of a Castle* is a chronicle of historical change in an English fortress from medieval times to the present day. John S. Goodall shows both interior and exterior views reflecting not just architectural evolution but changes in ways of life. The castle is shown as an imposing stronghold, a stately residence, the site of august social gatherings, a hospital for injured World War I soldiers, and a refuge for children evacuated during World War II. Front endpapers provide brief descriptions of the watercolor illustrations. Fans of this graphic history will definitely want to sample Goodall's similarly designed *The Story of an English Village* (1979). (Ages 6–11.)

19. *The City.* By Douglas Florian. (Crowell Junior Books, 1982.) Double-page spreads show a woman buying artwork from an outdoor vendor. Carrying it home in a shopping bag, she travels through the city, strolling by parks, shops, and museums, and rides on a subway, before getting the painting to her apartment. When she arrives, readers will note that this is no reluctant urbanite because it is a cityscape that she hangs on her wall. Children who like this book will also enjoy Douglas Florian's *City Street* (1990), which also uses strong images to capture glimpses of urban life. The gifted artist also has written and illustrated books of children's poetry, most notably *Dinothesaurus: Prehistoric Poems and Paintings* (2009). (Ages 4–8.)

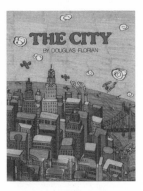

20. *The Inside-Outside Book of New York City.* By Roxie Munro. (Dodd, Mead, 1985.) Bright, detailed illustrations show the insides and outsides of some of the Big Apple's most famous landmarks, including the Statue of Liberty, the American Museum of Natural History, the New York Stock Exchange, the subway station at Times Square, Madison Square Garden, St. Patrick's Cathedral, and the Bronx Zoo. Roxie Munro's unusual vantage points set her book apart from other visual tours of the city. The *New York Times* named *The Inside-Outside Book of New York City* to its annual list of the best illustrated children's books. Munro has created a series of similar inside-outside books that cover Paris, London, Texas, and Washington, as well as books on the interiors and exteriors of libraries and dinosaurs. (Ages 5–10.)

21. *Journey to the Moon.* By Erich Fuchs. (Delacorte Press, 1969.) Spare text and abstract expressionist paintings by German artist Erich Fuchs tell the exciting day-by-day story of man's historic trip to the moon, the greatest technological accomplishment in human history. The paintings show Apollo 11 on the launch pad with a large crowd in attendance, the rocket's launch and staged separation, the achievement of lunar orbit, and the momentous first steps

on the moon on July 20, 1969. The return flight culminates in a picture of the space capsule parachuting down to earth, then being scooped up by a helicopter and taken to a recovery ship. This rendering of the Apollo mission does more to communicate the magnitude of the achievement than most photographic accounts. (Ages 4–8.)

22. *The Inside-Outside Book of Texas.* By Roxie Munro. (Chronicle Books, 2001.) As with the other titles in her inside-outside series, Roxie Munro does a masterful job of highlighting the best that her chosen venue has to offer. With captions of two or three words, Monro's guided journey through the Lone Star state includes pictures of the Dallas skyline, Houston's Lyndon B. Johnson Space Center, San Antonio's River Walk, and the Rio Grande, plus illustrations of the oil industry, cattle raising, cowboy hat and boot manufacturing, ranching, and the state's indigenous animals, including the coyote, jackrabbit, and roadrunner. This large-format book has a cowboy riding a bucking bronco on its cover, correctly signaling that readers will enjoy an exciting ride. (Ages 5–10.)

CHAPTER 26

Leaps of Imagination

I think books for children should be wild and adventurous. They should offer you something you can escape into, something you don't get later on.

—Emma Chichester Clark

1. *Sidewalk Circus.* By Paul Fleischman and Kevin Hawkes. (Candlewick Press, 2007.) A girl arrives in the morning at a city bus stop and watches a man hanging posters proclaiming that the world-renowned Garibaldi Circus is coming to town! In a book that is wordless except for what is printed on the posters and theater marquee, the girl imagines the circus is already underway. Everyday activities are cleverly cast in a new light as the man with the circus posters becomes the ringmaster, a man on a high steel girder becomes a tightrope walker, a brawny delivery-man transforms into the traveling show's strongman, and skate-boarding boys serve as clowns. When the girl boards her bus, a boy replaces her, ready to engage in his own leaps of imagination. (Ages 3–8.)

2. *The Chicken Thief.* By Beatrice Rodriguez. (Enchanted Lion Books, 2010.) In many children's stories, foxes are the unequivocal villains, preying on the defenseless for their selfish ends. But in this slight twist, a fox snatches a hen, who is at first alarmed but then is at peace with being abducted. When a bear,

rabbit, and rooster give chase, they race from the forest through the mountains to the sea, finally finding the fox and chicken playing chess by candlelight in the fox's burrow. The story line is certainly surprising and interesting, but is this a case of sweet, cross-species love or Stockholm syndrome? Beatrice Rodriguez makes one thing clear: the rooster is not at all happy with this romantic development. *The Chicken Thief* is the first title in Enchanted Lion Books' Stories without Words series. (Ages 4–8.)

3. *Shadow.* By Suzy Lee. (Chronicle Books, 2010.) Using only two colors, black with a touch of yellow, Suzy Lee attractively investigates the world of inventive play, where a little girl in a dark storage room shines a light on everyday objects, turning them into wild animals. As wordless artists are so prone to do, Lee smudges the boundaries between reality and the imagination, making a simple hose become a snake and transforming splayed hands into birds. One unique feature of *Shadow* is that objects from the page top are cast as inverted shadows down below. Children will leave the book eager to click off the lights and conduct their own make-believe experiments in the secret world of shadows. (Ages 4–8.)

4. *The Boy and the Airplane.* By Mark Pett. (Simon & Schuster Books for Young Readers, 2013.) If patience is a virtue, then Mark Pett has created a story about the world's most virtuous man. When a boy receives a toy airplane as a gift, he goes outside and immediately gets the toy stuck on a roof. After several unsuccessful attempts to recover the beloved toy, using a water hose, ladder, and other devices, he observes a seed fall from a tree and gets an idea. He plants the seed nearby and waits several decades to climb it to recover the airplane, finding that now he is too old to play with it. Children will be charmed by this unusual story but are likely to wonder why he gave up on using the ladder and to ask why he didn't ask someone for help. (Ages 4–9.)

5. *The Tooth Fairy.* By Peter Collington. (Knopf Books for Young Readers, 1995.) When a girl loses a baby tooth, she follows the time-honored tradition of placing it under her pillow in a little box. After forging a silver coin, the tiny tooth fairy travels from her mysterious realm to swap the coin for the tooth. But what does she do with all these collected mouth bones? Is she a hoarder? Peter Collington's creative answer is that she converts the teeth into keys for her piano. Kids worried about the fate of their precious cargo can take comfort in the belief that it is being nicely repurposed. As a bonus, the publisher has included a tooth box at the back of the book, with some cutting and assembly required. (Ages 4–8.)

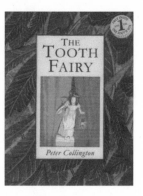

6. *April Wilson's Magpie Magic: A Tale of Colorful Mischief.* By April Wilson. (Dial, 1999.) In this clever story, a boy draws a bird that comes to life, flying off the page and causing chaos. The young artist responds by drawing two red cherries to entice the magpie back to eat them. In a postmodern move, the bird gets into the act and starts sketching things himself. The boy tries to cage the bird artistically, but the resourceful magpie uses an eraser to escape and even succeeds in redrawing himself with colored feathers. Children will love the artistic battle of wits won mostly by April Wilson's magpie. The book's only words are the color names that appear at the end. (Ages 4–8.)

7. *Fox and Hen Together.* By Beatrice Rodriguez. (Enchanted Lion Books, 2011.) In *The Chicken Thief* (2010), a hostage situation ends in a romantic connection between a fox and a chicken he has abducted, but can this bizarre acquisition of a mate result in true and lasting love? Apparently it does, because the hen has somehow managed to lay an egg. In this curious sequel, the hen leaves home looking for food because the refrigerator is bare, leaving the fox behind to mind the egg. Accompanied by her friend Crab, she goes fishing and has a run-in with a sea monster and

giant birds. Undaunted, she returns home to find a cracked and empty eggshell and a skillet on the table! She is about to dispatch the fox with the skillet, when she notices that he is holding a cute hen-fox baby! (Ages 4–8.)

8. *Un-brella.* By Scott E. Franson. (Roaring Brook Press, 2007.) Dressed for winter in the midst of summer, a little girl opens her umbrella and is able to make snowmen and build snow angels. Switch to winter, and her umbrella creates a microclimate appropriate for swimming and sunbathing. Scott E. Franson's magical *Un-brella* gives his bug-eyed, pig-tailed protagonist a portable canopy with the power to reverse the weather, at least in her immediate vicinity. This clever fantasy generates endless possibilities for a child to do the opposite of what Mother Nature has in mind. *Un-brella* is truly a book for all seasons. Kids will love imagining their own tiny blizzard on a hot day or creating their own miniature oasis in the depths of winter. (Ages 3–7.)

9. *The Conductor.* By Laetitia Devernay. (Chronicle Books, 2011.) From the top of a tall tree, a music conductor waves his baton, transforming leaves from a grove of trees into birds that swirl along the pages. Like a musical score, the birds glide, dance, and multiply, suggesting rhythm, sound, and movement in a way that both art and music lovers will appreciate. At the end of the piece, the formally clad orchestra director bows to an unseen audience and climbs down from the tree, as the birds return to the trees, covering them once again in leaves. This elegant book concludes with the conductor planting his baton in the soil, bringing forth new life in the forest. *The Conductor* won the United Kingdom's prestigious V&A Illustration Award. (Ages 4–8.)

10. *Mirror.* By Suzy Lee. (Seven Footer Kids, 2010.) A dejected girl sits alone until she spots her reflection in a mirror. She displays a range of emotions, from loneliness to surprise to exuberance, as she frolics with her reflected image until the reflection takes on a life of its own. When she loses control of her likeness, her delight turns to anger, causing her to shove the mirror and shatter the glass into pieces. Sadly, she is alone again. This sparsely illustrated, well-told story will resonate with some readers and leave others nonplussed by its bleak conclusion. *Mirror* will be useful in launching discussions about the expectations of companionship and the emotional need to be in control. (Ages 4–9.)

11. *The Line.* By Paula Bossio. (Kids Can Press, 2013.) A girl finds a pencil line and uses her imagination to transform it into many shapes. At first she follows the line, but then she makes it into a slide, bubble, and jungle vine. Seeming to take on a life of its own, the line morphs into a monster that is scared away by a bear, who then becomes a cute teddy bear. The final page shows the line leading to the creator of these endless possibilities, an amused boy artist with a pencil. Kids will love the simple premise of this inventive book and will be eager to use their own pencils for flights of fancy. (Ages 4–7.)

12. *Leaf.* By Stephen Michael King. (Roaring Brook Press, 2009.) Instead of submitting to a haircut, a mop-top boy and his dog romp around outside until something quite unusual happens. Australian artist Stephen Michael King's small-format book is not small in imagination, as it shows a red bird dropping a seed in a boy's unruly hair, where it begins to grow. Boy and dog try to take care of the sprout, but it does not flourish until they plant it in the ground. Time passes, and a tall tree grows, with the red bird perched

with another seed, ready to start the process over again. Kids who have been warned that their hair is so long that something will grow there will take comfort in this happy outcome. (Ages 4–9.)

13. *I See a Song.* By Eric Carle. (Thomas Y. Crowell, 1973.) Spectacular dancing colors and wild imagery for arousing children's artistic talents are the raison d'être of this visual depiction of the experience of music. Eric Carle shows an old man playing a violin to conjure up vivid swirls and shapes, inviting leaps of the imagination. When the musician takes a bow at the conclusion of his production, readers will notice that he has taken on the colors and designs seen earlier in the book. *I See a Song* has been made into a music video and is widely available online. Carle is a legendary illustrator best known for his classics *The Very Hungry Caterpillar* (1987), *Brown Bear, Brown Bear* (1992), *The Grouchy Ladybug* (1996), and *The Tiny Seed* (1997). (Ages 2–6.)

14. *Bubble Bubble.* By Mercer Mayer. (Parents' Magazine Press, 1973.) A lad dressed in old-fashioned garb buys bubble fluid from a street vendor, and magical things begin to happen. The boy is able to blow incredible shapes and animals, such as an airplane, car, boat, bird, jack-in-the-box, kangaroo, and more. The animals come to life and begin chasing one another. When one bubble turns into a snake, the boy blows a bubble cat to chase the snake away, and when an elephant is formed, he creates a mouse to frighten it. When the creatures begin to threaten him, he dumps the magic liquid on the ground, and a bubble monster appears sad that the fun is over. (Ages 3–7.)

15. *Rainy Day Dream.* By Michael Chesworth. (Farrar, Straus & Giroux, 1992.) Children will be pleased to follow the flight of an umbrella-wielding boy swept up by the autumn wind and sent on an amazing cross-country flight. The traveler passes over a variety of landscapes that readers view close-up and from a bird's-eye perspective. He flies over dams, trains, ships, waterfalls, forests, cities, streams, and oceans, then back to the park where his extraordinary journey began. The panoramic watercolor pictures are so stunningly captured that youngsters will feel they are aloft with the boy in this magnificent adventure. The book's evocative imagery will make readers of all ages long for the smell and feel of a real rainy day. (Ages 3–8.)

16. *The Great Cat Chase.* By Mercer Mayer. (Four Winds Press, 1974.) Kids who like adventure or enjoy games of dress up will appreciate this engaging story about a girl who dresses in her mother's clothes and pushes a carriage with a cat dressed as a baby. The cat escapes this playful captivity and is chased by the girl and two boys, one of them dressed like a policeman. They follow the cat on a bruising romp through a storm pipe, up a hill, and into a tree. When the policeman climbs the tree to get the cat, the branch breaks, leading the girl to dress up as a nurse. To everyone's delight, she serves cookies and lemonade, and one of the boys takes a turn in the baby carriage. *The Great Cat Chase* was reprinted with text and color in 1994. (Ages 4–8.)

17. *Animals Home Alone.* By Loes Riphagen. (Seven Footer Kids, 2011.) Originally published in the Netherlands, Loes Riphagen's almost wordless book reveals what children have long suspected: when humans are away, animals magically play. As a father and his young daughter depart their tranquil home, a cat sleeps on a chair and animals appear in framed pictures on the wall. Soon strange mischief arises as the cat makes a telephone call, the goldfish leaves his bowl, animals exit their paintings, cockroaches splash toilet water on the cat, and a possible romance ensues between an elephant and a bunny, who spends time applying makeup. This imaginative take on what animals do when home alone is a sure winner that children will return to many times to appreciate all the shenanigans. (Ages 4–8.)

18. *Higher! Higher!* By Leslie Patricelli. (Candlewick Press, 2010.) Told with few words, this is a simple story of an exuberant and expressive girl on a swing asking her smiling father to push her higher and higher. As the pig-tailed girl ascends to greater heights, so too does her imagination, as she conjures views from the perspective of a giraffe, mountaintop, airplane, and outer space, even giving high-fives to a single-eyed green alien. When the spectacular ride ends, she naturally wants to do it again! This Booklist Editor's Choice and Boston Globe–Horn Book selection would be ideal for sharing with an audience of toddlers. *Higher! Higher!* is also available in an English- and Spanish-text edition. (Ages 2–5.)

19. *When Night Didn't Come.* By Poly Bernatene. (Meadowside Children's, 2010.) When the sun goes down, the night does not arrive. With no darkness, no moon, and no stars, a man with some authority in these important matters discovers a group of children playing around in the universe's control room. He rounds them up and averts a calamity of epic proportions. For those interested in glimpsing the backstage of the universe, Argentinian artist Poly Bernatene has created a dreamy and gorgeously imagined world in the setting of a medieval town. Switching from comic strip panels to two-page spreads, this book reveals the considerable thought and amazing machinery at work behind the scenes in our clockwork universe. This story would make Isaac Newton proud and will provide young cosmologists one working theory of how everything works. (Ages 5–9.)

20. *Robot-Bot-Bot.* By Fernando Krahn. (Dutton Juvenile, 1979.) When father brings home a pint-size household robot, he and his wife are delighted as it mops the floor, does the dishes, empties the garbage, and even gets dad's slippers. Their daughter is not as sanguine about this new arrangement, so she rewires the machine, generating catastrophic results. The robot goes wild and careens out the window and into the trash can. Dad has another go at the robot's electrical system, giving it the ability to play Ping-Pong with the now satisfied girl. This sprightly black-and-white offering could be the book that gets preschoolers started on a lifetime of science fiction. (Ages 4–8.)

21. *Will's Mammoth.* By Rafe Martin and Stephen Gammell. (PaperStar, 1997.) Will believes in big wooly mammoths, but his parents do not, considering that these elephant ancestors have been extinct for thousands of years. To prove his point, Will goes outside one winter morning and imagines a mammoth into existence, along with an appropriate supporting prehistoric cast of wolves, saber-toothed tigers, and cave-dwelling humans, who are shown building snow-mammoths. The adventure ends when Will is called back home for dinner in the reality of the twentieth century, but he promises to return to the wild and ancient past. This story is breathtakingly abundant in illustrations, lofty in imagination, and short in words, with dialog only at the book's beginning and end. (Ages 4–8.)

22. *A Whole World.* By Antonin Louchard and Katy Couprie. (Milet, 2002.) First published in France, this unusual awarding-winning picture book uses mixed media—paintings, drawings, and photographs—to invite various imaginative interpretations rather than telling an overarching story. Its goal is apparently to show the interconnections of everyday people and objects in a kind of stream-of-consciousness compilation. This is the type of book designed to spur creative thinking and could be used as a writing prompt. A first glance, it might appear as a hodgepodge collection, but closer inspection will reveal chains of associations, such as a raindrop leading to a brook where a young man and woman are sitting and fish are swimming. *A Whole World* is original, but it might be a bit too abstract and indefinable for many children. (Ages 5–8.)

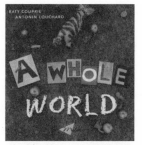

23. *Lola & Fred.* By Christoph Heuer. (4N Publishing, 2005.) Originally published in Switzerland, *Lola & Fred* is about a turtle and a frog who want to fly. They make several unsuccessful attempts at getting airborne using a rocket, a big rubber band, multiple balloons, and a catapult, until a kite finally lifts them into the sky. The unlikely copilots end up in a gondola held aloft by a hot-air balloon, where they meet a circus monkey destined to share top billing with them in the sequel *Lola & Fred & Tom* (2007). Christoph Heuer creates wordless children's books to avoid the practical difficulties posed by living in a country with four national languages: German, French, Italian, and Romansh, with the latter spoken in the southeastern Swiss canton of Grisons. (Ages 3–7.)

24. *Hi Fly.* By Pat Ross and John C. Wallner. (Crown Publishers, 1988.) One of the refreshing features of older picture books for young children is that their creators do not always feel obliged to make the protagonists cute and cuddly. The stars of this book, both quite homely, are a girl and fly that she spots on the kitchen ceiling. She shrinks down to his tiny size, and they go on an adventure fraught with dangers known only to the very small, taking a ride on a cup in the dishwasher, dancing on a record turntable, and barely escaping close calls with a spider, a cat, and a man's foot. The only thing missing in this inventive story is the chance for the pair to become proverbial flies on the wall, in fulfillment of the common expression. (Ages 4–8.)

25. *Trucks Trucks Trucks.* By Peter Sís. (Greenwillow Books, 2004.) Selected as a Notable Children's Book by the American Library Association, *Trucks Trucks Trucks* shows a little boy named Matt having some imaginative fun when he is asked to put away the trucks in his room. There are a total of nine brightly colored mechanized vehicles, including a dump truck, a plow, and a bulldozer, that Matt pretends to operate, providing a one-word description of what they do (digging, plowing, pushing, scooping, and rolling, etc.). In this attractive follow-up to *Fire Truck* (1998), the Caldecott-winning artist ends this cheerful truck fantasy with the boy and his mom going outside to encounter real trucks. (Ages 2–5.)

CHAPTER 27

Weird Encounters

Why, sometimes I've believed as many as six impossible things before breakfast.

—Lewis Carroll

1. *Bow-Wow Bugs a Bug*. By Mark Newgarden and Megan Montague Cash. (HMH Books for Young Readers, 2007.) In this first of the award-winning Bow-Wow book series, Mark Newgarden and Megan Montague Cash craft a story about an intrepid terrier with an insect problem. Following a pesky flea, which is no more than a little dark speck, over the course of a day around the neighborhood, the dog and the irksome bug have some comical and weird meetings, including a run-in with their identical twins and an encounter with an army of giant flies, ants, centipedes, and beetles all pursuing tiny dogs. Comic-strip panels combine with full-page layouts to make for a surreal and varied visual romp, ending with the pooch fast asleep next to the pesky bug that is now his friend. (Ages 3–7.)

2. *Jack and the Night Visitors*. By Pat Schories. (Front Street Press, 2006.) Seeing a light through the bedroom window, Jack the dog and his boy companion, each of them freckle faced, discover that a miniature spaceship has landed on the roof. The ship belongs to a good-humored crew of shiny little robots. The aliens playfully explore the boy's bed-

178

room, check out his toys, and eat some cornflakes, before the boy captures one of them in a jar. How rude! This is no way to treat a visitor to our planet, so Jack releases the alien, much to the dismay of his all-too-human accomplice. The aliens return to the starry sky as Jack and the boy smilingly gaze out the window. (Ages 2–7.)

3. *The Shadow.* By Donna Diamond. (Candlewick, 2010.) This pictorial narrative about facing down fear may have the opposite effect by making some children more fearful. In a series of seventeen excellent paintings, Donna Diamond tells the story of a girl whom a shadow has followed home and up to her bedroom. It is a menacing apparition with glowing eyes that mimics her every move. Instead of cowering, she bravely confronts the shadow, but in the end we see its sinister shining eyes peering out from under the bed, still threatening to haunt her. Diamond apparently intends to show that fear is never fully overcome, but she does it in a way that epitomizes every child's worse nightmare. (Ages 9–12.)

4. *The Night Riders.* By Matt Furie. (McSweeney's/ McMullens, 2012.) A long-legged, bicycle-riding frog and his sidekick mouse awaken late at night and decide to have a meal. As they sit together at a kitchen table, the frog stuffs his mouth with colorful and disgusting bugs, while the mouse nibbles at a healthy salad. With the frog peddling and the mouse tucked into a basket, they set out on a surreal bike adventure through strange surroundings populated by weird and scary creatures, the most fearsome being a dragon that turns out to be quite companionable. The frog, mouse, and dragon add a bat-human hybrid to their group and continue on their otherworldly odyssey, finally taking a break to watch the sunrise. (Ages 5–9.)

5. *The Creepy Thing.* By Fernando Krahn. (Clarion Books, 1982.) A young boy, fishing leisurely in the countryside, hooks something from a stream that looks like a clump of weeds or perhaps a tangled wig that has just been removed from a washing machine. He discards the green clump, but when he plays his harmonica, the creepy thing begins to dance to the music. There is no fun in leaving this slimy mystery behind, so he takes it home, where it escapes and causes panic in the town. Police arrive to subdue the runaway clump, but the boy saves the day by again playing his harmonica. It's not clear why the towns-folk are so terrorized by this hairy little thing—it lacks arms, legs, or even a face—but the pandemonium makes for good comedy. (Ages 4–8.)

6. *Full Moon Soup.* By Alastair Graham. (Dial Books, 1991.) There is a full moon, and children will immediately notice that it is producing some very strange events in the hotel depicted from attic to basement in cross section. The densely illustrated cartoons start out with the staff and guests acting normally, but when a cook takes a fateful sip of magic green soup, he turns into a werewolf. Dozens of weird incidents unfold, with goblins appearing in the attic, lovers falling from the balcony, hotel paintings coming to life, and a space ship crashing on the hotel roof. Kids will spend hours tracking the madness, both subtle and obvious. Boxer Books published another edition of *Full Moon Soup* in 2009 that contains text. (Ages 5–10.)

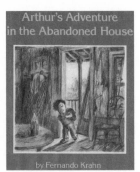

7. *Arthur's Adventure in the Abandoned House.* By Fernando Krahn. (Dutton Juvenile, 1981.) Arthur is curious about a dilapidated house located on the edge of a cliff. He goes inside to explore and finds a man tied to a chair in the basement and thuggish robbers using the abandoned house as a hideaway. When the gun-carrying thieves lock Arthur and the released prisoner in the attic, resourceful Arthur shoots a paper airplane message through a hole in the roof to a construction crew down below. The book ends with the arrest of the sinister criminals and the bulldozing of the abandoned house. Fernando Krahn's expert illustrations provide the full effect of the decrepitude of the building and the emotional range of the characters. (Ages 5–8.)

8. *The West Wing.* By Edward Gorey. (Simon & Schuster, 1963.) This darkly ominous book contains thirty drawings of room interiors in a gloomy Victorian mansion (not the offices of the president of the United States). The empty and sparsely furnished rooms have eerie images, such as a candle levitating in the air; a man sprawled on the floor; a nude man standing before a balcony; three abandoned shoes; limp, shredded wallpaper; images of ghostly faces; an open chasm in a flowered carpet; and more. At first glance, these bafflingly surreal illustrations do not seem related to one another, but they will captivate and challenge readers to tie them together nonetheless. Edward Gorey produced scores of illustration for dozens of books, and his *West Wing* pictures are often considered his best. (Ages 12+.)

9. *Bow-Wow's Nightmare Neighbors.* By Mark Newgarden and Megan Montague Cash. (Roaring Brook Press, 2014.) Bow-Wow's neighbor cats have stolen the dog's soft green bed, and he must go to the spooky house next door to retrieve it. The house is full of ghostly cats, trap doors, secret passageways, pictures with moving eyes, a robber, and other scary things, including a giant cat. In this follow-up to *Bow-Wow Bugs a Bug* (2007), the orange canine finds his purloined bed but has his tail bitten by the impish cats along the way. Funny and mysterious rather than genuinely frightening, Mark Newgarden and Megan Montague Cash's comic-style book is a perfect Halloween or campfire read, with enough surprises to keep everyone's attention without the risk of nightmares. (Ages 4–8.)

CHAPTER 28

Social and Environmental Awareness

In every generation, children's books mirror the society from which they arise; children always get the books their parents deserve.

—Leonard S. Marcus

1. *Window.* By Jeannie Baker. (Walker Books, 2002.) Beautiful pictures tell the depressing story of what we are doing to our planet with urban sprawl. Jeannie Baker's provocative book chronicles the life of a boy as his environment devolves from a pristine wilderness into a polluted and overcrowded cityscape. The entire story is told through the dramatic changes seen from the same window over the span of twenty years. With carefully rendered multimedia collages, *Window* powerfully raises our mindfulness of the impact human activity has on the landscape. Chosen as a School Library Journal Best Book and a Notable Trade Book in the Field of Social Studies, this compelling picture book would be ideal for anchoring a discussion about the relationship between humans and the environment. (Ages 5–9.)

2. *Home.* By Jeannie Baker. (Greenwillow Books, 2004.) This is a tale of a girl born in a destitute neighborhood who grows up to see it converted into a wonderful place to live. *Home*, a companion book to *Window*, uses the same device of depicting environmental changes through the vantage of a single window, this time showing the scenery being restored rather than debased. This American Library Association Notable Children's Book shows how a neglected and impoverished city street is transformed and made into a place where plants thrive and birds sing. In a succession of views, smog, garbage, and graffiti gradually give way to a final perspective of a rich, clean vista and a vibrant neighborhood made possible by an active citizenry. Jeannie Baker's tribute to community and environmental activism points the way to a beautiful place anyone would be proud to call home. In Australia, where Baker resides, *Home* was published under the title *Belonging* (2004). (Ages 5–9.)

3. *Mirror.* By Jeannie Baker. (Candlewick Press, 2010.) Jeannie Baker, known for her richly detailed collage work and her abiding concern for the environment, makes another noteworthy addition to her body of work with this inventive book, which is actually two books in one. Designed for both left-to-right and right-to-left reading, parallel narratives follow the lives of two boys and their families, one from Sydney, Australia, the other from an isolated village in Morocco. Children will be struck by the cultural differences and common humanity mirrored in their average days. They will be pleased to find the Moroccan dad selling a carpet that ends up being purchased by the Australian father on the other side of the world. *Mirror* is almost wordless except for a concise bilingual introduction in both English and Arabic. (Ages 4–8.)

4. *Why?* By Nikolai Popov. (Michael Neugebauer, 1998.) The wordless picture book genre is populated by dreamy adventures and feel-good friendships, but this bold, cautionary tale about the ugliness of war distinguishes itself by being neither. Russian artist Nikolai Popov's *Why?* begins innocently with a frog sitting in a meadow enjoying the fragrance of a flower. His peaceful repose is destroyed when a mouse with an umbrella appears and seizes the flower. The frog goes after him, takes his umbrella, and hostilities escalate. Soon more frogs and mice join the conflict in all-out, armed warfare. They devastate the verdant environment, transforming it into a scorched and smoky ruin. The spoils of war in this important allegory are a broken umbrella and a withered flower. Children will be eager to discuss the book and will want to know why wars happen. (Ages 5–9.)

5. *No!* By David McPhail. (Roaring Brook Press, 2009.) David McPhail's book is wordless except for its strong title word, which for a young boy becomes the vocal tipping point for speaking out against the horrors of war and standing up to a neighborhood bully. A boy sets out to deliver a letter to the president and along the way witnesses soldiers running amok, planes dropping bombs, tanks attacking buildings, and finally a bully about to give him a beating. When he shouts, "No!" the bully has a change of heart, which has a ripple effect on the boy's return home. He now observes the soldiers distributing gifts, tanks plowing fields, and planes dropping bicycles rather than bombs. *No!* should not be confused with David Shannon's *No, David!* (1998), a less serious picture book about a chronically misbehaving boy (who could grow into the neighborhood bully). (Ages 4–8.)

6. *The Flower Man: A Wordless Picture Book.* By Mark Ludy. (Green Pastures Publishing, 2005.) An unassuming elderly man enters a gray, depressed, and colorless neighborhood and transforms it through random acts of kindness, when everything he touches is infused with life. He begins by fixing up his house, planting a garden, and giving a flower to a little girl, who radiates color like everything he touches. Through a series of miraculous changes, the whole town is dramatically altered in constructive ways. This richly detailed book is no quick read. It deserves multiple examinations to unearth the hidden characters and interpret the many micro-narratives that play out beautifully in its pages. This inspiring story about one person making a difference sends just the kind of message that impressionable children need. (Ages 4–10.)

7. *Waterloo & Trafalgar.* By Olivier Tallec. (Enchanted Lion Books, 2012.) Olivier Tallec's story about the folly of war shows two soldiers continually spying on each other from across a field through their spyglasses. Each named for a lost Napoleonic battle, these stumpy enemies spend day and night locked in a cold war. Dressed in vibrantly different orange and blue, these combatants get angry over a misunderstanding and are about to shoot each other, when a small bird intercedes. Tinted with both of their adversarial colors, this symbol of peace forces them to face each other, resolve their conflict, and touchingly embrace. Still, not everything about this antiwar polemic is deadly serious. Tallec's cartoons have a slapstick quality, and he often makes his squat soldiers appear silly. (Ages 6–10.)

8. *Cool Cat.* By Nonny Hogrogian. (Roaring Brook Press, 2009.) Led by a creative and enterprising feline, animals revitalize a neighborhood presumably made lifeless and shabby by humans. Using paints and brushes from an old wooden box, the black-and-white cat beautifies the scenery in a series of increas-

ingly attractive spreads. This painter-community organizer recruits his animal buddies to help with the cleanup and artistry, and pretty soon a mouse, bird, rabbit, squirrel, and turtle are working together to create a masterpiece. When the work is done, the cool cat takes time for a nap and to smell the roses. Children, especially those who live in blighted neighborhoods, will be inspired by the message of self-help and cooperation. (Ages 3–7.)

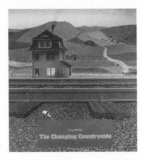

9. *The Changing Countryside.* By Jörg Müller. (Atheneum Publishers, 1977.) Swiss artist Jörg Müller's portfolio of seven precisely drawn foldouts is a thoughtful examination of what rampant industrialization and commercialization have done to a pastoral landscape and a tranquil life. The large color pictures show the same German village as it is transformed from the 1950s to the 1970s. The pictures begin with a Victorian farmhouse and a small town that over a number of years is crowded out of existence, finally giving way to a four-lane highway and large discount stores and factories. *The Changing Countryside* would be helpful in framing a classroom discussion about the meaning of social and economic progress and what is lost and what is gained in modern life. (Ages 7–10.)

10. *OK Go.* By Carin Berger. (Greenwillow Books, 2009.) When the glut of cars produces so much smog that it blacks out the sky, Carin Berger playfully suggests green alternatives to our frenetic path to environmental destruction. In this nearly wordless book, the word "Go!" is used repeatedly to convey the ever-growing carbon load brought on by excessive reliance on fossil fuels. Berger shows cars finally coming to a "Stop!" and uses rhymes to suggest other sensible modes of living, such as "Take a hike, Spike," "Use it again, Jen," "Use the bus, Gus," "Save the planet, Janet," "Use your feet, Pete," and so forth. Kids will respond to this simple plea to conserve our natural resources, while parents will groove on the inspiration apparently provided by Paul Simon's song "50 Ways to Leave Your Lover." Naturally, Berger's collages were constructed from recycled materials. (Ages 4–8.)

11. *An Edwardian Summer.* By John S. Goodall. (Macmillan, 1979.) John S. Goodall, lover of all things connected to the reign of England's Edward VII, provides another charming stroll down nostalgia lane in *An Edwardian Summer.* As usual, the beloved illustrator does not recognize the Dickensian aspects of British society, preferring to paint pictures of the peace and prosperity of the moneyed classes who lead a carefree existence. This romanticized rendering of a summer day in the Edwardian era shows a young girl and boy shopping, watching a cricket match, visiting friends, going to school, and attending a flower show, all images of fashionable leisure often associated with this period. This book could spark an interesting discussion about the masses of working-class people who did not lead such privileged and sheltered lives. (Ages 5–9.)

12. *A Flying Saucer Full of Spaghetti.* By Fernando Krahn. (E. P. Dutton, 1970.) Seven kindly elves see a hungry girl inside a shack seated at a table with no food in sight. Taking a page from the Robin Hood legend, they go to a mansion and take a large plate of spaghetti from a rich girl, flying it across town to the bewilderment of the people below. The airborne pasta is such a spectacle that it causes a few mishaps, but the gnomish little men accomplish their goal, and the poor child enjoys a filling meal. Most young readers will cheer this compassionate redistribution of wealth, while budding conservatives will insist that simply taking property from a well-heeled family is neither fair nor legal. (Ages 4–8.)

13. *The Great War: July 1, 1916: The First Day of the Battle of the Somme: An Illustrated Panorama.* By Joe Sacco. (W. W. Norton, 2013.) The most infamous day in World War I is the subject of Joe Sacco's epic twenty-four-foot-long panorama detailing the events surrounding what became one of the bloodiest mass

slaughters in human history. Packaged in a slipcase like a book, this accordion-fold, extended-graphic narrative depicts one of the world's first trench battles pitting overconfident, mostly British troops against an entrenched German army in a way that gives new significance to the war that was supposed to end all wars. Sacco's tiny black-and-white drawings, rendered from a bird's eye perspective, provide a sense of the scale of the massacre that had produced a million casualties by the conclusion of the offensive. Included in the slipcase is a sixteen-page booklet essay by historian Adam Hochschild. (Ages 12+.)

14. *If You Lived Here, You'd Be Home by Now.* By Ed Briant. (Roaring Brook Press, 2009.) After reading a book about animals, a young boy dreams about a forested park and starts searching for them. When he jumps into a pile of leaves, a friendly leafy creature emerges. They read the book together, locate the animals, and come upon a foreboding construction site encroaching on this natural domain. Flash forward a few decades to a future with flying cars, and the boy is now a father with a son of his own. They return to the park and camp out, and the son spots the mysterious leafy creature. Ed Briant's tribute to the unspoiled wilderness is underscored by the book's colorful cover, showing a boy and his father standing on a city street cramped with cars and row houses, with no evidence of nature except a handful of leaves. (Ages 3–6.)

15. *The Changing City.* By Jörg Müller. (Atheneum Publishers, 1977.) This portfolio of eight beautifully rendered foldout pictures depicts the same neighborhood as it devolves from quaint old row houses and shops into an unattractive and impersonal cityscape. The process, tracked from 1953 to 1976, shows renovations leading to skyscrapers and parking lots, sometimes over the protests of people who do not like what is happening. Children will have no difficulty discerning Jörg Müller's message, but some adults may prefer a less nostalgic and more nuanced presentation of social and technological change. *The Changing City* is a companion to *The Changing Countryside* (1977). Both titles lament the loss of character and personality that comes with urban development. (Ages 7–10.)

16. *Ben's Bunny Trouble.* By Daniel Wakeman and Dirk Van Stralen. (Orca Book Publishers, 2007.) In this sequel to *Ben's Big Dig* (2005), Ben lives with his mother and two pet rabbits in a future world that has lost its life-supporting greenery. He is a stargazer who uses his telescope to locate a planet that would be a better home for his bunnies and sets out in a rocket to transport them there. So as not to alarm his mother, Ben leaves her a map with his intended destination. After making stops at a few planets unsuitably inhabited by snails, sea monkeys, and the like, he finally finds a lush green planet with giant carrots. Ben departs for home, leaving behind a colony that by this point includes a multitude of rabbits. His mother is glad to see him, but it is not clear how they and other humans are going to continue living on a planet that was so ill suited for their pets. (Ages 4–8.)

CHAPTER 29

Graphic Novels for Children

People are so afraid to say the word "comic." . . . Change it
to "graphic novel" and that disappears.

—Marjane Satrapi

1. *The Adventures of Polo.* By Regis Faller. (Roaring Brook Press, 2006.) Well equipped with a backpack full of supplies, fearless dog Polo travels from one exciting adventure to another, always ready to make the best of every situation. Starting out from his island tree house, this resourceful pooch travels to the tropics and the Artic, under the ocean, and into outer space. Traveling by cloud, boat, plane, balloon, submarine, spaceship, and more, Polo never fails to impress with his ingenuity. When he crashes near an erupting volcano, the plucky canine roasts hot dogs over the lava flow. First published in France and lengthy by picture book standards, *The Adventures of Polo* will strongly appeal to would-be explorers, leaving them wishing for more. (Ages 4–8).

2. *Robot Dreams.* By Sara Varon. (First Second, 2007.) A dog buys a robot through the mail, he assembles his mechanical companion, and they become fast friends. Sara Varon's charming graphic novel shows them going to the library, watching movies, and making an ill-fated trip to the beach. The corrosive seawater immobilizes the robot, and the dog is forced to abandon him there. Time passes, both of them struggling to fill the emotional void. The dog tries out new friends, including unsatisfying relationships with a duck, a snowman, and an anteater. The inert robot suffers the damaging effects of weather and is only able to dream. This poignant story is packed with powerful existential questions having to do with loneliness, friendship, loss, and guilt, made accessible through Varon's clean and simple art. (Ages 8–12.)

3. *The Silver Pony: A Story in Pictures.* By Lynd Ward. (Houghton Mifflin, 1973.) This New York Times Best Illustrated Book features the travels of a farm boy and his magical winged horse. When the boy first spots the Pegasus, he tells his father, who reacts by spanking him. Lynd Ward's illustrations, sketched beautifully in black-and-white lithographic style, show the boy deciding to leave his cows, pigs, and chickens behind to mount the mythical horse. He travels to exciting, faraway places, doing good deeds, delivering an apple to an ice-fishing Eskimo, and giving a sunflower to a girl in a watchtower. Literally and metaphorically, *The Silver Pony* succeeds in tapping into the universal urge to spread our wings and explore the world. Ward is chiefly known for his woodcut artistry. He was awarded the Caldecott Medal for *The Biggest Bear* (1952) and has illustrated several Newbery Medal and Honor books. (Ages 6–10.)

4. *Polo: The Runaway Book.* By Regis Faller. (Roaring Brook Press, 2007.) When a little green alien steals his book, the hero of *The Adventures of Polo* (2006) embarks on a new set of fantastic escapades and predicaments. Rich, colorful panels tell the story of the flop-eared dog falling asleep and awakening to find that his brand-new book has been pilfered by a green glowing creature. Wearing his signature backpack, Polo gives chase up to a cotton-candy cloud, through fun-house mirrors, aboard hot-air balloons, and over desert and jungle terrain, mak-

ing friends as he goes along. In a nod to the story of Jack and the Beanstalk, the dog plants a magic seed that grows into an enormous plant, which he climbs. The adventure ends when the canine finally catches up with the alien at story time, finding the stick-legged extraterrestrial sharing the book with friends. (Ages 4–8.)

5. *Here I Am.* By Patti Kim and Sonia Sanchez. (Capstone Young Readers, 2014.) As with *The Arrival* (2007), *Here I Am*'s wordless format is the perfect vehicle for capturing the experience of recent immigrants who may feel silent and clueless in their strange new environment. In this graphic novel, a young Asian boy, new to life in an American city, is shown clinging to a red seed, a keepsake from his past, that falls out of his apartment window to the street below. A girl picks up the seed, and when he hunts for her, exploring the area, he is drawn out of his loneliness and isolation toward an important friendship. *Here I Am* may enable children to feel empathy for those who are alone and struggling to survive in an alien culture. (Ages 5–10.)

6. *Polo and Lily.* By Regis Faller. (Roaring Brook Press, 2009.) In this somewhat quiet tale in the Polo adventure series, we find Polo, the floppy-eared dog protagonist, living peaceably on his small island, watering his garden, tending to his tomatoes, eating his meal, and then sleeping in his bed, when a cloud carrying a rabbit collides with his tree house, landing the plucky visitor in his bedroom. Lily's sudden arrival produces surprise, smiles, and an enjoyable interruption in the canine's solitary life. They spend a fun day together, and their friendship blossoms. When Lily departs, she leaves a phone behind so that the fast friends can stay in touch. *Polo and Lily* is the perfect first graphic novel for beginners and an excellent introduction to the multipaneled comic book format. (Ages 4–8.)

7. *Polo and the Dragon.* By Regis Faller. (Roaring Brook Press, 2007.) Polo, the amicable dog hero featured in many adventures, goes sailing on a wintery day so cold that his boat gets stuck in the ice. He escapes his predicament by using a magic quill to draw a door leading to a forest. Polo enters a cave, encounters a little dragon, and runs away from him. The creature turns out to be friendly, following Polo not to harm him but to return the backpack the dog has left behind. Fortunately, the dragon is also a fire breather, just what is needed to free the boat from the ice. The little dragon and dog sail back to Polo's home and celebrate their new friendship by having a nice meal together. Regis Faller's book is a good beginning graphic novel. His protagonist is appealing, and his comic panels are saturated with color and easy to follow. (Ages 4–8.)

8. *Korgi Book 1: Sprouting Wings!* By Christian Slade. (Top Shelf Productions, 2007.) This beautifully drawn woodland fantasy adventure features a raven-haired young girl named Ivy and her dog, Sprout. Ivy belongs to a race of fairies who inhabit a Tolkien-esque world filled with action and suspense and populated with all types of monsters. In this first installment in the Korgi series, former Disney animator Christian Slade has Ivy and Spout facing danger from giant spiders and an ogre after they follow a winged insect away from their town. Thanks to Sprout's ability to breathe fire and Ivy's ability to fly, they escape unharmed, but not without attracting the attention of other sinister creatures. Children will be impressed with this auspicious beginning and will be eager to continue with this graphic novel series. (Ages 5–9.)

9. *Polo and the Magic Flute.* By Regis Faller. (Roaring Brook Press, 2009.) Polo, a dog who lives in an island tree house, is always having an adventure, and this one starts out with an unassuming boat trip looking for fish. Before you know it, the floppy-eared pup is upended by a wave from a splashing whale and gets shipwrecked on another island,

where a strange koala bear gives him a flute and then disappears. Polo waits at a bus stop, gets picked up by a large snail bus, and is taken to a mystical pagoda, where he finds the koala sitting on the roof. The bear shows him the secret to playing the flute, and the two of them fly on enchanted carpets to Polo's home. The final frame shows them flying away over the ocean, still playing their charmed musical instruments. (Ages 4–8.)

10. *Owly & Wormy, Bright Lights and Starry Nights.* By Andy Runton. (Atheneum Books for Young Readers, 2012.) Owly and Wormy go on a camping trip to gaze at the stars with their telescope, but things do not go as planned. Their view of the sky is blocked by dense foliage; then they are driven by rain into a cave, hear scary noises, and lose their telescope! When the big-eyed owl goes back into the forest to retrieve it, he meets three nice bats, who help set the friends' minds at ease. This graphic novel is a strong model for the power of friendship, and it will help children cope with fear of the dark. It concludes with fright finally giving way to joy at the sight of a sky filled with bright stars. (Ages 4–7.)

11. *Polo and the Magician!* By Regis Faller. (Roaring Brook Press, 2009.) In bright, color-saturated comic panels, Regis Faller takes readers on another exciting Polo adventure, with the magic beginning, as in all of his books, in Polo's island tree house. When a flood takes him and his easy chair to another island, the intrepid dog (who sometimes resembles a rabbit) joins the circus and soon occupies center stage as magician and tiger tamer. Managing to thrill the crowd and save the day, Polo will fascinate young readers with his derring-do. *Magician* is not the best in the Polo series, but fans will still want to add it to their libraries. (Ages 4–8.)

12. *Owly: The Way Home & The Bittersweet Summer.* By Andy Runton. (Top Shelf, 2004.) Andy Runton's graphic novel series gets off to a good start with two charming novellas. In *The Way Home*, Owly does not concern himself with the fact that Wormy is a soft-bodied earthworm and ideal source of food and instead rescues him from a rainstorm, takes care of him, and helps him find his way home. In *The Bittersweet Summer*, the big-hearted owl and the cute invertebrate team up to make friends with a pair of hummingbirds, but they are sad when the tiny birds must fly south for the winter. Owly and Wormy learn that all good-byes are not final when they see the hummingbirds returning from their seasonal migration. (Ages 7–11.)

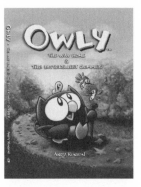

13. *A Wish for Elves.* By Mark Gonyea. (Henry Holt, 2010.) In this graphic novel aimed at children in the early and middle grades, a boy makes a holiday wish for some elves to help him with household chores and homework, but his bonanza puts a crimp in Santa's Christmas schedule. The elves are put to work cleaning the boy's room, doing the laundry, and fixing his meals, but the Christmas pixies turn out to be more trouble than they are worth. Meanwhile, Santa is behind schedule and has put up posters to locate his missing workers. To rid himself of his unwanted guests, the boy attaches some of the elves to helium balloons, and one of them lands at the North Pole. Thus alerted, Santa reclaims the other elves, and Christmas is saved. Mark Gonyea's illustrations are simple geometric forms colored in red, green, yellow, black, and white. (Ages 5–10.)

14. *Happy Halloween, Li'l Santa.* By Thierry Robin and Lewis Trondheim. (NBM Publishing, 2003.) Originally published in France, this energetic sequel to *Li'l Santa* (2002) shows Santa teaming up with Halloween characters to thwart environmental disaster near his home at the North Pole. In this graphic novel, some very unpleasant lumberjack monster machines are engaged in mass logging of Christmas trees in order to make matches. Santa's

ghoulish buddies come to his aid in an epic battle that naturally ends in the defeat of this frightening corporate invader. Fans of traditional Christmas narratives might be turned off by this odd marriage of Christmas and Halloween, created in the tradition of Tim Burton's 1993 movie *The Nightmare before Christmas*. (Ages 6–10.)

15. *Korgi Book 2: The Cosmic Collector.* By Christian Slade. (Top Shelf Books, 2008.) This graphic novel series, featuring a plucky girl fairy named Ivy and her cute dog sidekick, Sprout, continues with adventures that are more perilous and dark than in the first installment. The two live in magical Korgi Hollow, home to fairylike Mollies and fire-breathing Korgis, who resemble corgis, which are Welsh herding dogs. In this episode, alien creatures are clipping the wings off Mollies, and Ivy and Sprout try to get to the bottom of the mystery in the surrounding woodlands. Children who like this world of fantasy adventure will eventually want to graduate to *The Lord of the Rings* (2005) and *The Chronicles of Narnia* (2004). (Ages 6–11.)

16. *I'm Not a Plastic Bag.* By Rachel Hope Allison. (Archaia Entertainment, 2012.) There is no more potent testimony to the collective human disregard for the planet than the grotesque floating island of trash known as the "Great Pacific Garbage Patch." Instead of providing a discourse about environmental stewardship or a lecture about an expanse of garbage that is double the size of Texas, Rachel Hope Allison has brilliantly chosen to draw attention to this global eyesore in a sympathetic graphic novel about loneliness. Composed of plastic bags, cigarette butts, old tires, and all manner of disposable waste, this sentient trash stew longs for company. Like Frankenstein, this man-made trash island exists as a monster that is discarded, loathed, and sad. Allison's beautifully illustrated book is well suited to focusing the attention of youngsters on the problem of ocean pollution. (Ages 8+.)

17. *Don't Look Now.* By Ed Briant. (Roaring Brook Press, 2009.) Lively illustrations done in the style of a graphic novel tell the story of two brothers who employ the old "don't-look-now" prank to distract one another and grab each other's toys and treats. Starting out in an inflatable wading pool, one sibling steals a sailboat after pointing to a garden hose, suggesting that it is a frightening snake. This "what's-behind-you" contest escalates to include tricycles and bowls of ice cream, when the siblings are suddenly swallowed up in a jungle fantasy world rife with monsters, requiring cooperation rather than competition to escape. Parents will be able to use this book to discuss the merits of working together as well as the perennial need for kids to respect each other's belongings. (Ages 5–10.)

18. *Li'l Santa.* By Thierry Robin and Lewis Trondheim. (NBM Publishing, 2002.) In this silent comic book story, Santa must surmount many obstacles to succeed in performing his yearly duty, but his everyday activities carry the most appeal. For example, he is awakened in the morning by an alarm clock in the shape of a small igloo, activated when a teddy bear pops out blowing his horn. Sleepy Santa hits the snooze button a few times and is presented with increasingly louder alarms in the form of a frog and then an octopus sounding multiple horns. While he is still in his pajamas, birds and rabbits dress the sleepwalking gift giver in his red pants and black boots and even brush his teeth. With the aid of his elves and other friends, he manages to save Christmas Day. *Li'l Santa* would be an excellent first graphic novel for kindergarteners and elementary school students. (Ages 5–10.)

19. *Korgi Book 3: A Hollow Beginning.* By Christian Slade. (Top Shelf Productions, 2011.) In his third graphic novel in the Korgi series, Christian Slade reveals the origins of Korgi Hollow, a fantasy world featuring Ivy, a winged fairy, and Sprout, a fire-breathing dog modeled on a Welsh corgi. The two find a strange shard of stained glass window imprinted with the image of a castle, which leads them

to Wart, a magic toad and librarian, who provides surprising revelations about the origins of their world. Slade uses intricate black-and-white cross-hatching to make this imaginary universe seem real. This almost wordless tale includes a helpful introduction, character sketches, and Korgi Hollow map. Darker and scarier than the first two adventurers, *A Hollow Beginning* is a better fit for elementary school–age children than for preschoolers. (Ages 6–12.)

20. *Steam Park*. By Filippo Neri and Piero Ruggeri. (Simply Read Books, 2006.) In this silent graphic novel, a group of kids looking for a jaunt in a deserted amusement park find more than they bargained for, when a villainous man who sold them their admission tickets imprisons them. After boarding a roller coaster, the five youngsters are captured and forced to work as slaves to keep the steam machinery running in the creepy park. They are freed from captivity by a pumpkin-headed creature, a drunken clown, and others who must do battle with the evil caretaker who kidnapped the children. This Scooby-Doo-like adventure comes to a happy ending when the park is reopened, and people are seen moving about enjoying the food and amusements. (Ages 8–12.)

21. *Owly: Just a Little Blue*. By Andy Runton. (Top Shelf Productions, 2005.) Compassionate Owly and clever Wormy try to help a family of bluebirds but are driven off, even after the best friends have constructed a new home for the birds, having given up some of their own wood to fashion a birdhouse. Realizing that the bluebird's nest is in danger, the two pack away the home in the owl's closet for later use. When rain imperils the bluebirds, Owly and Wormy are there to save the day! Like the first graphic novel in the series, *Just a Little Blue* celebrates the virtue of kindness, even when it would be easier to choose a different path. This heartwarming story is a lesson in how to be a friend. (Ages 7–11.)

22. *Lio: There's a Monster in My Socks.* By Mark Tatulli. (Andrews McMeel Publishing, 2012.) This collection of short comics is culled from Mark Tatulli's daily newspaper strip with an eye to selecting the ones most appealing to kids. Lio, an ingenious little boy, not only has monsters in his socks but regularly encounters dragons, aliens, robots, zombies, and other bizarre creatures. Tatulli employs a scratchy pen-and-ink style to capture the lively imagination of a boy who lives with his father and pets. Adventure-loving school-age children will love the over-the-top humor and the quirky protagonist's basic good heartedness, particularly when he stands up to bullies. The *Lio* comics have a passing resemblance to *Calvin and Hobbes*, but they are much edgier. (Ages 8–12.)

23. *Hello Kitty: Surprise!* By Jacob Chabot, Ian McGinty, Jorge Monlongo, and Anastassia Neislotova. (Perfect Square, 2014.) This graphic novel is ostensibly an adventure story about a cheery moon-faced cat, but it is also part of an advertising campaign for a product line that includes shoes, bracelets, earrings, watches, tote bags, wallets, luggage, clothing, beauty supplies, hats, headbands, travel mugs, toys, backpacks, trading cards, jigsaw puzzles, pillows, art supplies, stationery, stickers, candy, DVDs, phone cases, hairbrushes, alarm clocks, and other merchandise too numerous to list. Hello Kitty is a comprehensive marketing effort aimed at preteen girls, and the uplifting Hello Kitty books are part of a brand and lifestyle that promote the consumption of consumer goods. The main surprise in *Hello Kitty: Surprise!* is that so many libraries are on board with this sales operation. (Ages 6–12.)

24. *Owly: Flying Lessons.* By Andy Runton. (Top Shelf Productions, 2006.) The beloved vegetarian owl and his faithful worm pal make friends with a flying squirrel in this third installment of the Owly series. It is not love at first sight, however, as the squirrel fears that Owly might be a predator. He is an owl, after all. When Wormy accidentally gets hurt, the squirrel sees how the owl tends to his buddy, becoming convinced

of the bird's gentle and compassionate nature. The friendship is sealed when the squirrel offers to teach Owly to fly, something that the puffball owl has never mastered. Some children's books contain warnings that the content may be too violent. In Owly's case, the admonition would have to be that he might be too sweet. (Ages 5–10.)

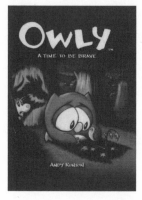

25. *Owly: A Time to Be Brave.* By Andy Runton. (Top Shelf Productions, 2007.) Owly fans know that the big-eyed bird is kindly beyond words, making him a natural for a feel-good graphic novel series. In this book, Wormy, his faithful sidekick, becomes frightened by a story involving dragons. Owl helps him overcome his fears by focusing on an opossum in need and involving him with nursing a damaged tree back to health. The cartoony Owly books are a perfect introduction to graphic novels for the younger set, with each book teaching a new lesson about character and friendship. Arguably, their only drawback is that Andy Runton does his drawings in black and white. (Ages 5–10.)

26. *Yam: Bite-Size Chunks.* By Corey Barba. (Top Shelf Productions, 2008.) This pantomime graphic novel is the first in a series about the strange adventures of a young boy and his quirky friends who live on the distant tropical island of Leche de la Luna, which means "Milk of the Moon." Yam, who wears a backpack over his orange-hooded footy pajamas, has a kitten for a friend and a television set for a pet. The noseless boy sleeps with his TV and uses the remote to change the channel when his pet has bad dreams. Corey Barba's book has a special page on how to draw Yam. Fans of the Korgi and Owly graphic novel series will want to give *Yam* a try but will find it gentler and more whimsical. Some of the *Yam* comics previously appeared in *Nickelodeon Magazine*. (Ages 6–10.)

CHAPTER 30

Graphic Novels for Teens

Comics are a gateway drug to literacy.

—Art Spiegelman

1. *Blood Song: A Silent Ballad.* By Eric Drooker. (Dark Horse Originals, 2009.) In this graphic novel, a young woman is forced to abandon her war-torn, forested island home in a nameless Southeast Asian country to journey across the ocean. Landing in a big Western city, she encounters another kind of oppression. She falls in love with a saxophone player who is senselessly arrested by the police for playing his music, leaving the couple with a bleak and uncertain future. American Book Award winner Eric Drooker works in a palette of only black, white, gray, and blue to a stunning effect. His political commentary on the abuses of government authority, coupled with his pictorially bold storytelling, will have strong appeal for many teenagers and adults. (Ages 12+.)

2. *Weathercraft.* By Jim Woodring. (Fantagraphics Books, 2010.) *Weathercraft* is set in a fictional universe called the "Unifactor" and features Jim Woodring's well-known characters Frank, Manhog, and Whim. Manhog, a miserable part-man, part-hog creature, normally plays a supporting role in Woodring's Frank-centered comic strips, but in *Weathercraft* he is the main protagonist. Manhog undergoes

immense suffering, heads out on a transformative trek to seek enlightenment, and returns to confront the always smiling, malevolent Whim. *Weathercraft* is the artist's first graphic novel. Its dust jacket is packed with explanatory text, tacitly acknowledging that newcomers to Woodring's universe might need more than pictures to figure out what is going on. Even Unifactor aficionados may need to return to the book a few times to get its full meaning. (Ages 12+.)

3. *Sticks and Stones.* By Peter Kuper. (Three Rivers Press, 2004.) In this allegorical story about the folly of hubris and empire building, a stone giant is brought to life from a volcano in a desolate land and demands that the people follow him. They construct a stone castle for him and help him invade, plunder, and enslave a nearby stick civilization, which had been living in peace. Not everyone submits to the despot, and an epic struggle ensues, led by a woman from the stone city and a man from the stick civilization. The man and woman are imprisoned and alone escape disaster. Peter Kuper received an award from the Society of Newspaper Designers for *Sticks and Stones* and is best known for doing the *Spy vs. Spy* comics for *Mad* magazine. (Ages 12+.)

4. *The Number: 73304-23-4153-6-96-8.* By Thomas Ott. (Fantagraphics Books, 2014.) When an electric chair operator pockets a slip of paper that he finds at the scene of an execution, the combination of numbers on it horribly transforms his life. The executioner notices it turning up everywhere—in a phone number, on a clock, on a dog tag, and in an address—and decides to place his fate in the hands of these mysterious numerals. At first the man has good fortune, gambling with the aid of the numbers in a casino and winning a large sum of money. He also meets a woman, briefly creating the hope of romantic fulfillment for this solitary figure, but the next morning she is gone, and so is the money. His search for her and the money send him spiraling into an abyss and to his ultimate demise. *The Number: 73304-23-4153-6-96-8* is done with detailed black-and-white scratchboard illustrations, demonstrating mastery of the medium. (Ages 12+.)

5. *Fox Bunny Funny.* By Andy Hartzell. (Top Shelf Productions, 2007.) While the title suggests that this is a cute little baby book, *Fox Bunny Funny* actually deals with the mature themes of violence, desire, and identity. In this society of anthropomorphized foxes and bunnies, the foxes rule with torture and violence and consume the bunnies for food. White bunnies suffer at the hands of their black oppressors in the cruelest ways imaginable. Yet the main character in the story, a fox, is haunted by a burning secret: he yearns to be a bunny. Privately, he dresses up in a bunny suit and struggles to mask his true nature and feelings. He eventually finds a place where foxes and bunnies live together amicably, but violence still lurks beneath the surface. *Fox Bunny Funny* provides ample opportunities for discussion of homophobia and other forms of bias and oppression. It belongs on the shelf of every school and community library. (Ages 12+.)

6. *Fran.* By Jim Woodring. (Fantagraphics Books, 2013.) In this sequel to *Congress of the Animals* (2011), Frank, the main character in Jim Woodring's surreal graphic novel series, gets a girlfriend. Readers actually encounter Fran toward the end of *Congress* and learn comparatively little about her in this book. *Fran* is mostly about providing more emotional depth and complexity to Frank, especially by showing how he becomes despondent after foolishly pushing Fran away. Regretting what he has done, Frank sets out on a dreamlike journey to find her, which takes him through a bizarre alternative universe with menacing creatures, the kind of freakish landscape that Woodring fans savor. The story ends with Frank and Fran settling down to a life of happy companionship. *Fran* received the Lynd Ward Graphic Novel Prize. (Ages 12+.)

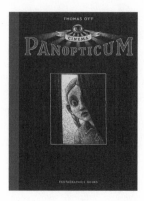

7. *Cinema Panopticum.* By Thomas Ott. (Fantagraphics Books, 2005.) *Cinema Panopticum* is a collection of five graphic novelettes: *The Hotel, The Champion, The Experiment, The Prophet,* and *The Girl.* The first story frames and introduces the other four. The Swiss cartoonist's tales are dark and bizarre, beginning with a young girl at a carnival who finds the only amusement she can afford is the Cinema Panopticum, which has coin-operated machines for viewing silent films, which in turn become Thomas Ott's subsequent stories. In *The Champion,* a Mexican wrestler engages in a fight against death itself, and in *The Prophet,* a homeless man foresees the end of the world and tries to warn everyone, but nobody heeds his message. Ott's haunting pictures are rendered in a detailed, black-and-white scratchboard style. (Ages 12+.)

8. *The Middle Passage: White Ships / Black Cargo.* By Tom Feelings. (Dial Books, 1995.) *The Middle Passage* is an unflinching pictorial history of enslaved Africans during their capture and torturous Atlantic journey to America. Showing men, women, and children packed into overcrowded slave vessels, Tom Feelings powerfully bears witness to conditions that were so cruel and horrific that only a third of the captives survived. Rendered in sixty-four paintings of muted black and white, this visceral record of the European slave trade includes scenes of beatings, brandings, rapes, suicides, and the summary disposal of dead bodies into the shark-infested sea. This graphic history will do more to communicate the earliest history of black America than any conventional textbook. It should be part of every American middle and high school curriculum. (Ages 12+.)

9. *The Sanctuary.* By Nate Neal. (Fantagraphics Books, 2010.) Nate Neal's imaginative graphic novel about cavemen and cavewomen ambitiously explores the role of art in society and other heady subjects. The story involves an outcast cave-dwelling artist and his nomad girl companion who are caught up in power struggles between opposing tribal groups.

Illustrated in black and white, this gloomy Paleo-lithic tale raises thoughtful questions about power, truth, morality, and artists' essential role in bringing inconvenient truths to the attention of an often cor-rupt social order. Teenagers will enjoy this inventive prehistory and its implicit claim that graphic art has always been central to the human condition. Neal invents a crude language for the cave people, which he conveys phonetically. (Ages 12+.)

10. *Age of Reptiles Omnibus*, Vol. 1. By Ricardo Delgado. (Dark Horse Books, 2011.) In brilliant cinematic spreads, Ricardo Delgado's volume brings his dinosaurs to life in realistic detail by infusing them with just enough love, hate, revenge, and violence to make the book irresistible to young adults. Compris-ing work originally published in comic book form over a period of sixteen years, this glossy paperback consistently delivers action and drama, aiming more to entertain than to educate. The omnibus collec-tion shows Delgado's artistic development from his initial use of an almost garish color pallet to more muted earth tones in the final section. Delgado's di-nosaurs are apparently based on solid paleontological research, challenging serious students of the ancient reptiles to identify all of them. (Ages 12+.)

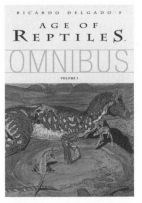

11. *Monsters! and Other Stories*. By Gustavo Duarte. (Dark Horse Books, 2014.) Gustavo Duarte's book comprises three previously published graphic novellas, each brimming with humor and horror. In the title story, three giant beasts from the depths of the ocean cut a swath though a city in a manner that would make Godzilla proud; in another story, aliens abduct a hapless pig farmer. The collection is rounded off by a nightmarish tale of two bird office workers being picked off by the Angel of Death. With minimal color, the Brazilian cartoonist's stories unfold with unusual sight gags, expressive characters, breathtaking perspec-tives, and unexpected twists and turns. *Monsters! and Other Stories* is an excellent addition to the burgeoning genre of silent graphic storytelling. (Ages 12+.)

12. *Dead End.* By Thomas Ott. (Fantagraphics Books, 2002.) Swiss cartoonist Thomas Ott, one of the leading lights of the silent comic format, is known for his dark tales of suspense and horror drawn on starkly contrasting, black-and-white scratchboard. The two short stories in *Dead End* deliver on the title's promise, each providing dead endings and karmic twists. In the "The Millionaires," Ott seems to channel *The Twilight Zone*'s Rod Serling in a tale about a suitcase full of cash that moves from one greedy hand to another, leading to a series of gruesome deaths. In "Washing Day," there is just one death, but a more compelling story, as a dwarf assassin tries to kill a former magician, who is also a little person. (Ages 12+.)

13. *The Frank Book.* By Jim Woodring. (Fantagraphics Books, 2003.) This omnibus collection of comic strips dating from 1991 center on Frank, a curious anthropoid resembling a cat, and a cast of weird characters, including the repugnant part-man, part-hog Manhog; Pupshaw, a loyal pet to Frank; and Whim, a smiling, moonfaced devil. The comics chronicle Frank's bizarre wanderings in a strange and dangerous world known as the "Unifactor." Film director Francis Ford Coppola provides the introduction to this hefty volume, which is an unexpected bonus. *The Frank Book* is a treasure trove of unique, lavish, and hallucinogenic cartoons that will leave a few viewers confused but most of them captivated. Hardcore fans of graphic storytelling will be hooked by Jim Woodring's inventive and surreal imaginings and eager to move on to his other books. (Ages 12+.)

14. *Congress of the Animals.* By Jim Woodring. (Fantagraphics Books, 2011.) This finalist for the Los Angeles Times Book Prize for Graphic Novels deals with Jim Woodring's signature character, Frank, and the question of what happens when he leaves the surreal world of the Unifactor. In this second book in the series, Frank loses his house, escapes a factory job, finds a giant statue of himself on a remote island, encounters nightmarish monsters, and finds a female version of himself, who becomes the subject of Woodring's next graphic novel. *Congress of the Animals* is a bizarre trip and not for the uninitiated. The best way to acclimate yourself to Frank and his world is to start at the beginning with *The Frank Book* (2003) and then get up to speed with *Weathercraft* (2010). (Ages 12+.)

15. *Adventures of a Japanese Businessman.* By José Domingo, Isabel Mancebo, Alex Spiro, and Sam Arthur. (Nobrow Press, 2012.) This English-language debut of a gifted Spanish cartoonist chronicles the crazy odyssey of a Japanese businessman who heads home after a day at the office. The unfortunate protagonist encounters a mind-boggling series of situations more resembling a dreamy stream of consciousness than a story. José Domingo's dense panels are rich with nonstop mayhem and humor that includes avoiding gun-wielding mobsters, inhaling something that turns the protagonist into a monster, encountering a family of cannibals, getting transformed by a witch, traveling to the bowels of the earth, and going to hell and back. This book-length comic, in which anything can happen, will bring hours of enjoyment to middle and high school audiences. (Ages 12+.)

16. *Combustion: A Story without Words.* By Chris Lanier. (Fantagraphics Books, 1999.) Chris Lanier's fifty-six-page graphic novel tells the story of a soldier lost behind enemy lines. Created in the traditional expressionistic woodcut style, this antiwar polemic focuses on the experience of a military man who discovers atonement when he defies his country's actions, suggesting to readers that they should also question the origins of war and violence. Lanier's book invites comparison to *All Quiet on the Western Front* (1982) and *The Thin Red Line* (1962), both dealing with the harsh realities of combat. Fans of the bold scratchboard style will admire Lanier's artistry and see it as a good fit with the book's strong

message. Nonetheless, this graphic parable of the horrors of war may be a little too intense for some middle schoolers. (Ages 12+.)

17. *Greetings from Hellville.* By Thomas Ott. (Fantagraphics Books, 2002.) *Greetings from Hellville* has the kind of cringe-inducing title that makes some parents and teachers averse to graphic novels. Yet Thomas Ott's dramatic style, reminiscent of Lynd Ward's woodcuts, is well within the bounds of the mainstream tradition of the horror genre. Yes, his scratchboard images are startling and more than a little creepy, but in this collection of four silent comics, they illuminate the anguish felt by solitary and desperate people. In one story, a white supremacist comes to a violent end because a voodoo spell has been cast on him; in another, a man repeatedly tries to take his own life but is finally undone by a nuclear blast. Ott's horror comics are well known to European audiences. *Greetings from Hellville* is his first book published in the United States. (Ages 12+.)

18. *Jinchalo.* By Matthew Forsythe. (Drawn and Quarterly, 2012.) Matthew Forsythe, the Canadian creator of *Ojingogo* (2009), has published a follow-up tale featuring the same little girl from the earlier book. In this surreal adventure, the girl's father sends her to the market for food after she has eaten everything in sight. She acquires a magic egg that hatches Jinchalo, a mischievous shape-shifter. The two of them go from one strange and dreamlike meeting to another, encountering robots, giant hummingbirds, headless monsters, and other grotesque creatures. In one of the book's surprising twists, the girl comically shape-shifts into an old woman. Forsythe's manga-influenced books are rooted in Korean mythology. Readers should resist the temptation to breeze through this comic and instead savor the intricate details. (Ages 12+.)

19. *R.I.P.: Best of 1985–2004.* By Thomas Ott. (Fantagraphics Books, 2011.) You can forget happy endings in Thomas Ott's dark and twisted tales of murder, suicide, pain, madness, and torment. Rendered in black-and-white scratchboard style, the stories are all nightmarish cartoons featuring characters with contorted faces and psyches. In one vignette, a man strangles someone to death, then tries to wipe away the evidence of his crime. The police discover him wearing an apron and looking quite mad, obsessively cleaning the silverware, dishes, picture frames, and everything else in sight. Serious collectors and newcomers will want to read this omnibus collection of new and previously published material, culled from almost two decades of work, including *Greetings from Hellville* (2002), *Dead End* (2002), and *Tales of Error* (2003). (Ages 12+.)

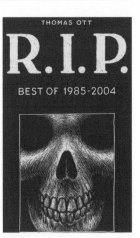

20. *Pebble Island.* By Jon McNaught. (Nobrow Press, 2012.) British illustrator Jon McNaught based *Pebble Island* on his childhood recollections of growing up in the Falkland Islands off the coast of Argentina. This beautifully understated graphic novel contains two stories of solitude and adventure. Muted colors and simple panels convey a vast, barren landscape and communicate the rhythms of life on a remote island. Images of children playing in peat bogs and wandering sheep evoke feelings of profound quietude, not the sort of thing usually found in a genre known for melodrama and action. McNaught somehow makes uneventful things seem fascinating, such as when he shows a fisherman watching television when the power goes out, requiring him to refill the generator. (Ages 12+.)

21. *Metronome.* By Véronique Tanaka. (NBM Publishing, 2008.) Chosen by *New York* magazine as one of its top ten graphic novels of the year, this existential, erotically charged book is actually the creation of British comic book artist Bryan Talbot. Under the pseudonym Véronique Tanaka, Talbot describes a love affair between a musician and his girlfriend doomed

by misunderstanding and miscommunication, which are mostly his fault. There are a few lovemaking scenes that make the book unsuitable for children. The novel comprises identical square panels, four rows to a page, which mark time like the equal intervals of a metronome. Long after readers finish with Talbot's book, they will feel its black-and-white images of a failed relationship embedded in their memories. (Ages 14+.)

22. *Almost Silent.* By Jason. (Fantagraphics Books, 2010.) In *Almost Silent*, the Norwegian cartoonist John Arne Sæterøy, who works under the pen name Jason, collects four previously published graphic novels: *Tell Me Something* (2003), *You Can't Get There from Here* (2004), *Meow Baby!* (2005), and *The Living and the Dead* (2007). His distinctive protagonists are invariably long and lean with animal heads and include zombies, vampires, werewolves, and other monsters. One story in the collection involves a love triangle between Dr. Frankenstein, his monster, and a bride for the monster who becomes the object of the mad scientist's affection. Jason originally began creating almost wordless graphic novels in order to reach audiences outside Norway. (Ages 12+.)

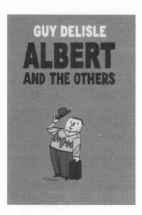

23. *Albert and the Others.* By Guy Delisle. (Drawn and Quarterly, 2008.) *Albert and the Others* is not the kind of book you expect to see on a recommended reading list or as part of a library collection. It's more like the kind of book that kids find on their own and furtively swap in class, until the teacher confiscates it, disapproving of every page. Why? The book is a disturbing collection of comics intended as a humorous take on the perversities and neuroses of the modern male. In twenty-six alphabetically arranged strips, Guy Delisle regales readers with such things as a woman being tied to railroad tracks, a woman getting dismembered and sewn back together, and a fisherman who catches and releases a naked woman after measuring her and finding that she does not meet the legal limit. This misogynist title has a companion volume, *Aline and the Others* (2006). (Ages 15+.)

24. *House.* By Josh Simmons. (Fantagraphics Books, 2007.) A young man and two teenage girls meet in the middle of the forest to explore an old abandoned mansion and discover its secrets. The man and one of the girls are romantically involved and the other girl seems jealous. Curiosity drives them to explore the house's empty rooms and hallways, and we notice a portrait of a grim old man on the wall, which also serves the book's cover. The group's desire for adventure soon gives way to claustrophobic anxiety and growing alarm as they become separated and lost in a maze of passageways. Terror and panic radiate from their faces as the blackness envelops them. *House* was nominated for an Ignatz Award in the category of outstanding graphic novel. (Ages 12+.)

25. *Bye, Bye Birdie.* By Shirley Hughes. (Jonathan Cape, 2009.) This is the first graphic novel for teenagers and adults by Shirley Hughes, an award-winning London illustrator recognized for her work writing and illustrating children's books. When a young dandy takes an attractive woman home, perhaps to be his wife, she undergoes a nightmarish transformation into a falcon-faced predatory bird. The bird-woman chases him around the house, creating havoc and ripping furniture with her sharp beak. Rendered in vibrant black-and-white drawings, the book has a retro feel reminiscent of a silent comedy film, adding to its attractiveness. Readers looking to sample the graphic novel format for the first time would be well advised to start here. (Ages 12+.)

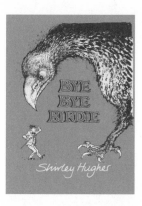

26. *Aline and the Others.* By Guy Delisle. (Drawn and Quarterly, 2006.) Guy Delisle, best known for *Pyongyang: A Journey in North Korea* (2007), *Shenzhen: A Travelogue from China* (2012), and other excellent travelogues, shows a different side of himself in *Aline and the Others.* In this collection of twenty-six comic strips—one each for different women and letters of the alphabet, beginning with Aline—the artist makes it clear that if there is a battle of the sexes, women are winning. His darkly humorous

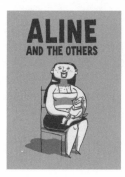

depictions of the plight of women are strange and racy, aimed at teenagers and adults, but definitely not everyone's cup of tea. *Aline and the Others* is intended as an amusing commentary on women and men, but the women come across as a collection of body parts. (Ages 15+.)

27. *H Day*. By Renée French. (PictureBox, 2010.) *H Day* is inspired by the artist's recurring migraine headaches and an invasion of tiny black Argentinean ants. Haunting, smudgy, and yet somehow beautiful, the drawings create a world that is part fantasy and part autobiography. The headache and ant stories run concurrently, facing each other on left- and right-hand pages. Grotesquely deformed heads communicate the pain and struggle of her chronic condition, while the menacing ants take over a block city and wrap up the inhabitants. While the relationship between the two narratives is not clear, the overall effect is to generate feelings of horror and oppression. Excerpts of *H Day* are included in *The Best American Comics 2012* (2012). (Ages 12+.)

28. *Gon*. By Masashi Tanaka. (Paradox Press, 1996.) Gon, a feisty little dinosaur with a big head and tiny arms, has made it his mission to protect weaker animals from the strong and predatory. As the last of his kind, this prehistoric anomaly fearlessly battles larger creatures in black-and-white drawings that show him as somewhat cartoonish compared to the more realistically depicted animals and environments. This first book in the multivolume Japanese manga series features three stories: "Gon Eats and Sleeps," "Gon Goes Flying," and "Gon Glares." Fiercely combative, this lizardly protagonist reveals himself to be also kindhearted in his rescue of a threatened baby bird. Gon is also a popular video game and cartoon character. (Ages 12+.)

29. *A.L.I.E.E.E.N.* By Lewis Trondheim. (First Second, 2006.) This comic-style book, cleverly presented by French cartoonist Lewis Trondheim as the very first graphic document of extraterrestrial origin, at first glance seems light and childlike, but it turns out to be darkly humorous, containing toilet humor and violence better suited to a teenage mentality. *A.L.I.E.E.E.N.*, which stands for "Archives of Lost Issues and Earthly Editions of Extraterrestrial Novelties," is designed to look like a worn and tattered artifact found by Trondheim while on vacation. Paging through the purportedly alien publication, readers will see cruel things happening to cute creatures. Trondheim has filled his stories with nonsensical alien dialog, adding a touch of authenticity to a book built on a very solid imaginative premise. (Ages 12+.)

30. *The System.* By Peter Kuper. (PM Press, 2014.) Set in a gritty modern-day New York City, Peter Kuper's cleverly intertwined visual narrative supports the six-degrees-of-separation theory or some variation of the notion that we are all somehow connected. Kuper shows us a city populated by corrupt police, ominous serial killers, dishonest politicians, and shady stockbrokers all caught up in a world of small coincidences and consequential results. Fresh and vibrant illustrations tell the story of an ugly metropolis with drug dealers, strippers, homeless people, and dangerous bombers whose chance meetings are all part of a vast system that privileges the rich and powerful and oppresses everyone else. (Ages 12+.)

31. *Speechless.* By Peter Kuper. (Top Shelf Productions, 2001.) This retrospective of Peter Kuper's career as a graphic artist places him at the forefront of his field. While Kuper first made his name in alternative magazines, his work appears regularly in publications such as the *New York Times, New Yorker, Village Voice, New York Daily News, Mother Jones, Newsweek, Time, Entertainment Weekly,* and *Mad* magazine, with many examples from these publications included in *Speechless.* This attractive

coffee-table book includes Kuper's political cartoons, magazine covers, and graphic novel excerpts. In addition to its wordless content, the book also has essays and anecdotes. *Speechless* is a collectable item for graphic artists, social activists, and teenagers who know Kuper through his work on *Mad*'s popular *Spy vs. Spy* comics. (Ages 12+.)

32. *Ojingogo.* By Matthew Forsythe. (Drawn and Quarterly, 2009.) Named book of the year by *Quill & Quire* magazine, this black-and-white graphic novel is described by the artist as a kind of "Korean-flavored Alice in Wonderland." Its fantastical, dream-like adventures focus on a young girl, her pet squid, and an octopus that has stolen her camera. The book is not easy to interpret, and like a dream it is clearly not a linear narrative. Teens and preteens will appreciate the unusual cast of monsters that contend with the anime heroine, who is diminutive but physically robust. *Ojingogo* was originally published as an Internet comic when Matthew Forsythe was living in South Korea teaching English. (Ages 12+.)

33. *Speechless = Sans Paroles = Sin Palabras: World History without Words.* By Polyp. (New Internationalist, 2009.) If the idea of storytelling without words is an artist's conceit, then the notion that you can collapse the whole of human history into a series of cartoons is vain beyond the pale. Still, the artist's whimsically ambitious project is irresistible because readers will want to see what he has included and consider what he has left out. The book provides much for readers to consider: images of the 9/11 attack on the World Trade Center, the Holocaust and Nazi Germany, the war for Iraqi oil, the Tiananmen Square protests, evolution, space travel, nuclear detonations, deforestation, colonization, and more convey a sense of world history from a left-leaning, environmentalist perspective. Teachers should encourage students to compare *Speechless* to conventional written histories. (Ages 12+.)

34. *The Man Who Grew His Beard.* By Olivier Schrauwen. (Fantagraphics Books, 2011.) Belgian cartoonist Olivier Schrauwen's spare-narration, seven-story comic collection is an almost inscrutable exploration of the worlds of strange, often isolated men. The first story, "Chromo Congo," is apparently a take on European colonialism, featuring three white hunters in Africa but omitting any Africans. Many of the illustrations are self-referential, showing characters with pens, pencils, or brushes, keeping readers thinking about the process of image creation rather than following actual stories. These absurdist comedic vignettes with titles such as "Hair Types" and "Outside/Inside" are absorbing combinations of fantasy and reality that will require several readings to discern an overarching theme or individual story lines. *The Man Who Grew His Beard* is Schrauwen's first graphic novel published in the United States. (Ages 12+.)

CHAPTER 31

Woodcut Novels

I have always held that the individual who "reads" a pictorial narrative should feel completely free to develop his own interpretation and end up with something that is right for him.

—Lynd Ward

1. *Mad Man's Drum: A Novel in Woodcuts.* By Lynd Ward. (Dover Publications, 2005.) Originally published in 1930, this complex pictorial narrative tells the story of a slave trader who steals a drum from an African he has murdered, with dire consequences for him and his family. Executed in 118 black-and-white wood engravings, the book exudes outrage over the social evil perpetrated by the rich trader who displays the demon-faced drum and the murder weapon in his mansion. When he tries to return to Africa, the man is lost at sea, but the drum's curse continues to haunt his bookish son, who becomes a scientist. Through despair, death, and insanity, the son and his family continue to atone for the grave injustice of slavery and murder. (Ages 12+.)

2. *Let That Bad Air Out: Buddy Bolden's Last Parade.* By Stefan Berg. (Porcupine's Quill, 2007.) Using linocut relief prints, this silent novel tells the tragic story of nineteenth-century jazz pioneer Buddy Bolden, known to jazz enthusiasts as the first bandleader to play this distinctly American brand of improvised music. The career of the New Orleans "first man of jazz" came to an end during a Labor Day parade, when a blood vessel erupted, causing a mental breakdown and leading to institutionalization for the rest of his life. Canadian artist Stefan Berg's first illustration-only graphic novel comprises seventy linocut images. His book is a tribute both to the legendary cornet player and to the unique musical culture of New Orleans. (Ages 12+.)

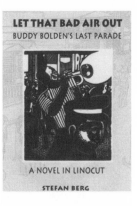

3. *He Done Her Wrong.* By Milt Gross. (Fantagraphics Books, 2005.) Originally published in 1930 by legendary cartoonist Milt Gross and abridged and re-issued in 1983 as *Heart of Gold*, *He Done Her Wrong* is one of the first graphic novels. The slapstick story is about a young lumberjack, a coonskin-cap-wearing bumpkin, who falls in love with a fair damsel, loses her to a perfidious rascal, locates the girl in the big city, and of course defeats the villain. Gross intended the book as a parody of Lynd Ward's popular *Gods' Man* (1929), suggesting that the woodcut novel was both melodramatic and pretentious, but *He Done Her Wrong* has gained the stature of a classic in its own right. Gross's cartoons have the feel of a silent film, due perhaps to Gross's involvement with the early film industry; he worked with Charlie Chaplin on the soundless classic *The Circus*. (Ages 12+.)

4. *Vertigo: A Novel in Woodcuts.* By Lynd Ward. (Dover Publications, 2009.) Originally published in the midst of the Great Depression, *Vertigo* is a stinging indictment of capitalism. This last and best of Lynd Ward's woodcut novels comprises three interconnected stories focusing on a young woman who aspires to be a great musician, a desperate young man who hopes to become a builder, and an ailing old industri-

alist whose company engages in brutal union busting. The stories underscore the tragedies of unemployment, poverty, and shattered dreams created by a corrupt economic system. Ward is considered one of the pre-eminent artists of the twentieth century. He earned a Caldecott Medal and Library of Congress Award, and an annual prize for the best graphic novel of the year is now given in his name. *Vertigo* is often considered Ward's greatest novel. (Ages 12+.)

5. *Destiny: A Novel in Pictures.* By Otto Nückel. (Dover Publications, 2012.) With its first English publication in 1930, *Destiny* contains seventeen short chapters that tell the unyieldingly grim story of a young woman whose life seems nothing more than a succession of tragedies. In over two hundred prints, the German illustrator chronicles the suffering of an unnamed woman whose poverty and misfortune lead her to parental abuse, birth out of wedlock, infanti-cide, murder, imprisonment, prostitution, and a vio-lent death. The story line is so wretched and melodra-matic that it borders on parody. *Destiny*, done in lead cuts rather than the more common woodcuts, is one of the world's first graphic novels. Otto Nückel is also known for his satirical political artwork published in *Der Simpl.* He became a painter and illustrator after dropping out of medical school. (Ages 14+.)

6. *Wild Pilgrimage: A Novel in Woodcuts.* By Lynd Ward. (Dover Publications, 2008.) In 105 stark images alternating between monochromatic blacks and reds, Lynd Ward's compelling narrative follows the existential torment of a factory worker raging against life in an unjust mass-industrial society. He seeks freedom in the forest, works for a farmer, and attempts to sexually assault the farmer's wife. He es-capes the husband's wrath, finding temporary refuge with a hermit, but then returns to the factory to start a worker rebellion. This anticapitalist morality tale shows the man witnessing a lynching scene. Lonely and struggling to the end, the protagonist is killed in a confrontation between police and striking laborers. Readers who wish to purchase all of Ward's wordless masterpieces will find them conveniently collected in *Six Novels in Woodcuts* (2010). (Ages 14+.)

7. *Book of Hours: A Wordless Novel Told in 99 Wood Engravings.* By George A. Walker. (Porcupine's Quill, 2010.) Award-winning wood engraver George A. Walker's tribute to the victims of the September 11, 2001, terrorist attacks depicts everyday life leading up to the tragedy. Walker aims to capture the routine lives of individuals unprepared for one of the most shocking events in US history. Innocent and on autopilot, people brush their teeth, drink coffee, answer phones, and wait in traffic, absorbed in mundane comfort and security, before their lives are abruptly ended with the destruction of the Twin Towers. Walker's intricate woodcuts are the perfect medium for freezing these moments in time, reminding us to savor our existence and live as if every day were our last. (Ages 12+.)

8. *Southern Cross: A Novel of the South Seas.* By Laurence Hyde. (Drawn and Quarterly, 2007.) First published in 1951, this replica of the original edition consists of 118 wood engravings conveying the British-Canadian artist's outrage over the US military's atomic bomb testing in the South Pacific following World War II. The peaceful lives of Polynesian islanders are irrevocably destroyed when they are forced from their homes prior to the blast. A native fisherman kills a drunken sailor who has tried to rape his wife and is forced to flee with her and his child into the jungle. The detonation produces environmental devastation, and the small family, not evacuated from the island, suffers a horrible death due to radiation poisoning. *Southern Cross* was Laurence Hyde's only wordless novel. (Ages 14+.)

9. *The City: A Vision in Woodcuts.* By Frans Masereel. (Dover Publications, 2006.) First published in 1925, *The City* is a compelling look at European urban existence in the time between the world wars. Presented in one hundred woodcuts, Frans Masereel's book might be characterized as a pictorial ethnography of the banalities, decadence, and occasional joys of everyday big-city life. This stark collection of black-and-white images is noteworthy not for telling a story but for providing a glimpse of the mood and atmosphere of the time. His numerous images of crowds, factories, and city streets seem comparable to the work of a documentary photographer. The Flemish artist's woodcut creations are among the earliest forerunners of the modern graphic novel. Masereel had a great influence on subsequent woodcut illustrators. (Ages 12+.)

10. *Prelude to a Million Years & Song without Words: Two Graphic Novels.* By Lynd Ward. (Dover Publications, 2010.) Originally published separately in 1933 and 1936, both novels reflect Lynd Ward's empathy for the plight of working people and the need to achieve social justice. In thirty pictures, *Prelude* tells the story of a sculptor who is focused on capturing in stone the beauty of an idealized woman. In one memorable scene, a military officer grips the alienated and despairing artist by the neck and forces him onto his knees to bow to the American flag. *Song without Words* uses only twenty-one images to narrate a tale about an expectant mother who is so concerned about the specter of fascism that she is unsure whether to bring her baby into such a world. The book has a helpful introduction by woodcut and comic historian David A. Beronä. (Ages 12+.)

11. *The Mysterious Death of Tom Thomson.* By George A. Walker. (Porcupine's Quill, 2012.) In 109 wood engravings, George A. Walker tells the story of landscape painter Tom Thomson's life, his contribution to Canadian art, and the curious circumstances of his death in 1917. As art critic Tom Smart states in the book's introduction, "Walker's engravings chart [Thomson's] life, relationships and journeys as he made a living as a commercial artist in early twentieth-century Toronto, a painter who found creative inspiration in the hinterland of lakes and forests." The iconic Canadian painter drowned while canoeing in Algonquin Park, leading to theories about the cause of his death, including murder and suicide. *The Mysterious Death of Tom Thomson* was nominated for several art and book design awards in Canada and Germany. (Ages 12+.)

12. *Passionate Journey: A Vision in Woodcuts.* By Frans Masereel. (Dover Publications, 2007.) *Passionate Journey*, the most popular of Frans Masereel's text-free novels, was first published in Switzerland in 1919. This influential precursor to the graphic novel is a primer in how to tell a story and show emotion without using words. Illustrated with black-and-white woodcut prints, the book delves into the life and loves of a prototypical young man living in a modern city. When he first arrives by train, he engages in the normal activities of life before traveling to Africa, China, and elsewhere. Upon his return, he is a changed man. The man eventually leaves the city for the solitude of the woods, a persistent theme among later woodcut artists. The most audacious picture in this seminal work shows the man urinating from the roof of a city building. *Passionate Journey* was first made available in the United States under the title *My Book of Hours* (1922). (Ages 14+.)

13. *White Collar: A Novel in Linocuts.* By Giacomo Patri. (Celestial Arts, 1975.) *White Collar* tells the story of a family's decline from comfort into poverty during the Great Depression. Giacomo Patri published the book with his wife in limited numbers prior to World War II to support the labor movement and unionization of white-collar workers. The monochromatic novel focuses on the life of an artist following the stock market crash of 1929; he is unable to find work, becoming homeless just as he finds out that his wife is pregnant. Patri was motivated to produce a wordless novel out of a desire to make his socialist message

accessible to a wider audience. The Italian-born artist also worked for the *San Francisco Chronicle* and operated his own art school for working people. (Ages 12+.)

14. *Walking Shadows: A Novel without Words.* By Neil Bousfield. (Manic D Press, 2010.) British artist Neil Bousfield's award-winning woodcut novel is about the bleak existence of a modern-day, working-class family that struggles with money, gambling, violence, alcohol, drugs, crime, and soul-numbing work. The people are stuck in an all-too-common destructive cycle learned in childhood and replicated in adulthood. Bousfield's labor-intensive drawings are extraordinarily detailed and beautifully rendered, even as the story conveys the ugly social realism of poverty and despair. Stylistically and politically, *Walking Shadows* is a continuation of the noble tradition of earlier woodcut novelists. Originally titled *The Cycle*, the book took two years to complete, with the artist hand-printing only a dozen copies on its first run. (Ages 12+.)

15. *The Sun / The Idea / Story without Words: Three Graphic Novels.* By Frans Masereel. (Dover Publications, 2009.) In *The Sun*, the legendary woodcut novelist uses sixty-three woodcuts to depict a man's resolute struggle to reach the sun. The story begins with Frans Masereel shown sitting at his desk and then dreaming of an Icarus figure going too near the sun and falling to earth in flames, landing on the artist's desk. In *The Idea*'s eighty-three woodcuts, Masereel pictures himself conjuring the idea of a naked woman in a sequence of images that is considered an allegory about the struggle between repression and artistic creation. Rich in romantic symbolism, *Story without Words* uses sixty wood engravings to show a man trying various strategies to gain the affections of a woman. He finally succeeds in getting her to love him but then pulls away, leaving her dejected. These novels were originally published in 1919 and 1920. (Ages 14+.)

CHAPTER 32

Special Interests

A man's interest in a single bluebird is worth more than a
complete but dry list of the fauna and flora of a town.

—Henry David Thoreau

Art

- *April Wilson's Magpie Magic: A Tale of Colorful Mischief.* By April Wilson.
- *Chalk.* By Bill Thomson.
- *Cool Cat.* By Nonny Hogrogian.
- *Draw!* By Raúl Colón.
- *Gods' Man.* By Lynd Ward.
- *Hanimals.* By Mario Mariotti.
- *Harold and the Purple Crayon.* By Crockett Johnson.
- *The Hero of Little Street.* By Gregory Rogers.
- *Journey.* By Aaron Becker.
- *The Line.* By Paula Bossio.
- *The Mysterious Death of Tom Thomson.* By George A. Walker.
- *Picturescape.* By Elisa Gutiérrez.
- *Polo and the Dragon.* By Regis Faller.
- *Quest.* By Aaron Becker.
- *The Red Thread.* By Tord Nygren.
- *Sector 7.* By David Wiesner.
- *Yam: Bite-Size Chunks.* By Corey Barba.
- *You Can't Take a Balloon into the Metropolitan Museum.* By Jacqueline Preiss Weitzman and Robin Preiss Glasser.
- *You Can't Take a Balloon into the Museum of Fine Arts.* By Jacqueline Preiss Weitzman and Robin Preiss Glasser.

Books

- *The Bored Book.* By David Michael Slater and Doug Keith.
- *Free Fall.* By David Wiesner.
- *If You Lived Here, You'd Be Home by Now.* By Ed Briant.
- *The Little Red Fish.* By Tae-Eun Yoo.
- *The Numbers.* By Monique Felix.
- *Polo: The Runaway Book.* By Regis Faller.
- *The Red Book.* By Barbara Lehman.
- *The Wind.* By Monique Felix.

Caldecott Awards and Honors

- *Alphabet City.* By Stephen T. Johnson.
- *A Ball for Daisy.* By Chris Raschka.

- *Blackout.* By John Rocco.
- *Color Zoo.* By Lois Ehlert.
- *Flora and the Flamingo.* By Molly Idle.
- *Flotsam.* By David Wiesner.
- *Free Fall.* By David Wiesner.
- *Freight Train.* By Donald Crews.
- *The Grey Lady and the Strawberry Snatcher.* By Molly Bang.
- *Journey.* By Aaron Becker.
- *The Lion & the Mouse.* By Jerry Pinkney.
- *Mr. Wuffles!* By David Wiesner.
- *My Friend Rabbit.* By Eric Rohmann.
- *No, David!* By David Shannon.
- *Noah's Ark.* By Peter Spier.
- *The Red Book.* By Barbara Lehman.
- *Sector 7.* By David Wiesner.
- *Time Flies.* By Eric Rohmann.
- *Truck.* By Donald Crews.
- *Tuesday.* By David Wiesner.
- *Yo! Yes?* By Chris Raschka.

Chase Scenes

- *The Boy, the Bear, the Baron, the Bard.* By Gregory Rogers.
- *Bye, Bye Birdie.* By Shirley Hughes.
- *Catch That Cat!* By Fernando Krahn.
- *The Chicken Thief.* By Beatrice Rodriguez.
- *The Chimp and the Clown.* By Ruth Carroll.
- *Coyote Run.* By Gaetan Dorémus.
- *Crocodile and Pierrot.* By Russell Hoban and Sylvie Selig.
- *The Great Cat Chase.* By Mercer Mayer.
- *The Great Escape.* By Philippe Dupasquier.
- *The Grey Lady and the Strawberry Snatcher.* By Molly Bang.
- *The Hero of Little Street.* By Gregory Rogers.
- *Hot on the Scent.* By Bente Bech and Peter Lind.
- *Jack Wants a Snack.* By Pat Schories.
- *Octopus Soup.* By Mercer Mayer.
- *Oink Oink.* By Arthur Geisert.
- *Once upon a Banana.* By Jennifer Armstrong and David Small.
- *Sunday Love.* By Alison Paul.
- *The Train.* By Witold Generowicz.

- *Where's Walrus?* By Stephen Savage.
- *Winterbird.* By Alfred Olschewski.

Circus and Clowns

- *The Adventures of Paddy Pork.* By John S. Goodall.
- *The Chimp and the Clown.* By Ruth Carroll.
- *Clown.* By Quentin Blake.
- *Crocodile and Pierrot.* By Russell Hoban and Sylvie Selig.
- *The Farmer and the Clown.* By Marla Frazee.
- *The Midnight Circus.* By Peter Collington.
- *Polo and the Magician!* By Regis Faller.
- *The Red Scarf.* By Anne Villeneuve.
- *Sidewalk Circus.* By Paul Fleischman and Kevin Hawkes.
- *Steam Park.* By Filippo Neri and Piero Ruggeri.

Cities

- *Alphabet City.* By Stephen T. Johnson.
- *Anno's Italy.* By Mitsumasa Anno.
- *The Arrival.* By Shaun Tan.
- *Beaver Is Lost.* By Elisha Cooper.
- *Blood Song: A Silent Ballad.* By Eric Drooker.
- *The Changing City.* By Jörg Müller.
- *Chicken and Cat.* By Sara Varon.
- *The City.* By Douglas Florian.
- *City by Numbers.* By Stephen T. Johnson.
- *Gods' Man.* By Lynd Ward.
- *Here I Am.* By Patti Kim and Sonia Sanchez.
- *Home.* By Jeannie Baker.
- *The Inside-Outside Book of New York City.* By Roxie Munro.
- *Is It Red? Is It Yellow? Is It Blue? An Adventure in Color.* By Tana Hoban.
- *Just in Passing.* By Susan Bonners.
- *Sidewalk Circus.* By Paul Fleischman and Kevin Hawkes.
- *The System.* By Peter Kuper.
- *Window.* By Jeannie Baker.
- *Wow! City!* By Robert Neubecker.
- *Yellow Umbrella.* By Jae-Soo Lui.
- *You Can't Take a Balloon into the Metropolitan Museum.* By Jacqueline Preiss Weitzman and Robin Preiss Glasser.

- *You Can't Take a Balloon into the Museum of Fine Arts*. By Jacqueline Preiss Weitzman and Robin Preiss Glasser.

Courage

- *Bluebird*. By Bob Staake.
- *The Boys*. By Jeff Newman.
- *The Giant Seed*. By Arthur Geisert.
- *Good Night, Garden Gnome*. By Jamichael Henterly.
- *A Growling Place*. By Thomas Aquinas Maguire.
- *Jacko*. By John S. Goodall.
- *Naughty Nancy Goes to School*. By John S. Goodall.
- *The Shadow*. By Donna Diamond.

Cultural Diversity

- *Anno's Italy*. By Mitsumasa Anno.
- *Anno's Journey*. By Mitsumasa Anno.
- *Anno's Spain*. By Mitsumasa Anno.
- *The Arrival*. By Shaun Tan.
- *Here I Am*. By Patti Kim and Sonia Sanchez.
- *Holland*. By Charlotte Dematons.
- *How Anansi Obtained the Sky God's Stories*. By Janice Skivington.
- *The Inside-Outside Book of Texas*. By Roxie Munro.
- *Mary Had a Little Lamb*. By Jonas Sickler.
- *Mirror*. By Jeannie Baker.
- *Ocean Whisper / Susurro del océano*. By Dennis Rockhill.
- *Polar Slumber / Sueño polar*. By Dennis Rockhill.
- *Unspoken: A Story from the Underground Railroad*. By Henry Cole.
- *Yo! Yes?* By Chris Raschka.
- *Yum! Yuck! A Foldout Book of People Sounds*. By Linda Sue Park, Julia Durango, and Sue Ramá.

Curiosity

- *The City*. By Douglas Florian.
- *Deep in the Forest*. By Brinton Turkle.
- *Flashlight*. By Lizi Boyd.

- *Flotsam*. By David Wiesner.
- *Mr. Wuffles!* By David Wiesner.
- *An Ocean World*. By Peter Sis.
- *School*. By Emily Arnold McCully.

Dinosaurs

- *Chalk*. By Bill Thomson.
- *Dinosaur!* By Peter Sis.
- *Fossil*. By Bill Thomson.
- *Gon*. By Masashi Tanaka.
- *Time Flies*. By Eric Rohmann.
- *Uh-oh!* By Mary Newell DePalma.

Drama

- *Age of Reptiles Omnibus*, Vol. 1. By Ricardo Delgado.
- *Blood Song: A Silent Ballad*. By Eric Drooker.
- *Cinema Panopticum*. By Thomas Ott.
- *Combustion: A Story without Words*. By Chris Lanier.
- *Dead End*. By Thomas Ott.
- *Greetings from Hellville*. By Thomas Ott.
- *House*. By Josh Simmons.
- *Metronome*. By Véronique Tanaka.
- *The Number: 73304-23-4153-6-96-8*. By Thomas Ott.
- *R.I.P.: Best of 1985–2004*. By Thomas Ott.
- *The Sanctuary*. By Nate Neal.
- *Southern Cross: A Novel of the South Seas*. By Laurence Hyde.
- *The System*. By Peter Kuper.

Extraterrestrial Beings

- *A.L.I.E.E.E.N.* By Lewis Trondheim.
- *Ben's Bunny Trouble*. By Daniel Wakeman and Dirk Van Stralen.
- *Flotsam*. By David Wiesner.
- *Higher! Higher!* By Leslie Patricelli.
- *Jack and the Night Visitors*. By Pat Schories.
- *Korgi Book 2: The Cosmic Collector*. By Christian Slade.

- *Lio: There's a Monster in My Socks.* By Mark Tatulli.
- *Mr. Wuffles!* By David Wiesner.
- *Polo: The Runaway Book.* By Regis Faller.
- *The World of Mamoko in the Year 3000.* By Aleksandra Mizielińska and Daniel Mizieliński.

Fables and Fairy Tales

- *Amanda and the Mysterious Carpet.* By Fernando Krahn.
- *Amanda's Butterfly.* By Nick Butterworth.
- *Anno's Journey.* By Mitsumasa Anno.
- *Creepy Castle.* By John S. Goodall.
- *Deep in the Forest.* By Brinton Turkle.
- *A Flying Saucer Full of Spaghetti.* By Fernando Krahn.
- *How Anansi Obtained the Sky God's Stories.* By Janice Skivington.
- *Hunters of the Great Forest.* By Dennis Nolan.
- *The Knight and the Dragon.* By Tomie DePaola.
- *Korgi Book 1: Sprouting Wings!* By Christian Slade.
- *Korgi Book 2: The Cosmic Collector.* By Christian Slade.
- *Korgi Book 3: A Hollow Beginning.* By Christian Slade.
- *The Lion & the Mouse.* By Jerry Pinkney.
- *Little Red Riding Hood.* By John S. Goodall.
- *Midsummer Knight.* By Gregory Rogers.
- *Polo: The Runaway Book.* By Regis Faller.
- *Puss in Boots.* By John S. Goodall.
- *Sea of Dreams.* By Dennis Nolan.
- *The Silver Pony: A Story in Pictures.* By Lynd Ward.
- *The Tooth Fairy.* By Peter Collington.
- *The Tortoise & the Hare.* By Jerry Pinkney.

Families

- *Alphabet House.* By Nancy Elizabeth Wallace.
- *The Bear and the Fly.* By Paula Winter.
- *Blackout.* By John Rocco.
- *Breakfast for Jack.* By Pat Schories.
- *Carl Makes a Scrapbook.* By Alexandra Day.
- *The Chicken's Child.* By Margaret A. Hartelius.
- *The Christmas We Moved to the Barn.* By Cooper Edens and Alexandra Day.

- *Coming Home.* By Greg Ruth.
- *Don't Look Now.* By Ed Briant.
- *Early Birdy Gets the Worm.* By Bruce Lansky and Bill Bolton.
- *An Edwardian Christmas.* By John S. Goodall.
- *An Edwardian Holiday.* By John S. Goodall.
- *Flood.* By Alvaro F. Villa.
- *Fox and Hen Together.* By Beatrice Rodriguez.
- *Have You Seen My Duckling?* By Nancy Tafuri.
- *He's My Jumbo!* By Claude K. Dubois.
- *Hug.* By Jez Alborough.
- *I Can't Sleep.* By Philippe Dupasquier.
- *Man's Work!* By Annie Kubler.
- *Mirror.* By Jeannie Baker.
- *Moonlight.* By Jan Ormerod.
- *New Baby.* By Emily Arnold McCully.
- *Our House on the Hill.* By Philippe Dupasquier.
- *Peter Spier's Christmas!* By Peter Spier.
- *Peter Spier's Rain.* By Peter Spier.
- *Picnic.* By Emily Arnold McCully.
- *Robot-Bot-Bot.* By Fernando Krahn.
- *Sea of Dreams.* By Dennis Nolan.
- *A Special Birthday.* By Symeon Shimin.
- *The Spring Hat.* By Madelaine Gill.
- *Sunshine.* By Jan Ormerod.
- *The Surprise Picnic.* By John S. Goodall.
- *Tall.* By Jez Alborough.
- *Thunderstorm.* By Arthur Geisert.
- *Waiting for Baby.* By Annie Kubler.
- *What Whiskers Did.* By Ruth Carroll.
- *The Zoo.* By Suzy Lee.

Famous Landmarks

- *Anno's Britain.* By Mitsumasa Anno.
- *Anno's Italy.* By Mitsumasa Anno.
- *Anno's Journey.* By Mitsumasa Anno.
- *Anno's Spain.* By Mitsumasa Anno.
- *Anno's U.S.A.* By Mitsumasa Anno.
- *Balloon Trip.* By Ronald Wegen.
- *The Boy, the Bear, the Baron, the Bard.* By Gregory Rogers.

- *Frere Jacques.* By Jonas Sickler.
- *The Inside-Outside Book of New York City.* By Roxie Munro.
- *The Inside-Outside Book of Texas.* By Roxie Munro.
- *Picturescape.* By Elisa Gutiérrez.
- *The Yellow Balloon.* By Charlotte Dematons.
- *You Can't Take a Balloon into the Metropolitan Museum.* By Jacqueline Preiss Weitzman and Robin Preiss Glasser.
- *You Can't Take a Balloon into the Museum of Fine Arts.* By Jacqueline Preiss Weitzman and Robin Preiss Glasser.

Food

- *Ben's Big Dig.* By Daniel Wakeman and Dirk Van Stralen.
- *A Birthday Wish.* By Ed Emberley.
- *Bow-Wow Orders Lunch.* By Mark Newgarden and Megan Montague Cash.
- *The Chicken's Child.* By Margaret A. Hartelius.
- *A Circle of Friends.* By Giora Carmi.
- *A Flying Saucer Full of Spaghetti.* By Fernando Krahn.
- *Foxly's Feast.* By Owen Davey.
- *Frere Jacques.* By Jonas Sickler.
- *Frog Goes to Dinner.* By Mercer Mayer.
- *Hot on the Scent.* By Bente Bech and Peter Lind.
- *Hunters of the Great Forest.* By Dennis Nolan.
- *Jack Wants a Snack.* By Pat Schories.
- *Letter Lunch.* By Elisa Gutiérrez.
- *Mister I.* By Lewis Trondheim.
- *The Night Riders.* By Matt Furie.
- *Oink.* By Arthur Geisert.
- *Oink Oink.* By Arthur Geisert.
- *Pancakes for Breakfast.* By Tomie DePaola.
- *Sunday Love.* By Alison Paul.
- *Yum! Yuck! A Foldout Book of People Sounds.* By Linda Sue Park, Julia Durango, and Sue Ramá.

Good Deeds

- *Amanda's Butterfly.* By Nick Butterworth.
- *The Boys.* By Jeff Newman.
- *Carl's Christmas.* By Alexandra Day.

- *The Christmas We Moved to the Barn.* By Cooper Edens and Alexandra Day.
- *A Circle of Friends.* By Giora Carmi.
- *Clown.* By Quentin Blake.
- *A Day, a Dog.* By Gabrielle Vincent.
- *Don't Forget Me, Santa Claus.* By Virginia Mayo.
- *The Farmer and the Clown.* By Marla Frazee.
- *The Flower Man: A Wordless Picture Book.* By Mark Ludy.
- *Fly, Little Bird.* By Tina Burke.
- *A Flying Saucer Full of Spaghetti.* By Fernando Krahn.
- *Four Hungry Kittens.* By Emily Arnold McCully.
- *Fox's Garden.* By Princesse Camcam.
- *The Girl and the Bicycle.* By Mark Pett.
- *Here Comes Alex Pumpernickel!* By Fernando Krahn.
- *The Lion and the Bird.* By Marianne Dubuc.
- *Little Bird.* By Germano Zullo and Albertine.
- *Out of the Blue.* By Alison Jay.
- *Owly: Flying Lessons.* By Andy Runton.
- *Owly: Just a Little Blue.* By Andy Runton.
- *Owly: A Time to Be Brave.* By Andy Runton.
- *Owly: The Way Home & The Bittersweet Summer.* By Andy Runton.
- *The Silver Pony: A Story in Pictures.* By Lynd Ward.
- *Sing, Pierrot, Sing: A Picture Book in Mime.* By Tomie DePaola.
- *South.* By Patrick McDonnell.
- *The Special String.* By Harald Bakken and Mischa Richter.
- *The Surprise.* By Sylvia van Ommen.
- *Unspoken: A Story from the Underground Railroad.* By Henry Cole.
- *The Wonder Ring: A Fantasy in Silhouette.* By Holden Wetherbee.

History

- *Anno's Britain.* By Mitsumasa Anno.
- *Anno's Flea Market.* By Mitsumasa Anno.
- *Anno's Italy.* By Mitsumasa Anno.
- *Anno's Journey.* By Mitsumasa Anno.
- *Anno's Spain.* By Mitsumasa Anno.
- *Anno's U.S.A.* By Mitsumasa Anno.
- *The Boy, the Bear, the Baron, the Bard.* By Gregory Rogers.
- *The Changing City.* By Jörg Müller.
- *The Changing Countryside.* By Jörg Müller.
- *An Edwardian Summer.* By John S. Goodall.

- *The Great War: July 1, 1916: The First Day of the Battle of the Somme: An Illustrated Panorama.* By Joe Sacco.
- *The Heartaches of a French Cat.* By Barbara McClintock.
- *Hot Air: The (Mostly) True Story of the First Hot-Air Balloon Ride.* By Marjorie Priceman.
- *Journey to the Moon.* By Erich Fuchs.
- *Lavinia's Cottage.* By John S. Goodall.
- *Let That Bad Air Out: Buddy Bolden's Last Parade.* By Stefan Berg.
- *The Middle Passage: White Ships / Black Cargo.* By Tom Feelings.
- *The Mysterious Death of Tom Thomson.* By George A. Walker.
- *Southern Cross: A Novel of the South Seas.* By Laurence Hyde.
- *Speechless = Sans Paroles = Sin Palabras: World History without Words.* By Polyp.
- *The Story of a Castle.* By John S. Goodall.
- *The Story of a Farm.* By John S. Goodall.
- *Unspoken: A Story from the Underground Railroad.* By Henry Cole.
- *Will's Mammoth.* By Rafe Martin and Stephen Gammell.
- *The Yellow Balloon.* By Charlotte Dematons.
- *You Can't Take a Balloon into the Museum of Fine Arts.* By Jacqueline Preiss Weitzman and Robin Preiss Glasser.

Machines

- *1, 2, 3 to the Zoo.* By Eric Carle.
- *Boat.* By Barbara Remington.
- *Dig, Drill, Dump, Fill.* By Tana Hoban.
- *Freight Train.* By Donald Crews.
- *Happy Halloween, Li'l Santa.* By Thierry Robin and Lewis Trondheim.
- *Hocus Pocus Takes the Train.* By Sylvie Desrosiers and Rémy Simard.
- *Hogwash.* By Arthur Geisert.
- *Journey to the Moon.* By Erich Fuchs.
- *Lights Out.* By Arthur Geisert.
- *Lola & Fred.* By Christoph Heuer.
- *Robot Dreams.* By Sara Varon.
- *Robot-Bot-Bot.* By Fernando Krahn.
- *Ship Ahoy!* By Peter Sis.
- *Snow Sounds: An Onomatopoeic Story.* By David A. Johnson.
- *The Train.* By Witold Generowicz.
- *Truck.* By Donald Crews.
- *Trucks Trucks Trucks.* By Peter Sis.

Magic

- *Animals Home Alone*. By Loes Riphagen.
- *Bluebird*. By Bob Staake.
- *Bubble Bubble*. By Mercer Mayer.
- *The Conductor*. By Laetitia Devernay.
- *The Flying Grandmother*. By Naomi Kojima.
- *Flying Jake*. By Lane Smith.
- *Full Moon Soup*. By Alastair Graham.
- *Harold and the Purple Crayon*. By Crockett Johnson.
- *Harry Potter and the Sorcerer's Stone: A Deluxe Pop-Up Book*. By J. K. Rowling and Jill Daniels.
- *Hocus Pocus*. By Sylvie Desrosiers and Rémy Simard.
- *Hocus Pocus Takes the Train*. By Sylvie Desrosiers and Rémy Simard.
- *How Santa Claus Had a Long and Difficult Journey Delivering His Presents*. By Fernando Krahn.
- *I See a Song*. By Eric Carle.
- *Jinchalo*. By Matthew Forsythe.
- *Little Bird*. By Germano Zullo and Albertine.
- *The Midnight Adventures of Kelly, Dot, and Esmeralda*. By John S. Goodall.
- *Ojingogo*. By Matthew Forsythe.
- *Polo and the Magician!* By Regis Faller.
- *Rooster's Revenge*. By Beatrice Rodriguez.
- *The Secret Box*. By Barbara Lehman.
- *Silent Night*. By Sandy Turner.
- *The Silver Pony: A Story in Pictures*. By Lynd Ward.
- *The Snowman*. By Raymond Briggs.
- *Three Little Dreams*. By Thomas Aquinas Maguire.
- *Trainstop*. By Barbara Lehman.
- *The Treasure Bath*. By Dan Andreasen.
- *Tuesday*. By David Wiesner.
- *Up and Up*. By Shirley Hughes.
- *Wings*. By Shinsuke Tanaka.
- *Wonder Bear*. By Tao Nyeu.
- *The Wonder Ring: A Fantasy in Silhouette*. By Holden Wetherbee.

Museums

- *The Hero of Little Street*. By Gregory Rogers.
- *Museum Trip*. By Barbara Lehman.

- *Picturescape*. By Elisa Gutiérrez.
- *Time Flies*. By Eric Rohmann.
- *You Can't Take a Balloon into the Metropolitan Museum*. By Jacqueline Preiss Weitzman and Robin Preiss Glasser.
- *You Can't Take a Balloon into the Museum of Fine Arts*. By Jacqueline Preiss Weitzman and Robin Preiss Glasser.

Persistence

- *Changes, Changes*. By Pat Hutchins.
- *Do You Want to Be My Friend?* By Eric Carle.
- *Flood*. By Alvaro F. Villa.
- *Hank Finds an Egg*. By Rebecca Dudley.
- *Ice*. By Arthur Geisert.
- *Lola & Fred*. By Christoph Heuer.
- *Mighty Mizzling Mouse and the Red Cabbage House*. By Friso Henstra.
- *Mister O*. By Lewis Trondheim.
- *Mouse Letters: A Very First Alphabet Book*. By Jim Arnosky.
- *The Tortoise & the Hare*. By Jerry Pinkney.

Play

- *Ball*. By Mary Sullivan.
- *A Ball for Daisy*. By Chris Raschka.
- *Beach Day*. By Helen Oxenbury.
- *Blackout*. By John Rocco.
- *A Boy, a Dog, and a Frog*. By Mercer Mayer.
- *Bubble Bubble*. By Mercer Mayer.
- *Carl's Afternoon in the Park*. By Alexandra Day.
- *Carl's Snowy Afternoon*. By Alexandra Day.
- *Carl's Summer Vacation*. By Alexandra Day.
- *Dancing Boy*. By Ronald Himler.
- *Dreams*. By Peter Spier.
- *Dylan's Day Out*. By Peter Catalanotto.
- *First Snow*. By Emily Arnold McCully.
- *Follow Carl!* By Alexandra Day.
- *The Happy Dog*. By Hideyuki Tanaka.
- *Hi Fly*. By Pat Ross and John C. Wallner.
- *Higher! Higher!* By Leslie Patricelli.

- *Island Dog.* By Rebecca Goodale.
- *Kitten for a Day.* By Ezra Jack Keats.
- *Leaf.* By Stephen Michael King.
- *The Line.* By Paula Bossio.
- *Mirror.* By Suzy Lee.
- *Mudkin.* By Stephen Gammell.
- *Peter Spier's Rain.* By Peter Spier.
- *Rainstorm.* By Barbara Lehman.
- *Red Hat.* By Lita Judge.
- *Red Sled.* By Lita Judge.
- *Rolling Downhill.* By Ruth Carroll.
- *Shadow.* By Suzy Lee.
- *The Snowman.* By Raymond Briggs.
- *The Spring Hat.* By Madelaine Gill.
- *The Tree House.* By Marije Tolman and Ronald Tolman.
- *Up to Ten and Down Again.* By Lisa Campbell Ernst.
- *What If?* By Laura Vaccaro Seeger.

Problem Solving

- *Abstract Alphabet: A Book of Animals.* By Paul Cox.
- *Arthur's Adventure in the Abandoned House.* By Fernando Krahn.
- *Boat.* By Barbara Remington.
- *The Boy and the Airplane.* By Mark Pett.
- *Carl Goes to Daycare.* By Alexandra Day.
- *Hippo! No, Rhino!* By Jeff Newman.
- *My Friend Rabbit.* By Eric Rohmann.
- *Tall.* By Jez Alborough.
- *What If?* By Laura Vaccaro Seeger.

Religion

- *Anno's Italy.* By Mitsumasa Anno.
- *Noah: A Wordless Picture Book.* By Mark Ludy.
- *Noah's Ark.* By Peter Spier.
- *Peter Spier's Christmas!* By Peter Spier.
- *A Small Miracle.* By Peter Collington.

School

- *Bedtime and New School.* By Anna Cunningham and Melanie Sharp.
- *Boom Boom.* By Sarvinder Naberhaus and Margaret Chodos-Irvine.
- *Carl Goes to Daycare.* By Alexandra Day.
- *Naughty Nancy Goes to School.* By John S. Goodall.
- *Peep!* By Kevin Luthardt.
- *School.* By Emily Arnold McCully.
- *The Secret Box.* By Barbara Lehman.
- *Sector 7.* By David Wiesner.
- *Yellow Umbrella.* By Jae-Soo Lui.

Science

- *Age of Reptiles Omnibus*, Vol. 1. By Ricardo Delgado.
- *The Apple and the Butterfly.* By Iela Mari and Enzo Mari.
- *In the Woods.* By Ermanno Cristini, Luigi Puricelli, and Renato Pegoraro.
- *Is It Rough? Is It Smooth? Is It Shiny?* By Tana Hoban.
- *Journey to the Moon.* By Erich Fuchs.
- *Looking Down.* By Steve Jenkins.
- *Sun's Up.* By Teryl Euvremer.
- *The Umbrella.* By Ingrid and Dieter Schubert.

Seasons and Weather

- *Boom Boom.* By Sarvinder Naberhaus and Margaret Chodos-Irvine.
- *Circle of Seasons.* By Gerda Muller.
- *Clementina's Cactus.* By Ezra Jack Keats.
- *Flood.* By Alvaro F. Villa.
- *The Girl and the Bicycle.* By Mark Pett.
- *Inside Outside.* By Lizi Boyd.
- *Mudkin.* By Stephen Gammell.
- *Our House on the Hill.* By Philippe Dupasquier.
- *Out of the Blue.* By Alison Jay.
- *Peter Spier's Rain.* By Peter Spier.
- *Rainstorm.* By Barbara Lehman.
- *Rainy Day Dream.* By Michael Chesworth.

- *Tabby: A Story in Pictures*. By Aliki.
- *Thunderstorm*. By Arthur Geisert.
- *The Umbrella*. By Ingrid and Dieter Schubert.
- *Un-brella*. By Scott E. Franson.
- *The Wind*. By Monique Felix.

Seek and Find

- *The 46 Little Men*. By Jan Mogensen.
- *Anno's Alphabet: An Adventure in Imagination*. By Mitsumasa Anno.
- *Anno's Animals*. By Mitsumasa Anno.
- *Anno's Britain*. By Mitsumasa Anno.
- *Anno's Flea Market*. By Mitsumasa Anno.
- *Anno's Italy*. By Mitsumasa Anno.
- *Anno's Journey*. By Mitsumasa Anno.
- *Anno's Spain*. By Mitsumasa Anno.
- *Anno's U.S.A.* By Mitsumasa Anno.
- *The Birthday Cake Mystery*. By Thé Tjong-Khing.
- *Find the Duck*. By Stephen Cartwright.
- *Have You Seen My Duckling?* By Nancy Tafuri.
- *Holland*. By Charlotte Dematons.
- *The Hunter and the Animals: A Wordless Picture Book*. By Tomie DePaola.
- *In the Woods*. By Ermanno Cristini, Luigi Puricelli, and Renato Pegoraro.
- *Invisible*. By Katja Kamm.
- *One, Two, Where's My Shoe?* By Tomi Ungerer.
- *Picture a Letter*. By Brad Sneed.
- *The Red Thread*. By Tord Nygren.
- *We Hide, You Seek*. By Jose Aruego and Ariane Dewey.
- *Welcome to Mamoko*. By Aleksandra Mizielińska and Daniel Mizieliński.
- *Where Is the Cake?* By Thé Tjong-Khing.
- *Where Is the Cake Now?* By Thé Tjong-Khing.
- *Where's Waldo? The Wonder Book*. By Martin Handford.
- *Where's Walrus?* By Stephen Savage.
- *The World of Mamoko in the Time of Dragons*. By Aleksandra Mizielińska and Daniel Mizieliński.
- *The World of Mamoko in the Year 3000*. By Aleksandra Mizielińska and Daniel Mizieliński.
- *The Yellow Balloon*. By Charlotte Dematons.

Shapes and Colors

- *Beach Ball.* By Peter Sis.
- *Blue Sea.* By Robert Kalan and Donald Crews.
- *Circles, Triangles, and Squares.* By Tana Hoban.
- *Color Zoo.* By Lois Ehlert.
- *The Colors.* By Monique Felix.
- *Freight Train.* By Donald Crews.
- *Is It Red? Is It Yellow? Is It Blue? An Adventure in Color.* By Tana Hoban.
- *My Very First Book of Shapes.* By Eric Carle.
- *Shadows and Reflections.* By Tana Hoban.
- *Shapes, Shapes, Shapes.* By Tana Hoban.
- *Snail, Where Are You?* By Tomi Ungerer.
- *So Many Circles, So Many Squares.* By Tana Hoban.
- *Spirals, Curves, Fanshapes & Lines.* By Tana Hoban.

Snow

- *Carl's Snowy Afternoon.* By Alexandra Day.
- *First Snow.* By Emily Arnold McCully.
- *Ice.* By Arthur Geisert.
- *The Lion and the Bird.* By Marianne Dubuc.
- *One Scary Night.* By Antoine Guilloppé.
- *Polar Slumber / Sueño polar.* By Dennis Rockhill.
- *Polo and the Dragon.* By Regis Faller.
- *The Red Book.* By Barbara Lehman.
- *Red Sled.* By Lita Judge.
- *The Self-Made Snowman.* By Fernando Krahn.
- *Small, Medium & Large.* By Jane Monroe Donovan.
- *Snow Day.* By Daniel Peddle.
- *Snow Sounds: An Onomatopoeic Story.* By David A. Johnson.
- *The Snowman.* By Raymond Briggs.
- *The Snowy Path: A Christmas Journey.* By Lark Carrier.
- *Will's Mammoth.* By Rafe Martin and Stephen Gammell.
- *Winterbird.* By Alfred Olschewski.

Strange Worlds

- *Adventures of a Japanese Businessman*. By José Domingo, Isabel Mancebo, Alex Spiro, and Sam Arthur.
- *The Adventures of Polo*. By Regis Faller.
- *Almost Silent*. By Jason.
- *Bow-Wow Bugs a Bug*. By Mark Newgarden and Megan Montague Cash.
- *Bow-Wow's Nightmare Neighbors*. By Mark Newgarden and Megan Montague Cash.
- *Congress of the Animals*. By Jim Woodring.
- *Fox Bunny Funny*. By Andy Hartzell.
- *Fran*. By Jim Woodring.
- *The Frank Book*. By Jim Woodring.
- *H Day*. By Renée French.
- *I'm Not a Plastic Bag*. By Rachel Hope Allison.
- *Jinchalo*. By Matthew Forsythe.
- *Korgi Book 1: Sprouting Wings!* By Christian Slade.
- *Korgi Book 2: The Cosmic Collector*. By Christian Slade.
- *Korgi Book 3: A Hollow Beginning*. By Christian Slade.
- *Monsters! and Other Stories*. By Gustavo Duarte.
- *Polo and Lily*. By Regis Faller.
- *Polo and the Dragon*. By Regis Faller.
- *Polo and the Magic Flute*. By Regis Faller.
- *Sticks and Stones*. By Peter Kuper.
- *Weathercraft*. By Jim Woodring.

Theft

- *The Angel and the Soldier Boy*. By Peter Collington.
- *Arthur's Adventure in the Abandoned House*. By Fernando Krahn.
- *The Birthday Cake Mystery*. By Thé Tjong-Khing.
- *Bobo's Dream*. By Martha Alexander.
- *Bow-Wow's Nightmare Neighbors*. By Mark Newgarden and Megan Montague Cash.
- *Crocodile and Pierrot*. By Russell Hoban and Sylvie Selig.
- *The Flying Grandmother*. By Naomi Kojima.
- *The Grey Lady and the Strawberry Snatcher*. By Molly Bang.
- *He's My Jumbo!* By Claude K. Dubois.
- *Jack and the Missing Piece*. By Pat Schories.
- *Paddy's New Hat*. By John S. Goodall.

- *Red Hat.* By Lita Judge.
- *Shrewbettina Goes to Work.* By John S. Goodall.
- *Shrewbettina's Birthday.* By John S. Goodall.
- *The Train.* By Witold Generowicz.
- *Where Is the Cake?* By Thé Tjong-Khing.
- *Where Is the Cake Now?* By Thé Tjong-Khing.

Time Travel

- *The Boy, the Bear, the Baron, the Bard.* By Gregory Rogers.
- *Dinosaur!* By Peter Sis.
- *The Hero of Little Street.* By Gregory Rogers.
- *The Secret Box.* By Barbara Lehman.
- *Time Flies.* By Eric Rohmann.
- *The World of Mamoko in the Time of Dragons.* By Aleksandra Mizielińska and Daniel Mizieliński.
- *The World of Mamoko in the Year 3000.* By Aleksandra Mizielińska and Daniel Mizieliński.
- *The Yellow Balloon.* By Charlotte Dematons.

Toys

- *The Angel and the Soldier Boy.* By Peter Collington.
- *The Boy and the Airplane.* By Mark Pett.
- *Changes, Changes.* By Pat Hutchins.
- *The Christmas Gift.* By Emily Arnold McCully.
- *Clown.* By Quentin Blake.
- *He's My Jumbo!* By Claude K. Dubois.
- *Hocus Pocus Takes the Train.* By Sylvie Desrosiers and Rémy Simard.
- *How Santa Claus Had a Long and Difficult Journey Delivering His Presents.* By Fernando Krahn.
- *Jack and the Missing Piece.* By Pat Schories.
- *Li'l Santa.* By Thierry Robin and Lewis Trondheim.
- *The Midnight Adventures of Kelly, Dot, and Esmeralda.* By John S. Goodall.
- *The Midnight Circus.* By Peter Collington.
- *Mine!* By Shutta Crum and Patrice Barton.
- *Muffel and Plums.* By Lilo Fromm.
- *My Friend Rabbit.* By Eric Rohmann.
- *REM: Rapid Eye Movement.* By Istvan Banyai.

- *Trucks Trucks Trucks*. By Peter Sis.
- *Where's My Monkey?* By Dieter Schubert.

Work and Business

- *Anno's Flea Market*. By Mitsumasa Anno.
- *Chicken and Cat Clean Up*. By Sara Varon.
- *The Girl and the Bicycle*. By Mark Pett.
- *Happy Halloween, Li'l Santa*. By Thierry Robin and Lewis Trondheim.
- *Inside Outside*. By Lizi Boyd.
- *Man's Work!* By Annie Kubler.
- *Mighty Mizzling Mouse and the Red Cabbage House*. By Friso Henstra.
- *Mirror*. By Jeannie Baker.
- *No Dogs Allowed!* By Linda Ashman and Kristin Sorra.
- *Paddy Pork: Odd Jobs*. By John S. Goodall.
- *Snow Sounds: An Onomatopoeic Story*. By David A. Johnson.
- *Sun's Up*. By Teryl Euvremer.

Zoo

- *Color Zoo*. By Lois Ehlert.
- *Good Night, Gorilla*. By Peggy Rathmann.
- *Hippo! No, Rhino!* By Jeff Newman.
- *Welcome to the Zoo*. By Alison Jay.
- *Where's Walrus?* By Stephen Savage.
- *The Zoo*. By Suzy Lee.

CHAPTER 33

24 Wordless Book Artists You Should Know

Fairy tales are more than true: not because they tell us that dragons exist, but because they tell us that dragons can be beaten.

—G. K. Chesterton

Wonderfully Wordless: The 500 Most Recommended Graphic Novels and Picture Books is a uniquely authoritative best-book guide that aggregates the views of an extraordinary cross section of literary, journalistic, and library expertise from around the world. The five hundred books that emerge from this composite of opinion are in a class by themselves, but the works of some author-illustrators in this elite collection are so compelling or their output has been so prolific that they demand more recognition. What follows are sketches of twenty-four individuals, briefly touching upon their educations, careers, and awards. The artists are listed alphabetically, with each profile beginning with those works cited among the five hundred most recommended reads.

Courtesy of Mikoto Takahashi.

MITSUMASA ANNO (B. 1926)

Topsy-Turvies: Pictures to Stretch the Imagination (1970)
Anno's Alphabet: An Adventure in Imagination (1975)
Anno's Counting Book (1977)
Anno's Animals (1979)
Anno's Italy (1980)
Anno's Counting House (1982)

243

Anno's Britain (1982)
Anno's U.S.A. (1983)
Anno's Flea Market (1984)
Anno's Journey (1997)
Anno's Spain (2004)

Mitsumasa Anno is an internationally acclaimed artist best known for his children's books with drawings that are intricately detailed; densely populated; rich in mathematical, scientific, and cultural knowledge; and rife with subtle visual humor. He grew up in a small town in Japan and was drafted into the Japanese army during World War II. Following the war, Anno attended the Yamaguchi Teacher Training College and taught mathematics to elementary students for ten years before he started creating children's books.

His first book, *Topsy-Turvies: Pictures to Stretch the Imagination*, first published in Japan in 1968, explores visual perspective. Anno established himself as a world-class artist with his series of illustration-only "Journey" books beginning with *Anno's Journey*, first released in 1977, and continuing with similar titles focused on various foreign cultures. In these travelogues, a small figure journeys through a country's landscape visiting sites of artistic, cultural, and historical significance. *Anno's Journey* was based on a trip that Anno made in the 1960s through Scandinavia, Germany, and England. Anno's picture books have a universal appeal, accomplishing the extraordinary task of capturing the complexity of a range of many different societies and imparting an impressive store of historical and cultural knowledge, without the use of language.

Anno has received many awards for his work, including the international Hans Christian Andersen Medal for his lasting contribution to children's literature and Japan's Person of Cultural Merit Award for enriching his country's cultural life. In the United States, he has been recognized through the Boston Globe–Horn Book Awards, the New York Times Best Book of the Year citations, and the American Library Association Notable Book honors.

AARON BECKER (B. 1974)

Journey (2013)
Quest (2014)

Few contemporary book artists have had such suddenly ascending careers as Aaron Becker. His first picture book, *Journey*, earned Caldecott Honors in 2014 and was named by the *New York Times* as one of the best-illustrated books, leading the newspaper to ask him to illustrate the cover of its prestigious Book

Review section. *Journey* got another boost when it was among a few books purchased by President Barack Obama in a much publicized bookstore visit with his daughters, and it has already been named to *Time* magazine's list of the hundred best children's books of all time. *Quest*, Becker's second book in a planned trilogy, has received even more glowing reviews than his debut volume.

While Becker nurtured an early passion for image making, he somehow managed to graduate from Baltimore City College High School as its valedictorian without taking a single art class. He attended Pomona College in Claremont, California, intending to major in international relations and move to Japan, but realized that his true calling was in art. He attended the Art Center in Pasadena for the first two terms of its eight-term program, leaving when an opportunity to work in the film industry arose. He worked on several films, including an adaptation of Chris Van Allsburg's *The Polar Express* (1985). Becker then moved to Amherst, Massachusetts, where he started working part-time on *Journey* and doing freelance work until Disney shut down the studio where he worked. Undaunted, Becker turned this layoff into an opportunity by moving with his wife and child to the southern coast of Spain to complete work on his book.

Becker credits the drawing books of Ed Emberley—himself a creator of wordless picture books—as the single greatest influence on the development of his craft. The next book in the *Journey* trilogy will be *Return*.

Courtesy of Peter Collington.

PETER COLLINGTON (B. 1948)

Little Pickle (1986)
The Angel and the Soldier Boy (1987)
The Midnight Circus (1992)
The Tooth Fairy (1995)
A Small Miracle (2011)

Praised by the *Chicago Tribune* as a "master of wordless picture books," Peter Collington was raised on the south coast of England by a father who was a draftsman and a mother who worked as a social worker. He developed an interest in art at an early age and studied photography for three years at the Bournemouth College of Art before turning his attention to painting and drawing while in his early twenties. He now lives in Dorset, England, but has also resided in New York, London, and Madison, Wisconsin.

Collington's first book, *Little Pickle*, illustrated over a span of nine months, was based on his young daughter Sasha. He got the idea for the book from her reactions to drawings he did for her amusement. The book was shortlisted for England's prestigious Mother Goose Award. Collington's other work has also been critically recognized, with *The Angel and the Soldier Boy* (1987), *On Christmas Eve* (1990), and *The Tooth Fairy* (1995) all being shortlisted for the Nestlé Smarties Book Prize. Italy's Bologna Children's Book Fair, one of the leading professional fairs of its kind in the world, honored *The Coming of Surfman* (1994).

Although not widely recommended in the United States, *On Christmas Eve* is one of Collington's most noteworthy wordless titles. It describes Santa Claus's journey to get presents to all children on Christmas Eve, even those without chimneys. Collington is also author of *My Darling Kitten* (1988) and *Clever Cat* (2000).

Courtesy of Sandra Darling.

ALEXANDRA DAY (B. 1941)

Carl's Christmas (1990)
Carl's Afternoon in the Park (1991)
Carl Goes Shopping (1992)
Carl's Masquerade (1992)
Carl Goes to Daycare (1993)
Carl Makes a Scrapbook (1994)
Good Dog, Carl (1996)
Carl's Birthday (1997)
The Christmas We Moved to the Barn (1997)
Follow Carl! (1998)
Carl's Summer Vacation (2008)
Carl's Snowy Afternoon (2009)

Alexandra Day, pseudonym for Sandra Louise Woodward Darling, is the well-known creator of Carl the Rottweiler series, a founder of Green Tiger Press, and owner of Laughing Elephant, a publisher and producer of greeting cards, stationery, and vintage paper products located in an old nunnery in Seattle, Washington.

The daughter of a painter, Day grew up in a creative environment well stocked with art supplies and books that were critical to her later development. After majoring in English literature at Swarthmore College, Day took art classes in New York City and worked as a crafts teacher.

When she and her husband Harold Darling were on a trip to Switzerland, they came across an old story about a poodle and a baby who instead of napping played with her dog, which became the core idea of her very successful Carl books. Day modeled Carl after her pet Rottweiler and fashioned the baby after her granddaughter, Madeleine. In almost all the Carl books, Day makes the lovable dog responsible for babysitting Madeleine. When the girl should be taking a nap, she and her canine accomplice get into all kinds of mischief.

Day has illustrated many other books besides the Carl series, most notably her first book, *The Teddy Bears' Picnic* (1983), based on a popular song, and three titles featuring a bear named Frank and an elephant named Ernest. In her first book about this comic duo, *Frank and Ernest* (1988), they learn how to run a diner.

This artist and entrepreneur has received a Children's Choice Award from the International Reading Association and a lifetime achievement award from the Pacific Northwest Booksellers Association. She has also been recognized by the Bologna Children's Book Fair.

Day will publish at least two more Carl titles, *Carl and the Lost Kitten* (2015) and *Carl's Halloween* (2015).

Courtesy of Eric Drooker.

ERIC DROOKER (B. 1958)

Flood! A Novel in Pictures (1992)
Blood Song: A Silent Ballad (2009)

Eric Drooker is a political activist, painter, graphic novelist, street artist, and regular cover artist for the *New Yorker*. His work can be seen in the *Village Voice*, the *Nation*, the *Progressive*, the *Guardian*, and the *New York Times*.

A lifelong resident of New York City, he attended the Downtown Community School in Manhattan's East Village and graduated from the fine arts department of Cooper Union, where he studied sculpture. He has been influenced by the work of the early twentieth-century woodcut artists and by the underground comics.

Drooker designed the animation for the film *Howl* (2010) and illustrated *Howl: A Graphic Novel* (2010), both projects based Allen Ginsberg's epic countercultural poem, which rages against the materialism, conformity, and dehumanization of American society. Drooker also collaborated with the Beat generation icon in *Illuminated Poems* (1996).

Drooker's *Flood! A Novel in Pictures* received the American Book Award and was an editor's pick for the *New York Times*. The Library of Congress acquired the book's artwork to become part of its public prints collection. While it has not received such formal recognition, *Blood Song: A Silent Ballad* is one of the most widely respected wordless graphic novels.

Drooker's paintings are part of many collections, although he disdains identification with the mainstream art establishment. His artwork has been used on album covers for Rage against the Machine and other rock bands. Underscoring his identity as a political provocateur, Drooker has also published *Slingshot: 32 Postcards* (2008) and *Street Posters and Ballads* (1998), chronicling some of his contributions to New York City's political protests and uprisings.

Courtesy of Enchanted Lion Books.

ARTHUR GEISERT (B. 1941)

Oink (1991)
Oink Oink (1993)
Lights Out (2005)
Hogwash (2008)
Ice (2011)
The Giant Seed (2012)
Thunderstorm (2013)

Although he has distinguished himself by drawing pigs and farms, Arthur Geisert claims never to have actually seen a pig until he was an adult. Although he grew up in Los Angeles, he now resides in a little farm village in Iowa and lives on the main street in a building that was once a bank. His bedroom is in the bank vault. When the award-winning artist launched *Thunderstorm*, he had a daylong book party in a bar across the street from his converted bank home, which was covered by National Public Radio. Hundreds of people showed up to obtain signed copies of the book.

Geisert's artistic method is even more distinctive than his approach to book promotion. He creates his picture books with a complex etching process that takes several months to complete. He scratches through wax on copper plates, which requires multiple soakings in acid baths. After the plates are inked and rolled onto heavy paper, he hand colors them. Over a career of more than thirty years, this laborious process has permitted him to produce about one book per year. His first book, *Pa's Balloon and Other Pig Tales* (1984), contained three short stories about a porcine family.

Geisert received an undergraduate degree in teaching and was trained to etch at the Otis Art Institute in Los Angeles. He also holds a master's from the University of California and an honorary doctorate from Concordia University. Geisert gives lectures at universities, and his work is exhibited in museum collections. His books have received Parents' Choice and Boston Globe–Horn Book awards, and the *New York Times* has often named Geisert's work to its annual lists of best-illustrated books.

JOHN S. GOODALL (1908–1996)

The Adventures of Paddy Pork (1968)
Jacko (1972)
Paddy Pork's Holiday (1973)
Creepy Castle (1975)
The Surprise Picnic (1977)
An Edwardian Holiday (1979)
An Edwardian Summer (1979)
Paddy's New Hat (1980)
An Edwardian Christmas (1981)
Shrewbettina Goes to Work (1981)
Lavinia's Cottage (1983)
Paddy Pork: Odd Jobs (1983)
Paddy Under Water (1984)
Naughty Nancy Goes to School (1985)
The Story of a Castle (1986)
Little Red Riding Hood (1988)
The Story of a Farm (1989)
Puss in Boots (1990)
Shrewbettina's Birthday (1998)
The Midnight Adventures of Kelly, Dot, and Esmeralda (1999)
Naughty Nancy (1999)

While plenty of artists have, over the years, committed themselves to producing wordless and almost wordless books, John S. Goodall emerges as the genre's most prolific master and its most resolute purist.

Goodall was immersed in Victorian art and culture in the Royal Academy Schools, Britain's first and most prestigious art school, established by King George III in 1768. During the 1930s Goodall worked as a magazine illustrator, and he was stationed in India during World War II. He was married and was a constant presence and caregiver to his wife, Margaret, who beginning in 1970 was ill and bedridden. For many years, Goodall worked by her bedside, leading a secluded life in a country cottage such as those pictured in several of his books.

The artist consistently drew Victorian and Edwardian scenes featuring the British upper classes. The books radiate nostalgia for an idealized aristocracy and seem to reflect the zeitgeist of the Margaret Thatcher era. Goodall's style was distinctive in his use of a small-book format and the technique of alternating half and full pages. He was considered one of England's best watercolorists and a kind of social historian. Many of his titles, including *Great Days of a Country House* (1992), are an education in the elegance and manners of privileged British society.

The Adventures of Paddy Pork won the Boston Globe–Horn Book Award, while the *New York Times* selected *The Surprise Picnic* as one the best illustrated children's books of the year.

TANA HOBAN (1917–2006)

Circles, Triangles, and Squares (1974)
Dig, Drill, Dump, Fill (1975)
Take Another Look (1981)
I Read Symbols (1983)
Is It Rough? Is It Smooth? Is It Shiny? (1984)
Is It Larger? Is It Smaller? (1985)
Shapes, Shapes, Shapes (1986)
Dots, Spots, Speckles, and Stripes (1987)
Is It Red? Is It Yellow? Is It Blue? An Adventure in Color (1987)
Look! Look! Look! (1988)
Of Colors and Things (1989)
Exactly the Opposite (1990)
Shadows and Reflections (1990)
Spirals, Curves, Fanshapes & Lines (1992)
What Is That? (1994)
Who Are They? (1994)
So Many Circles, So Many Squares (1998)
Over, Under & Through (2008)

Tana Hoban had an accomplished career as a photographer beginning in the 1940s before publishing her first children's book at age fifty-three. She went on to publish scores of titles and established herself as the foremost creator of photography concept books for young children.

Featuring everyday scenes, her books usually have few or no words and occasionally have cutout pages that revealed only a portion of a photograph, inviting children to guess the object before turning the page to view it in full.

Tana Hoban was born in Philadelphia, attended the public schools outside the city in Lansdale, Pennsylvania, and graduated from the School of Design for Women, now the Moore College of Art and Design.

Early in her career, Hoban was considered one of the top women photographers in America. Her work was exhibited at the Museum of Modern Art alongside the photographs of such legendary masters as Margaret Bourke-White and Dorothea Lange. Hoban's work was represented in the historic exhibition "The Family of Man" curated by Edward Steichen, her photos appeared in *Look*, *Life*, *McCall's*, and other major magazines, and she did advertising photos.

In the late 1960s, Hoban was a photography instructor at the University of Pennsylvania, and in the 1980s she moved to Paris, where she lived for over twenty years. She received many accolades, including notable book recognitions from the American Library Association, Boston Globe–Horn Book awards and honors, and a lifetime achievement award from the American Society of Media Photographers.

Courtesy of the Krahn family.

FERNANDO KRAHN (1935–2010)

A Flying Saucer Full of Spaghetti (1970)
April Fools (1974)
The Self-Made Snowman (1974)
Who's Seen the Scissors? (1975)
Catch That Cat! (1978)
Robot-Bot-Bot (1979)
Arthur's Adventure in the Abandoned House (1981)
Here Comes Alex Pumpernickel! (1981)
The Creepy Thing (1982)
Amanda and the Mysterious Carpet (1985)
How Santa Claus Had a Long and Difficult Journey Delivering His Presents (1988)

Born in Santiago, Chile, Fernando Krahn was internationally known as a political caricaturist whose work appeared in many magazines and newspapers. He was recognized as a distinguished writer and illustrator of humorous children's books and celebrated as one of the pioneers of wordless books. His cartoons appeared in *Esquire*, the *New Yorker*, the *Atlantic Monthy*, *El país*, *Die Zeit*, *La repubblica*, *La vanguardia*, and the *International Herald Tribune*. Dozens of his books have been published in the United States and Spain.

Krahn's father was a lawyer and urged him to study law, which he did before turning his attention to drawing. In the early 1960s, he moved to New York to become a professional cartoonist, returning to his homeland in 1971. After the 1973 Chilean coup d'état, Krahn was forced to flee the country to avoid persecution, moving to Barcelona, Spain. Backed by the United States, the coup overthrew socialist president Salvador Allende, replacing him with a right-wing military junta. Thousands of leftists such as Krahn were arrested by the military in the years following the coup.

In 2001, he received the SM Ediciones International Illustration Prize and numerous awards and honors. Although popular in the United States, his work has not been given the critical recognition it deserves.

Photo by Holly Kuper.

PETER KUPER (B. 1958)

Speechless (2001)
Sticks and Stones (2004)
The System (2014)

Peter Kuper is an alternate cartoonist, writer, graphic novelist, political activist, and instructor at Harvard University and New York's School of Visual Arts. He attended Cleveland Heights High School and Kent State University before moving to New York, where he took classes at the Art Students League and the Pratt Institute. Kuper is best known for drawing *Mad* magazine's *Spy vs. Spy* comic.

Kuper has extensive experience residing in and traveling to different parts of the world. He lived in both Israel and Mexico and documented some of his travels in *ComicsTrips: A Journal of Travels through Africa and Southeast Asia* (1992).

A cofounder and editorial board member of graphics magazine *World War 3*, he has illustrated covers for *Time* and *Newsweek* and created the first comic strip ever to regularly appear in the *New York Times*. Kuper has illustrated adaptations of Franz Kafka's *The Metamorphosis* (2003) and Upton Sinclair's *The Jungle* (2004). His graphic novel *Sticks and Stones* won the New York Society of Illustrators Gold Medal. The Society of Newspaper Designers has honored him.

His *Stop Forgetting to Remember: The Autobiography of Walter Kurtz* (2007) is roughly Kuper's autobiography. Kuper's *Drawn to New York: An Illustrated Chronicle of Three Decades in New York City* (2013) is a personal tribute to the city, capturing its energy and recent history using different media. Fellow artist and activist Eric Drooker wrote the book's introduction.

SUZY LEE (B. 1974)

The Zoo (2007)
Wave (2008)
Mirror (2010)
Shadow (2010)

Courtesy of Suzy Lee.

It would be difficult to find a current book artist who is more internationally respected and critically acclaimed than South Korean artist Suzy Lee.

She earned an MA in book arts from London's Camberwell College of Arts and received a BFA in painting from Seoul National University.

This well-traveled speaker has lectured at professional conferences in Guadalajara, Mexico; Shanghai, China; Washington, DC; Bologna, Italy; and Mumbai, India. She has participated in workshops in Japan, Brazil, the Republic of Singapore, and her home country of South Korea. Lee's work has been exhibited in Germany, Portugal, Great Britain, the United States, France, and South Korea.

Lee's *Open This Little Book* (2014) was selected as one of the best books of the year by the Bank Street College of Education and has earned awards from Boston Globe–Horn Book and the Philadelphia Touch Museum. The *New York Times* selected both *Shadow* and *Wave* as best-illustrated books of the year; the latter title was also designated as a best book by *Kirkus Reviews, Publishers Weekly, School Library Journal,* and the Society of Illustrators. The National Council of Teachers of English placed both *Wave* and *The Zoo* on its annual notable books list. The United States National Book Festival selected Lee as its official poster artist in 2013.

BARBARA LEHMAN (B. 1963)

The Red Book (2004)
Museum Trip (2006)
Rainstorm (2007)
Trainstop (2008)
The Secret Box (2011)

Courtesy of Barbara Lehman and Houghton Mifflin Harcourt.

Barbara Lehman, an award-winning artist and commercial illustrator who grew up in New Jersey, learned to draw at an early age. Her father was an artist who hung his drawings over her crib, and she benefited from living close enough to New York City to visit its art museums.

Many of the inspirations for her books come from childhood memories. She earned a BFA in illustration from New York City's Pratt Institute.

Lehman has worked as an animator and graphic designer and has experience in an assortment of odd jobs, including window designer, movie theater ticket seller, ice-cream server, lifeguard, house painter, and jewelry maker.

The Red Book won Caldecott Honors and was designated a notable book by the American Library Association. *Museum Trip* was named a best book of the year by the Cooperative Children's Book Center at the University of Wisconsin, Madison. *Rainstorm* was one of *Kirkus Reviews* best children's books of the year. *Trainstop* garnered a Parents' Choice Award and best book of the year designation from the Bank Street College of Education. *The Secret Box* was a Junior Library Guild Selection and a *Kirkus Reviews* best children's book selection.

Lehman's work has been shown at the New York Public Library, the Society of Illustrators, the Chicago Art Institute, the Whitney Museum of American Art, and the Eric Carle Museum of Picture Book Art.

FRANS MASEREEL (1889–1972)

The City: A Vision in Woodcuts (2006)
Passionate Journey: A Vision in Woodcuts (2007)
The Sun / The Idea / Story without Words: Three Graphic Novels (2009)

Courtesy of the Frans-Masereel-Foundation.

Frans Masereel, generally regarded as the most influential woodcut artist of the twentieth century, was one of the earliest pioneers of the wordless graphic novel. Born in Belgium and educated at the Ghent Academy of Fine Art, Masereel worked mostly in France but also lived for a while in Switzerland and Germany.

He was a fervent humanist, pacifist, and antifascist critic whose work was burned and banned from German museums when the Nazis took power. Although he contributed to many left-wing publications, he eschewed political labels, preferring to think of himself as a foe of all forms of exploitation and oppression. His books were noteworthy for their bold depictions of nudity, prostitutes, and sexual activity.

The esteemed painter and woodcut artist was a member of the Belgian Royal Academy of the Sciences, Literature and the Fine Arts and the Academy of Fine Arts in East Berlin, and he has been the subject of several books, exhibitions, and research centers. The Frans Masereel Centrum in Belgium encourages graphic artistry by hosting exhibitions and offering residencies and workspace to artists, designers, and critics. Germany's Frans Masereel Foundation provides an

Internet portal with information on the artist's life and works. There is even a progressive Flemish cultural organization named after Masereel.

Masereel produced over fifty wordless books in his lifetime. *Passionate Journey: A Vision in Woodcuts* is usually considered his greatest work. Some of his other seminal wordless novels are *Danse macabre* (1942), *Route des hommes* (2006), and *The Passion of Man*, which is represented in the important collection *Graphic Witness: Four Wordless Graphic Novels* (2007), including works by Frans Masereel, Lynd Ward, Giacomo Patri, and Laurence Hyde.

Masereel exerted a strong influence on the American art community, particularly on Lynd Ward, Art Spiegelman, and Eric Drooker.

Courtesy of Mercer Mayer.

MERCER MAYER (B. 1943)

Bubble Bubble (1973)
The Great Cat Chase (1974)
Ah-choo (1976)
Hiccup (1976)
Oops (1978)
A Boy, a Dog, a Frog, and a Friend (1993)
A Boy, a Dog, and a Frog (2003)
Frog Goes to Dinner (2003)
Frog on His Own (2003)
Frog, Where Are You? (2003)
One Frog Too Many (2003)
Octopus Soup (2011)

Although Mercer Mayer is best known for his Little Critter and Little Monster book series, his place in the history of children's literature will probably be established by his pioneering work drawing wordless picture books, particularly his popular Boy, Dog, and Frog series.

Mayer was born in Little Rock, Arkansas, and recalls catching frogs in swamps near his home. Small wonder that his first book, originally published in 1967, was *A Boy, a Dog, and a Frog*.

Mercer's family moved to Hawaii when he was a teenager, and he attended the Honolulu Art Students' Academy for one year. Discouraged by the academy against pursuing a career in illustration, he persevered, moving to New York City and receiving instruction at the Art Students League. The inexhaustible artist has published over three hundred books in his career.

His first Little Critter book was *Just for You* (1975); recently he published *Little Critter: Just a Special Day* (2014), with more titles in the series planned for 2015. Mayer's Little Monster titles help children cope with fear. They include

There's a Nightmare in My Closet (1968), *There's an Alligator under My Bed* (1987), *There's Something in My Attic* (1988), and *There Are Monsters Everywhere* (2005). The artist has distinguished himself by employing a variety of styles ranging from simple cartoons to rich painterly masterpieces, such as *East of the Sun & West of the Moon* (1980).

In 2007, he was chosen as the National Book Festival Artist of the Year. His *A Boy, a Dog, and a Frog* received an award from the Association for Childhood Education, and the *New York Times* selected *Frog Goes to Dinner* for its annual best illustrated books list.

Courtesy of Emily
Arnold McCully.

EMILY ARNOLD MCCULLY (B. 1939)

Picnic (1984)
First Snow (1985)
School (1987)
New Baby (1988)
The Christmas Gift (2012)
Four Hungry Kittens (2013)

Writer, illustrator, actor, and feminist Emily Arnold McCully has produced dozens of award-winning books for preschoolers to adults, earning her the Caldecott Medal for *Mirette on the High Wire* (1993). She was born in Galesburg, Illinois, and grew up on Long Island, New York, the daughter of an actress, singer, and teacher mother and a father who wrote and produced radio shows. As a young girl, she says, she was a "daredevil" and entertained herself by illustrating what she heard on the radio, read in books, and constructed out of her own imagination, often binding her work into homemade books.

McCully has an undergraduate degree from Brown University, where she focused on theater, and a master's in art history from Columbia University. After receiving her graduate degree, she landed a secretarial job at an advertising agency and did freelance work, including the design of subway posters. When an editor saw her posters, he invited her to illustrate George Panetta's *Sea Beach Express* (1966), which led to other assignments and an accomplished career.

In the mid-1970s, McCully published a short story that was selected for an O. Henry best short stories collection, followed by two novels, *A Craving* (1982) and *Life Drawing* (1986).

After *Mirette on the High Wire*, McCully's interest in confronting sex role stereotypes for girls and women is most apparent in *The Bobbin Girl* (1996), a story about child labor in a nineteenth-century textile mill, and *The Ballot Box Battle* (1996), a tale of a young girl and women's rights activist Elizabeth Cady Stanton.

McCully illustrated *A Journey from Peppermint Street* (1968), winning the National Book Award. She received a Christopher Award for *Picnic* and received an honorary doctorate from Brown University.

Courtesy of Mark Pett.

MARK PETT (B. 1969)

The Boy and the Airplane (2013)
The Girl and the Bicycle (2014)

Mark Pett always wanted to be a cartoonist. At age nine he submitted his first comic strip to the *Salt Lake Tribune*, receiving the unwelcome reply that the newspaper only accepted syndicated material. Pett grew up in Utah, honing his craft by drawing caricatures of his teachers, and then attended the University of Pennsylvania, graduating with a degree in philosophy.

After graduation, he got a job teaching English in Prague, Czech Republic, where he penned editorial cartoons skewering the government. This teaching experience prepared Pett to take a sixth-grade teaching position in Mississippi as part of the Teach for America program. Challenged by the rigors of being a middle school teacher, he turned his experience into a syndicated comic strip called *Mr. Lowe* and subsequently published *Mr. Lowe: Cartoons from the Classroom* (2002). In order to prepare himself for the launch of another comic strip named *Lucky Cow* about a quirky fast-food restaurant, Pett briefly worked at McDonald's, yielding another book in 2005 named for this comic strip.

When he was visiting schools to promote his book *The Girl Who Never Made Mistakes* (2011), a little boy asked Pett, "How do you like being an authorstrator?" Pett was so smitten by this inventive new word, summing up his work as an author and illustrator, that he bought the Internet domain name for it and renamed his website Authorstrator.

Pett's wordless picture books have been very well received, propelling him to a new level of critical recognition. *The Boy and the Airplane* is a Junior Library Guild selection, and *The Girl and the Bicycle* made it to the New York Public Library's list of best picture books.

Photo by Sonya Sones.

CHRIS RASCHKA (B. 1959)

Yo! Yes? (2007)
A Ball for Daisy (2011)
Daisy Gets Lost (2013)

The multitalented Chris Raschka is an author, violist, and socially conscious artist who has thrice received America's most prestigious recognition from the American Library Association for producing the year's most distinguished picture books. First published in 1993, *Yo! Yes?* earned Raschka Caldecott Honors, while *The Hello, Goodbye Window* (2005) and *A Ball for Daisy* (2011) brought him Caldecott Medals.

Raschka was born in Pennsylvania, grew up in suburban Chicago, and received his undergraduate education at St. Olaf College in Minnesota, majoring in biology. Before deciding upon a career in writing and illustrating, he came within a hair's breadth of entering medical school. Having worked as an intern at a clinic in Germany, he was about to begin the medical program at the University of Michigan but changed his mind on the day of registration. Raschka also very nearly pursued a musical livelihood. He was a member of two different orchestras in Michigan, but tendonitis prevented him from continuing as a professional viola player.

Raschka has published dozens of excellent books, some of the standouts being books about fellow musicians, including *Charlie Parker Played Be Bop* (1992), *Mysterious Thelonious* (1997), *John Coltrane's Giant Steps* (2002), and *A Poke in the I* (2001). He has illustrated four books for bell hooks, a leading cultural critic: *Happy to Be Nappy* (1999), *Be Boy Buzz* (2002), *Skin Again* (2004), and *Grump Groan Growl* (2008).

ERIC ROHMANN (B. 1957)

Time Flies (1994)
My Friend Rabbit (2007)

Writer and illustrator Eric Rohmann was born in Riverside, Illinois, and grew up in suburban Chicago. As a boy, he made sense of the world around him by drawing it and exercising "attentive seeing." When he began to imagine stories, like many visual artists, Rohmann constructed his narratives as a sequence of pictures. He learned to draw by copying popular comics, then by studying the work of great illustrators such as Robert McCloskey, Maurice Sendak, Wanda Gag, and Chris Van Allsburg.

Rohmann graduated from Illinois State University with a bachelor's in art and a master's in studio art; at Arizona State University he received a second master's in printmaking and fine bookmaking. He has taught printmaking and bookmaking at Belvoir Terrace in Massachusetts and at St. Olaf College in Minnesota.

Time Flies was Rohmann's first book, earning him a Caldecott Honor and notable book designations from both the American Library Association and the *New York Times*. *My Friend Rabbit* yielded the Caldecott Medal and recognition from various parenting organizations.

Rohmann has illustrated books for some of the most outstanding writers on the contemporary scene, including Candace Fleming's *Oh, No!* (2012) and *Bulldozer's Big Day* (2015), Lois Lowry's *Bless This Mouse* (2011), and Phillip Pullman's *His Dark Materials* trilogy (1995).

To keep his art fresh, Rohmann pushes himself to try different media. For *The Cinder-Eyed Cats* (1997), for example, Rohmann used oil paints, for *My Friend Rabbit* (2007), he used woodcuts, and for *A Kitten Tale* (2008), he worked with new watercolor inks.

PAT SCHORIES (B. 1952)

Courtesy of Pat Schories.

Breakfast for Jack (2004)
Jack and the Missing Piece (2004)
Jack and the Night Visitors (2006)
Jack Wants a Snack (2008)

Pat Schories grew up in Ohio and lives in Cold Spring, New York, where, aside from art, her favorite pursuits are reading, gardening, swimming, climbing, biking, and hiking in woods and fields. This outdoorsy artist also likes to accompany her musician husband to fiddler camps. She has a bachelor's in fine arts from Kent University. Her five-book Jack series has established Schories as an important contributor to the wordless picture book genre.

The only book in the series that has been overlooked as a most recommended wordless title is *When Jack Goes Out* (2010). This charming Junior Library Guild selection is about the return of the friendly aliens from *Jack and the Night Visitors* (2006), Schories's most critically recognized book, judged to be one of the best children's books of the year by the Bank Street College of Education and recommended by the Cooperative Children's Book Center at the University of Wisconsin, Madison.

Schories has specialized in writing and illustrating books for new and emergent readers. She has illustrated several early readers about an endearing puppy for Alyssa Satin Capucilli, including *Biscuit Goes Camping* (2015), *Biscuit Loves the Library* (2014), and *Biscuit's Christmas Storybook Collection* (2013), and recently published *Pants for Chuck* (2014), a whimsical basic reader about a woodchuck determined to squeeze into a pair of pants that are too tight.

Her first book, *Mouse Around* (1991), was a wordless tale about the unintentional travels of a young mouse who falls from his nest in the cellar into a plumber's pocket. Schories does school visits for young children in the New York City area, describing how she does her job and what art supplies she uses.

PETER SPIER (B. 1927)

Noah's Ark (1977)
Peter Spier's Rain (1982)
Peter Spier's Christmas! (1983)
Dreams (1986)

Peter Spier was born in Amsterdam, the Netherlands, and was raised in the small farming village that was the birthplace of Hans Christian Andersen. He attended art school in the Rijksacademie and served in the Royal Netherlands Navy immediately following World War II. During the war, Spier and his family were sent to Theresienstadt, a Nazi concentration camp, because his father was a Jewish journalist and cartoonist and had depicted Hitler in a satirical manner. Thousands of people died in Theresienstadt, located in Terezín, now part of the Czech Republic, but the Spier family survived and managed to emigrate to the United States.

Based in New York City, Peter Spier established himself as a capable commercial artist and illustrator of children's books, first writing and illustrating his own book, *The Fox Went Out on a Chilly Night* (1961), earning a Caldecott Honor. Spier received the Boston Globe–Horn Book Award for *London Bridge Is Falling Down* (1967), the Christopher Award for *The Erie Canal* (1970), and the Caldecott Medal for *Noah's Ark* (1977).

Spier has illustrated over a hundred books in the course of his career. In 2014, some of his most popular titles were reissued, including *Noah's Ark*, *The Fox Went Out on a Chilly Night*, *Dreams*, *The Erie Canal*, *The Star-Spangled Banner*, and *We the People*.

Most of Spier's books have text and images; yet he once observed that perfectly written books require no pictures and perfectly illustrated books require no words. This widely acclaimed illustrator, known for his beautiful imagery and careful research, has secured a place for himself in the pantheon of great illustrators of children's books.

Courtesy of Bill Thomson.

BILL THOMSON (B. 1963)

Chalk (2010)
Fossil (2013)

Bill Thomson, a professor of illustration at the University of Hartford, has distinguished himself as a teacher, artist, coach, and creator of some of the best wordless picture books on the current scene. His books and artwork have received scores of awards and nominations, with *Chalk* leading the way with praises from the American Library Association, the Bank Street College of Education, the New York Public Library, and the International Reading Association.

Born in Waterbury, Connecticut, he embarked on his illustrating career as a teenager when he contributed weekly editorial cartoons to a local newspaper. This led to his majoring in fine arts at Syracuse University, where he graduated with high honors. While at Syracuse he earned a varsity letter as a cross-country runner.

Before he graduated, Thomson was already doing freelance illustrations. His client list includes an impressive array of nationally known civic and commercial enterprises. With the flexibility that came from setting his own hours, Thomson also coached track at Southington High School, leading the team to multiple conference championships.

Thomson has collaborated with Carol Nevius in the publication of three sports books, *Karate Hour* (2004), *Baseball Hour* (2008), and *Soccer Hour* (2011), each providing exciting visual perspectives on a single hour of team exercises and practice.

As an artist, Thomson has participated in some of America's most prestigious juried illustration competitions, group exhibitions, and book events. He has received teaching awards from the University of Hartford. Another wordless picture book is planned for 2015, presumably with a dinosaur theme, creating a trilogy of illustration-only titles.

© Sara Varon, used with permission from First Second Books.

SARA VARON (B. 1971)

Chicken and Cat (2006)
Robot Dreams (2007)
Chicken and Cat Clean Up (2009)

Sara Varon, a graphic novel artist, illustrator, and printmaker originally from Chicago, graduated from that city's School of the Art Institute. She now lives in Brooklyn and is an instructor at New York City's School of Visual Arts, where she received her master's in fine arts.

When she moved into her Brooklyn apartment, there was an unattractive splotch of white paint on the wall that she transformed into a chicken, which she soon coupled with a now familiar feline, giving birth to *Chicken and Cat*, recognized with a Parents' Choice Award. *Chicken and Cat Clean Up* is a Junior Library Guild selection.

Varon's breakout hit was *Robot Dreams*, establishing her as a graphic novel star. The book has been listed as a best book by the New York Public Library, *Kirkus Reviews*, the *Bulletin of the Center for Children's Books*, the American Library Association, and the National Council of Teachers of English. Varon illustrated Cecil Castellucci's *Odd Duck* (2013), which was picked by the *School Library Journal* as one of the top ten graphic novels of the year, included by *Kirkus Reviews* on its annual list of best children's books, and nominated for an Eisner Award.

Varon's style is instantly recognizable, deploying deceptive simplicity and irresistible charm to create cartoon characters that are sweet but never excessively so. When she attends comic book conventions, she sells her books and handmade items, such as hats, prints, jewelry, bags, T-shirts, stationery, wallets, and greeting cards. She identifies herself as a runner, a recreational boxer, and a baker. She has a book titled *Bake Sale* (2011), which features a cupcake and his best friend, an eggplant, plus actual recipes at the back of the book.

Varon's first book was *Sweaterweather* (2003); it will be redesigned and expanded for a 2015 edition. Her upcoming graphic novel projects will feature a donkey shoemaker and a seafaring monkey.

LYND WARD (1905–1985)

The Silver Pony: A Story in Pictures (1973)
Gods' Man (2004)
Mad Man's Drum: A Novel in Woodcuts (2005)
Wild Pilgrimage: A Novel in Woodcuts (2008)
Vertigo: A Novel in Woodcuts (2009)
Prelude to a Million Years & Song without Words: Two Graphic Novels (2010)

Lynd Ward was a politically committed graphic artist best known for his six classic wordless wood-engraved novels originally published from 1929 to 1937. He also published one text-free book for children, *The Silver Pony*, for which he received the Lewis Carroll Shelf Award, the Children's Book Showcase Award, and recognition from the *New York Times* for creating one of the best illustrated books of the year.

Born in Chicago, he studied at Teachers College, Columbia University in New York and attended the National Academy of Graphic Arts in Leipsig, Germany. Visiting a bookstore in Leipsig, he encountered the work of Belgian woodcut engraver Frans Masereel, which had a profound effect on his career. Upon his return to America, he published *Gods' Man*, his first graphic novel. One of Ward's children's books, *The Biggest Bear* (1952), earned him the Caldecott Medal. *Frankenstein: The Lynd Ward Illustrated Edition* (2009) marries Mary Shelley's classic horror story to Ward's vivid woodcut engravings in a way that brings out the best features of both creative masters. Ward's illustrations for this book were drawn in 1934.

Besides wood engraving, Ward also worked in lithography, brush and ink, watercolor, and oil. He illustrated over a hundred children's books, several of which won Newbery Honors and Medals. The work of the legendary artist has been exhibited in many museums, including the Museum of Modern Art, the Smithsonian Institution, and the Library of Congress. He was a member of the National Academy of Design, the Society of Illustrators, and the Society of American Graphic Arts.

Like other artists in the woodcut tradition, Ward used his art to promote awareness of issues involving social and economic justice, racial inequality, and the challenges to organized labor. From 1937 to 1939, Ward directed the graphic arts division of the Federal Art Project, part of the New Deal's Works Progress Administration.

Courtesy of Peggy Morsch.

DAVID WIESNER (B. 1956)

Tuesday (1997)
Sector 7 (1999)
Flotsam (2006)
Free Fall (2008)
Mr. Wuffles! (2013)

When Virginia H. Richey and Kathryn E. Puckett published their seminal *Wordless / Almost Wordless Picture Books: A Guide* in 1992, they asked David Wiesner, already a recognized leader in this specialized genre, to write the foreword. Twenty-three years later, the award-winning artist has only solidified his reputation as a master of illustration-only narrative, becoming the most recommended wordless book artist in the English-speaking world. *Flotsam* is the single most popular wordless book, and his other books are not far behind.

Wiesner won the Caldecott Medal for *Tuesday* (1997), *The Three Pigs* (2001), and *Flotsam* (2006), making him only the second person in the history of the award to win three times. *Free Fall*, first published in 1999, *Sector 7*, and *Mr. Wuffles!* each earned Caldecott Honors. His other picture books include *Hurricane* (1990), *June 29, 1999* (1992), *Night of the Gargoyles* (1994), *The Loathsome Dragon* (2005), and *Art & Max* (2010). Wiesner's first book was *Honest Andrew* (1980), a picture book with text authored by Gloria Skurzynski.

Wiesner grew up in Bridgewater, New Jersey, and was drawing at an early age, realizing that he wanted to tell stories in pictures. He attended the Rhode Island School of Design and created a wordless picture book as his senior project.

The acclaimed artist is best known for his inventive fantasy themes, some having a dreamlike quality. In *Flotsam*, a curious boy finds a camera on the beach that contains fantastical images of an undersea world. In *Tuesday*, frogs magically rise into the air on their lily pads and fly through a suburban town while humans sleep. *Sector 7* features a boy on a school trip to the Empire State Building who is transported to a place where clouds are made.

Appendix 1
THE 500 MOST RECOMMENDED BOOKS BY OVERALL RANK

1. *Flotsam*. By David Wiesner. (Clarion Books, 2006.)
2. *The Snowman*. By Raymond Briggs. (Random House, 1978.)
3. *The Red Book*. By Barbara Lehman. (Houghton Mifflin, 2004.)
4. *The Lion & the Mouse*. By Jerry Pinkney. (Little, Brown, 2009.)
5. *Zoom*. By Istvan Banyai. (Viking, 1995.)
6. *Tuesday*. By David Wiesner. (Clarion Books, 1997.)
7. *A Ball for Daisy*. By Chris Raschka. (Schwartz & Wade Books, 2011.)
8. *Wave*. By Suzy Lee. (Chronicle Books, 2008.)
9. *Time Flies*. By Eric Rohmann. (Crown, 1994.)
10. *The Arrival*. By Shaun Tan. (Arthur A. Levine Books, 2007.)
11. *Pancakes for Breakfast*. By Tomie DePaola. (Harcourt, Brace, Jovanovich, 1978.)
12. *Free Fall*. By David Wiesner. (HarperCollins, 2008.)
13. *Chalk*. By Bill Thomson. (Marshall Cavendish Children, 2010.)
14. *You Can't Take a Balloon into the Metropolitan Museum*. By Jacqueline Preiss Weitzman and Robin Preiss Glasser. (Dial Books for Young Readers, 1998.)
15. *Rainstorm*. By Barbara Lehman. (Houghton Mifflin, 2007.)
16. *Sector 7*. By David Wiesner. (Clarion Books, 1999.)
17. *Good Dog, Carl*. By Alexandra Day. (Little Simon, 1996.)
18. *Journey*. By Aaron Becker. (Candlewick Press, 2013.)
19. *Changes, Changes*. By Pat Hutchins. (Aladdin Paperbacks, 1987.)
20. *Truck*. By Donald Crews. (Tupelo Books, 1997.)
21. *Museum Trip*. By Barbara Lehman. (Houghton Mifflin, 2006.)
22. *Window*. By Jeannie Baker. (Walker Books, 2002.)
23. *Home*. By Jeannie Baker. (Greenwillow Books, 2004.)
24. *Where's Walrus?* By Stephen Savage. (Scholastic Press, 2011.)
25. *Flora and the Flamingo*. By Molly Idle. (Chronicle Books, 2013.)

26. *A Boy, a Dog, and a Frog.* By Mercer Mayer. (Dial, 2003.)
27. *Sidewalk Circus.* By Paul Fleischman and Kevin Hawkes. (Candlewick Press, 2007.)
28. *Do You Want to Be My Friend?* By Eric Carle. (HarperFestival, 1995.)
29. *The Grey Lady and the Strawberry Snatcher.* By Molly Bang. (Aladdin Paperbacks, 1996.)
30. *Trainstop.* By Barbara Lehman. (Houghton Mifflin, 2008.)
31. *Anno's Journey.* By Mitsumasa Anno. (Puffin Books, 1997.)
32. *Re-zoom.* By Istvan Banyai. (Puffin Books, 1998.)
33. *The Chicken Thief.* By Beatrice Rodriguez. (Enchanted Lion Books, 2010.)
34. *Bluebird.* By Bob Staake. (Schwartz & Wade Books, 2013.)
35. *Frog Goes to Dinner.* By Mercer Mayer. (Dial, 2003.)
36. *Yellow Umbrella.* By Jae-Soo Lui. (Kane/Miller, 2002.)
37. *Deep in the Forest.* By Brinton Turkle. (Puffin Books, 1992.)
38. *The Adventures of Polo.* By Regis Faller. (Roaring Brook Press, 2006.)
39. *Clown.* By Quentin Blake. (Henry Holt, 1998.)
40. *The Boy, the Bear, the Baron, the Bard.* By Gregory Rogers. (Roaring Brook Press, 2004.)
41. *Unspoken: A Story from the Underground Railroad.* By Henry Cole. (Scholastic Press, 2012.)
42. *South.* By Patrick McDonnell. (Little, Brown Books for Young Readers, 2008.)
43. *The Secret Box.* By Barbara Lehman. (Houghton Mifflin, 2011.)
44. *Mr. Wuffles!* By David Wiesner. (Clarion Books, 2013.)
45. *Bow-Wow Bugs a Bug.* By Mark Newgarden and Megan Montague Cash. (HMH Books for Young Readers, 2007.)
46. *Robot Dreams.* By Sara Varon. (First Second, 2007.)
47. *Frog, Where Are You?* By Mercer Mayer. (Dial, 2003.)
48. *The Silver Pony: A Story in Pictures.* By Lynd Ward. (Houghton Mifflin, 1973.)
49. *Jack and the Night Visitors.* By Pat Schories. (Front Street Press, 2006.)
50. *Shadow.* By Suzy Lee. (Chronicle Books, 2010.)
51. *Sea of Dreams.* By Dennis Nolan. (Roaring Brook Press, 2011.)
52. *Mirror.* By Jeannie Baker. (Candlewick Press, 2010.)
53. *Dinosaur!* By Peter Sis. (Greenwillow Books, 2005.)
54. *The Other Side.* By Istvan Banyai. (Chronicle Books, 2005.)
55. *A Boy, a Dog, a Frog, and a Friend.* By Mercer and Marianna Mayer. (Puffin Books, 1993.)
56. *Sunshine.* By Jan Ormerod. (Frances Lincoln Children's Books, 2009.)
57. *Anno's U.S.A.* By Mitsumasa Anno. (Philomel, 1983.)
58. *Oops.* By Mercer Mayer. (Puffin Books, 1978.)

59. *Moonlight.* By Jan Ormerod. (Frances Lincoln Children's Books, 2004.)
60. *Frog on His Own.* By Mercer Mayer. (Dial, 2003.)
61. *The Boy and the Airplane.* By Mark Pett. (Simon & Schuster Books for Young Readers, 2013.)
62. *Four Hungry Kittens.* By Emily Arnold McCully. (StarWalk Kids Media, 2013.)
63. *Clementina's Cactus.* By Ezra Jack Keats. (Viking Juvenile, 1999.)
64. *Wonder Bear.* By Tao Nyeu. (Dial, 2008.)
65. *A Small Miracle.* By Peter Collington. (Dragonfly Books, 2011.)
66. *One Frog Too Many.* By Mercer and Marianna Mayer. (Dial, 2003.)
67. *Last Night.* By Hyewon Yum. (Farrar, Straus & Giroux, 2008.)
68. *The Umbrella.* By Ingrid and Dieter Schubert. (Lemniscaat USA, 2011.)
69. *The Last Laugh.* By Jose Aruego and Ariane Dewey. (Dial, 2006.)
70. *Inside Outside.* By Lizi Boyd. (Chronicle Books, 2013.)
71. *Daisy Gets Lost.* By Chris Raschka. (Schwartz & Wade Books, 2013.)
72. *Ice.* By Arthur Geisert. (Enchanted Lion Books, 2011.)
73. *The Tooth Fairy.* By Peter Collington. (Knopf Books for Young Readers, 1995.)
74. *Polo: The Runaway Book.* By Regis Faller. (Roaring Brook Press, 2007.)
75. *Bee & Bird.* By Craig Frazier. (Roaring Brook Press, 2011.)
76. *The Hunter and the Animals: A Wordless Picture Book.* By Tomie DePaola. (Holiday House, 1981.)
77. *Carl Goes Shopping.* By Alexandra Day. (Farrar, Straus & Giroux, 1992.)
78. *April Wilson's Magpie Magic: A Tale of Colorful Mischief.* By April Wilson. (Dial, 1999.)
79. *Why?* By Nikolai Popov. (Michael Neugebauer, 1998.)
80. *Owly & Wormy, Friends All Aflutter!* By Andy Runton. (Atheneum Books for Young Readers, 2011.)
81. *Noah's Ark.* By Peter Spier. (Doubleday, 1977.)
82. *Fox and Hen Together.* By Beatrice Rodriguez. (Enchanted Lion Books, 2011.)
83. *A Day, a Dog.* By Gabrielle Vincent. (Front Street Press, 1999.)
84. *Un-brella.* By Scott E. Franson. (Roaring Brook Press, 2007.)
85. *The Conductor.* By Laetitia Devernay. (Chronicle Books, 2011.)
86. *Anno's Counting Book.* By Mitsumasa Anno. (Crowell, 1977.)
87. *The Tree House.* By Marije Tolman and Ronald Tolman. (Lemniscaat, 2010.)
88. *Peter Spier's Rain.* By Peter Spier. (Doubleday, 1982.)
89. *Mirror.* By Suzy Lee. (Seven Footer Kids, 2010.)
90. *The Giant Seed.* By Arthur Geisert. (Enchanted Lion Books, 2012.)
91. *School.* By Emily Arnold McCully. (Harper & Row, 1987.)
92. *Peter Spier's Christmas!* By Peter Spier. (Doubleday, 1983.)
93. *Have You Seen My Duckling?* By Nancy Tafuri. (Greenwillow Books, 1984.)

94. *Creepy Castle*. By John S. Goodall. (Atheneum, 1975.)
95. *Welcome to the Zoo*. By Alison Jay. (Dial Books for Young Readers, 2008.)
96. *Hank Finds an Egg*. By Rebecca Dudley. (Peter Pauper Press, 2013.)
97. *Chicken and Cat*. By Sara Varon. (Scholastic Press, 2006.)
98. *Hocus Pocus*. By Sylvie Desrosiers and Rémy Simard. (Kids Can Press, 2011.)
99. *Bear Despair*. By Gaetan Dorémus. (Enchanted Lion Books, 2012.)
100. *Where Is the Cake?* By Thé Tjong-Khing. (Abrams Books for Young Readers, 2007.)
101. *Tabby: A Story in Pictures*. By Aliki. (HarperCollins, 1995.)
102. *Here I Am*. By Patti Kim and Sonia Sanchez. (Capstone Young Readers, 2014.)
103. *The Shadow*. By Donna Diamond. (Candlewick, 2010.)
104. *Polo and Lily*. By Regis Faller. (Roaring Brook Press, 2009.)
105. *The Midnight Adventures of Kelly, Dot, and Esmeralda*. By John S. Goodall. (Margaret K. McElderry, 1999.)
106. *Follow Carl!* By Alexandra Day. (Farrar, Straus & Giroux, 1998.)
107. *Chicken and Cat Clean Up*. By Sara Varon. (Scholastic Press, 2009.)
108. *The Boys*. By Jeff Newman. (Simon & Schuster Books for Young Readers, 2010.)
109. *The Yellow Balloon*. By Charlotte Dematons. (Front Street / Lemniscaat, 2003.)
110. *Blood Song: A Silent Ballad*. By Eric Drooker. (Dark Horse Originals, 2009.)
111. *You Can't Take a Balloon into the Museum of Fine Arts*. By Jacqueline Preiss Weitzman and Robin Preiss Glasser. (Penguin Group, 2002.)
112. *The Treasure Bath*. By Dan Andreasen. (Henry Holt, 2009.)
113. *Midsummer Knight*. By Gregory Rogers. (Allen & Unwin Children's Books, 2008.)
114. *The Surprise*. By Sylvia van Ommen. (Lemniscaat, 2007.)
115. *The Hero of Little Street*. By Gregory Rogers. (Roaring Brook Press, 2012.)
116. *Rooster's Revenge*. By Beatrice Rodriguez. (Enchanted Lion Books, 2011.)
117. *Peep!* By Kevin Luthardt. (Peachtree Publishers, 2012.)
118. *Good Night, Gorilla*. By Peggy Rathmann. (Putnam Juvenile, 1996.)
119. *Archie*. By Domenica More Gordon. (Bloomsbury USA Children's, 2012.)
120. *The Girl and the Bicycle*. By Mark Pett. (Simon & Schuster Books for Young Readers, 2014.)
121. *Sing, Pierrot, Sing: A Picture Book in Mime*. By Tomie DePaola. (Harcourt Children's Books, 1987.)
122. *First Snow*. By Emily Arnold McCully. (Harper & Row, 1985.)
123. *Polo and the Dragon*. By Regis Faller. (Roaring Brook Press, 2007.)

124. *The Mysteries of Harris Burdick.* By Chris Van Allsburg. (Houghton Mifflin, 1984.)
125. *Hogwash.* By Arthur Geisert. (HMH Books for Young Readers, 2008.)
126. *The Crocodile Blues.* By Coleman Polhemus. (Candlewick Press, 2007.)
127. *Hug.* By Jez Alborough. (Candlewick Press, 2002.)
128. *Carl's Masquerade.* By Alexandra Day. (Farrar, Straus & Giroux, 1992.)
129. *Breakfast for Jack.* By Pat Schories. (Boyds Mills Press, 2004.)
130. *Up and Up.* By Shirley Hughes. (Red Fox, 1991.)
131. *Anno's Britain.* By Mitsumasa Anno. (Philomel, 1982.)
132. *Small, Medium & Large.* By Jane Monroe Donovan. (Sleeping Bear Press, 2010.)
133. *Naughty Nancy.* By John S. Goodall. (Margaret K. McElderry, 1999.)
134. *Silent Night.* By Sandy Turner. (Atheneum, 2001.)
135. *No!* By David McPhail. (Roaring Brook Press, 2009.)
136. *Jack Wants a Snack.* By Pat Schories. (Boyds Mills Press, 2008.)
137. *Fossil.* By Bill Thomson. (Two Lions, 2013.)
138. *The Surprise Picnic.* By John S. Goodall. (Atheneum, 1977.)
139. *The Flower Man: A Wordless Picture Book.* By Mark Ludy. (Green Pastures Publishing, 2005.)
140. *The Birthday Cake Mystery.* By Thé Tjong-Khing. (Gecko Press, 2012.)
141. *Thunderstorm.* By Arthur Geisert. (Enchanted Lion Books, 2013.)
142. *Once upon a Banana.* By Jennifer Armstrong and David Small. (Simon & Schuster / Paula Wiseman Books, 2006.)
143. *The Line.* By Paula Bossio. (Kids Can Press, 2013.)
144. *Korgi Book 1: Sprouting Wings!* By Christian Slade. (Top Shelf Productions, 2007.)
145. *The Angel and the Soldier Boy.* By Peter Collington. (Knopf Books for Young Readers, 1987.)
146. *The Island.* By Marije Tolman and Ronald Tolman. (Lemniscaat USA, 2012.)
147. *Gods' Man.* By Lynd Ward. (Dover Publications, 2004.)
148. *A Circle of Friends.* By Giora Carmi. (Star Bright Books, 2006.)
149. *The Wind.* By Monique Felix. (Creative Editions, 2012.)
150. *Carl's Birthday.* By Alexandra Day. (Farrar, Straus & Giroux, 1997.)
151. *The Adventures of Paddy Pork.* By John S. Goodall. (Harcourt, Brace & World, 1968.)
152. *Where Is the Cake Now?* By Thé Tjong-Khing. (Abrams Books for Young Readers, 2009.)
153. *Polo and the Magic Flute.* By Regis Faller. (Roaring Brook Press, 2009.)
154. *Octopus Soup.* By Mercer Mayer. (Marshall Cavendish Children, 2011.)
155. *Waterloo & Trafalgar.* By Olivier Tallec. (Enchanted Lion Books, 2012.)

156. *Owly & Wormy, Bright Lights and Starry Nights.* By Andy Runton. (Atheneum Books for Young Readers, 2012.)
157. *Leaf.* By Stephen Michael King. (Roaring Brook Press, 2009.)
158. *Jacko.* By John S. Goodall. (Harcourt Children's Books, 1972.)
159. *Anno's Counting House.* By Mitsumasa Anno. (Philomel, 1982.)
160. *Jack and the Missing Piece.* By Pat Schories. (Boyds Mills Press, 2004.)
161. *Hello, Mr. Hulot.* By David Merveille. (NorthSouth, 2013.)
162. *Shapes, Shapes, Shapes.* By Tana Hoban. (Greenwillow Books, 1986.)
163. *Good Night, Garden Gnome.* By Jamichael Henterly. (Dial, 2001.)
164. *The Christmas Gift.* By Emily Arnold McCully. (StarWalk Kids Media, 2012.)
165. *Weathercraft.* By Jim Woodring. (Fantagraphics Books, 2010.)
166. *Topsy-Turvies: Pictures to Stretch the Imagination.* By Mitsumasa Anno. (Tuttle Publishing, 1970.)
167. *Look What I Can Do.* By Jose Aruego. (Aladdin Books, 1988.)
168. *Shrewbettina's Birthday.* By John S. Goodall. (Margaret K. McElderry, 1998.)
169. *Red Sled.* By Lita Judge. (Atheneum Books for Young Readers, 2011.)
170. *Polo and the Magician!* By Regis Faller. (Roaring Brook Press, 2009.)
171. *Look! Look! Look!* By Tana Hoban. (Greenwillow Books, 1988.)
172. *Owly: The Way Home & The Bittersweet Summer.* By Andy Runton. (Top Shelf, 2004.)
173. *New Baby.* By Emily Arnold McCully. (Harper & Row, 1988.)
174. *Carl's Christmas.* By Alexandra Day. (Farrar, Straus & Giroux, 1990.)
175. *Little Star.* By Antonin Louchard. (Hyperion Books for Children, 2003.)
176. *Anno's Flea Market.* By Mitsumasa Anno. (Philomel Books, 1984.)
177. *Letter Lunch.* By Elisa Gutiérrez. (Owlkids Books, 2014.)
178. *Gem.* By Holly Hobbie. (Little, Brown, 2012.)
179. *The Self-Made Snowman.* By Fernando Krahn. (J. B. Lippincott, 1974.)
180. *Flood.* By Alvaro F. Villa. (Picture Window Books, 2013.)
181. *Rosie's Walk.* By Pat Hutchins. (Red Fox, 2010.)
182. *Early Morning in the Barn.* By Nancy Tafuri. (Greenwillow Books, 1983.)
183. *Cool Cat.* By Nonny Hogrogian. (Roaring Brook Press, 2009.)
184. *Sticks and Stones.* By Peter Kuper. (Three Rivers Press, 2004.)
185. *Carl's Afternoon in the Park.* By Alexandra Day. (Farrar, Straus & Giroux, 1991.)
186. *Beaver Is Lost.* By Elisha Cooper. (Schwartz & Wade Books, 2010.)
187. *The Story of a Farm.* By John S. Goodall. (Margaret K. McElderry, 1989.)
188. *The Bear and the Fly.* By Paula Winter. (Crown Publishers, 1976.)
189. *April Fools.* By Fernando Krahn. (E. P. Dutton, 1974.)
190. *Naughty Nancy Goes to School.* By John S. Goodall. (Atheneum, 1985.)

191. *Anno's Spain.* By Mitsumasa Anno. (Philomel Books, 2004.)
192. *Hiccup.* By Mercer Mayer. (Dial, 1976.)
193. *Looking Down.* By Steve Jenkins. (Houghton Mifflin, 1995.)
194. *The Wrong Side of the Bed.* By Edward Ardizzone. (Doubleday, 1970.)
195. *Just in Passing.* By Susan Bonners. (Lothrop, Lee & Shepard Books, 1989.)
196. *The Colors.* By Monique Felix. (Creative Editions, 2013.)
197. *Is It Larger? Is It Smaller?* By Tana Hoban. (Greenwillow Books, 1985.)
198. *Holland.* By Charlotte Dematons. (Lemniscaat, 2013.)
199. *Coyote Run.* By Gaetan Dorémus. (Enchanted Lion Books, 2014.)
200. *Hocus Pocus Takes the Train.* By Sylvie Desrosiers and Rémy Simard. (Kids Can Press, 2013.)
201. *Fish on a Walk.* By Eva Muggenthaler. (Enchanted Lion Books, 2011.)
202. *The Little Red Fish.* By Tae-Eun Yoo. (Dial, 2007.)
203. *The Night Riders.* By Matt Furie. (McSweeney's/McMullens, 2012.)
204. *Carl Goes to Daycare.* By Alexandra Day. (Farrar, Straus & Giroux, 1993.)
205. *Anno's Italy.* By Mitsumasa Anno. (Collins, 1980.)
206. *The 46 Little Men.* By Jan Mogensen. (Greenwillow Books, 1991.)
207. *Ah-choo.* By Mercer Mayer. (Dial, 1976.)
208. *Where's My Monkey?* By Dieter Schubert. (Dial Books for Young Readers, 1987.)
209. *Shadows and Reflections.* By Tana Hoban. (Greenwillow Books, 1990.)
210. *An Ocean World.* By Peter Sis. (Greenwillow Books, 1992.)
211. *The Numbers.* By Monique Felix. (Creative Education, 1992.)
212. *Little Pickle.* By Peter Collington. (E. P. Dutton, 1986.)
213. *A Wish for Elves.* By Mark Gonyea. (Henry Holt, 2010.)
214. *Invisible.* By Katja Kamm. (North-South Books, 2006.)
215. *Circles, Triangles, and Squares.* By Tana Hoban. (Macmillan, 1974.)
216. *I See a Song.* By Eric Carle. (Thomas Y. Crowell, 1973.)
217. *Flicks.* By Tomie DePaola. (Harcourt Brace Jovanovich, 1979.)
218. *The Changing Countryside.* By Jörg Müller. (Atheneum Publishers, 1977.)
219. *Bubble Bubble.* By Mercer Mayer. (Parents' Magazine Press, 1973.)
220. *Up to Ten and Down Again.* By Lisa Campbell Ernst. (Lothrop, Lee & Shepard Books, 1986.)
221. *Bobo's Dream.* By Martha Alexander. (Dial, 1970.)
222. *Welcome to Mamoko.* By Aleksandra Mizielińska and Daniel Mizieliński. (Big Picture Press, 2013.)
223. *The Red Scarf.* By Anne Villeneuve. (Tundra Books, 2010.)
224. *The Farmer and the Clown.* By Marla Frazee. (Beach Lane Books, 2014.)
225. *Rainy Day Dream.* By Michael Chesworth. (Farrar, Straus & Giroux, 1992.)
226. *Paddy Under Water.* By John S. Goodall. (Atheneum, 1984.)

227. *Mister O.* By Lewis Trondheim. (NBM / Nantier, Beall, Minoustchine, 2004.)
228. *OK Go.* By Carin Berger. (Greenwillow Books, 2009.)
229. *Paddy Pork's Holiday.* By John S. Goodall. (Atheneum, 1973.)
230. *Our House on the Hill.* By Philippe Dupasquier. (Viking Kestrel, 1988.)
231. *Fox Bunny Funny.* By Andy Hartzell. (Top Shelf Productions, 2007.)
232. *One Scary Night.* By Antoine Guilloppé. (Milk & Cookies Press, 2004.)
233. *Fran.* By Jim Woodring. (Fantagraphics Books, 2013.)
234. *The Marvelous Misadventures of Fun-Boy.* By Ralph Cosentino. (Viking, 2006.)
235. *I Can't Sleep.* By Philippe Dupasquier. (Walker Books, 1999.)
236. *Mad Man's Drum: A Novel in Woodcuts.* By Lynd Ward. (Dover Publications, 2005.)
237. *Little Red Riding Hood.* By John S. Goodall. (Margaret K. McElderry, 1988.)
238. *Is It Red? Is It Yellow? Is It Blue? An Adventure in Color.* By Tana Hoban. (Mulberry Books, 1987.)
239. *How Santa Claus Had a Long and Difficult Journey Delivering His Presents.* By Fernando Krahn. (Dell Publishing, 1988.)
240. *Fox's Garden.* By Princesse Camcam. (Enchanted Lion Books, 2014.)
241. *Happy Halloween, Li'l Santa.* By Thierry Robin and Lewis Trondheim. (NBM Publishing, 2003.)
242. *The Great Cat Chase.* By Mercer Mayer. (Four Winds Press, 1974.)
243. *Fly, Little Bird.* By Tina Burke. (Kane/Miller, 2006.)
244. *Cinema Panopticum.* By Thomas Ott. (Fantagraphics Books, 2005.)
245. *Flood! A Novel in Pictures.* By Eric Drooker. (Four Walls Eight Windows, 1992.)
246. *An Edwardian Christmas.* By John S. Goodall. (Atheneum, 1981.)
247. *Anno's Alphabet: An Adventure in Imagination.* By Mitsumasa Anno. (Crowell, 1975.)
248. *The Christmas We Moved to the Barn.* By Cooper Edens and Alexandra Day. (HarperCollins, 1997.)
249. *Hunters of the Great Forest.* By Dennis Nolan. (Roaring Brook Press, 2014.)
250. *Balloon Trip.* By Ronald Wegen. (Houghton Mifflin, 1981.)
251. *Picturescape.* By Elisa Gutiérrez. (Simply Read Books, 2005.)
252. *Draw!* By Raúl Colón. (Simon & Schuster, 2014.)
253. *Amanda and the Mysterious Carpet.* By Fernando Krahn. (Clarion Books, 1985.)
254. *Little Bird.* By Germano Zullo and Albertine. (Enchanted Lion Books, 2012.)
255. *1, 2, 3 to the Zoo.* By Eric Carle. (Puffin, 1998.)

256. *The Creepy Thing*. By Fernando Krahn. (Clarion Books, 1982.)
257. *We Hide, You Seek*. By Jose Aruego and Ariane Dewey. (Greenwillow Books, 1979.)
258. *The Tortoise & the Hare*. By Jerry Pinkney. (Little, Brown, 2013.)
259. *The Red Thread*. By Tord Nygren. (Farrar, Straus & Giroux, 1988.)
260. *Take Another Look*. By Tana Hoban. (Greenwillow Books, 1981.)
261. *Sunday Love*. By Alison Paul. (HMH Books for Young Readers, 2010.)
262. *Let That Bad Air Out: Buddy Bolden's Last Parade*. By Stefan Berg. (Porcupine's Quill, 2007.)
263. *The Secret of Love*. By Sarah Emmanuelle Burg. (Penguin Young Readers Group, 2006.)
264. *Red Hat*. By Lita Judge. (Atheneum Books for Young Readers, 2013.)
265. *Polar Slumber / Sueño polar*. By Dennis Rockhill. (Raven Tree Press, 2004.)
266. *Dig, Drill, Dump, Fill*. By Tana Hoban. (Greenwillow Books, 1975.)
267. *The Story of a Castle*. By John S. Goodall. (Margaret K. McElderry, 1986.)
268. *Paddy Pork: Odd Jobs*. By John S. Goodall. (Atheneum, 1983.)
269. *Korgi Book 2: The Cosmic Collector*. By Christian Slade. (Top Shelf Books, 2008.)
270. *Catch That Cat!* By Fernando Krahn. (Dutton, 1978.)
271. *The Midnight Circus*. By Peter Collington. (Knopf, 1992.)
272. *Of Colors and Things*. By Tana Hoban. (Greenwillow Books, 1989.)
273. *In the Woods*. By Ermanno Cristini, Luigi Puricelli, and Renato Pegoraro. (Scholastic, 1990.)
274. *Full Moon Soup*. By Alastair Graham. (Dial Books, 1991.)
275. *I'm Not a Plastic Bag*. By Rachel Hope Allison. (Archaia Entertainment, 2012.)
276. *The Bored Book*. By David Michael Slater and Doug Keith. (Simply Read Books, 2009.)
277. *Hot on the Scent*. By Bente Bech and Peter Lind. (Gareth Stevens, 1992.)
278. *The Great Escape*. By Philippe Dupasquier. (Houghton Mifflin, 1988.)
279. *Alphabet City*. By Stephen T. Johnson. (Viking, 1995.)
280. *Freight Train*. By Donald Crews. (Greenwillow Books, 1978.)
281. *An Edwardian Summer*. By John S. Goodall. (Macmillan, 1979.)
282. *Sun's Up*. By Teryl Euvremer. (Crown Publishers, 1987.)
283. *Dylan's Day Out*. By Peter Catalanotto. (Orchard Books, 1989.)
284. *The City*. By Douglas Florian. (Crowell Junior Books, 1982.)
285. *The Middle Passage: White Ships / Black Cargo*. By Tom Feelings. (Dial Books, 1995.)
286. *Arthur's Adventure in the Abandoned House*. By Fernando Krahn. (Dutton Juvenile, 1981.)

287. *The Wonder Ring: A Fantasy in Silhouette.* By Holden Wetherbee. (Doubleday, 1978.)
288. *Animals Home Alone.* By Loes Riphagen. (Seven Footer Kids, 2011.)
289. *Snow Sounds: An Onomatopoeic Story.* By David A. Johnson. (Houghton Mifflin, 2006.)
290. *Amanda's Butterfly.* By Nick Butterworth. (Collins, 1991.)
291. *No Dogs Allowed!* By Linda Ashman and Kristin Sorra. (Sterling Children's Books, 2011.)
292. *Higher! Higher!* By Leslie Patricelli. (Candlewick Press, 2010.)
293. *The Snowy Path: A Christmas Journey.* By Lark Carrier. (Picture Book Studio, 1989.)
294. *What Whiskers Did.* By Ruth Carroll. (Scholastic Books, 1965.)
295. *The Sanctuary.* By Nate Neal. (Fantagraphics Books, 2010.)
296. *Age of Reptiles Omnibus*, Vol. 1. By Ricardo Delgado. (Dark Horse Books, 2011.)
297. *The Rabbits Are Coming!* By Kathleen Bullock. (Simon & Schuster Books for Young Readers, 1991.)
298. *Muffel and Plums.* By Lilo Fromm. (Macmillan, 1972.)
299. *Good News, Bad News.* By Jeff Mack. (Chronicle Books, 2012.)
300. *Mouse Letters: A Very First Alphabet Book.* By Jim Arnosky. (Clarion Books, 1999.)
301. *He Done Her Wrong.* By Milt Gross. (Fantagraphics Books, 2005.)
302. *Monsters! and Other Stories.* By Gustavo Duarte. (Dark Horse Books, 2014.)
303. *Lights Out.* By Arthur Geisert. (Houghton Mifflin, 2005.)
304. *Is It Rough? Is It Smooth? Is It Shiny?* By Tana Hoban. (Greenwillow Books, 1984.)
305. *Dead End.* By Thomas Ott. (Fantagraphics Books, 2002.)
306. *The Inside-Outside Book of New York City.* By Roxie Munro. (Dodd, Mead, 1985.)
307. *Hot Air: The (Mostly) True Story of the First Hot-Air Balloon Ride.* By Marjorie Priceman. (Atheneum Books for Young Readers, 2005.)
308. *The Frank Book.* By Jim Woodring. (Fantagraphics Books, 2003.)
309. *When Night Didn't Come.* By Poly Bernatene. (Meadowside Children's, 2010.)
310. *A Flying Saucer Full of Spaghetti.* By Fernando Krahn. (E. P. Dutton, 1970.)
311. *Don't Forget Me, Santa Claus.* By Virginia Mayo. (Barrons Juveniles, 1993.)
312. *Wiggle! March!* By Kaaren Pixton. (Workman Publishing, 2009.)
313. *Dancing Boy.* By Ronald Himler. (Star Bright Books, 2005.)
314. *Congress of the Animals.* By Jim Woodring. (Fantagraphics Books, 2011.)
315. *The Zoo.* By Suzy Lee. (Kane/Miller, 2007.)
316. *The Chimp and the Clown.* By Ruth Carroll. (H. Z. Walck, 1968.)

317. *The Apple and the Butterfly.* By Iela Mari and Enzo Mari. (Price Stern Sloan, 2013.)

318. *The Chicken's Child.* By Margaret A. Hartelius. (Doubleday, 1975.)

319. *Harry Potter and the Sorcerer's Stone: A Deluxe Pop-Up Book.* By J. K. Rowling and Jill Daniels. (Scholastic, 2001.)

320. *Carl's Summer Vacation.* By Alexandra Day. (Farrar, Straus & Giroux, 2008.)

321. *Frere Jacques.* By Jonas Sickler. (Workman Publishing, 2011.)

322. *Vertigo: A Novel in Woodcuts.* By Lynd Ward. (Dover Publications, 2009.)

323. *Beach Day.* By Helen Oxenbury. (Dial Very First Books, 1982.)

324. *Ship Ahoy!* By Peter Sis. (Greenwillow Books, 1999.)

325. *Adventures of a Japanese Businessman.* By José Domingo, Isabel Mancebo, Alex Spiro, and Sam Arthur. (Nobrow Press, 2012.)

326. *Quest.* By Aaron Becker. (Candlewick Press, 2014.)

327. *The World of Mamoko in the Year 3000.* By Aleksandra Mizielińska and Daniel Mizieliński. (Big Picture Press, 2014.)

328. *Travel.* By Yuichi Yokoyama. (PictureBox, 2008.)

329. *Mudkin.* By Stephen Gammell. (Carolrhoda Books, 2011.)

330. *Early Birdy Gets the Worm.* By Bruce Lansky and Bill Bolton. (Meadowbrook, 2014.)

331. *Man's Work!* By Annie Kubler. (Child's Play International, 1999.)

332. *Don't Look Now.* By Ed Briant. (Roaring Brook Press, 2009.)

333. *A Special Birthday.* By Symeon Shimin. (McGraw-Hill, 1976.)

334. *Picture a Letter.* By Brad Sneed. (Dial Books, 2002.)

335. *Snail, Where Are You?* By Tomi Ungerer. (Blue Apple Books, 2005.)

336. *The West Wing.* By Edward Gorey. (Simon & Schuster, 1963.)

337. *Sir Andrew.* By Paula Winter. (Random House, 1984.)

338. *Robot-Bot-Bot.* By Fernando Krahn. (Dutton Juvenile, 1979.)

339. *Pssst! Doggie—.* By Ezra Jack Keats. (Franklin Watts, 1973.)

340. *Flashlight.* By Lizi Boyd. (Chronicle, 2014.)

341. *Combustion: A Story without Words.* By Chris Lanier. (Fantagraphics Books, 1999.)

342. *Oh!* By Josse Goffin. (Kalandraka, 2007.)

343. *The Number: 73304-23-4153-6-96-8.* By Thomas Ott. (Fantagraphics Books, 2014.)

344. *Journey to the Moon.* By Erich Fuchs. (Delacorte Press, 1969.)

345. *Mouse Numbers: A Very First Counting Book.* By Jim Arnosky. (Clarion Books, 1999.)

346. *Lavinia's Cottage.* By John S. Goodall. (Margaret K. McElderry, 1983.)

347. *The Great War: July 1, 1916: The First Day of the Battle of the Somme: An Illustrated Panorama.* By Joe Sacco. (W. W. Norton, 2013.)

348. *A Long Piece of String.* By William Wondriska. (Chronicle Books, 2010.)
349. *Greetings from Hellville.* By Thomas Ott. (Fantagraphics Books, 2002.)
350. *Li'l Santa.* By Thierry Robin and Lewis Trondheim. (NBM Publishing, 2002.)
351. *Flying Jake.* By Lane Smith. (Macmillan, 1988.)
352. *Korgi Book 3: A Hollow Beginning.* By Christian Slade. (Top Shelf Productions, 2011.)
353. *He's My Jumbo!* By Claude K. Dubois. (Viking Kestrel, 1990.)
354. *The Knight and the Dragon.* By Tomie DePaola. (Puffin Books, 1998.)
355. *Exactly the Opposite.* By Tana Hoban. (Greenwillow Books, 1990.)
356. *Kitten for a Day.* By Ezra Jack Keats. (Perfection Learning, 2008.)
357. *Jinchalo.* By Matthew Forsythe. (Drawn and Quarterly, 2012.)
358. *Destiny: A Novel in Pictures.* By Otto Nückel. (Dover Publications, 2012.)
359. *Island Dog.* By Rebecca Goodale. (Two Dog Press, 1999.)
360. *Here Comes Alex Pumpernickel!* By Fernando Krahn. (Little, Brown, 1981.)
361. *Color Zoo.* By Lois Ehlert. (HarperFestival, 1997.)
362. *The Heartaches of a French Cat.* By Barbara McClintock. (D. R. Godine, 1989.)
363. *Graham Oakley's Magical Changes.* By Graham Oakley. (Atheneum, 1980.)
364. *Carl Makes a Scrapbook.* By Alexandra Day. (Farrar, Straus & Giroux, 1994.)
365. *The Good Bird.* By Peter Wezel. (Harper & Row, 1964.)
366. *Flutter! Fly!* By Kaaren Pixton. (Workman Publishing, 2009.)
367. *Splat! Starring the Vole Brothers.* By Roslyn Schwartz. (Owlkids Books, 2014.)
368. *An Edwardian Holiday.* By John S. Goodall. (Atheneum, 1979.)
369. *Dots, Spots, Speckles, and Stripes.* By Tana Hoban. (Greenwillow Books, 1987.)
370. *Carl's Snowy Afternoon.* By Alexandra Day. (Farrar, Straus & Giroux, 2009.)
371. *Wild Pilgrimage: A Novel in Woodcuts.* By Lynd Ward. (Dover Publications, 2008.)
372. *Book of Hours: A Wordless Novel Told in 99 Wood Engravings.* By George A. Walker. (Porcupine's Quill, 2010.)
373. *The Flying Grandmother.* By Naomi Kojima. (Crowell, 1981.)
374. *Boat.* By Barbara Remington. (Doubleday, 1975.)
375. *Alligator's Toothache.* By Diane de Groat. (Crown, 1977.)
376. *A Birthday Wish.* By Ed Emberley. (Little, Brown, 1977.)
377. *Yo! Yes?* By Chris Raschka. (Scholastic, 2007.)
378. *Ben's Big Dig.* By Daniel Wakeman and Dirk Van Stralen. (Orca Book Publishers, 2005.)

379. *Mighty Mizzling Mouse and the Red Cabbage House.* By Friso Henstra. (Little, Brown, 1984.)
380. *Beach Ball.* By Peter Sis. (Greenwillow Books, 1990.)
381. *Wings.* By Shinsuke Tanaka. (Purple Bear Books, 2006.)
382. *Steam Park.* By Filippo Neri and Piero Ruggeri. (Simply Read Books, 2006.)
383. *Who Are They?* By Tana Hoban. (Greenwillow Books, 1994.)
384. *Ball.* By Mary Sullivan. (Houghton Mifflin Harcourt Books for Children, 2013.)
385. *Paddy's New Hat.* By John S. Goodall. (Atheneum, 1980.)
386. *Albert B. Cub and Zebra: An Alphabet Storybook.* By Anne F. Rockwell. (Crowell, 1977.)
387. *No, David!* By David Shannon. (Blue Sky Press, 1998.)
388. *Winterbird.* By Alfred Olschewski. (Houghton Mifflin, 1969.)
389. *The Train.* By Witold Generowicz. (Dial, 1982.)
390. *Will's Mammoth.* By Rafe Martin and Stephen Gammell. (PaperStar, 1997.)
391. *Shrewbettina Goes to Work.* By John S. Goodall. (Atheneum, 1981.)
392. *A Whole World.* By Antonin Louchard and Katy Couprie. (Milet, 2002.)
393. *The Special String.* By Harald Bakken and Mischa Richter. (Prentice Hall, 1981.)
394. *Who's Seen the Scissors?* By Fernando Krahn. (Dutton, 1975.)
395. *Southern Cross: A Novel of the South Seas.* By Laurence Hyde. (Drawn and Quarterly, 2007.)
396. *Anno's Animals.* By Mitsumasa Anno. (Collins, 1979.)
397. *What Is That?* By Tana Hoban. (Greenwillow Books, 1994.)
398. *Bang.* By Leo Timmers. (Gecko Press, 2013.)
399. *Oink.* By Arthur Geisert. (HMH Books for Young Readers, 1991.)
400. *Uh-oh!* By Mary Newell DePalma. (Eerdmans Books for Young Readers, 2011.)
401. *The City: A Vision in Woodcuts.* By Frans Masereel. (Dover Publications, 2006.)
402. *The Spring Hat.* By Madelaine Gill. (Simon & Schuster Books for Young Readers, 1993.)
403. *Flora and the Penguin.* By Molly Idle. (Chronicle Books, 2014.)
404. *Spirals, Curves, Fanshapes & Lines.* By Tana Hoban. (Greenwillow Books, 1992.)
405. *Moo!* By David LaRochelle and Mike Wohnoutka. (Walker Books for Young Readers, 2013.)
406. *Who?* By Leo Lionni. (Pantheon, 1983.)
407. *Puss in Boots.* By John S. Goodall. (Margaret K. McElderry Books, 1990.)

408. *So Many Circles, So Many Squares.* By Tana Hoban. (Greenwillow Books, 1998.)
409. *Rolling Downhill.* By Ruth Carroll. (H. Z. Walck, 1973.)
410. *Mister I.* By Lewis Trondheim. (NBM Publishing, 2007.)
411. *R.I.P.: Best of 1985–2004.* By Thomas Ott. (Fantagraphics Books, 2011.)
412. *Prelude to a Million Years & Song without Words: Two Graphic Novels.* By Lynd Ward. (Dover Publications, 2010.)
413. *Pebble Island.* By Jon McNaught. (Nobrow Press, 2012.)
414. *Owly: Just a Little Blue.* By Andy Runton. (Top Shelf Productions, 2005.)
415. *Blackout.* By John Rocco. (Disney-Hyperion, 2011.)
416. *Ocean Whisper / Susurro del océano.* By Dennis Rockhill. (Raven Tree Press, 2008.)
417. *The Mysterious Death of Tom Thomson.* By George A. Walker. (Porcupine's Quill, 2012.)
418. *My Friend Rabbit.* By Eric Rohmann. (Square Fish, 2007.)
419. *I Read Symbols.* By Tana Hoban. (Greenwilllow Books, 1983.)
420. *What If?* By Laura Vaccaro Seeger. (Roaring Brook Press, 2010.)
421. *Noah: A Wordless Picture Book.* By Mark Ludy. (Plough Publishing, 2014.)
422. *Passionate Journey: A Vision in Woodcuts.* By Frans Masereel. (Dover Publications, 2007.)
423. *Alphabet House.* By Nancy Elizabeth Wallace. (Two Lions, 2005.)
424. *Metronome.* By Véronique Tanaka. (NBM Publishing, 2008.)
425. *Boom Boom.* By Sarvinder Naberhaus and Margaret Chodos-Irvine. (Beach Lane Books, 2014.)
426. *Lola & Fred.* By Christoph Heuer. (4N Publishing, 2005.)
427. *Bow-Wow's Nightmare Neighbors.* By Mark Newgarden and Megan Montague Cash. (Roaring Brook Press, 2014.)
428. *Lio: There's a Monster in My Socks.* By Mark Tatulli. (Andrews McMeel Publishing, 2012.)
429. *Kite in the Park.* By Lucy Cousins. (Candlewick, 1992.)
430. *Almost Silent.* By Jason. (Fantagraphics Books, 2010.)
431. *If You Lived Here, You'd Be Home by Now.* By Ed Briant. (Roaring Brook Press, 2009.)
432. *Albert and the Others.* By Guy Delisle. (Drawn and Quarterly, 2008.)
433. *House.* By Josh Simmons. (Fantagraphics Books, 2007.)
434. *Bye, Bye Birdie.* By Shirley Hughes. (Jonathan Cape, 2009.)
435. *Hippo! No, Rhino!* By Jeff Newman. (Little, Brown, 2006.)
436. *Aline and the Others.* By Guy Delisle. (Drawn and Quarterly, 2006.)
437. *Hi Fly.* By Pat Ross and John C. Wallner. (Crown Publishers, 1988.)
438. *Harold and the Purple Crayon.* By Crockett Johnson. (HarperCollins, 2005.)
439. *Coming Home.* By Greg Ruth. (Feiwel & Friends, 2014.)

440. *H Day*. By Renée French. (PictureBox, 2010.)

441. *Gon*. By Masashi Tanaka. (Paradox Press, 1996.)

442. *Abstract Alphabet: A Book of Animals*. By Paul Cox. (Chronicle Books, 2001.)

443. *Foxly's Feast*. By Owen Davey. (Templar, 2010.)

444. *A.L.I.E.E.E.N.* By Lewis Trondheim. (First Second, 2006.)

445. *Find the Duck*. By Stephen Cartwright. (Usborne, 2000.)

446. *Oink Oink*. By Arthur Geisert. (HMH Books for Young Readers, 1993.)

447. *Dreams*. By Peter Spier. (Doubleday, 1986.)

448. *10 Minutes till Bedtime*. By Peggy Rathmann. (Puffin, 2004.)

449. *City by Numbers*. By Stephen T. Johnson. (Puffin, 2003.)

450. *Hello Kitty: Surprise!* By Jacob Chabot, Ian McGinty, Jorge Monlongo, and Anastassia Neislotova. (Perfect Square, 2014.)

451. *The Changing City*. By Jörg Müller. (Atheneum Publishers, 1977.)

452. *The Lion and the Bird*. By Marianne Dubuc. (Enchanted Lion Books, 2014.)

453. *Blue Sea*. By Robert Kalan and Donald Crews. (Greenwillow Books, 1992.)

454. *Where's Al?* By Byron Barton. (Clarion, 1972.)

455. *The Happy Dog*. By Hideyuki Tanaka. (Atheneum, 1983.)

456. *Ben's Bunny Trouble*. By Daniel Wakeman and Dirk Van Stralen. (Orca Book Publishers, 2007.)

457. *How Anansi Obtained the Sky God's Stories*. By Janice Skivington. (Children's Press, 1991.)

458. *Bedtime and New School*. By Anna Cunningham and Melanie Sharp. (Franklin Watts, 2011.)

459. *White Collar: A Novel in Linocuts*. By Giacomo Patri. (Celestial Arts, 1975.)

460. *Crocodile and Pierrot*. By Russell Hoban and Sylvie Selig. (Charles Scribner's Sons, 1975.)

461. *Hanimals*. By Mario Mariotti. (Green Tiger Press, 1984.)

462. *The Alphabet Parade*. By Seymour Chwast. (Harcourt Brace Jovanovich, 1991.)

463. *Out of the Blue*. By Alison Jay. (Barefoot Books, 2014.)

464. *Yum! Yuck! A Foldout Book of People Sounds*. By Linda Sue Park, Julia Durango, and Sue Ramá. (Charlesbridge, 2005.)

465. *Wow! City!* By Robert Neubecker. (Disney-Hyperion, 2004.)

466. *Archie's Vacation*. By Domenica More Gordon. (Bloomsbury, 2014.)

467. *Where's Waldo? The Wonder Book*. By Martin Handford. (Candlewick Press, 1997.)

468. *The Inside-Outside Book of Texas*. By Roxie Munro. (Chronicle Books, 2001.)

469. *Walking Shadows: A Novel without Words*. By Neil Bousfield. (Manic D Press, 2010.)

470. *The System*. By Peter Kuper. (PM Press, 2014.)
471. *Waiting for Baby*. By Annie Kubler. (Child's Play International, 2000.)
472. *Trucks Trucks Trucks*. By Peter Sis. (Greenwillow Books, 2004.)
473. *Animal Alphabet*. By Bert Kitchen. (Dial Books, 1984.)
474. *Over, Under & Through*. By Tana Hoban. (Aladdin, 2008.)
475. *Three Little Dreams*. By Thomas Aquinas Maguire. (Simply Read Books, 2009.)
476. *The Sun / The Idea / Story without Words: Three Graphic Novels*. By Frans Masereel. (Dover Publications, 2009.)
477. *Circle of Seasons*. By Gerda Muller. (Duttons Children's Books, 1995.)
478. *Stick Man's Really Bad Day*. By Steve Mockus. (Chronicle Books, 2012.)
479. *A Growling Place*. By Thomas Aquinas Maguire. (Simply Read Books, 2007.)
480. *Owly: Flying Lessons*. By Andy Runton. (Top Shelf Productions, 2006.)
481. *REM: Rapid Eye Movement*. By Istvan Banyai. (Viking, 1997.)
482. *(Mostly) Wordless*. By Jed Alexander. (Alternative Comics, 2014.)
483. *Picnic*. By Emily Arnold McCully. (Harper & Row, 1984.)
484. *Owly: A Time to Be Brave*. By Andy Runton. (Top Shelf Productions, 2007.)
485. *Speechless*. By Peter Kuper. (Top Shelf Productions, 2001.)
486. *One, Two, Where's My Shoe?* By Tomi Ungerer. (Phaidon Press, 2014.)
487. *My Very First Book of Shapes*. By Eric Carle. (Philomel, 2005.)
488. *Yam: Bite-Size Chunks*. By Corey Barba. (Top Shelf Productions, 2008.)
489. *Ojingogo*. By Matthew Forsythe. (Drawn and Quarterly, 2009.)
490. *My New Baby*. By Annie Kubler. (Child's Play International, 2000.)
491. *Tall*. By Jez Alborough. (Candlewick Press, 2005.)
492. *Baby! Baby!* By Vicky Ceelen. (Random House, 2008.)
493. *Mrs. Mustard's Baby Faces*. By Jane Wattenberg. (Chronicle Books, 2007.)
494. *The World of Mamoko in the Time of Dragons*. By Aleksandra Mizielińska and Daniel Mizieliński. (Big Picture Press, 2014.)
495. *Mine!* By Shutta Crum and Patrice Barton. (Knopf Books for Young Readers, 2012.)
496. *Mary Had a Little Lamb*. By Jonas Sickler. (Workman Publishing, 2010.)
497. *Snow Day*. By Daniel Peddle. (Doubleday, 2000.)
498. *Bow-Wow Orders Lunch*. By Mark Newgarden and Megan Montague Cash. (Red Wagon Books, 2007.)
499. *Speechless = Sans Paroles = Sin Palabras: World History without Words*. By Polyp. (New Internationalist, 2009.)
500. *The Man Who Grew His Beard*. By Olivier Schrauwen. (Fantagraphics Books, 2011.)

Appendix 2
THE 500 MOST RECOMMENDED BOOKS BY CHAPTER

CHAPTER 1: CLASSIC TITLES

1. *Flotsam*. By David Wiesner. (Clarion Books, 2006.)
2. *The Snowman*. By Raymond Briggs. (Random House, 1978.)
3. *The Lion & the Mouse*. By Jerry Pinkney. (Little, Brown, 2009.)
4. *Truck*. By Donald Crews. (Tupelo Books, 1997.)
5. *The Arrival*. By Shaun Tan. (Arthur A. Levine Books, 2007.)
6. *Anno's Journey*. By Mitsumasa Anno. (Puffin Books, 1997.)
7. *Deep in the Forest*. By Brinton Turkle. (Puffin Books, 1992.)
8. *Noah's Ark*. By Peter Spier. (Doubleday, 1977.)
9. *Gods' Man*. By Lynd Ward. (Dover Publications, 2004.)
10. *The Adventures of Paddy Pork*. By John S. Goodall. (Harcourt, Brace & World, 1968.)
11. *Little Red Riding Hood*. By John S. Goodall. (Margaret K. McElderry, 1988.)
12. *Flood! A Novel in Pictures*. By Eric Drooker. (Four Walls Eight Windows, 1992.)
13. *The Tortoise & the Hare*. By Jerry Pinkney. (Little, Brown, 2013.)
14. *What Whiskers Did*. By Ruth Carroll. (Scholastic Books, 1965.)
15. *Harry Potter and the Sorcerer's Stone: A Deluxe Pop-Up Book*. By J. K. Rowling and Jill Daniels. (Scholastic, 2001.)
16. *Puss in Boots*. By John S. Goodall. (Margaret K. McElderry Books, 1990.)
17. *Harold and the Purple Crayon*. By Crockett Johnson. (HarperCollins, 2005.)
18. *How Anansi Obtained the Sky God's Stories*. By Janice Skivington. (Children's Press, 1991.)
19. *Where's Waldo? The Wonder Book*. By Martin Handford. (Candlewick Press, 1997.)

CHAPTER 2: FOR AND ABOUT BABIES

1. *New Baby.* By Emily Arnold McCully. (Harper & Row, 1988.)
2. *Of Colors and Things.* By Tana Hoban. (Greenwillow Books, 1989.)
3. *Frere Jacques.* By Jonas Sickler. (Workman Publishing, 2011.)
4. *Who Are They?* By Tana Hoban. (Greenwillow Books, 1994.)
5. *Wiggle! March!* By Kaaren Pixton. (Workman Publishing, 2009.)
6. *Flutter! Fly!* By Kaaren Pixton. (Workman Publishing, 2009.)
7. *What Is That?* By Tana Hoban. (Greenwillow Books, 1994.)
8. *Kite in the Park.* By Lucy Cousins. (Candlewick, 1992.)
9. *Find the Duck.* By Stephen Cartwright. (Usborne, 2000.)
10. *Waiting for Baby.* By Annie Kubler. (Child's Play International, 2000.)
11. *My New Baby.* By Annie Kubler. (Child's Play International, 2000.)
12. *Baby! Baby!* By Vicky Ceelen. (Random House, 2008.)
13. *Mrs. Mustard's Baby Faces.* By Jane Wattenberg. (Chronicle Books, 2007.)
14. *Mary Had a Little Lamb.* By Jonas Sickler. (Workman Publishing, 2010.)

CHAPTER 3: CONCEPTS GALORE

1. *Shapes, Shapes, Shapes.* By Tana Hoban. (Greenwillow Books, 1986.)
2. *Look! Look! Look!* By Tana Hoban. (Greenwillow Books, 1988.)
3. *Is It Larger? Is It Smaller?* By Tana Hoban. (Greenwillow Books, 1985.)
4. *The Colors.* By Monique Felix. (Creative Editions, 2013.)
5. *Shadows and Reflections.* By Tana Hoban. (Greenwillow Books, 1990.)
6. *Circles, Triangles, and Squares.* By Tana Hoban. (Macmillan, 1974.)
7. *Is It Red? Is It Yellow? Is It Blue? An Adventure in Color.* By Tana Hoban. (Mulberry Books, 1987.)
8. *Freight Train.* By Donald Crews. (Greenwillow Books, 1978.)
9. *Dylan's Day Out.* By Peter Catalanotto. (Orchard Books, 1989.)
10. *Is It Rough? Is It Smooth? Is It Shiny?* By Tana Hoban. (Greenwillow Books, 1984.)
11. *Snail, Where Are You?* By Tomi Ungerer. (Blue Apple Books, 2005.)
12. *Exactly the Opposite.* By Tana Hoban. (Greenwillow Books, 1990.)
13. *Color Zoo.* By Lois Ehlert. (HarperFestival, 1997.)
14. *Beach Ball.* By Peter Sis. (Greenwillow Books, 1990.)
15. *Spirals, Curves, Fanshapes & Lines.* By Tana Hoban. (Greenwillow Books, 1992.)
16. *So Many Circles, So Many Squares.* By Tana Hoban. (Greenwillow Books, 1998.)
17. *I Read Symbols.* By Tana Hoban. (Greenwilllow Books, 1983.)

18. *Blue Sea*. By Robert Kalan and Donald Crews. (Greenwillow Books, 1992.)
19. *My Very First Book of Shapes*. By Eric Carle. (Philomel, 2005.)
20. *Bow-Wow Orders Lunch*. By Mark Newgarden and Megan Montague Cash. (Red Wagon Books, 2007.)

CHAPTER 4: NUMBERS AND LETTERS

1. *Anno's Counting Book*. By Mitsumasa Anno. (Crowell, 1977.)
2. *Anno's Counting House*. By Mitsumasa Anno. (Philomel, 1982.)
3. *Letter Lunch*. By Elisa Gutiérrez. (Owlkids Books, 2014.)
4. *The Numbers*. By Monique Felix. (Creative Education, 1992.)
5. *Up to Ten and Down Again*. By Lisa Campbell Ernst. (Lothrop, Lee & Shepard Books, 1986.)
6. *Anno's Alphabet: An Adventure in Imagination*. By Mitsumasa Anno. (Crowell, 1975.)
7. *1, 2, 3 to the Zoo*. By Eric Carle. (Puffin, 1998.)
8. *Alphabet City*. By Stephen T. Johnson. (Viking, 1995.)
9. *Mouse Letters: A Very First Alphabet Book*. By Jim Arnosky. (Clarion Books, 1999.)
10. *Picture a Letter*. By Brad Sneed. (Dial Books, 2002.)
11. *Mouse Numbers: A Very First Counting Book*. By Jim Arnosky. (Clarion Books, 1999.)
12. *A Long Piece of String*. By William Wondriska. (Chronicle Books, 2010.)
13. *Albert B. Cub and Zebra: An Alphabet Storybook*. By Anne F. Rockwell. (Crowell, 1977.)
14. *Alphabet House*. By Nancy Elizabeth Wallace. (Two Lions, 2005.)
15. *City by Numbers*. By Stephen T. Johnson. (Puffin, 2003.)
16. *Abstract Alphabet: A Book of Animals*. By Paul Cox. (Chronicle Books, 2001.)
17. *The Alphabet Parade*. By Seymour Chwast. (Harcourt Brace Jovanovich, 1991.)
18. *Animal Alphabet*. By Bert Kitchen. (Dial Books, 1984.)

CHAPTER 5: BEST AT BEDTIME

1. *Sunshine*. By Jan Ormerod. (Frances Lincoln Children's Books, 2009.)
2. *Moonlight*. By Jan Ormerod. (Frances Lincoln Children's Books, 2004.)
3. *Tabby: A Story in Pictures*. By Aliki. (HarperCollins, 1995.)
4. *Good Night, Gorilla*. By Peggy Rathmann. (Putnam Juvenile, 1996.)

5. *Breakfast for Jack.* By Pat Schories. (Boyds Mills Press, 2004.)
6. *The Angel and the Soldier Boy.* By Peter Collington. (Knopf Books for Young Readers, 1987.)
7. *The Wind.* By Monique Felix. (Creative Editions, 2012.)
8. *Jacko.* By John S. Goodall. (Harcourt Children's Books, 1972.)
9. *Good Night, Garden Gnome.* By Jamichael Henterly. (Dial, 2001.)
10. *Carl's Afternoon in the Park.* By Alexandra Day. (Farrar, Straus & Giroux, 1991.)
11. *Just in Passing.* By Susan Bonners. (Lothrop, Lee & Shepard Books, 1989.)
12. *Flicks.* By Tomie DePaola. (Harcourt Brace Jovanovich, 1979.)
13. *I Can't Sleep.* By Philippe Dupasquier. (Walker Books, 1999.)
14. *Sun's Up.* By Teryl Euvremer. (Crown Publishers, 1987.)
15. *Snow Sounds: An Onomatopoeic Story.* By David A. Johnson. (Houghton Mifflin, 2006.)
16. *Lights Out.* By Arthur Geisert. (Houghton Mifflin, 2005.)
17. *The Chimp and the Clown.* By Ruth Carroll. (H. Z. Walck, 1968.)
18. *Man's Work!* By Annie Kubler. (Child's Play International, 1999.)
19. *Flashlight.* By Lizi Boyd. (Chronicle, 2014.)
20. *The Spring Hat.* By Madelaine Gill. (Simon & Schuster Books for Young Readers, 1993.)
21. *Blackout.* By John Rocco. (Disney-Hyperion, 2011.)
22. *Wow! City!* By Robert Neubecker. (Disney-Hyperion, 2004.)
23. *A Growling Place.* By Thomas Aquinas Maguire. (Simply Read Books, 2007.)
24. *Snow Day.* By Daniel Peddle. (Doubleday, 2000.)

CHAPTER 6: ANIMALS APLENTY

1. *Welcome to the Zoo.* By Alison Jay. (Dial Books for Young Readers, 2008.)
2. *Hug.* By Jez Alborough. (Candlewick Press, 2002.)
3. *Fish on a Walk.* By Eva Muggenthaler. (Enchanted Lion Books, 2011.)
4. *Welcome to Mamoko.* By Aleksandra Mizielińska and Daniel Mizieliński. (Big Picture Press, 2013.)
5. *We Hide, You Seek.* By Jose Aruego and Ariane Dewey. (Greenwillow Books, 1979.)
6. *Red Hat.* By Lita Judge. (Atheneum Books for Young Readers, 2013.)
7. *Hot on the Scent.* By Bente Bech and Peter Lind. (Gareth Stevens, 1992.)
8. *No Dogs Allowed!* By Linda Ashman and Kristin Sorra. (Sterling Children's Books, 2011.)
9. *Anno's Animals.* By Mitsumasa Anno. (Collins, 1979.)

10. *Who?* By Leo Lionni. (Pantheon, 1983.)
11. *My Friend Rabbit.* By Eric Rohmann. (Square Fish, 2007.)
12. *Hippo! No, Rhino!* By Jeff Newman. (Little, Brown, 2006.)
13. *Hanimals.* By Mario Mariotti. (Green Tiger Press, 1984.)
14. *Tall.* By Jez Alborough. (Candlewick Press, 2005.)

CHAPTER 7: CHRISTMAS CHEER

1. *A Small Miracle.* By Peter Collington. (Dragonfly Books, 2011.)
2. *Peter Spier's Christmas!* By Peter Spier. (Doubleday, 1983.)
3. *Small, Medium & Large.* By Jane Monroe Donovan. (Sleeping Bear Press, 2010.)
4. *Silent Night.* By Sandy Turner. (Atheneum, 2001.)
5. *The Christmas Gift.* By Emily Arnold McCully. (StarWalk Kids Media, 2012.)
6. *Carl's Christmas.* By Alexandra Day. (Farrar, Straus & Giroux, 1990.)
7. *The Christmas We Moved to the Barn.* By Cooper Edens and Alexandra Day. (HarperCollins, 1997.)
8. *The Snowy Path: A Christmas Journey.* By Lark Carrier. (Picture Book Studio, 1989.)
9. *Don't Forget Me, Santa Claus.* By Virginia Mayo. (Barrons Juveniles, 1993.)
10. *How Santa Claus Had a Long and Difficult Journey Delivering His Presents.* By Fernando Krahn. (Dell Publishing, 1988.)
11. *An Edwardian Christmas.* By John S. Goodall. (Atheneum, 1981.)

CHAPTER 8: CHARACTER VALUES

1. *Changes, Changes.* By Pat Hutchins. (Aladdin Paperbacks, 1987.)
2. *Four Hungry Kittens.* By Emily Arnold McCully. (StarWalk Kids Media, 2013.)
3. *Inside Outside.* By Lizi Boyd. (Chronicle Books, 2013.)
4. *A Day, a Dog.* By Gabrielle Vincent. (Front Street Press, 1999.)
5. *Hank Finds an Egg.* By Rebecca Dudley. (Peter Pauper Press, 2013.)
6. *The Girl and the Bicycle.* By Mark Pett. (Simon & Schuster Books for Young Readers, 2014.)
7. *The Red Scarf.* By Anne Villeneuve. (Tundra Books, 2010.)
8. *Early Birdy Gets the Worm.* By Bruce Lansky and Bill Bolton. (Meadowbrook, 2014.)
9. *Noah: A Wordless Picture Book.* By Mark Ludy. (Plough Publishing, 2014.)
10. *Coming Home.* By Greg Ruth. (Feiwel & Friends, 2014.)

CHAPTER 9: FABULOUS FRIENDSHIPS

1. *Flora and the Flamingo*. By Molly Idle. (Chronicle Books, 2013.)
2. *Do You Want to Be My Friend?* By Eric Carle. (HarperFestival, 1995.)
3. *Bluebird*. By Bob Staake. (Schwartz & Wade Books, 2013.)
4. *Clown*. By Quentin Blake. (Henry Holt, 1998.)
5. *Owly & Wormy, Friends All Aflutter!* By Andy Runton. (Atheneum Books for Young Readers, 2011.)
6. *Chicken and Cat*. By Sara Varon. (Scholastic Press, 2006.)
7. *Chicken and Cat Clean Up*. By Sara Varon. (Scholastic Press, 2009.)
8. *The Boys*. By Jeff Newman. (Simon & Schuster Books for Young Readers, 2010.)
9. *Peep!* By Kevin Luthardt. (Peachtree Publishers, 2012.)
10. *An Ocean World*. By Peter Sis. (Greenwillow Books, 1992.)
11. *The Farmer and the Clown*. By Marla Frazee. (Beach Lane Books, 2014.)
12. *Little Bird*. By Germano Zullo and Albertine. (Enchanted Lion Books, 2012.)
13. *The Secret of Love*. By Sarah Emmanuelle Burg. (Penguin Young Readers Group, 2006.)
14. *Muffel and Plums*. By Lilo Fromm. (Macmillan, 1972.)
15. *Good News, Bad News*. By Jeff Mack. (Chronicle Books, 2012.)
16. *Pssst! Doggie—*. By Ezra Jack Keats. (Franklin Watts, 1973.)
17. *Kitten for a Day*. By Ezra Jack Keats. (Perfection Learning, 2008.)
18. *Mighty Mizzling Mouse and the Red Cabbage House*. By Friso Henstra. (Little, Brown, 1984.)
19. *Yo! Yes?* By Chris Raschka. (Scholastic, 2007.)
20. *Ball*. By Mary Sullivan. (Houghton Mifflin Harcourt Books for Children, 2013.)

CHAPTER 10: COMEDY CAPERS

1. *Where's Walrus?* By Stephen Savage. (Scholastic Press, 2011.)
2. *Oops*. By Mercer Mayer. (Puffin Books, 1978.)
3. *Hocus Pocus*. By Sylvie Desrosiers and Rémy Simard. (Kids Can Press, 2011.)
4. *Follow Carl!* By Alexandra Day. (Farrar, Straus & Giroux, 1998.)
5. *Jack Wants a Snack*. By Pat Schories. (Boyds Mills Press, 2008.)
6. *Once upon a Banana*. By Jennifer Armstrong and David Small. (Simon & Schuster / Paula Wiseman Books, 2006.)

7. *Octopus Soup.* By Mercer Mayer. (Marshall Cavendish Children, 2011.)
8. *Hello, Mr. Hulot.* By David Merveille. (NorthSouth, 2013.)
9. *Look What I Can Do.* By Jose Aruego. (Aladdin Books, 1988.)
10. *Red Sled.* By Lita Judge. (Atheneum Books for Young Readers, 2011.)
11. *Rosie's Walk.* By Pat Hutchins. (Red Fox, 2010.)
12. *The Bear and the Fly.* By Paula Winter. (Crown Publishers, 1976.)
13. *April Fools.* By Fernando Krahn. (E. P. Dutton, 1974.)
14. *Naughty Nancy Goes to School.* By John S. Goodall. (Atheneum, 1985.)
15. *Hiccup.* By Mercer Mayer. (Dial, 1976.)
16. *Hocus Pocus Takes the Train.* By Sylvie Desrosiers and Rémy Simard. (Kids Can Press, 2013.)
17. *Ah-choo.* By Mercer Mayer. (Dial, 1976.)
18. *Mister O.* By Lewis Trondheim. (NBM / Nantier, Beall, Minoustchine, 2004.)
19. *Paddy Pork's Holiday.* By John S. Goodall. (Atheneum, 1973.)
20. *The Marvelous Misadventures of Fun-Boy.* By Ralph Cosentino. (Viking, 2006.)
21. *Sunday Love.* By Alison Paul. (HMH Books for Young Readers, 2010.)
22. *Paddy Pork: Odd Jobs.* By John S. Goodall. (Atheneum, 1983.)
23. *The Great Escape.* By Philippe Dupasquier. (Houghton Mifflin, 1988.)
24. *The Rabbits Are Coming!* By Kathleen Bullock. (Simon & Schuster Books for Young Readers, 1991.)
25. *Dancing Boy.* By Ronald Himler. (Star Bright Books, 2005.)
26. *Splat! Starring the Vole Brothers.* By Roslyn Schwartz. (Owlkids Books, 2014.)
27. *Carl's Snowy Afternoon.* By Alexandra Day. (Farrar, Straus & Giroux, 2009.)
28. *The Train.* By Witold Generowicz. (Dial, 1982.)
29. *Who's Seen the Scissors?* By Fernando Krahn. (Dutton, 1975.)
30. *Bang.* By Leo Timmers. (Gecko Press, 2013.)
31. *Uh-oh!* By Mary Newell DePalma. (Eerdmans Books for Young Readers, 2011.)
32. *Yum! Yuck! A Foldout Book of People Sounds.* By Linda Sue Park, Julia Durango, and Sue Ramá. (Charlesbridge, 2005.)
33. *Mister I.* By Lewis Trondheim. (NBM Publishing, 2007.)
34. *Stick Man's Really Bad Day.* By Steve Mockus. (Chronicle Books, 2012.)

CHAPTER 11: ACTS OF KINDNESS

1. *South.* By Patrick McDonnell. (Little, Brown Books for Young Readers, 2008.)

2. *The Hunter and the Animals: A Wordless Picture Book.* By Tomie DePaola. (Holiday House, 1981.)
3. *A Circle of Friends.* By Giora Carmi. (Star Bright Books, 2006.)
4. *Fox's Garden.* By Princesse Camcam. (Enchanted Lion Books, 2014.)
5. *Fly, Little Bird.* By Tina Burke. (Kane/Miller, 2006.)
6. *Amanda's Butterfly.* By Nick Butterworth. (Collins, 1991.)
7. *The Good Bird.* By Peter Wezel. (Harper & Row, 1964.)
8. *The Special String.* By Harald Bakken and Mischa Richter. (Prentice Hall, 1981.)
9. *Boom Boom.* By Sarvinder Naberhaus and Margaret Chodos-Irvine. (Beach Lane Books, 2014.)
10. *The Lion and the Bird.* By Marianne Dubuc. (Enchanted Lion Books, 2014.)

CHAPTER 12: LOST AND FOUND

1. *A Ball for Daisy.* By Chris Raschka. (Schwartz & Wade Books, 2011.)
2. *Daisy Gets Lost.* By Chris Raschka. (Schwartz & Wade Books, 2013.)
3. *School.* By Emily Arnold McCully. (Harper & Row, 1987.)
4. *Have You Seen My Duckling?* By Nancy Tafuri. (Greenwillow Books, 1984.)
5. *Beaver Is Lost.* By Elisha Cooper. (Schwartz & Wade Books, 2010.)
6. *Where's My Monkey?* By Dieter Schubert. (Dial Books for Young Readers, 1987.)
7. *Catch That Cat!* By Fernando Krahn. (Dutton, 1978.)
8. *The Zoo.* By Suzy Lee. (Kane/Miller, 2007.)
9. *Where's Al?* By Byron Barton. (Clarion, 1972.)
10. *Crocodile and Pierrot.* By Russell Hoban and Sylvie Selig. (Charles Scribner's Sons, 1975.)
11. *Picnic.* By Emily Arnold McCully. (Harper & Row, 1984.)

CHAPTER 13: GALA GATHERINGS

1. *The Crocodile Blues.* By Coleman Polhemus. (Candlewick Press, 2007.)
2. *Naughty Nancy.* By John S. Goodall. (Margaret K. McElderry, 1999.)
3. *Carl's Birthday.* By Alexandra Day. (Farrar, Straus & Giroux, 1997.)
4. *Shrewbettina's Birthday.* By John S. Goodall. (Margaret K. McElderry, 1998.)
5. *A Special Birthday.* By Symeon Shimin. (McGraw-Hill, 1976.)
6. *A Birthday Wish.* By Ed Emberley. (Little, Brown, 1977.)
7. *Alligator's Toothache.* By Diane de Groat. (Crown, 1977.)
8. *Foxly's Feast.* By Owen Davey. (Templar, 2010.)

CHAPTER 14: PET MISCHIEF

1. *Good Dog, Carl.* By Alexandra Day. (Little Simon, 1996.)
2. *Frog Goes to Dinner.* By Mercer Mayer. (Dial, 2003.)
3. *Frog, Where Are You?* By Mercer Mayer. (Dial, 2003.)
4. *Frog on His Own.* By Mercer Mayer. (Dial, 2003.)
5. *Carl Goes Shopping.* By Alexandra Day. (Farrar, Straus & Giroux, 1992.)
6. *Carl's Masquerade.* By Alexandra Day. (Farrar, Straus & Giroux, 1992.)
7. *Jack and the Missing Piece.* By Pat Schories. (Boyds Mills Press, 2004.)
8. *Carl's Summer Vacation.* By Alexandra Day. (Farrar, Straus & Giroux, 2008.)
9. *Carl Makes a Scrapbook.* By Alexandra Day. (Farrar, Straus & Giroux, 1994.)
10. *10 Minutes till Bedtime.* By Peggy Rathmann. (Puffin, 2004.)

CHAPTER 15: AQUATIC ADVENTURES

1. *Wave.* By Suzy Lee. (Chronicle Books, 2008.)
2. *A Boy, a Dog, and a Frog.* By Mercer Mayer. (Dial, 2003.)
3. *Dinosaur!* By Peter Sis. (Greenwillow Books, 2005.)
4. *A Boy, a Dog, a Frog, and a Friend.* By Mercer and Marianna Mayer. (Puffin Books, 1993.)
5. *The Tree House.* By Marije Tolman and Ronald Tolman. (Lemniscaat, 2010.)
6. *Peter Spier's Rain.* By Peter Spier. (Doubleday, 1982.)
7. *The Treasure Bath.* By Dan Andreasen. (Henry Holt, 2009.)
8. *Hogwash.* By Arthur Geisert. (HMH Books for Young Readers, 2008.)
9. *Paddy Under Water.* By John S. Goodall. (Atheneum, 1984.)
10. *Beach Day.* By Helen Oxenbury. (Dial Very First Books, 1991.)
11. *Ship Ahoy!* By Peter Sis. (Greenwillow Books, 1999.)
12. *Mudkin.* By Stephen Gammell. (Carolrhoda Books, 2011.)
13. *Rolling Downhill.* By Ruth Carroll. (H. Z. Walck, 1973.)
14. *Ocean Whisper / Susurro del océano.* By Dennis Rockhill. (Raven Tree Press, 2008.)
15. *What If?* By Laura Vaccaro Seeger. (Roaring Brook Press, 2010.)
16. *The Happy Dog.* By Hideyuki Tanaka. (Atheneum, 1983.)
17. *Out of the Blue.* By Alison Jay. (Barefoot Books, 2014.)
18. *(Mostly) Wordless.* By Jed Alexander. (Alternative Comics, 2014.)

CHAPTER 16: WONDERS OF NATURE

1. *Clementina's Cactus*. By Ezra Jack Keats. (Viking Juvenile, 1999.)
2. *Gem*. By Holly Hobbie. (Little, Brown, 2012.)
3. *Flood*. By Alvaro F. Villa. (Picture Window Books, 2013.)
4. *In the Woods*. By Ermanno Cristini, Luigi Puricelli, and Renato Pegoraro. (Scholastic, 1990.)
5. *The Apple and the Butterfly*. By Iela Mari and Enzo Mari. (Price Stern Sloan, 2013.)
6. *Island Dog*. By Rebecca Goodale. (Two Dog Press, 1999.)
7. *Dreams*. By Peter Spier. (Doubleday, 1986.)
8. *Circle of Seasons*. By Gerda Muller. (Duttons Children's Books, 1995.)

CHAPTER 17: RURAL REWARDS

1. *Pancakes for Breakfast*. By Tomie DePaola. (Harcourt, Brace, Jovanovich, 1978.)
2. *Thunderstorm*. By Arthur Geisert. (Enchanted Lion Books, 2013.)
3. *Early Morning in the Barn*. By Nancy Tafuri. (Greenwillow Books, 1983.)
4. *Our House on the Hill*. By Philippe Dupasquier. (Viking Kestrel, 1988.)
5. *The Story of a Farm*. By John S. Goodall. (Margaret K. McElderry, 1989.)
6. *The Chicken's Child*. By Margaret A. Hartelius. (Doubleday, 1975.)
7. *Wings*. By Shinsuke Tanaka. (Purple Bear Books, 2006.)
8. *Oink*. By Arthur Geisert. (HMH Books for Young Readers, 1991.)
9. *Moo!* By David LaRochelle and Mike Wohnoutka. (Walker Books for Young Readers, 2013.)
10. *Oink Oink*. By Arthur Geisert. (HMH Books for Young Readers, 1993.)

CHAPTER 18: CREATIVE JOURNEYS

1. *Journey*. By Aaron Becker. (Candlewick Press, 2013.)
2. *Trainstop*. By Barbara Lehman. (Houghton Mifflin, 2008.)
3. *The Secret Box*. By Barbara Lehman. (Houghton Mifflin, 2011.)
4. *Sea of Dreams*. By Dennis Nolan. (Roaring Brook Press, 2011.)
5. *The Umbrella*. By Ingrid and Dieter Schubert. (Lemniscaat USA, 2011.)
6. *The Giant Seed*. By Arthur Geisert. (Enchanted Lion Books, 2012.)
7. *The Island*. By Marije Tolman and Ronald Tolman. (Lemniscaat USA, 2012.)
8. *Draw!* By Raúl Colón. (Simon & Schuster, 2014.)

9. *The Bored Book*. By David Michael Slater and Doug Keith. (Simply Read Books, 2009.)
10. *Hot Air: The (Mostly) True Story of the First Hot-Air Balloon Ride*. By Marjorie Priceman. (Atheneum Books for Young Readers, 2005.)
11. *Quest*. By Aaron Becker. (Candlewick Press, 2014.)

CHAPTER 19: DREAMY DEPARTURES

1. *Wonder Bear*. By Tao Nyeu. (Dial, 2008.)
2. *Last Night*. By Hyewon Yum. (Farrar, Straus & Giroux, 2008.)
3. *Little Star*. By Antonin Louchard. (Hyperion Books for Children, 2003.)
4. *The Little Red Fish*. By Tae-Eun Yoo. (Dial, 2007.)
5. *Little Pickle*. By Peter Collington. (E. P. Dutton, 1986.)
6. *Polar Slumber / Sueño polar*. By Dennis Rockhill. (Raven Tree Press, 2004.)
7. *The Midnight Circus*. By Peter Collington. (Knopf, 1992.)
8. *Three Little Dreams*. By Thomas Aquinas Maguire. (Simply Read Books, 2009.)
9. *REM: Rapid Eye Movement*. By Istvan Banyai. (Viking, 1997.)

CHAPTER 20: FASHIONABLE FAVORITES

1. *Archie*. By Domenica More Gordon. (Bloomsbury USA Children's, 2012.)
2. *Sing, Pierrot, Sing: A Picture Book in Mime*. By Tomie DePaola. (Harcourt Children's Books, 1987.)
3. *Sir Andrew*. By Paula Winter. (Random House, 1984.)
4. *Lavinia's Cottage*. By John S. Goodall. (Margaret K. McElderry, 1983.)
5. *The Heartaches of a French Cat*. By Barbara McClintock. (D. R. Godine, 1989.)
6. *An Edwardian Holiday*. By John S. Goodall. (Atheneum, 1979.)
7. *Paddy's New Hat*. By John S. Goodall. (Atheneum, 1980.)
8. *Shrewbettina Goes to Work*. By John S. Goodall. (Atheneum, 1981.)
9. *Archie's Vacation*. By Domenica More Gordon. (Bloomsbury, 2014.)

CHAPTER 21: FASCINATING FANTASIES

1. *The Red Book*. By Barbara Lehman. (Houghton Mifflin, 2004.)
2. *Time Flies*. By Eric Rohmann. (Crown, 1994.)
3. *Chalk*. By Bill Thomson. (Marshall Cavendish Children, 2010.)

4. *Sector 7.* By David Wiesner. (Clarion Books, 1999.)
5. *Mr. Wuffles!* By David Wiesner. (Clarion Books, 2013.)
6. *Ice.* By Arthur Geisert. (Enchanted Lion Books, 2011.)
7. *The Midnight Adventures of Kelly, Dot, and Esmeralda.* By John S. Goodall. (Margaret K. McElderry, 1999.)
8. *Up and Up.* By Shirley Hughes. (Red Fox, 1991.)
9. *Fossil.* By Bill Thomson. (Two Lions, 2013.)
10. *The Surprise Picnic.* By John S. Goodall. (Atheneum, 1977.)
11. *The Self-Made Snowman.* By Fernando Krahn. (J. B. Lippincott, 1974.)
12. *The 46 Little Men.* By Jan Mogensen. (Greenwillow Books, 1991.)
13. *Hunters of the Great Forest.* By Dennis Nolan. (Roaring Brook Press, 2014.)
14. *The Wonder Ring: A Fantasy in Silhouette.* By Holden Wetherbee. (Doubleday, 1978.)
15. *The World of Mamoko in the Year 3000.* By Aleksandra Mizielińska and Daniel Mizieliński. (Big Picture Press, 2014.)
16. *Flying Jake.* By Lane Smith. (Macmillan, 1988.)
17. *The Flying Grandmother.* By Naomi Kojima. (Crowell, 1981.)
18. *Ben's Big Dig.* By Daniel Wakeman and Dirk Van Stralen. (Orca Book Publishers, 2005.)
19. *The World of Mamoko in the Time of Dragons.* By Aleksandra Mizielińska and Daniel Mizieliński. (Big Picture Press, 2014.)

CHAPTER 22: MARVELOUS MYSTERIES

1. *Tuesday.* By David Wiesner. (Clarion Books, 1997.)
2. *Free Fall.* By David Wiesner. (HarperCollins, 2008.)
3. *Rainstorm.* By Barbara Lehman. (Houghton Mifflin, 2007.)
4. *The Grey Lady and the Strawberry Snatcher.* By Molly Bang. (Aladdin Paperbacks, 1996.)
5. *Creepy Castle.* By John S. Goodall. (Atheneum, 1975.)
6. *Where Is the Cake?* By Thé Tjong-Khing. (Abrams Books for Young Readers, 2007.)
7. *The Surprise.* By Sylvia van Ommen. (Lemniscaat, 2007.)
8. *Rooster's Revenge.* By Beatrice Rodriguez. (Enchanted Lion Books, 2011.)
9. *The Mysteries of Harris Burdick.* By Chris Van Allsburg. (Houghton Mifflin, 1984.)
10. *The Birthday Cake Mystery.* By Thé Tjong-Khing. (Gecko Press, 2012.)
11. *Where Is the Cake Now?* By Thé Tjong-Khing. (Abrams Books for Young Readers, 2009.)
12. *One Scary Night.* By Antoine Guilloppé. (Milk & Cookies Press, 2004.)

13. *Amanda and the Mysterious Carpet.* By Fernando Krahn. (Clarion Books, 1985.)
14. *Boat.* By Barbara Remington. (Doubleday, 1975.)

CHAPTER 23: PICTORIAL PERSPECTIVES

1. *Zoom.* By Istvan Banyai. (Viking, 1995.)
2. *Re-zoom.* By Istvan Banyai. (Puffin Books, 1998.)
3. *Yellow Umbrella.* By Jae-Soo Lui. (Kane/Miller, 2002.)
4. *The Other Side.* By Istvan Banyai. (Chronicle Books, 2005.)
5. *Bee & Bird.* By Craig Frazier. (Roaring Brook Press, 2011.)
6. *Topsy-Turvies: Pictures to Stretch the Imagination.* By Mitsumasa Anno. (Tuttle Publishing, 1970.)
7. *Looking Down.* By Steve Jenkins. (Houghton Mifflin, 1995.)
8. *Invisible.* By Katja Kamm. (North-South Books, 2006.)
9. *Balloon Trip.* By Ronald Wegen. (Houghton Mifflin, 1981.)
10. *Take Another Look.* By Tana Hoban. (Greenwillow Books, 1981.)
11. *Travel.* By Yuichi Yokoyama. (PictureBox, 2008.)
12. *Oh!* By Josse Goffin. (Kalandraka, 2007.)
13. *Graham Oakley's Magical Changes.* By Graham Oakley. (Atheneum, 1980.)
14. *Dots, Spots, Speckles, and Stripes.* By Tana Hoban. (Greenwillow Books, 1987.)
15. *Over, Under & Through.* By Tana Hoban. (Aladdin, 2008.)
16. *One, Two, Where's My Shoe?* By Tomi Ungerer. (Phaidon Press, 2014.)

CHAPTER 24: DIFFICULT CHALLENGES

1. *One Frog Too Many.* By Mercer and Marianna Mayer. (Dial, 2003.)
2. *The Last Laugh.* By Jose Aruego and Ariane Dewey. (Dial, 2006.)
3. *Bear Despair.* By Gaetan Dorémus. (Enchanted Lion Books, 2012.)
4. *First Snow.* By Emily Arnold McCully. (Harper & Row, 1985.)
5. *The Wrong Side of the Bed.* By Edward Ardizzone. (Doubleday, 1970.)
6. *Coyote Run.* By Gaetan Dorémus. (Enchanted Lion Books, 2014.)
7. *Carl Goes to Daycare.* By Alexandra Day. (Farrar, Straus & Giroux, 1993.)
8. *Bobo's Dream.* By Martha Alexander. (Dial, 1970.)
9. *He's My Jumbo!* By Claude K. Dubois. (Viking Kestrel, 1990.)
10. *The Knight and the Dragon.* By Tomie DePaola. (Puffin Books, 1998.)
11. *Here Comes Alex Pumpernickel!* By Fernando Krahn. (Little, Brown, 1981.)
12. *No, David!* By David Shannon. (Blue Sky Press, 1998.)

13. *Winterbird.* By Alfred Olschewski. (Houghton Mifflin, 1969.)
14. *Flora and the Penguin.* By Molly Idle. (Chronicle Books, 2014.)
15. *Bedtime and New School.* By Anna Cunningham and Melanie Sharp. (Franklin Watts, 2011.)
16. *Mine!* By Shutta Crum and Patrice Barton. (Knopf Books for Young Readers, 2012.)

CHAPTER 25: EDIFYING EXPLOITS

1. *You Can't Take a Balloon into the Metropolitan Museum.* By Jacqueline Preiss Weitzman and Robin Preiss Glasser. (Dial Books for Young Readers, 1998.)
2. *Museum Trip.* By Barbara Lehman. (Houghton Mifflin, 2006.)
3. *The Boy, the Bear, the Baron, the Bard.* By Gregory Rogers. (Roaring Brook Press, 2004.)
4. *Unspoken: A Story from the Underground Railroad.* By Henry Cole. (Scholastic Press, 2012.)
5. *Anno's U.S.A.* By Mitsumasa Anno. (Philomel, 1983.)
6. *The Yellow Balloon.* By Charlotte Dematons. (Front Street / Lemniscaat, 2003.)
7. *You Can't Take a Balloon into the Museum of Fine Arts.* By Jacqueline Preiss Weitzman and Robin Preiss Glasser. (Penguin Group, 2002.)
8. *Midsummer Knight.* By Gregory Rogers. (Allen & Unwin Children's Books, 2008.)
9. *The Hero of Little Street.* By Gregory Rogers. (Roaring Brook Press, 2012.)
10. *Anno's Britain.* By Mitsumasa Anno. (Philomel, 1982.)
11. *Anno's Flea Market.* By Mitsumasa Anno. (Philomel Books, 1984.)
12. *Anno's Spain.* By Mitsumasa Anno. (Philomel Books, 2004.)
13. *Holland.* By Charlotte Dematons. (Lemniscaat, 2013.)
14. *Anno's Italy.* By Mitsumasa Anno. (Collins, 1980.)
15. *Picturescape.* By Elisa Gutiérrez. (Simply Read Books, 2005.)
16. *The Red Thread.* By Tord Nygren. (Farrar, Straus & Giroux, 1988.)
17. *Dig, Drill, Dump, Fill.* By Tana Hoban. (Greenwillow Books, 1975.)
18. *The Story of a Castle.* By John S. Goodall. (Margaret K. McElderry, 1986.)
19. *The City.* By Douglas Florian. (Crowell Junior Books, 1982.)
20. *The Inside-Outside Book of New York City.* By Roxie Munro. (Dodd, Mead, 1985.)
21. *Journey to the Moon.* By Erich Fuchs. (Delacorte Press, 1969.)
22. *The Inside-Outside Book of Texas.* By Roxie Munro. (Chronicle Books, 2001.)

CHAPTER 26: LEAPS OF IMAGINATION

1. *Sidewalk Circus*. By Paul Fleischman and Kevin Hawkes. (Candlewick Press, 2007.)
2. *The Chicken Thief.* By Beatrice Rodriguez. (Enchanted Lion Books, 2010.)
3. *Shadow*. By Suzy Lee. (Chronicle Books, 2010.)
4. *The Boy and the Airplane*. By Mark Pett. (Simon & Schuster Books for Young Readers, 2013.)
5. *The Tooth Fairy*. By Peter Collington. (Knopf Books for Young Readers, 1995.)
6. *April Wilson's Magpie Magic: A Tale of Colorful Mischief.* By April Wilson. (Dial, 1999.)
7. *Fox and Hen Together*. By Beatrice Rodriguez. (Enchanted Lion Books, 2011.)
8. *Un-brella*. By Scott E. Franson. (Roaring Brook Press, 2007.)
9. *The Conductor*. By Laetitia Devernay. (Chronicle Books, 2011.)
10. *Mirror*. By Suzy Lee. (Seven Footer Kids, 2010.)
11. *The Line*. By Paula Bossio. (Kids Can Press, 2013.)
12. *Leaf.* By Stephen Michael King. (Roaring Brook Press, 2009.)
13. *I See a Song*. By Eric Carle. (Thomas Y. Crowell, 1973.)
14. *Bubble Bubble*. By Mercer Mayer. (Parents' Magazine Press, 1973.)
15. *Rainy Day Dream*. By Michael Chesworth. (Farrar, Straus & Giroux, 1992.)
16. *The Great Cat Chase*. By Mercer Mayer. (Four Winds Press, 1974.)
17. *Animals Home Alone*. By Loes Riphagen. (Seven Footer Kids, 2011.)
18. *Higher! Higher!* By Leslie Patricelli. (Candlewick Press, 2010.)
19. *When Night Didn't Come*. By Poly Bernatene. (Meadowside Children's, 2010.)
20. *Robot-Bot-Bot*. By Fernando Krahn. (Dutton Juvenile, 1979.)
21. *Will's Mammoth*. By Rafe Martin and Stephen Gammell. (PaperStar, 1997.)
22. *A Whole World*. By Antonin Louchard and Katy Couprie. (Milet, 2002.)
23. *Lola & Fred*. By Christoph Heuer. (4N Publishing, 2005.)
24. *Hi Fly*. By Pat Ross and John C. Wallner. (Crown Publishers, 1988.)
25. *Trucks Trucks Trucks*. By Peter Sis. (Greenwillow Books, 2004.)

CHAPTER 27: WEIRD ENCOUNTERS

1. *Bow-Wow Bugs a Bug*. By Mark Newgarden and Megan Montague Cash. (HMH Books for Young Readers, 2007.)
2. *Jack and the Night Visitors*. By Pat Schories. (Front Street Press, 2006.)
3. *The Shadow*. By Donna Diamond. (Candlewick, 2010.)

4. *The Night Riders*. By Matt Furie. (McSweeney's/McMullens, 2012.)
5. *The Creepy Thing*. By Fernando Krahn. (Clarion Books, 1982.)
6. *Full Moon Soup*. By Alastair Graham. (Dial Books, 1991.)
7. *Arthur's Adventure in the Abandoned House*. By Fernando Krahn. (Dutton Juvenile, 1981.)
8. *The West Wing*. By Edward Gorey. (Simon & Schuster, 1963.)
9. *Bow-Wow's Nightmare Neighbors*. By Mark Newgarden and Megan Montague Cash. (Roaring Brook Press, 2014.)

CHAPTER 28: SOCIAL AND ENVIRONMENTAL AWARENESS

1. *Window*. By Jeannie Baker. (Walker Books, 2002.)
2. *Home*. By Jeannie Baker. (Greenwillow Books, 2004.)
3. *Mirror*. By Jeannie Baker. (Candlewick Press, 2010.)
4. *Why?* By Nikolai Popov. (Michael Neugebauer, 1998.)
5. *No!* By David McPhail. (Roaring Brook Press, 2009.)
6. *The Flower Man: A Wordless Picture Book*. By Mark Ludy. (Green Pastures Publishing, 2005.)
7. *Waterloo & Trafalgar*. By Olivier Tallec. (Enchanted Lion Books, 2012.)
8. *Cool Cat*. By Nonny Hogrogian. (Roaring Brook Press, 2009.)
9. *The Changing Countryside*. By Jörg Müller. (Atheneum Publishers, 1977.)
10. *OK Go*. By Carin Berger. (Greenwillow Books, 2009.)
11. *An Edwardian Summer*. By John S. Goodall. (Macmillan, 1979.)
12. *A Flying Saucer Full of Spaghetti*. By Fernando Krahn. (E. P. Dutton, 1970.)
13. *The Great War: July 1, 1916: The First Day of the Battle of the Somme: An Illustrated Panorama*. By Joe Sacco. (W. W. Norton, 2013.)
14. *If You Lived Here, You'd Be Home by Now*. By Ed Briant. (Roaring Brook Press, 2009.)
15. *The Changing City*. By Jörg Müller. (Atheneum Publishers, 1977.)
16. *Ben's Bunny Trouble*. By Daniel Wakeman and Dirk Van Stralen. (Orca Book Publishers, 2007.)

CHAPTER 29: GRAPHIC NOVELS FOR CHILDREN

1. *The Adventures of Polo*. By Regis Faller. (Roaring Brook Press, 2006.)
2. *Robot Dreams*. By Sara Varon. (First Second, 2007.)
3. *The Silver Pony: A Story in Pictures*. By Lynd Ward. (Houghton Mifflin, 1973.)
4. *Polo: The Runaway Book*. By Regis Faller. (Roaring Brook Press, 2007.)

5. *Here I Am*. By Patti Kim and Sonia Sanchez. (Capstone Young Readers, 2014.)
6. *Polo and Lily*. By Regis Faller. (Roaring Brook Press, 2009.)
7. *Polo and the Dragon*. By Regis Faller. (Roaring Brook Press, 2007.)
8. *Korgi Book 1: Sprouting Wings!* By Christian Slade. (Top Shelf Productions, 2007.)
9. *Polo and the Magic Flute*. By Regis Faller. (Roaring Brook Press, 2009.)
10. *Owly & Wormy, Bright Lights and Starry Nights*. By Andy Runton. (Atheneum Books for Young Readers, 2012.)
11. *Polo and the Magician!* By Regis Faller. (Roaring Brook Press, 2009.)
12. *Owly: The Way Home & The Bittersweet Summer*. By Andy Runton. (Top Shelf, 2004.)
13. *A Wish for Elves*. By Mark Gonyea. (Henry Holt, 2010.)
14. *Happy Halloween, Li'l Santa*. By Thierry Robin and Lewis Trondheim. (NBM Publishing, 2003.)
15. *Korgi Book 2: The Cosmic Collector*. By Christian Slade. (Top Shelf Books, 2008.)
16. *I'm Not a Plastic Bag*. By Rachel Hope Allison. (Archaia Entertainment, 2012.)
17. *Don't Look Now*. By Ed Briant. (Roaring Brook Press, 2009.)
18. *Li'l Santa*. By Thierry Robin and Lewis Trondheim. (NBM Publishing, 2002.)
19. *Korgi Book 3: A Hollow Beginning*. By Christian Slade. (Top Shelf Productions, 2011.)
20. *Steam Park*. By Filippo Neri and Piero Ruggeri. (Simply Read Books, 2006.)
21. *Owly: Just a Little Blue*. By Andy Runton. (Top Shelf Productions, 2005.)
22. *Lio: There's a Monster in My Socks*. By Mark Tatulli. (Andrews McMeel Publishing, 2012.)
23. *Hello Kitty: Surprise!* By Jacob Chabot, Ian McGinty, Jorge Monlongo, and Anastassia Neislotova. (Perfect Square, 2014.)
24. *Owly: Flying Lessons*. By Andy Runton. (Top Shelf Productions, 2006.)
25. *Owly: A Time to Be Brave*. By Andy Runton. (Top Shelf Productions, 2007.)
26. *Yam: Bite-Size Chunks*. By Corey Barba. (Top Shelf Productions, 2008.)

CHAPTER 30: GRAPHIC NOVELS FOR TEENS

1. *Blood Song: A Silent Ballad*. By Eric Drooker. (Dark Horse Originals, 2009.)
2. *Weathercraft*. By Jim Woodring. (Fantagraphics Books, 2010.)
3. *Sticks and Stones*. By Peter Kuper. (Three Rivers Press, 2004.)

4. *The Number: 73304-23-4153-6-96-8.* By Thomas Ott. (Fantagraphics Books, 2014.)
5. *Fox Bunny Funny.* By Andy Hartzell. (Top Shelf Productions, 2007.)
6. *Fran.* By Jim Woodring. (Fantagraphics Books, 2013.)
7. *Cinema Panopticum.* By Thomas Ott. (Fantagraphics Books, 2005.)
8. *The Middle Passage: White Ships / Black Cargo.* By Tom Feelings. (Dial Books, 1995.)
9. *The Sanctuary.* By Nate Neal. (Fantagraphics Books, 2010.)
10. *Age of Reptiles Omnibus*, Vol. 1. By Ricardo Delgado. (Dark Horse Books, 2011.)
11. *Monsters! and Other Stories.* By Gustavo Duarte. (Dark Horse Books, 2014.)
12. *Dead End.* By Thomas Ott. (Fantagraphics Books, 2002.)
13. *The Frank Book.* By Jim Woodring. (Fantagraphics Books, 2003.)
14. *Congress of the Animals.* By Jim Woodring. (Fantagraphics Books, 2011.)
15. *Adventures of a Japanese Businessman.* By José Domingo, Isabel Mancebo, Alex Spiro, and Sam Arthur. (Nobrow Press, 2012.)
16. *Combustion: A Story without Words.* By Chris Lanier. (Fantagraphics Books, 1999.)
17. *Greetings from Hellville.* By Thomas Ott. (Fantagraphics Books, 2002.)
18. *Jinchalo.* By Matthew Forsythe. (Drawn and Quarterly, 2012.)
19. *R.I.P.: Best of 1985–2004.* By Thomas Ott. (Fantagraphics Books, 2011.)
20. *Pebble Island.* By Jon McNaught. (Nobrow Press, 2012.)
21. *Metronome.* By Véronique Tanaka. (NBM Publishing, 2008.)
22. *Almost Silent.* By Jason. (Fantagraphics Books, 2010.)
23. *Albert and the Others.* By Guy Delisle. (Drawn and Quarterly, 2008.)
24. *House.* By Josh Simmons. (Fantagraphics Books, 2007.)
25. *Bye, Bye Birdie.* By Shirley Hughes. (Jonathan Cape, 2009.)
26. *Aline and the Others.* By Guy Delisle. (Drawn and Quarterly, 2006.)
27. *H Day.* By Renée French. (PictureBox, 2010.)
28. *Gon.* By Masashi Tanaka. (Paradox Press, 1996.)
29. *A.L.I.E.E.E.N.* By Lewis Trondheim. (First Second, 2006.)
30. *The System.* By Peter Kuper. (PM Press, 2014.)
31. *Speechless.* By Peter Kuper. (Top Shelf Productions, 2001.)
32. *Ojingogo.* By Matthew Forsythe. (Drawn and Quarterly, 2009.)
33. *Speechless = Sans Paroles = Sin Palabras: World History without Words.* By Polyp. (New Internationalist, 2009.)
34. *The Man Who Grew His Beard.* By Olivier Schrauwen. (Fantagraphics Books, 2011.)

CHAPTER 31: WOODCUT NOVELS

1. *Mad Man's Drum: A Novel in Woodcuts.* By Lynd Ward. (Dover Publications, 2005.)
2. *Let That Bad Air Out: Buddy Bolden's Last Parade.* By Stefan Berg. (Porcupine's Quill, 2007.)
3. *He Done Her Wrong.* By Milt Gross. (Fantagraphics Books, 2005.)
4. *Vertigo: A Novel in Woodcuts.* By Lynd Ward. (Dover Publications, 2009.)
5. *Destiny: A Novel in Pictures.* By Otto Nückel. (Dover Publications, 2012.)
6. *Wild Pilgrimage: A Novel in Woodcuts.* By Lynd Ward. (Dover Publications, 2008.)
7. *Book of Hours: A Wordless Novel Told in 99 Wood Engravings.* By George A. Walker. (Porcupine's Quill, 2010.)
8. *Southern Cross: A Novel of the South Seas.* By Laurence Hyde. (Drawn and Quarterly, 2007.)
9. *The City: A Vision in Woodcuts.* By Frans Masereel. (Dover Publications, 2006.)
10. *Prelude to a Million Years & Song without Words: Two Graphic Novels.* By Lynd Ward. (Dover Publications, 2010.)
11. *The Mysterious Death of Tom Thomson.* By George A. Walker. (Porcupine's Quill, 2012.)
12. *Passionate Journey: A Vision in Woodcuts.* By Frans Masereel. (Dover Publications, 2007.)
13. *White Collar: A Novel in Linocuts.* By Giacomo Patri. (Celestial Arts, 1975.)
14. *Walking Shadows: A Novel without Words.* By Neil Bousfield. (Manic D Press, 2010.)
15. *The Sun / The Idea / Story without Words: Three Graphic Novels.* By Frans Masereel. (Dover Publications, 2009.)

Bibliography

"5 Great Wordless Picture Books of 2013." *Book News and Reviews*. Bullitt County Public Library. Last modified January 3, 2014. http://bcplreviews.blogspot.com/2014/01/flash-reviews-5-great-wordless-picture.html.

"15 Wonderful Wordless Picture Books." *What Do We Do All Day?* Last modified April 18, 2013. http://www.whatdowedoallday.com/2013/04/tips-for-reading-wordless-picture-books.html.

"2014 Notable Children's Books." Association for Library Service to Children, American Library Association. Accessed June 6, 2014. http://www.ala.org/alsc/awardsgrants/notalists/ncb.

Anno, Mitsumasa. *Upside Downers: Pictures to Stretch the Imagination*. New York: Walker/Weatherhill, 1971.

Ardizzone, Edward. *Johnny's Bad Day*. London: Bodley Head, 1970.

Arnold [McCully], Emily. *A Craving*. New York: Avon Books, 1982.

———. *Life Drawing*. New York: Delacorte Press, 1986.

Arnosky, Jim. *All about Alligators*. New York: Scholastic, 2008.

———. *All about Deer*. New York: Scholastic, 1996.

———. *Mouse Numbers and Letters*. San Diego, CA: Harcourt Children's Books, 1982.

———. *Tooth and Claw: The Wild World of Big Predators*. New York: Sterling Children's Books, 2014.

Baker, Jeannie. *Belonging*. London: Walker Books, 2004.

Beecher, Alyson. "My Top Ten Favorite Wordless Picture Books That Require a Second or Third Read." *Kid Lit Frenzy*. Last modified August 10, 2013. http://www.kidlitfrenzy.com/2013/08/august-10-for-10-picture-book-post-my.html.

Beronä, David A. *Wordless Books: The Original Graphic Novels*. New York: Abrams, 2008.

"Best Sellers and Other Lists." Public Library of New London. Accessed June 14, 2014. http://catalog.lioninc.org/search~S15.

"Beyond Words! Picture Books without Words." Waltham Public Library. Accessed May 31, 2014. http://www.waltham.lib.ma.us/children/wordless.php.

"Book Lists—Wordless Picture Books." Louisville Free Public Library. Last modified October 5, 2007. http://www.lfpl.org/kids/kids-booklist-wordless.htm.

"Booklists—Stories without Words." Hennepin County Library. Accessed May 29, 2014. http://www.hclib.org/birthto6/booklistaction.cfm?list_num=184.

Brochtrup, William A. "Too Good for Words: An Annotated Bibliography of Wordless Children's Books." ERIC Document. Pacific Western University. Accessed May 22, 2014. http://files.eric.ed.gov/fulltext/ED112379.pdf.

Bunting, Eve. *Night of the Gargoyles*. Illustrated by David Wiesner. Boston: Clarion Books, 1994.

Capucilli, Alyssa Satin. *Biscuit Goes Camping*. Illustrated by Pat Schories. New York: HarperCollins Children's Books, 2015.

———. *Biscuit Loves the Library*. Illustrated by Pat Schories. New York: HarperCollins Children's Books, 2014.

———. *Biscuit's Christmas Storybook Collection*. Illustrated by Pat Schories. New York: HarperCollins Children's Books, 2013.

Carle, Eric. *The Grouchy Ladybug*. New York: HarperCollins, 1996.

———. *My Very First Book of Shapes = Mi primer libro de figuras*. New York: Philomel, 2013.

———. *The Tiny Seed*. Natick, MA: Picture Book Studio, 1987.

———. *The Very Hungry Caterpillar*. New York: Philomel Books, 1987.

Cassady, Judith K. "Wordless Books: No-Risk Tools for Inclusive Middle-Grade Classrooms." *Journal of Adolescent & Adult Literacy* 41, no. 6 (March 1998).

Castellucci, Cecil. *Odd Duck*. Illustrated by Sara Varon. New York: First Second, 2013.

"Children's Lit—Library Guides." University of the Cumberlands. Accessed June 2, 2014. http://ucumberlands.libguides.com/content.php?pid=407072&sid=3332159.

"Children's Picture Book Database at Miami University." Accessed May 30, 2014. http://dlp.lib.miamioh.edu/picturebook.

"Children's Picture Books—Wordless." Powell's Books. Accessed June 13, 2014. http://www.powells.com/section/childrens-picture-books/wordless.

Chwast, Seymour, and Martin Moskof. *Still Another Number Book*. Mineola, NY: Dover Publications, 2013.

Codell, Esmé Raji. *How to Get Your Child to Love Reading*. Chapel Hill, NC: Algonquin Books, 2003.

Collington, Peter. *The Coming of Surfman*. New York: Knopf, 1994.

———. *On Christmas Eve*. New York: Knopf, 1990.

"Comics without Words." Amazon. Accessed June 15, 2014. http://www.amazon.com/s/ref=nb_sb_noss?url=search-alias%3Dstripbooks&field-keywords=comics+without+words&rh=n%3A283155%2Ck%3Acomics+without+words.

"Core Collection of Graphic Novels—2012 Update." Association for Library Service to Children, American Library Association. Accessed June 14, 2014. http://www.ala.org/alsc/compubs/booklists/grphcnvls.

Cormier, Beth, and Bill Glaister. "Graphic Novels in the Classroom: Suggested Titles, Teaching Strategies & Resources." University of Lethbridge. Last modified February 2013. http://www.uleth.ca/education/sites/education/files/GN%20handout.pdf.

Cousins, Lucy. *Flower in the Garden*. Somerville, MA: Candlewick Press, 1992.

————. *Hen on the Farm*. Somerville, MA: Candlewick Press, 1992.

————. *Teddy in the House*. Somerville, MA: Candlewick Press, 1992.

Crews, Donald. *Freight Train*. New York: Greenwillow Books, 1996.

Cristini, Ermanno, and Luigi Puricelli. *In My Garden*. Natick, MA: Picture Book Studio USA, 1985.

————. *In the Pond*. Natick, MA: Picture Book Studio USA, 1984.

Cunningham, Anna, and Trevor Dunton. *Rocket Ship and The Planet*. London: Hodder & Stoughton, 2012.

Cunningham, Anna, and Barbara Vagnozzi. *Stormy Day and Snowy Day*. London: Franklin Watts, 2011.

"Current JLG Selections." Junior Library Guild. Accessed June 13, 2014. http://www.juniorlibraryguild.com/www/dcms/files/resources/pdf/cat-jlg-2014spring-s.pdf.

Dahl, Roald. *The BFG*. Illustrated by Quentin Blake. New York: Farrar, Straus & Giroux, 1982.

————. *Matilda*. New York: Viking Kestrel, 1988.

————. *The Witches*. New York: Farrar, Straus & Giroux, 1983.

Dales, Brenda. "USBBY's 2014 Outstanding International Books List." *School Library Journal*. Last modified February 24, 2014. http://www.slj.com/2014/02/collection-development/passport-to-a-world-of-reading-usbbys-2014-outstanding-international-books-list-introduces-readers-to-the-global-community/#_.

Day, Alexandra. *Carl and the Lost Kitten*. New York: Square Fish, 2015.

————. *Carl's Halloween*. New York: Farrar, Straus & Giroux, 2015.

————. *Frank and Ernest*. New York: Scholastic, 1988.

DeJong, Meindert. *A Journey from Peppermint Street*. Illustrated by Emily Arnold McCulley. New York: Harper & Row, 1968.

Dematons, Charlotte, and Jesse Goossens. *A Thousand Things about Holland*. New York: Lemniscaat, 2013.

DePalma, Mary Newell. *Bow, Wow Wiggle-Waggle*. Grand Rapids, MI: Eerdmans Books for Young Readers, 2012.

————. *Two Little Birds*. Grand Rapids, MI: Eerdmans Books for Young Readers, 2014.

DePaola, Tomie. *Strega Nona*. Englewood Cliffs, NJ: Prentice Hall, 1975.

Donovan, Jane Monroe. *Winter's Gift*. Chelsea, MI: Sleeping Bear Press, 2004.

Dowhower, Sarah. "Wordless Books: Promise and Possibilities, a Genre Come of Age." *American Reading Forum Online Yearbook* 17 (1997). Accessed May 18, 2014. http://www.americanreadingforum.org/yearbook/yearbooks/97_yearbook/pdf/06_Dowhower.pdf.

Drake, Jim. "Stories without Words." Saskatoon Public Library. Last modified February 2014. http://www.saskatoonlibrary.ca/node/1860.

Drooker, Eric. *Slingshot: 32 Postcards*. Oakland, CA: PM Press, 2008.

————. *Street Posters and Ballads*. New York: Seven Stories Press, 1998.

Dubois, Claude K. *Looking for Ginny*. New York: Viking Kestrel, 1990.

Dykstra, Jon. "More Wordless Wonders." *Really Good Reads*. Last modified June 7, 2014. http://www.reallygoodreads.com/search/label/wordless.

Eisner, Will. *Comics and Sequential Art: Principles and Practices from the Legendary Cartoonist*. New York: W. W. Norton, 2008.

———. *Expressive Anatomy for Comics and Narrative: Principles and Practices from the Legendary Cartoonist.* New York: W. W. Norton, 2008.

———. *Graphic Storytelling and Visual Narrative: Principles and Practices from the Legendary Cartoonist.* New York: W. W. Norton, 2008.

"Fantastic Picture Books with No Words." Huntley Area Public Library. Accessed May 30, 2014. http://huntley.bibliocommons.com/list/show/73495315_anthea_mark hampl/91804825_fantastic_picture_books_with_no_words.

Felix, Monique. *The Alphabet.* Mankato, MN: Creative Editions, 2012.

———. *The Boat.* Mankato, MN: Creative Editions, 1993.

———. *The House.* Mankato, MN: Creative Editions, 1993.

———. *The Opposites.* Mankato, MN: Creative Editions, 1993.

———. *The Plane.* San Diego: Harcourt Brace, 1995.

———. *The Valentine.* Mankato, MN: Creative Editions, 2013.

"Five Great Comics without Words." Richland Library. Last modified June 5, 2013. http://www.richlandlibrary.com/recommend/five-great-comics-without-words.

Fleming, Candace. *Bulldozer's Big Day.* Illustrated by Eric Rohmann. New York: Atheneum Books for Young Readers, 2015.

———. *Oh, No!* Illustrated by Eric Rohmann. New York: Schwartz & Wade Books, 2012.

Florian, Douglas. *Dinothesaurus: Prehistoric Poems and Paintings.* New York: Atheneum Books for Young Readers, 2009.

Ford, Deborah B. "Wordless Picture Books That Speak Volumes | JLG's [Junior Library Guild] on the Radar." *School Library Journal.* Last modified October 7, 2013. http://www.slj.com/2013/10/collection-development/on-the-radar/wordless-picture-books-that-speak-volumes-jlgs-on-the-radar/#_.

"Friday's Five: #Cybils Nominated Wordless Wonders." *5 Minutes for Books.* Accessed June 15, 2014. http://books.5minutesformom.com/34106/fridays-five-cybils-nominated-wordless-wonders.

Fuller, Rachael. *Waiting for Baby.* Swindon, UK: Child's Play International, 2009.

Fulton, Janet M., and National Center for Family Literacy. *Talking about Wordless Picture Books: A Tutor Strategy Supporting English Language Learners.* National Center for Families Learning. Accessed May 25, 2014. http://familieslearning.org/pdf/talking-about-wordless-picture-books.pdf.

Garces-Bacsal, Myra. "List of Wordless Picture Books: A Gathering Books Recommendation." *Gathering Books.* Last modified December 27, 2011. http://gatheringbooks.wordpress.com/2011/12/27/list-of-wordless-picture-books.

Geisert, Arthur. *Pa's Balloon and Other Pig Tales.* Boston: Houghton Mifflin, 1984.

———. *Pigs from A to Z.* Boston: Houghton Mifflin, 1986.

Ginsberg, Allen. *Howl: A Graphic Novel.* Illustrated by Eric Drooker. New York: Harper Perennial, 2010.

———. *Illuminated Poems.* Illustrated by Eric Drooker. New York: Four Walls Eight Windows, 1996.

Glasser, Debbie. "Books without Words May Help Boost Your Child's Language." *Psychology Today.* Last modified June 8, 2013. http://www.psychologytoday.com/blog/parenting-news-you-can-use/201306/books-without-words-may-help-boost-your-childs-language.

Goffin, Josse. *Oh! Coloring Book.* New York: Harry N. Abrams, 1994.

Goodall, John S. *Edwardian Entertainments.* New York: Atheneum, 1982.

———. *An Edwardian Season.* New York: Atheneum, 1980.

———. *Great Days of a Country House.* New York: Margaret K. McElderry Books, 1992.

———. *The Story of an English Village.* New York: Atheneum, 1979.

Gordon, Domenica More. *Archie's Holiday.* London: Bloomsbury, 2013.

Graham, Alastair. *Full Moon Soup.* London: Boxer Books, 2009.

"Graphic Novel Reading List." Takoma Park Maryland Library. Last updated March 20, 2010. http://www.takomapark.info/library/books/archives/002181.html.

Gross, Milt. *Heart of Gold.* New York: Abbeville Press, 1983.

"Grown-Ups (Boring!)—Wordless Picture Books." Denver Library. Accessed May 29, 2014. http://kids.denverlibrary.org/grownups/results.cfm?genre=Wordless%20 Picture%20Books.

Gruber, Elise. "Stories without Words: Exploring Books with Preschoolers." *Parent Map.* Accessed May 29, 2014. http://www.parentmap.com/article/stories-without-words -exploring-books-with-preschoolers.

Hasting, A. "Great Wordless Books." Amazon. Accessed May 22, 2014. http://www .amazon.com/Great-Wordless-Books/lm/R3I8KCR3OLIXWD.

Hedeen, Katrina. "From the Guide: Wordless Picture Books." *The Horn Book.* Last modified March 24, 2014. http://www.hbook.com/2014/03/choosing-books/guide -wordless-picture-books/#_.

Henstra, Frisco. *Mighty Mizzling Mouse.* New York: Lippincott, 1983.

Heuer, Christoph. *Lola & Fred & Tom.* Long Island City, NY: 4N Publishing, 2005.

Hoban, Tana. *Look Again!* New York: Macmillan, 1971.

———. *Look Book.* New York: Greenwillow Books, 1997.

———. *What Is It?* New York: William Morrow, 1985.

hooks, bell. *Be Boy Buzz.* Illustrated by Chris Raschka. New York: Hyperion Books for Children, 2002.

———. *Grump Groan Growl.* Illustrated by Chris Raschka. New York: Hyperion Books for Children, 2008.

———. *Happy to Be Nappy.* Illustrated by Chris Raschka. New York: Hyperion Books for Children, 1999.

———. *Skin Again.* Illustrated by Chris Raschka. New York: Hyperion Books for Children, 2004.

"Imagine the Fun at Your Library—Wordless Picture Books." Idaho Commission for Libraries. Accessed May 30, 2014. http://libraries.idaho.gov/files/Booklists_Wordless PictureBooks.pdf.

Jalongo, Mary Renck, with Denise Dragich, Natalie K. Conrad, and Ann Zhang. "Using Wordless Picture Books to Support Emergent Literacy." *Early Childhood Education Journal* 29 (spring 2002). Accessed August 12, 2014. http://wordlesspbs.wikispaces .com/file/view/using+wordless+picture+books+to+support+emergent+literacy.pdf.

Janeczko, Paul B. *A Poke in the I.* Illustrated by Chris Raschka. Cambridge, MA: Candle-wick Press, 2001.

Jason. *The Living and the Dead.* Seattle, WA: Fantagraphics, 2007.

———. *Meow Baby!* Seattle, WA: Fantagraphics, 2005.

———. *Tell Me Something.* Seattle, WA: Fantagraphics, 2003.
———. *You Can't Get There from Here.* Seattle, WA: Fantagraphics, 2004.
Johannes, Shelley. "18 Wonderfully Wordless Picture Books." *The Book Diaries.* Last modified November 12, 2013. http://www.thebookdiariesblog.com/2013/11/18 -wonderfully-wordless-picture-books.html.
Jones, James. *The Thin Red Line.* New York: Scribner, 1962.
Juster, Norton. *The Hello, Goodbye Window.* Illustrated by Chris Raschka. New York: Michael di Capua Books / Hyperion Books for Children, 2005.
Kafka, Franz. *The Metamorphosis.* Illustrated by Peter Kuper. New York: Crown, 2003.
Kalan, Robert, and Donald Crews. *Rain.* New York: Greenwillow Books, 1991.
"KDL Recommends." Kent District Library. Accessed May 29, 2014. http://www.kdl .org/categories/print/3412.
Keane, Nancy. *The Big Book of Teen Reading Lists: 100 Great, Ready-to-Use Book Lists for Educators, Librarians, Parents, and Teens.* Santa Barbara, CA: Libraries Unlimited, 2006.
———. "Wordless Picture Books." *Nancy Keane's Children's Literature Webpage.* Accessed May 26, 2014. http://nancykeane.com/rl/317.htm.
Keats, Ezra Jack. *The Snowy Day.* New York: Viking Press, 1962.
Kennedy, Jimmy. *The Teddy Bears' Picnic.* Illustrated by Alexandra Day. La Jolla, CA: Green Tiger Press, 1983.
"Kidspace Wordless Picture Books." Public Library of Cincinnati and Hamilton County. Accessed May 31, 2014. http://kidspace.cincinnatilibrary.org/books/lists.aspx?id=41.
Killeen, Eriene Bishop. "What Will You Do with a Wordless Book?" *Teacher Librarian* 41 (June 2014). Accessed August 11, 2014. http://catalog.cumberlandcountylibraries. org:61080/ebsco-w-b/ehost/detail/detail?sid=06fa66a9-4557-4717-aab6-32e703e7c2 c9%40sessionmgr114&vid=0&hid=113&bdata=JnNpdGU9ZWhvc3QtbGl2ZQ%3 d%3d#db=f6h&AN=96678467.
Kitchen, Bert. *Animal Numbers.* New York: Dial, 1987.
Klausmeier, Jesse. *Open This Little Book.* Illustrated by Suzy Lee. San Francisco, CA: Chronicle Books, 2013.
Kleon, Austin. "Wordless Graphic Novels and Comics." Amazon. Accessed May 26, 2014. http://www.amazon.com/WORDLESS-GRAPHIC-NOVELS-COMICS/lm/ R12G4G0BQHCYZP.
Krahn, Fernando. *Sleep Tight, Alex Pumpernickel.* Boston: Little, Brown, 1982.
Kuper, Peter. *ComicsTrips: A Journal of Travels through Africa and Southeast Asia.* Northampton, MA: Tundra Publishing, 1992.
———. *Drawn to New York: An Illustrated Chronicle of Three Decades in New York City.* Oakland, CA: PM Press, 2013.
———. *Stop Forgetting to Remember: The Autobiography of Walter Kurtz.* New York: Crown, 2007.
Lenin, Vanessa J. "Jim Trelease: Wordless Picture Books." *Pre-K Pages.* Last modified July 7, 2013. http://www.pre-kpages.com/jim-trelease-wordless-picture-books.
Lionni, Leo. *Alexander and the Wind-Up Mouse.* New York: Dragonfly Books, 1974.
———. *Frederick.* New York: Dragonfly Books, 1973.
———. *Inch by Inch.* New York: HarperCollins, 1995.

———. *Swimmy*. New York: Dragonfly Books, 1973.

Lipson, Eden Ross. *The New York Times Parent's Guide to the Best Books for Children*. New York: Three Rivers Press, 2000.

"List of Excellent Wordless Picture Books." Orchard Ridge Elementary. Accessed May 31, 2014. http://madison.campusguides.com/wordlesspicturebooks.

Lovatt, Holly. "Wordless Graphic Novels: An Annotated Bibliography." Last updated November 18, 2009. http://abwgn.blogspot.com/2009/11/annotated-bibliography -wordless-graphic.html.

Lowry, Lois. *Bless This Mouse*. Illustrated by Eric Rohmann. Boston: Houghton Mifflin Books for Children, 2011.

Lukehart, Wendy. "Wordless Books—Picture Perfect." *School Library Journal*. Last modified April 1, 2011. http://www.slj.com/2011/04/collection-development/word less-books-picture-perfect.

Maguire, Thomas Aquinas. *The Wild Swans*. Vancouver, BC: Simply Read Books, 2012.

Marcus, Leonard S. "Chris Raschka Unleashed." *Horn Book Magazine* (July/August 2012): 32–35.

Mari, Iela, and Enzo Mari. *The Apple and the Moth*. New York: Pantheon Books, 1969.

Mariotti, Mario. *Hanimations*. Brooklyn, NY: Kane/Miller, 1989.

———. *Humages*. La Jolla, CA: Green Tiger Press, 1984.

———. *Humands*. La Jolla, CA: Green Tiger Press, 1982.

Martin, Bill. *Brown Bear, Brown Bear*. Illustrated by Eric Carle. New York: Henry Holt, 1992.

Martin, William Patrick. *A Lifetime of Fiction: The 500 Most Recommended Reads for Ages 2 to 102*. Lanham, MD: Rowman & Littlefield, 2014.

———. *The Mother of All Booklists: The 500 Most Recommended Nonfiction Reads for Ages 3 to 103*. Lanham, MD: Rowman & Littlefield, 2014.

Marvin, Maria. "Annotated Wordless Picture Book List." Goodling Institute for Research in Family Literacy. Accessed June 16, 2014. http://issuu.com/mmarvin/docs/ goodling_wordless_picture_book_list.

Masereel, Frans. *Danse macabre*. New York: Pantheon Books, 1942.

———. *Route des hommes*. Brussels, Belgium: La Lettre Volee, 2006.

Masereel, Frans, Lynd Ward, Giacomo Patri, and Laurence Hyde. *Graphic Witness: Four Wordless Graphic Novels*. Edited by George Walker. Buffalo, NY: Firefly Books, 2007.

May, Robert L., and David Wenzel. *Rudolph the Red-Nosed Reindeer*. New York: Grosset & Dunlap, 2001.

Mayer, Mercer. *East of the Sun & West of the Moon*. New York: Four Winds Press, 1980.

———. *Just for You*. New York: Golden Press, 1975.

———. *Little Critter: Just a Special Day*. New York: HarperCollins Publishers, 2014.

———. *There Are Monsters Everywhere*. New York: Dial Books for Young Readers, 2005.

———. *There's a Nightmare in My Closet*. New York: Dial Press, 1968.

———. *There's an Alligator under My Bed*. New York: Dial Books for Young Readers, 1987.

———. *There's Something in My Attic*. New York: Dial Books for Young Readers, 1988.

McCloud, Scott. *Understanding Comics: The Invisible Art*. New York: HarperPerennial, 1994.

McCully, Emily Arnold. *The Ballot Box Battle*. New York: Knopf, 1996.

———. *The Bobbin Girl*. New York: Dial Books for Young Readers, 1996.

———. *Mirette on the High Wire*. New York: G. P. Putnam's Sons, 1992.

McDonnell, Patrick. *Hug Time*. New York: Little, Brown, 2007.

———. *Me . . . Jane*. New York: Little, Brown, 2011.

Meyer, Nadean. "Eastern Washington University—Wordless Books." OCLC World-Cat. Accessed June 2, 2014. https://www.worldcat.org/profiles/EWU-Center/lists/2926719.

Monnin, Katie. *Teaching Graphic Novels: Practical Strategies for the Secondary ELA Classroom*. Gainesville, FL: Maupin House, 2013.

Mouly, Françoise, Jessica Abel, Matt Madden, and Charles Burns. *The Best American Comics 2012*. Boston: Houghton Mifflin Harcourt, 2012.

"Nearly Wordless." *LibraryThing*. Accessed June 14, 2014. http://www.librarything.com/tag/nearly+wordless.

Nevius, Carol. *Baseball Hour*. Illustrated by Bill Thomson. New York: Marshall Cavendish Children, 2008.

———. *Karate Hour*. Illustrated by Bill Thomson. New York: Marshall Cavendish Children, 2004.

———. *Soccer Hour*. Illustrated by Bill Thomson. Tarrytown, NY: Marshall Cavendish Children, 2011.

Newgarden, Mark, and Megan Montague Cash. *Bow-Wow Hears Things*. New York: Red Wagon Books, 2008.

———. *Bow-Wow Naps by Number*. New York: Red Wagon Books, 2007.

———. *Bow-Wow's Colorful Life*. Boston: HMH Books for Young Readers, 2009.

"Notable Children's Books of 2013." *New York Times Sunday Book Review*. Last modified November 27, 2013. http://www.nytimes.com/2013/12/08/books/review/notable-childrens-books-of-2013.html.

NoveList Plus. EBSCO Information Services. Accessed November 29, 2014. http://0-web.a.ebscohost.com.sierra.cumberlandcountylibraries.org/novp/search/novbasic?sid=6a30b9c0-c1d7-4acd-8bfa-ad50e7a1b09a%40sessionmgr4005&vid=1&hid=4109.

Ott, Thomas. *Tales of Error*. Seattle, WA: Fantagraphics, 2003.

Oxenbury, Helen. *Dressing*. New York: Wanderer Books, 1981.

———. *Family*. New York: Wanderer Books, 1981.

———. *Friends*. New York: Wanderer Books, 1981.

———. *The Helen Oxenbury Nursery Collection*. New York: Alfred A. Knopf, 2004.

Panetta, George. *Sea Beach Express*. Illustrated by Emily Arnold McCully. New York: Harper & Row, 1966.

"Past NCB Lists." Association for Library Service to Children, American Library Association. Accessed June 6, 2014. http://www.ala.org/alsc/awardsgrants/notalists/ncb/ncbpastlists.

Pett, Mark. *Lucky Cow*. Kansas City, MO: Andrews McMeel, 2005.

———. *Mr. Lowe: Cartoons from the Classroom*. Reno, NV: Cottonwood Press, 2002.

Pett, Mark, and Gary Rubinstein. *The Girl Who Never Made Mistakes*. Naperville, IL: Sourcebooks, 2011.

"Picture Book Titles." Cornwall Public Library. Accessed June 14, 2014. http://guides
.rcls.org/content.php?pid=549566.

"Picture Books without Words." Gumberg Library, Duquesne University. Accessed June
2, 2014. http://guides.library.duq.edu/content.php?pid=212027&sid=3241740.

"Picture This!" *Education World*. Last modified July 21, 2009. http://www.education
world.com/a_tsl/archives/04-1/lesson003.shtml.

Pixton, Kaaren. *Creep! Crawl!* New York: Workman Publishing, 2009.

———. *Plip-Plop Pond*. New York: Workman Publishing, 2010.

"Popular Wordless Picture Books Shelf." Goodreads. Accessed May 18, 2014. https://
www.goodreads.com/shelf/show/wordless-picture-books?page=1.

Puckett, Katharyn E., and Virginia H. Richey. *Using Wordless Picture Books: Authors and
Activities*. Englewood, CO: Libraries Unlimited, 1993.

Pullman, Philip. *His Dark Materials Trilogy*. Illustrated by Eric Rohmann. New York:
Knopf, 1995.

Raschka, Chris. *Charlie Parker Played Be Bop*. New York: Orchard Books, 1992.

———. *John Coltrane's Giant Steps*. New York: Atheneum, 2002.

———. *Mysterious Thelonious*. New York: Orchard Books, 1997.

Rathmann, Peggy. *Goodnight Gorilla*. New York: G. P. Putnam's Sons, 1993.

———. *Officer Buckle and Gloria*. New York: G. P. Putnam's Sons, 1995.

"Ready Readers: Talking—Wordless Picture Books." Sno-Isle Libraries. Accessed June
14, 2014. http://www.sno-isle.org/?ID=2631&lid=854.

"Recommended Reads—Wordless Picture Books." Davenport Public Library. Accessed
May 29, 2014. http://www.davenportlibrary.com/kids/recommended-reads/wordless
-picture-books.

"Recommended Wordless Picture Books." *Children's Books and Reading*. Accessed May
22, 2014. http://www.childrens-books-and-reading.com/wordless-picture-books.html.

Reese, Colleen. "Story Development Using Wordless Picture Books." *The Reading
Teacher*. Last modified October 1996. http://www.lesn.appstate.edu/fryeem/RE5130/
WordlessRT.pdf.

Remarque, Erich Maria. *All Quiet on the Western Front*. New York: Ballantine Books, 1982.

Remenar, Kristen. "Top Ten Wordless Picture Books." *Nerdy Book Club*. Last modified
March 30, 2013. http://nerdybookclub.wordpress.com/2013/03/30/top-ten-word
less-picture-books-by-kristen-remenar.

"Research Guide—Wordless Picture Books." Bank Street College Library. Last
modified September 10, 2013. http://libguides.bankstreet.edu/content.php?pid=452
453&sid=3716419.

Richey, Virginia H., and Katharyn E. Puckett. *Wordless / Almost Wordless Picture Books:
A Guide*. Santa Barbara, CA: Libraries Unlimited, 1992.

Ridinger, Sara. "Wordless Books." Loden-Daniel Library, Freed-Hardeman University.
Accessed June 1, 2014. http://fhu.worldcat.org/profiles/sarahridinger/lists/3044827.

Rippel, Marie. "Reading Wordless Picture Books with Your Children." *All about Learning Press*. Last modified November 11, 2013. http://blog.allaboutlearningpress.com/
wordless-picture-books.

Rivlin, Holly, Michael Cavanaugh, Brenn Jones, and Barnes & Noble. *The Barnes &
Noble Guide to Children's Books*. New York: Barnes & Noble Books, 1999.

Rodriguez, Beatrice. *The Treasure Thief.* Wellington, NZ: Gecko Press, 2011.

Rohmann, Eric. *The Cinder-Eyed Cats.* New York: Crown Publishers, 1997.

———. *A Kitten Tale.* New York: Knopf, 2008.

Ross-Degnan, Leslie, and Christina Silvi. "Why Wordless Books?" *Early Childhood News.* Accessed May 29, 2014. http://www.earlychildhoodnews.com/earlychildhood/article_view.aspx?ArticleID=690.

Salminen, Jane. "Using Wordless Books in Your ESL Classroom." ERIC Document. Last modified March 1998. http://files.eric.ed.gov/fulltext/ED423693.pdf.

Schories, Pat. *Mouse Around.* New York: Farrar Straus & Giroux, 1991.

———. *Pants for Chuck.* New York: Holiday House, 2014.

———. *When Jack Goes Out.* Honesdale, PA: Boyds Mills Press, 2010.

Schwartz, Roslyn. *The Complete Adventures of the Mole Sisters.* Toronto: Annick Press, 2004.

———. *The Vole Brothers.* Toronto: Owlkids Books, 2011.

Scieszka, Jon. *The Stinky Cheese Man and Other Fairly Stupid Tales.* Illustrated by Lane Smith. New York: Viking, 1992.

———. *The True Story of the Three Little Pigs.* New York: Viking, 1989.

Seuss, Dr. *How the Grinch Stole Christmas.* New York: Random House, 1957.

Shannon, David. *Duck on a Bike.* New York: Blue Sky Press, 2002.

Shaw, Nancy E., and Margot Apple. *Sheep in a Jeep.* Boston: Houghton Mifflin, 1986.

Shelley, Mary Wollstonecraft. *Frankenstein: The Lynd Ward Illustrated Edition.* Illustrated by Lynd Ward. Mineola, NY: Dover Publications, 2009.

"Shhh: 7 Amazing Wordless Picture Books." *Modern Parents, Messy Kids.* Accessed May 24, 2014. http://www.modernparentsmessykids.com/2013/08/shhh-7-amazing-wordless-picture-books.html

Sickler, Jonas. *Hey, Diddle Diddle.* New York: Workman Publishing, 2010.

"Silent / Wordless Graphic Novels." Goodreads. Accessed May 26, 2014. http://www.goodreads.com/list/show/4605.Silent_Wordless_Graphic_Novels.

Sinclair, Upton. *The Jungle.* Illustrated by Peter Kuper. New York: NBM ComicsLit, 2004.

Sis, Peter. *Fire Truck.* New York: Greenwillow Books, 1998.

———. *Humpty Dumpty.* New York: Workman Publishing, 2010.

Skurzynski, Gloria. *Honest Andrew.* Illustrated by David Wiesner. New York: Harcourt Brace Jovanovich, 1980.

Spier, Peter. *Dreams.* Great Neck, NY: StarWalk Kids Media, 2014.

———. *The Erie Canal.* Great Neck, NY: StarWalk Kids Media, 2014.

———. *The Fox Went Out on a Chilly Night.* New York: Doubleday Books for Young Readers, 2014.

———. *London Bridge Is Falling Down.* Garden City, NY: Doubleday, 1967.

———. *The Star-Spangled Banner.* New York: Doubleday Books for Young Readers, 2014.

———. *We the People.* New York: Doubleday Books for Young Readers, 2014.

Steig, William. *Doctor De Soto.* New York: Farrar, Straus & Giroux, 1982.

Steinberg, Rachel. "Wordless Wonders." *Publishers Weekly.* Last modified July 19, 2010. http://www.publishersweekly.com/pw/by-topic/new-titles/childrens-announcements/article/43866-wordless-wonders.html.

Stevenson, Robert Louis. *Treasure Island*. New York: HarperFestival, 2005.

"Stories without Words." Bodleian Library, University of Oxford. Accessed November 16, 2014. http://solo.bodleian.ox.ac.uk/primo_library/libweb/action/search.do?dscnt=1 &dum=true&dstmp=1402932311535&vl(freeText0)=stories%20without%20words &vid=OXVU1&fn=search&fromLogin=true.

"Stories without Words." Boston Public Library. Accessed November 14, 2014. http://bpl .bibliocommons.com/search?q=Stories%20without%20Words&t=subject&display _quantity=25&sort[field]=PUBLISHED_DATE&sort[type]=BIB_FIELDS&sort[di rection]=descending.

"Stories without Words." British Council Library India. Accessed November 15, 2014. http://www.library.britishcouncil.org.in/cgi-bin/koha/opac-search.pl?idx=kw& amp;q=stories%20without%20pictures&show=20.

"Stories without Words." British Library. Accessed October 14, 2014. http://explore. bl.uk/primo_library/libweb/action/search.do?srt=date&srtChange=true&fctN=facet _rtype&dscnt=0&rfnGrp=1&scp.scps=scope%3A(BLCONTENT)&fctV=books&fr bg=&tab=local_tab&dstmp=1402771015622&srt=rank&ct=facet&mode=Basic&vl (488279563UI0)=any&dum=true&tb=t&indx=1&rfnGrpCounter=1&vl(freeText0) =stories%20without%20words&fn=search&vid=BLVU1.

"Stories without Words." Cumberland County Library System. Accessed November 12, 2014. http://catalog.cumberlandcountylibraries.org/iii/encore/search?formids=target &lang=eng&suite=def&reservedids=lang%2Csuite&submitmode=&submitname=& target=stories+without+words.

"Stories without Words." Dover Public Library. Accessed October 30, 2014. http:// www.dover.lib.nh.us/childrens'room/Booklists/Wordless.pdf.

"Stories without Words." Goodreads. Accessed November 12, 2014. http://www .goodreads.com/shelf/show/stories-without-words.

"Stories without Words." Hong Kong Public Libraries. Accessed November 15, 2014. https://webcat.hkpl.gov.hk/search/query?match_1=MUST&field_1=&term_1=stories +without+words&sort=sort_ss_date%3Bdescending,sort_ss_author&theme=WEB.

"Stories without Words." Iowa City Public Library. Accessed November 15, 2014. http:// catpro.icpl.org/iii/encore/search?formids=target&lang=eng&suite=def&reservedids =lang%2Csuite&submitmode=&submitname=&target=stories+without+words&site search=&siteurl=http%3A%2F%2Fwww.icpl.org%2F.

"Stories without Words." *LibraryThing*. Accessed May 29, 2014. http://www.library thing.com/subject/Stories%20without%20words&all=1.

"Stories without Words." National Library of Australia. Accessed October 15, 2014. http://catalogue.nla.gov.au/Search/Home?lookfor=stories+without+words&type=sub ject&limit%5B%5D=&submit=Find&limit%5B%5D=format%3ABook&sort= sort_date_desc&page=1.

"Stories without Words." National Library of the Philippines. Accessed November 15, 2014. http://www.elib.gov.ph/results.php.

"Stories without Words." Olathe Public Library. Accessed November 14, 2014. http:// www.olathelibrary.org/kids/picture-book-finder-stories-without-words.

"Stories without Words." Public Library of Cincinnati & Hamilton County. Accessed November 14, 2014. http://catalog.cincinnatilibrary.org/iii/encore/search/C__SStories

%20without%20words.__Ff%3Afacetmediatype%3Aa%3Aa%3ABook%3A%3A
__O-date__X0?lang=eng&suite=cobalt.

"Stories without Words." Seattle Public Library. Accessed November 16, 2014. http://
seattle.bibliocommons.com/search?where=catalog&term=stories+without+words&t=
smart&q=stories+without+words&search_category=keyword&commit=search&sort%5
Bfield%5D=UGC_RATING&sort%5Btype%5D=UGC_FIELDS&sort%5Bdirection
%5D=descending&display_quantity=25&page=1.

"Stories without Words." Temple University Library. Accessed November 16, 2014.
http://diamond.temple.edu/search~S30/?searchtype=m&searcharg=stories+without+
words&searchscope=30&extended=0&SUBMIT=Search&searchlimits=&searchorig
arg=X.

"Stories without Words." Toronto Public Library. Accessed June 12, 2014. http://
www.torontopubliclibrary.ca/search.jsp?Erp=20&N=&Ns=p_pub_date_sort&Nso
=1&Ntk=Subject_Search_Interface&Ntt=Stories+without+words.&view=grid.

"Stories without Words." Townsend Memorial Library. Accessed September 12, 2014.
http://umhblib.umhb.edu/search~S0/?searchtype=d&searcharg=stories+without+
words&sortdropdown=r&SORT=D&extended=0&SUBMIT=Search&searchlimits=
&searchorigarg=dstories+without+words.

"Stories without Words." Trinity College Library Dublin. Accessed October 14, 2014.
http://stella.catalogue.tcd.ie/iii/encore/search?formids=target&lang=eng&suite=def&
reservedids=lang%2Csuite&submitmode=&submitname=&target=stories+without+
words&x=28&y=10.

"Stories without Words." University of Chicago Library. Accessed November 16, 2014.
https://libcat.uchicago.edu/ipac20/ipac.jsp?session=14J29340482T6.1247442&profil
e=ucpublic&uri=link=3100008~!3655888~!3100001~!3100002&aspect=subtab13&
menu=search&ri=3&source=~!horizon&term=Stories+without+words&index=.

"Stories without Words." Vancouver Public Library. Accessed June 14, 2014. http://
vpl.bibliocommons.com/search?t=keyword&q=stories+without+words&searchTarget
=cat.

"Stories without Words." Waupaca Area Public Library. Last modified November 11,
2008. http://info.infosoup.org/lists/withoutwords.asp?x=&y=1&r=no.

"Stories without Words: A Bibliography with Annotations." Michigan State Universities
Libraries. Accessed June 13, 2014. http://comics.lib.msu.edu/rhode/wordless.htm.

"Stories without Words for Children." Amazon. Accessed June 13, 2014. http://www
.amazon.com/s/ref=sr_st_date-desc-rank?keywords=stories+without+words+for+child
ren&qid=1402663048&rh=n%3A283155%2Ck%3Astories+without+words+for+
children&sort=date-desc-rank.

Sutherland, Zena. *Children and Books*. New York: Pearson, 1997.

Sutton, Roger, and Martha V. Parravano. *A Family of Readers: The Book Lover's Guide
to Children's and Young Adult Literature*. Somerville, MA: Candlewick Press, 2010.

Taylor, Melissa. "The Best Wordless Picture Books." *Imagination Soup*. Last modified
October 5, 2011. http://imaginationsoup.net/2011/10/wordless-picture-books-to-love.

"Themed Wordless Picture Book Lists." Rhode Island Teachers of English Language
Learners. Accessed June 3, 2014. http://www.ritell.org/Default.aspx?pageId=1513756.

Thomas, Rebecca L., and Carolyn W. Lima. *A to Zoo: Subject Access to Children's Picture Books*. New York: Libraries, 2014.

Tolkien, J. R. R. *The Hobbit*. New York: Ballantine Books, 1965.

———. *The Lord of the Rings*. New York: Ballantine Books, 1965.

Turner, Christine. "Encourage Learning with Wordless Picture Books." Harris County Public Library. Last modified April 25, 2012. http://www.hcpl.net/content/encourage -learning-wordless-picture-books.

Van Allsburg, Chris. *The Chronicles of Harris Burdick*. Boston: Houghton Mifflin Books for Children, 2011.

———. *The Garden of Abdul Gasazi*. Boston: Houghton Mifflin, 1979.

———. *Jumanji*. Boston: Houghton Mifflin, 1981.

———. *The Polar Express*. Houghton Mifflin, 1985.

Varon, Sara. *Bake Sale*. New York: First Second, 2011.

———. *Sweaterweather*. Gainesville, FL: Alternative Comics, 2003.

Walsh, Ellen Stoll. *Mouse Paint*. Boston: HMH Books for Young Readers, 1995.

Ward, Lynd. *The Biggest Bear*. Boston: Houghton Mifflin, 1952.

———. *Six Novels in Woodcuts*. New York: Library of America, 2010.

Waterreus, Adam. "December Graphic Novel Recommendations—(Almost) Wordless Books." Politics and Prose Bookstore. Accessed May 26, 2014. http://www.politics -prose.com/graphic-novels/dec10.

Wattenberg, Jane. *Mrs. Mustard's Beastly Babies*. San Francisco: Chronicle Books, 1990.

Wiesner, David. *Art & Max*. Boston: Clarion Books, 2010.

———. *Hurricane*. Boston: Clarion Books, 1990.

———. *June 29, 1999*. Boston: Clarion Books, 1992.

———. *The Loathsome Dragon*. Boston: Clarion Books, 2005.

———. *The Three Pigs*. Boston: Clarion Books, 2001.

"Wonderful Wordless Picture Books." *Storytime Standouts: Raising Children Who Love to Read*. Accessed June 2, 2014. http://www.storytimestandouts.com/wordless-picture -books.

"Wordless." *Children's Books Guide*. Accessed May 24, 2014. http://childrensbooksguide .com/wordless.

"Wordless / Nearly Wordless Picture Books." Nashville Public Library. Accessed May 31, 2014. http://npl.worldcat.org/profiles/nashvillelibrarykids/lists/1666070.

"Wordless Book List." Pennsylvania Center for the Book, Penn State University. Accessed June 14, 2014. http://pabook.libraries.psu.edu/familylit/bakersdozen/2010/ wordless.html.

"Wordless Books." OCLC WorldCat. Accessed June 2, 2014. https://www.worldcat.org/ profiles/ljerniga/lists/3093334.

"Wordless Books." *The Horn Book*. Accessed June 14, 2014. http://www.hbook.com/ tag/wordless-books/#_.

"Wordless Graphic Novels." *Readings*. Accessed May 26, 2014. http://www.readings .com.au/collection/wordless-graphic-novels.

"Wordless Picture Books." Andruss Library, Bloomsburg University. Last modified March 11, 2014. http://guides.library.bloomu.edu/content.php?pid=489981&sid=4058105.

"Wordless Picture Books." Ann Arbor District Library. Last updated December 5, 2011. http://www.aadl.org/user/lists/13182.

"Wordless Picture Books." Appalachian State University. Accessed November 9, 2014. http://www.lesn.appstate.edu/fryeem/RE5130/wordless_picture_books.htm.

"Wordless Picture Books." Bailey Library, Slippery Rock University. Last modified August 2010. http://www.sru.edu/academics/library/directory/imc/pages/wordless picturebooks.aspx.

"Wordless Picture Books." Barnes & Noble. Accessed November 19, 2014. http://www .barnesandnoble.com/s/?category_id=800138&csrftoken=SHkSC3j6rR7lrdiXK41cI5 gpKTR8f1eC&size=90&sort=R.

"Wordless Picture Books." Carnegie Library of Pittsburgh. Accessed November 22, 2014. http://www.clpgh.org/kids/books/showbooklist.cfm?list=wordlesspictures.

"Wordless Picture Books." Cedar Mill Library. Last modified February 10, 2012. http:// library.cedarmill.org/readers/book-lists/list-archive/wordless-picture-books.html.

"Wordless Picture Books." Department of Education, Training, and Development: Queensland Government. Accessed November 1, 2014. http://202.191.49.200/lib erty/opac/search.do?limit=All&action=topicSearch&branch=All&resourceCollection= All&available=false&dataFile=false&operator=AND&queryTerm=Wordless+picture+ books&mode=TOPIC_LIST&_open=1.

"Wordless Picture Books." Instructional Media Center, Long Island University. Last modified May 27, 2014. http://liu.cwp.libguides.com/content.php?pid=348700 &sid=3832318.

"Wordless Picture Books." Kim's Corner for Teacher Talk. Last updated November 14, 2007. http://www.kimskorner4teachertalk.com/bookstore/wordless.htm.

"Wordless Picture Books." National Library of New Zealand. Accessed June 15, 2014. http://natlib.govt.nz/items?utf8=&text=wordless+picture+books&direction=desc& sort=sort_date.

"Wordless Picture Books." New York Public Library. Accessed November 30, 2014. http:// nypl.bibliocommons.com/list/show/86806309_nypl_battery_park_city/93782944 _wordless_picture_books.

"Wordless Picture Books." Oklahoma State University. Last modified September 7, 2013. http://info.library.okstate.edu/content.php?pid=467309&sid=3825930.

"Wordless Picture Books." Pinterest. Accessed June 13, 2014. http://www.pinterest .com/books4yourkids/wordless-picture-books.

"Wordless Picture Books." Polk Library, University of Wisconsin at Oshkosh. Accessed November 30, 2014. http://www.uwosh.edu/library/emc/bibliographies/emc-bibliog raphies/wordless-picture-books.

"Wordless Picture Books." Social Sciences, Health, and Education Library, University of Illinois, Urbana-Champaign. Last modified April 17, 2014. http://www.library .illinois.edu/sshel/s-coll/findbks/s-collbibs/wordless.htm.

"Wordless Picture Books." Suffolk Public Library. Accessed May 29, 2014. http://www .suffolk.lib.va.us/Online-resources/booklists-1/childrens-booklists/wordless-picture -books.html.

"Wordless Picture Books." Weber County Library System. Accessed May 22, 2014. http://www.weberpl.lib.ut.us/wordless-picture-books.

"Wordless Picture Books Bibliography." University of British Columbia. Accessed June 1, 2014. http://guides.library.ubc.ca/friendly.php?s=bibwordless.

"Wordless Picture Books for Children." Amazon. Accessed May 24, 2014. http://www.amazon.com/s/ref=sr_kk_1?rh=i%3Astripbooks%2Ck%3Awordless+picture+books+for+children&keywords=wordless+picture+books+for+children&ie=UTF8&qid=1400960196.

"Wordless Picturebooks." Stanford University Libraries. Last modified November 6, 2014. http://library.stanford.edu/guides/wordless-picturebooks.

"Wordless Recommendations." Daniel Boone Regional Library. Accessed June 9, 2014. http://dbrl.bibliocommons.com/search?q=wordless&search_category=tag&t=tag.

"Wordless Wonders." Enfield Public Library. Accessed June 17, 2014. http://www.enfield-ct.gov/content/91/109/5448/5496/5515.aspx.

"Wordless Wonders." Scholastic. Accessed June 17, 2014. http://www.scholastic.com/browse/booklistcontent.jsp?id=11171.

Zvirin, Stephanie. *Read with Me: Best Books for Preschoolers*. Chicago: Huron Street Press, 2012.